# NEW APPROACHES TO HEDGING

## STUDIES IN PRAGMATICS

Series Editors: Bruce Fraser, Kerstin Fischer, Maj-Britt Mosegaard Hansen

The *Studies in Pragmatics* series is dedicated to publishing innovative, authoritative monographs and edited collections from all micro-, macro-, and meta-pragmatic linguistic perspectives. Rooted in the interdisciplinary spirit of the *Journal of Pragmatics*, it welcomes not only book proposals from linguistics proper but also pragmatically oriented proposals from neighboring disciplines such as interactional sociology, language philosophy, communication science, social psychology, cognitive science, and information science. The goal of the series is to provide a widely read and respected international forum for high-quality theoretical, analytical, and applied pragmatic studies of all types. By publishing leading-edge work on natural language practice, it seeks to extend our growing knowledge of the forms, functions, and foundations of human interaction.

---

***Other titles in this series*:**

| | |
|---|---|
| **FISCHER** | Approaches to Discourse Particles |
| **AIJMER & SIMON-VANDENBERGEN** | Pragmatic Markers in Contrast |
| **FETZER & FISCHER** | Lexical Markers of Common Grounds |
| **CAFFI** | Mitigation |
| **ROSSARI, RICCI & SPIRIDON** | Grammaticalization and Pragmatics: Facts, Approaches, Theoretical Issues |
| **FRASER & TURNER** | Language in Life, and a Life in Language: Jacob Mey – A Festschrift |
| **HANSEN & VISCONTI** | Current Trends in Diachronic Semantics and Pragmatics |
| **BARTH-WEINGARTEN, DEHÉ & WICHMANN** | Where Prosody Meets Pragmatics |

Proposals for the series are welcome. Please contact the Series Editor, Bruce Fraser: bfraser@bu.edu

# NEW APPROACHES TO HEDGING

EDITED BY

**GUNTHER KALTENBÖCK**
University of Wien, Austria

**WILTRUD MIHATSCH**
University of Bochum, Germany

**STEFAN SCHNEIDER**
University of Graz, Austria

Emerald

United Kingdom – North America – Japan
India – Malaysia – China

Emerald Group Publishing Limited
Howard House, Wagon Lane, Bingley BD16 1WA, UK

First edition 2010



**British Library Cataloguing in Publication Data**
A catalogue record for this book is available from the British Library

ISBN: 978-0-85724-247-1
ISSN: 1750-368X (Series)

# Studies in Pragmatics (SiP)

# Table of Contents

# List of Contributors


Gisle Andersen, Norwegian School of Economics and Business Administration (NHH), Norway

Antonio Briz, University of Valencia, Valencia, Spain

Claudia Caffi, University of Genova, Genova, Italy

Maria Estellés, University of Valencia, Valencia, Spain

Anita Fetzer, University of Würzburg, Würzburg, Germany

Bruce Fraser, Boston University, Boston, USA

Gunther Kaltenböck, Universität Wien, Wien, Austria

Elise Kärkkäinen, University of Oulu, Oulu, Finland

Eva Lavric, Universität Innsbruck, Innsbruck, Austria

Bernd Meyer, Universität Hamburg, Hamburg, Germany

Wiltrud Mihatsch, Ruhr-Universität Bochum, Bochum, Germany

Birte Pawlack, Universität Hamburg, Hamburg, Germany

Yongping Ran, Guangdong University of Foreign Studies, Guangdong, P.R. China

Stefan Schneider, Karl-Franzens-Universität Graz, Graz, Austria

# Acknowledgments

This volume is based on selected papers presented at the panel "Vague language: the use of approximators and hedges in spoken and written corpora" at the 10th International Pragmatics Conference in Göteborg and an additional chapter by Bruce Fraser. We thank all the participants of the panel for their contributions and stimulating discussions. We owe particular thanks to Bruce Fraser, who accepted our volume in this series and whose comments and constructive criticism have been of invaluable help. We also thank Karin Aijmer for her enlightening comments and useful suggestions. Bryan Jenner has helped us with stylistic revisions. We are indebted to Carina Zeiger for her competent assistance in the final stages of the editing process. Finally, we are grateful to Emerald for their friendly and efficient support.

Gunther Kaltenböck
Wiltrud Mihatsch
Stefan Schneider
*Editors*

# Announcement

Bruce Fraser, chief editor of the *Studies in Pragmatics* series, has decided to step down from his position as of June 30th, 2010, in order to have more time for his family and research. Bruce was a founding editor of the *Studies in Pragmatics* series, and helped give it a good start in 2006. He has since accompanied it calmly and wisely through the past five years. Bruce has worked hard to maintain the series' high scientific standard and reputation and to establish and preserve smooth, friendly, and efficient procedures between the authors, the publisher, and the editorial team. He has shaped the series' content and image, and much of its anchorage in the scientific community is due to his generous dedication to the success of the series. He has been a great colleague, and we will miss his wonderful sense of humor, his friendly ways, and his experience in all matters of life.

Kerstin Fischer Maj-Britt Mosegaard Hansen
*Series Editors, Studies in Pragmatics*

New Approaches to Hedging
Edited by Gunther Kaltenböck, Wiltrud Mihatsch and Stefan Schneider


# Introduction

*Gunther Kaltenböck, Wiltrud Mihatsch and Stefan Schneider*

## 1. Aim and Scope of the Volume

Although a relatively young term, the concept of hedging is already firmly established in linguistics. It is generally understood as a discourse strategy that reduces the force or truth of an utterance and thus reduces the risk a speaker runs when uttering a strong or firm assertion or other speech act. Typical examples of specialized markers signalling hedging, that is hedges, are Engl. *sort of, approximately, I think, I would suggest*. For some time, elements such as these were considered to be marginal, even redundant items that contribute little to the communication, but they are now generally acknowledged as playing a crucial role in both spoken and written discourse.

In its brief history in linguistics the term 'hedging' has already seen considerable change in its use. Originally introduced by Lakoff in 1972, it started out as a primarily semantic concept, which was later given a wider, pragmatic definition (cf. Section 2 for an overview, and Fraser, this volume). With this widening of the definition came an increase in attention from various linguistic disciplines, especially pragmatics and applied linguistics, which approached the notion of hedging from different (but overlapping) perspectives, such as speech act- and politeness-theory (e.g. Fraser, 1975; Brown and Levinson, 1978, 1987; House and Kasper, 1981; Wierzbicka, 1991, 2006; Terraschke and Holmes, 2007), genre-specific investigations (e.g. Markkanen and Schröder, 1992, 1997; Hyland, 1998), interactional pragmatics (e.g. Jucker *et al.*, 2003; Kärkkäinen, 2003; Kerbrat-Orecchioni, 2005) or studies of vague language (e.g. Channell, 1994; Cutting, 2007), which investigate a variety of linguistic means reducing precision, such as hedges, but also placeholders and indefinite quantifiers.

The present volume contributes to the discussion of hedging by bringing together studies from a variety of fields in an attempt to provide an up-to-date overview of current research on the topic.

In this, the focus has been on corpus-based approaches, a cross-linguistic perspective, and an inclusive, multi-level analysis of hedging and hedges. Let us look briefly at the rationale behind each of these objectives.

Most of the studies included in the volume involve some empirical data analysis, which represents an important basis for assessing existing theoretical categories (cf. Section 2 and Fraser, this volume, for an overview). Corpus-based approaches have, in fact, gained importance with the widening of the concept of hedging from semantics to pragmatics, and this has made it necessary to investigate genuinely attested language data rather than just invented sample sentences. Among the first to do this were Prince *et al.* (1982), whose classification of approximators (adaptors, rounders) and shields (plausibility, attribution) is based on a corpus of physician–physician interaction.

Corpus data are of course not only a useful basis for establishing categories, but also provide a good means of testing existing classification systems, and as such they may have an important corrective function. It is therefore one of the explicit aims of this volume to bring together studies that make a link between theory and language use by applying theoretical concepts to actual language data. This, in turn, can provide valuable feedback for the fine-tuning and adjustment of existing categories.

The advantages of corpus-based approaches are well-known. By providing frequency information both on the level of occurrence (e.g. in different text types) and co-occurrence (i.e. the 'company' a particular linguistic item keeps), corpora can enable the researcher to uncover patterns and regularities of use that are otherwise not easily noticed. Often even less frequent patterns or borderline cases provide valuable insights into the structure of a system and its dynamic qualities, as evidenced for instance in language change. At the same time, corpora give access to co(n)textual information of linguistic items, which provides an important basis for qualitative research. This is of particular value for the investigation of a pragmatic phenomenon such as hedging, whose precise function depends to a large extent on co(n)textual features, with different contexts giving rise to different implicatures. Most of the studies in the volume address this interaction between hedges and co(n)text and its effects on pragmatic interpretation.

Another objective of the present volume is to provide a cross-linguistic perspective of hedging devices, which allows for comparisons to be drawn between different linguistic manifestations of the same concept. By widening the scope of investigation to include different languages rather than limiting it to a single one, the book offers a more comprehensive view of hedging, which allows for the assessment of existing classification models in the light of different types of linguistic data and can shed light on similarities and differences between languages and cultures (as demonstrated for instance by Brown and Levinson (1978, 1987) and Blum-Kulka *et al.* (1989). The contributions included are investigations of hedging in single languages or varieties, such as American English (Fraser, Kärkkäinen), British English (Fetzer, Kaltenböck), Spanish (Briz and Estellés), Chinese (Ran), and Classical Greek (Caffi), but also cross-linguistic analyses involving two or more languages, such as English compared with Norwegian (Anderson), Brazilian

Portuguese and German (Meyer and Pawlack), or a comparison of several Romance languages (Lavric, Mihatsch, Schneider). The volume thus spans a wide range of analyses, from the detailed single language study to overviews of whole language groups.

To do justice to the multi-functionality of hedging and hedges, the present volume has allowed for an inclusive view of hedging, one that embraces a multi-level analysis of the phenomenon and includes functionally equivalent means such as placeholders and approximative quantifiers. Only by casting the net wide, as it were, is it possible to account for the multi-facetted nature of hedging and, methodologically speaking, to pre-empt the adoption of pre-conceived but empirically unfounded ideas. Hedging is a pragmatic function that involves all levels of linguistic analysis from prosody to morphology, syntax and semantics. Aspects of each of these are considered by the present collection of articles. Some also take into account the synchronic and diachronic relations among the different functions expressed by hedges, and this permits a new perspective on some existing classification systems. These intricate links between synchronic and diachronic views as well as other levels of analysis are easily overlooked and best studied on the basis of natural data, which may allow us to uncover non-prototypical and hitherto unknown uses.

Taking a broad view of hedging devices also means investigating their occurrence and use in different communicative settings and text types. While earlier research on hedging has focused almost exclusively on the use of hedges in casual spoken language, the field of investigation has now widened considerably and includes a variety of different genres and text types, both spoken and written. Along with these studies has come an increasing awareness of the close interdependence of hedging and context, in particular how the use of hedges is shaped to a large extent by the expectations and requirements of a particular discourse community. This volume, with its corpus-based focus, continues the trend of contextualization and diversification in research on hedging. While investigating concepts in the light of actual language use, the various contributions bring together a range of different text types, such as political interviews and political speeches (Fetzer), interpreters' discourse (Meyer and Pawlack), and various other forms of formal and informal spoken language (Andersen, Mihatsch, Kärkkäinen, Kaltenböck, Schneider) as well as a classical Greek dialogue (Caffi) and literary texts (Lavric, Ran).

The inclusive view of hedging adopted in this volume is also reflected in the range of linguistic devices covered by the different contributions. They discuss classic hedges such as the approximators *sort of*, *kind of*, *so to say* (e.g. Fetzer, Mihatsch, Meyer and Pawlack, Caffi), the shields *I think* and *I guess* (Kärkkäinen, Kaltenböck) and hedged performatives of the type *I would suggest* (Schneider) in a variety of languages, but also other linguistic expressions that 'make things fuzzy'. Among these are placeholder nouns such as *thing* (Andersen), discourse particles with attenuating function (Briz and Estellés) and approximative uses of numerals (Lavric, Ran). By allowing for a wide definition of hedges, this volume not only takes into account the multi-functionality of these expressions but also aims at highlighting their similarities in terms of pragmatic use.

## 2. A Brief Research History

As noted in the preceding section, the use of the term hedge has seen a change from a narrowly semantic concept to a wider pragmatic one. Lakoff (1972), who first proposed the term,[1] starts from a purely semantic perspective that reflects both Zadeh's (1965) fuzzy set theory and the development of prototype theory in the early 1970s (see Berlin and Kay, 1969; Rosch, 1973). Lakoff is primarily interested in the logical properties of expressions such as Engl. *sort of* and *kind of*, but also *technically speaking* or *strictly speaking*, for their capability to modify the category boundaries of a concept. For Lakoff (1972: 195) a hedge is a word 'whose job is to make things fuzzier or less fuzzy'. Nowadays, the term *hedge* is mainly used for approximating and attenuating expressions rather than for 'less fuzzy' hedges such as *strictly speaking* and reinforcing expressions. For instance, in a sentence such as Engl. *A penguin is sort of a bird* the peripheral and non-prototypical concept 'penguin' can be included within the category 'bird' owing to the use of the hedge *sort of*. A hedge such as Engl. *sort of* therefore affects the truth value of the propositional content (see Lakoff, 1972: 195; Prince *et al.*, 1982: 85).

Lakoff (1972: 213) paved the way for the introduction of hedges into pragmatics by stating that 'obviously hedges interact with felicity conditions for utterances and with rules of conversation' and mentioning the possibility that hedges may act on performatives. The first step in this process was to include means that modify the force of speech acts. Fraser (1975) developed the concept of 'hedged performative', that is, the idea that performatives can be hedged by modal verbs, as in Engl. *I can promise you that* p or *I must advise you that* p. Shortly afterwards, Brown and Levinson (1978) showed that hedging acts not only on the propositional content or on the explicit performative clause but also on illocutionary force and speaker commitment in general. Hedges are seen by Brown and Levinson as expressions which indicate primarily that the speaker is not adhering to one of Grice's (1975, 1978) maxims. Brown and Levinson (1978: 169–176) illustrated hedges on the maxims of quantity, of quality, of relevance and of manner and investigated their use mainly as means of negative politeness, only marginally as markers of positive politeness (see Brown and Levinson 1987: 116).

---

[1] Compare, however, also Weinreich (1963: 130), who notes that '[f]or every language, finally, stock must be taken of all meta-linguistic operators such as English *true, real, so-called, strictly speaking*, German *eigentlich*, and the most powerful extrapolator of all – *like* – which function as instructions for the loose or strict interpretation of designata'.

Thus, by 1978 the concept of 'hedge' was fully established in the domain of pragmatics. The conceptual changes of the term 'hedging' are reflected in the framework established by Prince *et al.* (1982: 85), who distinguish between two types of 'fuzziness': 'fuzziness within the propositional content proper' and 'fuzziness in the relationship between the propositional content and the speaker, that is, in the speaker's commitment to the truth of the proposition conveyed'. The former category is referred to as 'approximators' (as in Engl. *His feet were sort of blue*) and is further subdivided into 'adaptors' (markers such as *sort of* adapting an existing term to a new instance) and *rounders* (imprecision markers such as *approximately* used in connection with measurements). The latter category, indicating degree of speaker commitment, is referred to as *shields* (as in Engl. *I think his feet were blue*) and may be further subdivided into 'plausibility shields' (expressing doubt) and 'attribution shields' (attributing the belief to someone other than the speaker). A similar distinction was proposed by Hübler (1983), who, drawing on Hare (1970), distinguishes between understatements and hedges. In his view, understatements as in Engl. *It's a bit cold in here* modify the *phrastic*, that is the propositional content, whereas hedges, as in Engl. *It is cold in Alaska, I suppose*, modify the *neustic*, that is the speaker's attitude toward his or her utterance.

The bipartite distinction of Prince *et al.* (1982) and Hübler (1983) has more recently been expanded into a tripartite model by Caffi (1999, 2001, 2007). In her framework of mitigation devices, she distinguishes between *bushes*, *hedges* and *shields*. *Bushes* correspond with Prince *et al.*'s (1982) approximators and operate on the propositional content by making referring terms or predicates less precise (or by minimizing them). *Hedges*, in her terminology, cover both speaker commitment and indication of illocutionary force. As such, they subsume Prince *et al.*'s (1982) plausibility shields and Fraser's (1975) hedged performatives. *Shields*, finally, are comparable to Prince *et al.*'s (1982) attribution shields, but go beyond it since they may shift any deictic component of the utterance in various ways.

Table I.1 compares the different (and partly overlapping) categories illustrated in the preceding paragraphs.

Diewald (2006) returns to a binary model. In so doing, she draws on Hyland (1998), who distinguishes between content-oriented and reader-oriented hedges with the former being further subdivided into accuracy-oriented hedges (which can be of the attribute type or the reliability type) and writer-oriented hedges. Hyland's (1998) hierarchical system is criticized by Diewald (2006: 305–306) for including interpersonal communicative effects, which are difficult to capture, and for not clearly distinguishing between the subcategories. Instead, she suggests a distinction between two types of hedges, those that are 'charakterisierend' ('characterizing') and those that are 'perspektivierend' ('perspectivizing'). The former category relates to the referential accuracy of an expression and is thus reminiscent of Prince *et al.*'s (1982) approximators. The latter category assesses the validity, factuality or appropriateness of an utterance, thus reflecting Prince *et al.*'s (1982) shields.

**Table I.1.** Comparison of classification systems

| | **Propositional content** | **Illocutionary force indication** | **Felicity conditions (speaker commitment, etc.)** | **Evidence and source** |
|---|---|---|---|---|
| Lakoff (1972) | Hedge | | | |
| Fraser (1975) | | Hedged performative | | |
| Brown and Levinson (1978) | Hedge | Hedge | Hedge | |
| Prince *et al.* (1982) | Approximator (Adaptor, rounder) | | Plausibility shield | Attribution shield |
| Caffi (1999, 2001, 2007) | Bush | Hedge | Hedge | Shield |

The different classification systems have also met with criticism. Objections to Lakoff's semantic account of approximation were raised, for instance, by Sadock (1977), who instead provides a radical pragmatic account, treating approximations as almost unfalsifiable. In a similar vein, but still within bivalent (i.e. truth-conditional) semantics, Wachtel (1980) proposes a context-sensitive approach to account for the fact that a particular approximation may be appropriate in one context but not in another.[2] Prince *et al.*'s (1982) subdivision has been criticized as 'sustainable only in the abstract' (Skelton, 1988: 38). Such criticism does not seem to be entirely justified, since Prince *et al.*'s (1982) categories arose precisely out of an analysis of actual language data, namely physician–physician discourse. It is true, however, that in actual language use individual linguistic items may prove difficult to pigeon-hole, often as a result of their multi-functionality (cf. e.g. Caffi, 2007: 264 and Kaltenböck, this volume).

Another problem for the classification models is that hedging effects may also be achieved by employing semantically different mechanisms such as generic expressions (placeholders), for example, which can also play an important role in approximating constructions, see Andersen (this volume) or indefinite hyperbolic quantifying expressions, for example which tend to be

[2] Cf. also Channell (1980) for a critical response to Wachtel (1980).

derived from round numbers (see Lavric, this volume). As suggested by Markkanen and Schröder (1997: 6), 'almost any linguistic item or expression can be interpreted as a hedge'.

Despite the difficulties involved, it is clear that classificatory frameworks are necessary heuristic devices. It is one of the explicit aims of this volume, therefore, to contribute to the discussion and definition of the individual categories.

## 3. Overview of the Contributions

As outlined in the brief overview in Section 2, the study of hedges is a varied field for which a number of different but related (and often overlapping) categories have been proposed. The contributions to this volume reflect this variety, in accordance with the inclusive view of hedging adopted for the present collection (cf. the discussion in Section 1). The chapters thus span a range of different categories from approximators, shields, hedged performatives to placeholder nouns and approximative numerals. All contributions are, however, in some form concerned with the pragmatic functions and patterns of use of the different linguistic devices and base their investigations on empirical data analysis, typically derived from corpora. While this corpus-based approach provides a unifying element for the contributions, there is considerable variation in the text types and communicative settings discussed. In line with the cross-linguistic perspective of the volume (cf. Section 1), the contributions also involve a number of different languages. Table I.2 provides a brief, albeit somewhat crude, overview of the different languages, types of hedges, and language data discussed in the volume.

It is clear that contributions as varied as these are difficult to group thematically. The arrangement chosen for the present volume is therefore only a loose one, which follows, very roughly, the degree of semantic-pragmatic scope of the linguistic devices discussed. After an introductory overview chapter by Fraser, the first contribution is on expressions that typically lack scope over other items and function as placeholders for semantically more specific words (e.g. Engl. *thing*). The following discussions involve items with narrow scope, typically over a phrasal constituent, such as the classic English approximator *sort of*. The final contributions then move on to a discussion of hedges with wider scope (e.g. over an entire clause), such as the English shield *I think*.

The volume starts with a contribution by *Fraser*, who studies a central aspect of hedging, namely hedging as a rhetorical strategy, and the necessary pragmatic competence of speakers involved in hedging. After giving a detailed overview of the diverse linguistic means exploited for hedging in English, he discusses the interaction of hedging and related discourse phenomena such as vagueness, evasion, equivocation and politeness and their motivations by looking at highly varied examples taken from naturally occurring language data such as everyday conversation, formal academic writing and mass media. These examples illustrate the ubiquity of hedging and show the relevance of hedging as an important area in second-language teaching.

**Table I.2.** Overview of contributions

| Author | Languages | Hedging type | Data |
|---|---|---|---|
| Fraser | English (Am.) | Approximators, shields | Examples from everyday conversation, formal academic writing, and mass media |
| Andersen | Norwegian, English (mainly Brit.) | Placeholder nouns | Corpora of spoken Norwegian, *Oxford English Dictionary* |
| Fetzer | English (Brit.) | Approximators (*sort of, kind of*) | Political interviews and political speeches |
| Meyer & Pawlack | Brazilian Portuguese, German | Approximators, shields, expressions of vagueness | Corpus of expert talks translated into German |
| Mihatsch | French, Italian, Portuguese, Spanish | Approximators (adaptors and rounders) | Corpora of spoken language, e.g. *C-ORAL-ROM* |
| Lavric | French, Italian, Spanish, German and English | Indefinite quantifiers derived from numerals | Collection of attestations in novels, interviews with native speakers |
| Ran | Chinese | Approximative numerals | Examples taken from literary and non-literary texts |
| Caffi | Classical Greek | Approximators (*so to say*) | Plato's *Gorgias* |
| Kärkkäinen | English (Am.) compared to British English | Shields (*I think, I guess*, etc.) | *Santa Barbara Corpus of Spoken American English* |
| Kaltenböck | English (Brit.) | Shields, approximators | Spoken part of the British component of the *International Corpus of English* |

*Table I.2: (Continued)*

| Author | Languages | Hedging type | Data |
|---|---|---|---|
| Schneider | English, French, Italian, Spanish | Hedged performatives | Spoken language corpora of French, Italian, Spanish |
| Briz and Estellés | Spanish | Approximative discourse particles | *Diccionario de Partículas Discursivas del Español*, based on corpora of spoken language and press texts |

*Andersen* analyses Norwegian placeholder nouns, that is a means of vague language in a wider sense, and their usage patterns as placeholders in head position or rightmost component of an NP, as textual discourse marker, in specific lexicalized uses and in set-marking tags, that is in approximating devices, thus hedges in a narrower sense. The contrastive and diachronic study is based on five corpora of spoken Norwegian ranging from 1970 to 2005. The results are then compared to the English equivalents. Although the placeholder function can be observed for all countable general nouns analyzed, the function as a textual discourse marker shows some remarkable diachronic developments and a shift from the use of the now receding *sak* to the more recent use of *ting* and most recently *greie.* The latter is also found to exhibit a new meaning in expressions corresponding to 'not my thing'.

The classic English hedges *sort of* and *kind of* in the context of political discourse are investigated by *Fetzer*, who combines a quantitatively oriented corpus analysis with qualitatively oriented socio-pragmatics. The contribution presents a genre-specific analysis of *sort of* and *kind of* in political speeches and interviews, which accounts for their distribution, collocation patterns and scope and argues for *sort of* and *kind of* to be assigned the status of contextualization cues par excellence: when collocating with an NP, they can retain the literal lexical meaning and make the NP more fuzzy or, when used as an approximator, make it less fuzzy, depending on position, co-occurrence and sequential status. When collocating with a VP, they make the VP over which they have scope more fuzzy, and thus only show the hedging function.

Speakers tend to use hedges rather unconsciously, and hedges do not seem to be very salient in speech reception either. It therefore might be expected that interpreters do not translate hedges. However, *Meyer* and *Pawlack*, who analyse a specifically collected corpus of three Brazilian Portuguese expert talks translated into German by five interpreters, show that the reverse is also the case: interpreters introduce hedges in the target language where the source is more precise. The reason is that interpreters use hedging devices, that is approximators but also shields (in Prince *et al.*'s (1982) classification), as well as other means of vague language to adapt a source text to the audience's knowledge. Typical examples are the replacing of proper names by placeholders or the use of shields to soften strong claims in the source text and thus render the content more acceptable to the audience.

In her comparative and diachronic study, *Mihatsch* analyses the changes leading from adaptors to rounders (according to Prince *et al.*'s (1982) classification) and compares French-, Italian-, Portuguese- and Spanish-spoken corpus data. She detects strong unidirectional changes leading from lexical approximators, that is adaptors, to quantificational approximators, that is rounders, probably through shield functions, but not vice versa, and explains this restriction by showing the different communicative motivations, cognitive mechanisms and the different origins behind the use of adaptors and rounders.

*Lavric* undertakes a contrastive study of a specific type of indefinite quantifiers, that is those meaning 'very few' or 'very many', derived from cardinal numbers through expressive discourse strategies. Starting from a published collection of French number expressions taken from novels, Lavric investigates equivalent expressions in French, Italian, Spanish, German and English by conducting systematic interviews with native speakers. The study reveals three types of cardinals: (i) specific small cardinals leading to minimizing quantifiers, (ii) very high round cardinals as well as those just below and above round numerals (such as 99) leading to quantifiers indicating large amounts and (iii) cardinals between 7 and 40, which seem to be culturally determined and which can either become maximizing or minimizing quantifiers, depending on the context. The chapter shows both general cross-linguistic tendencies as well as culture-specific, often idiomatic, uses.

Another study of approximative uses of numerals is provided by *Ran* for Chinese. He shows that approximative numerals fall into two categories: those accompanied by the discourse marker *ba* and those without *ba*. While in the former category the approximative interpretation of the numeral arises through the use of *ba*, in the latter category the approximation results from conventional uses of numerical expressions. These conventionalized uses are shown to be highly culture-specific, as evidenced for instance in popular sayings and ancient poems. The chapter, however, also highlights the context-dependence of numerals, illustrating how the effects of approximative numerals may change in different contexts.

*Caffi*'s contribution is grounded in the assumption that the study of hedging operations can benefit from the analysis of language usage as it developed through the centuries in the field of rhetoric. She presents an in-depth analysis of the use of the approximation marker *so to say* in a passage taken from Plato's dialogue *Gorgias*. The contextualized analysis of the marker shows that it can be given two opposite interpretations: attenuating and reinforcing. In other words, the marker in question can be seen as both an approximator and an underscorer and illustrates a peculiar case of *enantiosemy*.

*Kärkkäinen* explores the use of epistemic phrases such as *I think, I don't know, I guess, I thought* and *I remember* in American English conversation, comparing unplanned everyday speech and planned institutional speech. Her study focuses on the scope of these expressions, more precisely whether they have 'forward scope' extending over material following the epistemic phrase, or 'backward scope', that is over what was verbalized immediately before. The corpus data show that, overall, there is a clear prevalence of clausal scope (i.e. covering an entire clause) over phrasal scope (i.e. covering a phrasal constituent) as well as a prevalence of forward scope over backward scope. The results are contrasted with findings for British English, and it is argued that the differences in scope reflect a deeper grammaticalization difference between the two varieties.

The scope of hedging devices is also a main focus in the contribution by *Kaltenböck*, who investigates the pragmatic function of parenthetical *I think* in spoken British English. Taking into account the parameter of scope together with position, prosody and co-occurrence facts, the study shows that *I think* exhibits great functional flexibility. The following core communicative functions are identified: shield, approximator, structural device and booster function. These seemingly disparate uses are accounted for in a unified way in a monosemous account, which relates the four functions to an underlying abstract core meaning. Depending on the concrete co-textual realization of *I think,* this abstract meaning is activated in different ways, thus providing a unifying semantic bracket for all different uses.

*Schneider* investigates the use of parenthetical hedged performatives in spoken English, French, Italian and Spanish. A corpus survey of forms actually occurring in spoken discourse shows that the performatives are mostly based on Engl. *say* and its equivalents in the three Romance languages. Because of their particular form, hedged performatives resemble descriptions of state of affairs rather than indications of illocutionary force. This formal resemblance results in an overt discrepancy, as they pretend to describe a speech act, which at the same time is being performed. The discrepancy violates a conversational maxim, which is resolved by a conversational implicature and reinterpreted as mitigation of speaker commitment.

*Briz* and *Estellés* provide evidence for the interaction between the meanings of Spanish discourse particles and their positions with respect to discourse units. Changes in position bring about changes in meaning and may also trigger or inhibit mitigation. There are some discourse particles whose core meaning is mitigating, and some others whose attenuating meaning arises in particular contexts. The former are *prototypically* attenuating, provided they are in the appropriate position with respect to their discourse unit. The latter, by contrast, may develop a contextual, peripheral attenuating meaning if their position in discourse is changed.

## References

Berlin, B. and P. Kay (1969). *Basic colour terms: Their universality and evolution.* Berkeley: University of California Press.

Blum-Kulka, J., J. House and G. Kasper (eds.) (1989). *Cross-cultural pragmatics: Requests and apologies*. Norwood (NJ): Ablex.

Brown, P. and S. Levinson (1978). "Universals in language usage: Politeness phenomena", in E. N. Goody (ed.), *Questions and politeness. Strategies in social interaction*. Cambridge: Cambridge University Press, 56–311.

Brown, P. and S. Levinson (1987). *Politeness: Some universals in language usage*. Cambridge: Cambridge University Press.

Caffi, C. (1999). "On mitigation". *Journal of Pragmatics* **31**: 881–909.

Caffi, C. (2001). *La mitigazione. Un approccio pragmatico alla comunicazione nei contesti terapeutici*. Münster: LIT.

Caffi, C. (2007). *Mitigation*. Amsterdam: Elsevier.

Channell, J. (1980). "More on approximators: A reply to Wachtel". *Journal of Pragmatics* **4**: 461–476.

Channell, J. (1994). *Vague language*. Oxford: Oxford University Press.

Cutting, J. (ed.) (2007). *Vague language explored*. Houndmills: Palgrave Macmillan.

Diewald, G. (2006). "Hecken und Heckenausdrücke. Versuch einer Neudefinition", in E. Calaresu, C. Guardiano and K. Hölker (eds.), *Italienisch und Deutsch als Wissenschaftssprachen. Bestandsaufnahmen, Analysen, Perspektiven*. Berlin: Lit Verlag, 295–315.

Fraser, B. (1975). "Hedged performatives", in P. Cole and J. L. Morgan (eds.), *Syntax and semantics. Vol. 3. Speech acts*. New York: Academic Press, 187–210.

Grice, H. P. (1975). "Logic and conversation", in P. Cole and J. L. Morgan (eds.), *Syntax and semantics. Vol. 3. Speech acts*. New York: Academic Press, 41–58.

Grice, H. P. (1978). "Further notes on logic and conversation", in P. Cole (ed.), *Syntax and semantics. Vol. 9. Pragmatics*. New York: Academic Press, 113–127.

Hare, R. M. (1970). "Meaning and speech acts". *Philosophical Review* **79**: 3–24.

House, J. and G. Kasper (1981). "Politeness markers in English and German", in F. Coulmas (ed.), *Conversational routine*. The Hague: Mouton de Gruyter, 157–185.

Hübler, A. (1983). *Understatements and hedges in English*. Amsterdam/Philadelphia: Benjamins.

Hyland, K. (1998). *Hedging in scientific research articles*. Amsterdam/Philadelphia: Benjamins.

Jucker, A. H., S. W. Smith and T. Lüdge (2003). "Interactive aspects of vagueness in conversation". *Journal of Pragmatics* **35**: 1737–1769.

Kärkkäinen, E. (2003). *Epistemic stance in English conversation. A description of its interactional functions, with a focus on "I think"*. Amsterdam/Philadelphia: Benjamins.

Kerbrat-Orecchioni, C. (2005). *Le discours en interaction*. Paris: Armand Colin.

Lakoff, G. (1972). "Hedges: A study in meaning criteria and the logic of fuzzy concepts", in P. M. Peranteau, J. N. Levi and G. C. Phares (eds.), *Papers from the Eighth Regional Meeting of the Chicago Linguistic Society*, Chicago Linguistic Society, Chicago, 183–228. Reprinted in *Journal of Philosophical Logic*, 1973, **2**: 458–508.

Markkanen, R. and H. Schröder (1992). "Hedging and its linguistic realization in English, German and Finnish philosophical texts: a case study", in M. Nordman (ed.), *Fachsprachliche Miniaturen*. Frankfurt/Main: Peter Lang, 121–130.

Markkanen, R. and H. Schröder (1997). "Hedging: A challenge for pragmatics and discourse analysis", in R. Markkanen and H. Schröder (eds.), *Hedging and discourse. Approaches to the analysis of a pragmatic phenomenon in academic texts*. Berlin/New York: Walter de Gruyter, 3–18.

Prince, E. F., J. Frader and C. Bosk (1982). "On hedging in physician-physician discourse", in R. J. Di Pietro (ed.), *Linguistics and the professions. Proceedings of the Second Annual Delaware Symposium on Language Studies*. Norwood (NJ): Ablex, 83–97.

Rosch, E. (1973). "Natural categories". *Cognitive Psychology* **4**: 328–350.

Sadock, J.M. (1977). "Truth and approximations". *Proceedings of the Third Annual Meeting of the Berkeley Linguistics Society*. Berkeley: Berkeley Linguistics Society, 430–439.

Skelton, J. (1988). "The care and maintenance of hedges". *ELT Journal* **42** (**1**): 37–43.

Terraschke, A. and J. Holmes (2007). " 'Und Tralala': Vagueness and General Extenders in German and New Zealand English", in J. Cutting (ed.), *Vague language explored*. Houndmills: Palgrave Macmillan, 198–220.

Wachtel, T. (1980). "Pragmatic approximations". *Journal of Pragmatics* **4**: 201–211.

Weinreich, U. (1963). "On the semantic structure of language", in J. H. Greenberg (ed.), *Universals of language*. Report of a conference held at Dobbs Ferry, New York, April 13–15, 1961. Cambridge (MA): MIT Press, 114–171.

Wierzbicka, A. (1991). *Cross cultural pragmatics. The semantics of human interaction*. Berlin: Mouton de Gruyter.

Wierzbicka, A. (2006). *English: Meaning and culture*. Oxford: Oxford University Press.

Zadeh, L. (1965). "Fuzzy sets". *Information and Control* **8**: 338–353.

New Approaches to Hedging
Edited by Gunther Kaltenböck, Wiltrud Mihatsch and Stefan Schneider


# 1

# Pragmatic Competence: The Case of Hedging

*Bruce Fraser*

## Abstract

This chapter looks at hedging as an aspect of pragmatic competence. After describing the evolution of the concept of hedging from 1972 to the present day, it reviews the principal properties of hedges and discusses the relationship between hedging and the discourse effects of vagueness, evasion, equivocation, and politeness. The final part of the chapter presents examples of hedging from a range of sources, illustrating the ubiquity of the concept.

## 1. Introduction

PRAGMATIC COMPETENCE is the ability to communicate your intended message with all its nuances in any socio-cultural context and to interpret the message of your interlocutor as it was intended. As critical as this ability is for communication success, it is often not given the emphasis it deserves in the teaching of a second language, with the result that second-language speakers, who lack pragmatic competence, may produce grammatically flawless speech that nonetheless fails to achieve its communicative aims.

One area in which the lack of pragmatic competence can create serious problems for a second-language speaker is that of HEDGING, a rhetorical strategy that attenuates either the full semantic value of a particular expression, as in *He's* ***sort of*** *nice*, or the full force of a speech act, as in *I must ask you to stop doing that.* When non-native speakers fail to hedge appropriately, they may be perceived as impolite, offensive, arrogant, or simply inappropriate. Failing to recognize a hedged utterance, they may misunderstand a native speaker's meaning. This is especially unfortunate when speakers are otherwise fluent, since people typically expect that someone who speaks their language well on the grammatical level has also mastered the pragmatic niceties.

In this chapter I look at hedging as an aspect of pragmatic competence. In Section 2, I describe the evolution of hedging from the point at which it was introduced into the linguistic literature in 1972 until today. In Section 3, I address the properties of hedges, the devices through which hedging is implemented, and in Section 4, I discuss the relationship between hedging and the discourse effects of vagueness, evasion, equivocation, and politeness. In Section 5, I present examples of hedging from a range of sources, including everyday conversation, formal academic writing, and mass media (radio and television). These examples illustrate the ubiquity of hedging and highlight the perils its misuse holds for non-native speakers.

## 2. The Evolution of the Concept of Hedging

As far as I can determine, Weinreich (1966: 163) was the first person to write about hedging in the linguistic research literature when he talked about "metalinguistic operators," arguing that

> for every language "metalinguistic operators" such as (in) English *true*, *real*, *so-called*, *strictly speaking*, and the most powerful extrapolator of all, *like*, function as instructions for the loose or strict interpretation of designata.

However, it was Lakoff (1972) who had the greatest initial impact, and it was his papers that popularized the concept. He drew on the work of Zadeh (1965), and that of Rosch (1973). Zadeh worked with fuzzy sets and noticed that categories such as animals, which were thought to have a fixed membership criteria, had a "continuum of classification grades." Rosch-Heider challenged the notion that properties defining a category are shared by all members equally. For example, a robin is not just a "sort of a bird" but rather a "bird par excellence," whereas a penguin is a "sort of bird."

Lakoff suggested that any attempt to limit truth conditions for natural language sentences to true, false, and "nonsense" would distort the natural language concepts by portraying them as having sharp rather than vaguely defined boundaries. Suggesting that this is an area that deserves study, he wrote that

> For me, some of the most interesting questions are raised by the study of ***words*** whose meaning implicitly involves fuzziness – words whose job it is to make things fuzzier or less fuzzy. (Lakoff, 1972: 195)

He was interested in the properties of words such as *rather* or *sort of* and how they make things fuzzy or less fuzzy (vague or less vague). For Lakoff, hedging involved the attenuation of the membership of a particular expression, for example,

(1) a) John is **sort of** smart.
    b) That is **technically** a bookcase.

or the reinforcement of the class membership, for example,[1]

(2) a) John is **very, very** smart.
b) I **really** love you.
c) What I tell you is the **absolute** truth.

Lakoff began with a semantic discussion of *sort of*, pointing out that this predicate modifier and others like it reveal different distinctions of category membership. In the sentences below,

(3) a) A robin is **sort of** a bird. [false, no questions it's a bird]
b) A chicken is **sort of** a bird. [true, or very close to true]
c) A penguin is **sort of** a bird. [true, or close to true]
d) A bat is **sort of** a bird. [false, or very close to false]
e) A cow is **sort of** a bird. [false]

the degree of truth must be "rejected" for a real bird, "possibly" accepted for a non-prototypical bird like a chicken or penguin, but "rejected" again when the animal of which *bird* was being predicated was simply not a bird or not much of a bird. Lakoff discussed other hedges such as *par excellence*, *typically*, *strictly speaking*, *loosely speaking*, and *in essence*, showing that these hedges interact with the term they modify, but in different ways. All his examples involved predicate adjectives or predicate nominals, and all were declarative sentences. This type of hedging I refer to as PROPOSITIONAL HEDGING, since it is the truth value of the proposition that is affected.

It is relevant that Lakoff was primarily interested in hedges, not hedging. He offered the following as examples of hedges in English.[2]

(4) *real, regular, actually, almost, as it were, basically, can be view as, crypto-, especially, essentially, exceptionally, for the most part, in a manner of speaking, in a real sense, in a sense, in a way, kind of, largely, literally, loosely speaking, more or less, mostly, often, on the tall side, par excellence, particularly, pretty much, principally, pseudo-, quintessentially, rather, really, relatively, roughly, so to say, somewhat, sort of, strictly speaking, technically, typically, very, virtually.*

He also showed that the interpretation of hedges is dependent on context and that the effect of hedging is a pragmatic not a semantic phenomenon. For example, the interpretation of (5),

(5) Technically, Dale and Lee are married.

---

[1] None of the examples in this chapter were invented but came from the BNC, texts, papers, overheard conversations, and the like. I sometimes made modifications in length. I have not cited the sources since I do not believe they are relevant for this chapter.

[2] Although he does not mention it, he presumably is aware that these terms were involved in hedging only some of the time.

depends crucially on the hearer's knowledge of the gender of the two subjects as well as what constitutes marriage.

Finally, Lakoff touched upon, but did not delve into, several notions that were developed later by others. For example, he wrote of hedges interacting with **performatives**, as in

(6) Technically, I *said* Harry was a bastard [ = I said Harry was a bastard, but I didn't mean it]

where *technically* is canceling the implication that if you say something, it is assumed that you mean it. He also attributes to Robin Lakoff the observation that certain verbs and syntactic constructions "convey hedged performatives – that is, they modify the force of a speech act" (195) For example, in

(7) I suppose that Harry is coming

we have a modified claim. He did not follow up on her observations, but Fraser (1975) and Brown and Levinson (1978, 1987) did so.

Fraser (1975) introduced the term HEDGED PERFORMATIVE, where certain performative verbs such as *apologize*, *promise*, and *request* when preceded by specific modals such as *can*, *must*, and *should*, as in

(8) a) I **should** apologize for running over your cat.
b) I **can** promise that I will never again smoke grass.
c) I **must** request that you sit down.

result in an attenuated illocutionary force of the speech act designated by the verb. In these examples, the modals were considered as hedges. Example (8a) is still an apology, just one less strong than if *should* were not present.

It was Brown and Levinson (1978, 1987) who developed fully the speech act aspect of hedging. Whereas Lakoff considered only propositional hedging, and Fraser touched only on performative verb hedging, Brown and Levinson treated the hedging of the illocutionary force of a speech act in great detail in their efforts to account for politeness phenomena. This second type of hedging I refer to as SPEECH ACT HEDGING.

They commented that in the literature,

> A hedge is a particle, word, or phrase that modifies the degree of membership of a predicate or noun phrase in a set; it says of that membership that it is *partial*, or true only in certain respect; or that it is *more* true and complete than perhaps might be expected. (145)

and then moved to a discussion involving illocutionary force hedging, where the hedge attenuates the strength of the speech act. They write:

> Now, the thrust of our argument is that ordinary communicative intentions are often potential threats to cooperative interaction. Communicative intentions are regulated and encoded in speech

> acts, and if one looks at the conditions on the felicitous use of speech acts, the sources of threat become clear ... Consequently, to hedge these assumptions – that is, to avoid commitment to them – is a primary and fundamental method of disarming routine interactional threats. (146)

It is interesting that Brown and Levinson maintain both the **attenuation** and the **reinforcement** aspects of hedging, although they wrote little of the latter aspect.

Prince *et al.* (1982) made a clear distinction between two types of hedging, one type that involves the propositional content and affects the truth condition of the proposition conveyed (propositional hedging), and a second type that involves the relationship between the propositional content and the speaker and serves as an index of the commitment of the speaker to the truth of the propositional content conveyed (speech act hedging).[3]

These authors divided up the hedging world into two classes. The first, APPROXIMATORS, operate on the propositional content proper and contribute to the interpretation by indicating some markedness, that is, non-prototype, with respect to class membership of a particular item. There are two subclasses: ADAPTORS (acknowledged to be what Lakoff called **hedges**), relate to class membership; for example, *somewhat, sort of, almost describable as, some, a little bit*, etc.,

(9) a) He also has a **somewhat** low interior larynx.
b) She noticed that he was **a little bit** blue.

and ROUNDERS, convey a range, where the term is typical, for example, *about, approximately, something around*, etc.

(10) a) His weight was **approximately** 3.2 kilograms.
b) The baby's blood pressure was **something** between forty and fifty.

Both sub-classes occur when the speaker is attempting to correlate an actual situation with some prototypical, goal-relevant situation, where the hedging indicates that actual situation is close to but not exactly the expression modified.

SHIELDS, their second class, change the relationship between propositional content and the speaker by implicating a level of uncertainty with respect to speaker's commitment. Here, again, there are two subclasses. PLAUSIBILITY SHIELDS are expressions that relate doubt, such as *I think, I take it, probably, as far as I can tell, right now, I have to believe, I don't see that*, etc., illustrated by the following.

(11) a) **I think** we can just slow him down to a little over maintenance.
b) **As far as I can tell**, you don't have anything to lose by taking that path.

[3] Although they discuss only statements in their chapter, their discussion can be easily extended to other syntactic types.

Prince *et al.* point out that whereas the unhedged versions imply that the speaker has knowledge via observations and/or logical reasoning, statements marked by a plausibility shield imply that the speaker is making the assertion based on plausible reasons.

The second subclass, ATTRIBUTION SHIELDS are expressions such as *according to her estimates*, *presumably*, *at least to X's knowledge*, etc., which attribute the responsibility of the message to someone other than the speaker, often via plausible reasoning.

(12) a) He was not very ill, **according to her estimates**.
b) There was no reason to worry, **as far as anyone knew**.

The authors also point out that one usually does not impose belief on another when the speaker believes that the proposition at issue is false. For example, in (13),

(13) **According to** Dr. Jenkins, we should take out the shunt before we move him.

the speaker is typically committed to the truth of the statement.[4]

Hübler (1983) made a similar two-way distinction of hedging, between what he called UNDERSTATEMENTS and HEDGES, although he uses UNDERSTATEMENT as a cover term for both. Understatement means that "the emotional negatability (of sentences) is restricted through the indetermination of the phrastic," that is, they concern the propositional content of the sentence. *It is **a bit** cold in here*, contains an understatement. HEDGING "is restricted through the indetermination of the neustic," that is, it concerns the speaker's attitude to the hearer regarding the proposition, the claim to validity of the proposition the speaker makes. *It is cold in Alaska, **I suppose***, contains a hedge. Hübler's division resembles that of Prince *et al.* (1982), whose APPROXIMATORS correspond to Hübler's UNDERSTATEMENTS and whose SHIELDS correspond to his HEDGES.

Finally, Caffi (1999, 2007) wrote about MITIGATION, the attenuation of unwelcome effects on the hearer (cf. Fraser, 1980), and proposed a classification of mitigating mechanisms (mostly hedging devices) based on her view of the three components of the utterance on which mitigation can operate: the proposition, the illocution, and the utterance source. She called these BUSHES, HEDGES, and SHIELDS, respectively.

(14) BUSHES, which are lexical expressions that reduce the commitment to the propositional content of the utterance and may introduce vagueness in the interpretation of the utterance and affect the truth value of the proposition.

[4] Brown and Levinson (1978, 1987) do acknowledge the existence of this last sub-class, Attribution Shields, but they do not call them hedges but rather refer to them as impersonal verbs (196); replacement of *I and you* by indefinites (202); pluralization of *I and you* (203); use of address terms as you avoidance (208); use of reference terms as I avoidance (209); and point-of-view distancing (209).

(15) **HEDGES**, which are lexical expressions whose scope is the illocutionary force of the speech act and attenuates the strength of the force by reducing the speaker's commitment.

(16) **SHIELDS**, which are devices to avoid the self-ascription to the utterance and realize an overall shift of responsibility, for instance by introducing a different speaker or by deleting the deictic origin of the utterance.

Caffi's mitigators covered the same concepts as Prince, Frader, and Bosk, although the labels are applied differently. However, Caffi was quite clear that mitigation is not the same as politeness. She wrote,

> Far from being limited to a matter of politeness, mitigation captures a rationally grounded behavior which is chiefly aimed at avoiding unnecessary risks, responsibilities and conflicts. At the same time, mitigation indexes the type of speaker we want to be taken for in a given encounter. (1999: 12)

and suggested that a mitigating speaker can be perceived as impolite, and conversely, a non-mitigating, direct speaker can be perceived as exquisitely polite. In Caffi's view, politeness is one of many possible effects of a mitigating operation, an effect that is both calculable and uncertain, that is, not guaranteed.

In Caffi's approach, there is no space for a sharp distinction between approximators belonging to semantics and shields to pragmatics. For her, the operation of bushes on the propositional content has repercussions on the whole speech act. In other words, a weakened (marked) precision in the reference act has the effect of weakening the commitment to the truth of the proposition, and this in turn has the effect of weakening the subscription to the whole speech act.

It is relevant that the Plausibility Shields and Attribution Shields of Prince, Frader, and Bosk and Hedges and Shields of Caffi have the same overall effect: they both attenuate the force of the speech act, the former of each applying to the scope of the speech act, the latter applying to the source of the contribution.

In the 1980s, there was considerable effort to sub-classify the class of hedges, based on certain class membership criteria. The following list reflects the array of proposals involving attenuating hedges.

(17) *adaptors, agent avoiders, approximators, attenuators, attribution shields, bushes, committers, compromisers, consultative devices, deintensifiers, diffusers, diminishers, down-toners forewarners, indicator of degrees of reliability, minimizers, mitigators, plausibility shields, play-downs, politeness markers, scope-staters, understaters, validity markers, vocal hesitators, weakeners, etc.*

Since the 1980s, there has also been an emphasis on the properties of individual hedges, for example, see Kay (1984), Aijmer (1984), and Fetzer (this volume). In addition, there has been considerable interest in exploring the use of hedging within different genres of language use, for example, the research article, mathematics talk, politician talk, negotiation talk, and the speech of language learners, to name but a few of the areas. I do not explore these areas (cf. Schröder and Zimmer, 1997).

## 3. Hedging Today

There is general agreement today that **HEDGING** is a rhetorical strategy, by which a speaker, using a linguistic device, can signal a lack of commitment to either the full semantic membership of an expression (**PROPOSITIONAL HEDGING**),

(18) a) He's really **like** a geek.
b) The pool has **sort of** a L-shaped design.
c) Peter's house is **almost** 100 feet wide.

or the full commitment to the force of the speech act being conveyed (**SPEECH ACT HEDGING**),

(19) a) Come over here, **can you**?
b) **I guess** I **should** leave now.
c) That type of comment isn't made around here. [Agentless passive]
d) **Perhaps** you would sit down a minute.

The notion of **REINFORCEMENT**, initially considered a part of hedging, has pretty much been laid aside. Thus, sentences such as

(20) a) **I certainly do insist** that you sit down.
b) He is **extremely** tall.

are not generally viewed today as instances of hedging but rather of reinforcement. I believe that the reason for this narrowing of the concept stems from the fact that the sense of hedging on the positive side of a concept (be it to involve a proposition or a speech act) seems counterintuitive: hedging is simply not a symmetrical notion, and it does not connote reinforcement.

Linguistic hedges include linguistic devices, both morphological and syntactic forms used in the process of hedging. These include

(21) adverbs, adjectives, impersonal pronouns, concessive conjunctions, indirect speech acts, introductory phrases, modal adverbs, modal adjectives, hedged performatives, modal nouns, modal verbs, epistemic verbs, negation, tag questions, agentless passives, parenthetic constructions, if clauses, progressive forms, tentative inference, hypothetical past, metalinguistic comments, etc.

Although I am concerned here with linguistic devices, for example, lexical expressions such as *sort of*, *technically*, and *I think*, and syntactic configurations such as agentless passive, tag question, and hedged performative, vocalizations such as *aww*, *uhhh*, and *weeellll*, and gestural devices such as a dismissive wave of the hand or a shrug of the head can be used in hedging as well. I am not discounting them, but they are not a focus of this chapter.

The fact that an expression may be used as a hedge is not part of its definition. In fact, an expression is usually only recognized as a hedge when it is used in hedging. Thus, it should not be surprising that there is no grammatical class of hedges, since hedging devices are drawn from every syntactic category. At best we might say that hedges form an open functional class. As Clemen (1997: 6) comments:

> There is no limit to the linguistic expressions that can be considered as hedges . . . The difficulty with these functional definitions is that almost any linguistic item or expression can be interpreted as a hedge . . . no linguistic items are inherently hedges but can acquire this quality depending on the communicative context or the co-text. This also means that no clear-cut lists of hedging expressions are possible.

Nevertheless, I offer below some examples of English hedges and their associated linguistic analysis, drawn from a variety of sources.

(22) a) Adverbs/Adjectives *approximately*, *roughly*, *about*, *often*, *occasionally*, *generally*, . . . )
He *looks* **sort of** sick.
b) Impersonal pronouns (one, it, . . . )
***One*** *can imagine that . . .*
c) Concessive conjunctions (*although*, *though*, *while*, *whereas*, *even though*, *even if*, . . . )
***Even though*** *you dislike the beach, it's worth going for the view.*
d) Hedged performative (use of modal to hedge performative verb)
I ***must*** *ask you to sit down.*
e) Indirect Speech Acts
*Could you speak a little louder?*
f) Introductory phrases (*I believe*, *to our knowledge*, *it is our view that*, *we feel that*, . . . )
***I believe*** *that he should go, if possible.*
g) Modal adverbs (*perhaps*, *possibly*, *probably*, *practically*, *presumably*, *apparently*, . . . )
*I can* ***possibly*** *do that,*
h) Modal adjectives (*possible*, *probable*, *un/likely*, . . . )
***It is possible*** *that . . .*

i) Modal noun (*assumption, claim, possibility, estimate, suggestion, ...* )
***The assumption*** here is that ...
j) Modal verbs (*might, can, would, could, ...* )
*John* ***might*** *leave now.*
k) Epistemic verbs (*to seem, to appear, to believe, to assume, to suggest, ...* )
***It seems that*** ...
l) Negative question convey positive hedged assertion
***Didn't*** *Harry leave? [I think Harry left]*
*I don't think I'm going. vs. I'm not going. [Former hedges the meaning of latter]*
m) Reversal tag
*He's coming,* ***isn't he****? [I think he's coming]*
n) Agentless Passive
*Many of the troops were injured ( ... )*
o) Conditional subordinators (*such as as long as, so long as, assuming that, given that*)
***Unless*** *the strike has been called off, there will be no trains tomorrow.*
p) Progressive form
*I* ***am hoping*** *you will come.*
q) Tentative Inference
*The mountains* ***should be*** *visible from here.*
r) Conditional clause refers to the condition under which the speaker makes the utterance.
***If you're going my way****, I need a lift back.*
s) Metalinguistic comment such as (*strictly speaking, so to say, exactly, almost, just about*)
*He has an idea, a hypothesis,* ***if you will****, that you* ***may*** *find interesting.*

In addition, Salager-Meyer (1995) proposed compound hedges such as the following:

(23) a) Modal with hedging verb (*It would appear that...*).
b) Hedging verb with hedging adverb/adjective (*It seems reasonable that...*).
c) Double hedges (*It may suggest that; This probably indicates that...*).
d) Treble hedges (*It seems reasonable to assume that...*).
e) Quadruple hedges (*It would seem somewhat unlikely that* John will tell anyone.

The focus of hedging may range from a single word to a speech act.

(24) a) Word – *He's* ***basically*** *a [bachelor.]*
b) Phrase – *He has a* ***somewhat*** *[elevated temperature.]*
c) Proposition – ***As far as I can tell****, [you won't have problems.]*
d) Speech Act – *I* ***must*** *[request] that you sit down.*

However, the focus of hedging is never an inference, an entailment, or a presupposition.

(25) a) An inference – *It's* ***sort of*** *warm in here* = > ***sort of*** *[Shut the window]*
b) An entailment – ***I think*** *that some of the boys stayed* = > ***I think that*** *[More than two of the boys stayed.]*
c) A presupposition – ***It could be*** *that Harry stopped beating his wife* = > ***It could be that*** *[Harry had been beating his wife.]*

The effect of hedging is found in the interpretation of the utterance rather than in the semantic meaning of the sentence uttered, where the interpretation depends on the context of utterance, the semantic meaning of the sentence uttered, the particular hedge(s) used, and the belief system of the hearer. Moreover, hedging often gives an indication of the speaker's intentions. For example, in (26),

(26) All I know is that smoking is harmful to your health.

the expression "All I know" indicates that the speaker is saying that the proposition following is true only as far as he can judge, not in any absolute sense. But the speaker is also indicating that Grice's Maxim of Quantity is being followed (cf. Grice, 1975). Finally, the effect of hedges in initial vs. medial vs. final utterance position often creates a different interpretation, but this has not been examined in great depth (cf. Fetzer, this volume; Schneider, 2007).

## 4. The Relationship of Hedging to Other Discourse Effects

Some instances of hedging give rise to other discourse effects. I address several of them here, recognizing that there are others not touched upon.

### 4.1. Vagueness

Most expressions are vague, although we do not realize it. The utterance *John is bald* is vague. How much hair must he have lost to be considered bald? It depends. Generally, we reduce our requirement of precision to accommodate the hearer, what we might call "common ground exploitation" (Jucker *et al.*, 2003).[5]

(27) a) John is bald [on top but has a fringe around the edges.]
b) John is bald [for one so young.]
c) John is [completely] bald.

---

[5] An expression is said to be ambiguous if it has at least two specific meanings that make sense in context whereas an expression is said to be vague if its meaning is not clear in context. If Jones does not know what is meant by a phrase, then that phrase is vague to him. He cannot identify exactly what the term is intended to mean or refer to. If Jones does not know which of two or more specific meanings is intended, then the term is ambiguous to him. Articles on vagueness include Channell (1994).

Simply stated, VAGUENESS, a perlocutionary effect (cf. Austin, 1962), occurs ***when the information you receive from a speaker lacks the expected precision***. For example, if two Americans encounter one another in Paris, and one asks the other where she lives, the answer *Boston* would be acceptable. In contrast, the answer *in the eastern part of the U.S.* would be vague. On the contrary, if these same two people met in Boston, the answer *Boston* to the query of where she lived would be heard as vague, and probably evasive.

Intentional vagueness occurs for a variety of reasons. For example, the non-vague contribution might offend someone, or the speaker does not know the precise details, or it really does not matter, or the intention is to evade. Worry of being charged with being wrong, might give rise to the hedged response *He visited Japan, Hong Kong, and so on* when asked *Where did he go on his trip*. The speaker, intending to evade when asked when she would return, might offer, *I'll be back sometime around noon*, whereas the desire to create an informal atmosphere might result in *Your dog, Aristotle, or whatever his name is, is welcome here*, said to an acquaintance standing at your front door.

Intentional vagueness also arises to accommodate memory loss (*thingamabob*, *whatsit*), or when there is a desire to imply shared knowledge, "You know what I mean." Finally, there are occasions when the speaker deliberately increases the vagueness, using terms like *and so on*, *in a way*, *or something like that*, *more or less*, *et cetera*, *in a sense*, *and things like that*, *or whatever*, *so to say*, *and so forth*, *somewhat*, *and everything*, and *stuff like*.

Propositional hedging may create propositional vagueness, as in

(28) a) He's **sort of** a geek.
b) I'll be there **around** six o'clock.

whereas speech act hedging, while creating a weakened illocutionary force, does not create vagueness, as the following show.

(29) a) **If you wouldn't mind**, help me up.
b) **It appears** that we should go.

Some hedging results in vagueness,

(30) a) A: What score did you receive on the test? B: I **kind of** messed up.
b) A: Exactly how wide is the porch? B: The porch is **about** 6 feet wide, give or take a foot.

whereas some hedging does not result in vagueness,

(31) a) Help me lift this box, **would you**.
b) [From an examining physician] **As far as I can tell**, you're in excellent shape.

and some vagueness does not come about from hedging

(32) a) He is bald.
b) I will come back sometime.

### 4.2. Evasion

EVASION occurs when the information you receive from the speaker fails to meet your expectation. Like vagueness, whether an utterance is evasive depends on the information provided by the speaker and the information expected by the hearer. Like vagueness, evasion is a property of hearer interpretation and, as such, is a perlocutionary effect. The answer *I think you'd better ask your mother* to the question *Can I go out tonight?* is potentially evasive, depending on the father's role in such matters.

Propositional hedging may result in vagueness, which may result in evasion,

(33) A: How is she? B: **In some ways** she is lovely.

and, unlike vagueness, speech act hedging may result in evasion.

(34) A: How much do you weigh? B: **One doesn't ask** a woman such things.

Sometimes vagueness can result in evasion, as mentioned earlier. Some hedging results in evasion,

(35) a) A: What time can we leave? B: I hope we can leave by noon.
b) A: Mr. President, what do you think of the general comment? B: **I think** it's a wonderful country when we all enjoy free speech.

some hedging does not result in evasion,

(36) A: Ok, doctor, what do you think. B: **As far as I can tell**, you're in excellent shape.

and some evasion does not come about from hedging

(37) A: Will you help me? B: I will have to consult with my principals.
A: Who is here? B: I'm not going to tell you.

There are a variety of ways to evade using language. The following list, taken primarily from Partington (2003), provides some examples.

(38) Ways of Evading
a) Bald, on record avoidance
A: Who is here? B: I'm not going to tell you.
b) Hedging, by providing a vague contribution
A: Exactly what time will you be here? B: Oh, about noon or so.
c) Claims of ignorance

A: Where is your daughter right now? B: Sorry, but I really don't know.
d) In response to a question, stating that the answer is well known
A: What is the policy on that? B: Oh, everybody is aware of the policy.
e) Referring the questioner to another
A: May I go out this evening. B: Go ask your father.
f) Challenging the questioner or the source
A: What will you do now? B: Who wants to know?

### 4.3. Equivocation

Equivocation is the use of a word with more than one meaning, where the intention is to mislead the hearer. For example,

(39) No child should work.
Every one is a child of someone.
Therefore, no one should work.

The term has been defined as "non-straightforward communication ... ambiguous, contradictory, tangential, obscure or even evasive" (Bavelas *et al.*, 1990: 28). I think that the ambiguous use, as shown in the examples below, is illustrative of the discourse use as typically viewed.

(40) a) Hubert Humphrey upon losing the 1968 election to Richard Nixon, said, "I'd always wanted to run for President in the worst way, and now I have."
b) President Clinton on being question about his relationship with Monica Lewinsky, said "I did not have sex with that woman."

I am not aware of examples where either propositional or speech act hedging results in equivocation, but there are numerous cases where equivocation does not arise from hedging.

(41) a) Well, that depends on what you call a good employee. (Person having to recommend someone he doesn't like for a job)
b) Our military operation in Panama was not, I repeat, not an invasion. That would violate the national sovereignty of one of our strongest friends and allies. "Operation Just Cause" was simply the result of my directing our armed forces to protect the lives of American citizens in Panama, to execute pre-planned missions in Panama, to conduct efforts to support the democratic processes in Panama, and to assure the integrity of the Panama Canal while creating an environment safe for American citizens. (President George H. Bush, 1989)

According to a theory of equivocation proposed by Bavelas *et al.* (1990), people typically equivocate when confronted with an avoidance–avoidance conflict, where they are posed a question to which all of the possible replies have potentially negative consequences, but where nevertheless a reply is expected. As far as I can tell, hedging does not result in equivocation.

### 4.4. Politeness

Brown and Levinson (1978, 1987) were concerned with two types of politeness: POSITIVE POLITENESS and NEGATIVE POLITENESS. Positive politeness is defined as redressive action directed to the addressee's positive face (the desire that his/her wants should be thought of as desirable), where redress consists in partially satisfying that desire by communicating that one's own wants are in some respects similar to the address's wants. Negative Politeness is defined as redressive action addressed to the addressee's negative face (the want to have his/her freedom of action unhindered and his attention unimpeded), where redress consists in partially satisfying that need by weakening a challenge to negative face.

Brown and Levinson focused primarily on negative politeness strategies that include (i) hedging the illocutionary force of an utterance; (ii) hedging any of the felicity conditions on the speech act; or (iii) hedging any of the four Gricean maxims. For example,

(42) a) Hedged performative
I **must** request that you sit down.
b) A felicity condition on requesting: hearer is able to carry out the act
Take the books off the table, **if you can manage it**.
c) The maxim of quality indicates full responsibility for truth of proposition
**I hope** the boat has already sailed.

Some hedging results in making the utterance more polite,

(43) a) **Would you be so kind as to** lift that up.
b) I **must** apologize for doing that.

whereas some hedging does not,

(44) a) The length of the curtains is **approximately** 48 inches.
b) Many of the soldiers were injured (**by the enemy**)

and some politeness does not result from hedging

(45) a) **Sir**, where is your hat.
b) What a beautiful hat, Myrna.

## 5. The Occurrence of Hedging

There are instances when an expression such as *kind of*, *in a way*, or *I think*, typically used as a hedge, is used with its literal meaning. This is not hedging. For example,

(46) a) I will be coming in **a few** minutes.
b) **I think** that politics is sleazy.

c) **Can** you see the deer over there.
d) I appreciate that **kind of** help.
e) Blair and I were able to talk **in a way** that reduced ambiguity.
f) I always admired the fact that a person who was **relatively** comfortable in life would be willing to help the less fortunate.

But I suggest that this literal use pales in comparison with the use of hedging in America's speech and writing. Although Americans view themselves as being direct, straightforward, and not beating around the bush, this is a myth. [*Note*: the previous statement is not hedged.] Hedging in American culture (and I assume most others) is necessary in many circumstances, lest the speaker be perceived as impolite, offensive, or arrogant. As I stated initially, successful performance and interpretation of hedging are a mark of pragmatic competence.

I present some of the many occasions where hedging is expected, if not required. These examples are taken from speech, newspapers, research articles, and TV. They are not intended to be systematic or complete, rather illustrative of the ubiquity of hedging in spoken and written English, both formal and informal.

The most obvious situation where hedging is used is one in which the speaker wishes to convey a negative message, as in (47).

(47) a) **It might be a good idea if we could** move on to the next speaker. [Teacher to a student giving a presentation]
b) I **must** insist that you leave.

A second situation occurs when the speaker wants to evade responsibility for the truth of a statement that potentially brings bad news to the hearer. This occurs, for example, when the doctor conveys (48a) rather than (48b) to a patient.

(48) a) **The CAT scan shows** that you have a lump in your liver.
b) There is a lump in your liver.

By doing this, the speaker is able to reference another authority. The more confident a speaker is about his/her own position vis-a-vis the interlocutor, the less need there is for hedging for the purposes of self-protection. The same evading of responsibility occurs in (49), which were statements made in a newspaper.

(49) a) A car was **reportedly** burglarized in the suburb of Nicola last night.
b) The **alleged** perpetrator fled the scene in a green Buick.

When authority is cited, it may be unclear where it ends and the writer resumes, as this quotation from *The Economist* exemplifies:

(50) The OECD acknowledges that there are risks. First, inflation **could** prove more stubborn in Germany. Second, Japanese firms **may** take longer to adjust their heavy

dept-burdens and lower asset-prices. Third, high unemployment **may** increase protectionist tendencies. **Even though** a GATT deal has been agreed, some governments **may still** try to protect individual industries.

Related is the use of hedging to evade responsibility for an action.

(51) a) The decision was made on Friday (**by Ø**).
b) **Someone** will let you know the outcome by 5 pm.

Another source of hedging is found in the language of negotiation. To appear conciliatory is not a sign of weakness but rather a strategy to appease the opposition and is often necessary for a successful resolution. In the following excerpt, a divorcing husband and wife are having a heated discussion about the sleeping arrangements during the time when their three-year-old son is with his father. The argument is not resolved until the wife conveys a hedged assertion that the issue is her business as well.

(52) W: Well, what if your girlfriend sleeps overnight. Then where is Jason going to sleep?
H: He'll sleep with me**, I guess**.
W: **I don't think** it's a good idea having him sleep between you and your girlfriend. **Wouldn't it be** a good plan for you to have another room for him?
H: Now listen, Jason is my son. What I do with my son is my business, not yours or anybody else's as long as he is taken care of . . .
W: Yes, it is your business. I agree. But, **without putting too fine a point on it**, **isn't it possibly** mine as well.
H: Well, I guess so. Ok, I'll arrange for a bed in another room.

The wife, by hedging her last statement, reduces the challenge to the husband.

In another divorcing negotiation (53), by hedging his question the husband expresses a conciliatory (hedged) stance and receives his wife's approval.

(53) W: Whatever you think, this child should be seeing you frequently.
H: Well I tried to make an effort to see her everyday but your mother kind of keeps me away.
W: Oh I love it . . . You would come down and see Rachel without telephoning that you were coming, you were coming in during Rachel's dinner time . . .
[More bickering]
H: So, **is what are you saying** Constance, **that is this a way of saying that**, that **if, there can be some kind of understanding and some kind of arrangement,** that you would not object to my seeing Rachel?
W: Yes.

Hedging may also occur when also occurs when the speaker asks a potentially sensitive question. The following examples are from White House press briefings.

(54) a) Q: The report, **I thought**, was clear about the medicinal value of **some of the compounds in** marijuana, so why the push back now?
b) Q: I want to go back to something previous. **I think** it's a fair question and **maybe** deserves a thoughtful answer.
c) Q: **If I remember correctly,** these negotiations – **and please correct me if I'm wrong** – weren't they seen as a way to avoid the situation was now find our self in? [Then the sentence is alright].

Not surprisingly, the president receives hedged questions when the topic is particularly sensitive.

(55) a) Q. Mr. President, the Prime Minister has referred to terrorism as, quote, "a crime", and he's referred to it **in part** as a law enforcement issue. So for you, **I'm wondering**, does that underscore **any sort of** philosophical difference … ?
b) Q. Putin said – **well, at least the quote said** that he "sees no evidence to suggest Iran wants to build a nuclear bomb." Were you disappointed with that message? And does that indicate **possibly** that international pressure is **not as great as you once thought** against Iran abandoning its nuclear program?

To the latter question, Mr. Bush replied that *Those are all legitimate questions that I'm sure historians will analyze*, a case of evasion without hedging.

Still another use of hedging is to show warmth and establish rapport with a stranger. This is illustrated in (56).

(56) a) **Could** I **just** ask you to take your clothes off and put on this silly gown? [Nurse to nervous young patient]
b) **Even though** you dislike the medicine, and I don't blame you, it's worthwhile taking it. [Nurse to reluctant patient]
c) This is **sort of** a different kind of school but one which **I think** you'll have no difficulty getting accustomed to. [Teacher to new student]

Being vague by hedging to conceal the truth is yet another hedging ploy.

(57) a) It is **possible** that he arrived when you were in the kitchen and you didn't hear him.
b) I don't know when exactly John will come home.

as is hedging to convey powerlessness and to elicit sympathy.

(58) a) **It seems** that the door is not going to open.
b) If you're going my way, could you possibly give me a lift back.

Another situation is in academic speech or writing when direct assertion of your point – *There is no doubt that this is the correct answer* – might well turn off the audience and cause them to cease engaging in the debate. To appear modest, conciliatory, or open for disagreement, it is often politic that the author hedge what any claims made. I have gone through this paper and found many cases of hedging for just these reasons. For example,

(59) a) **As far as I can determine**, Weinreich (1966) was the first person to write about hedging . . .
b) **There is general agreement today that** HEDGING is a rhetorical strategy, where a speaker, . . .
c) **I am not aware of examples** where either propositional or speech act hedging results in equivocation . . .

Finally, there are cases in which the language spoken has no equivalent hedging expression in the non-native speakers' language, and vice-versa. For example, English imperatives have a tag, as in (60)

(60) English: Help me, **can you**.

while this hedging device is absent in Spanish and German though there are alternative means to convey the same message.

## 6. Conclusion

Pragmatic competence is necessary if one is to communicate effectively in a language. This includes mastering the art of hedging, one feature of this pragmatic ability. Hedging is all around us, with messages being attenuated both on the propositional level and the speech act level. Not only does hedging appropriately help us achieve our communicative goals, but, failing to hedge where it is expected, as well as failing to understand the meaning of the hedging, has great potential for miscommunication.

I hope that this chapter has brought into focus what hedging is and how it is brought about, thereby furnishing language teachers and non-native speakers alike with a better understanding of this critical aspect of pragmatic competence.

## References

Aijmer, K. (1984). "*Sort of* and *kind of* in English conversation". *Studia Linguistica* **38** **(2)**: 118–128.
Austin, J. (1962). *How to do things with words*. London: Oxford University Press.

Bavelas, J. B., A. Black, N. Chovil and J. Mullett (1990). *Equivocal communication*. Newbury Park, CA: Sage.

Brown, P. and S. Levinson (1978). "Universals in language usage: Politeness phenomena", in E. N. Goody (ed.), *Questions and politeness. Strategies in social interaction*. Cambridge: Cambridge University Press, 56–311.

Brown, P. and S. Levinson (1987). *Politeness. Some universals in language usage*. Cambridge: Cambridge University Press.

Caffi, C. (1999). "On mitigation". *Journal of Pragmatics* **31**: 881–909.

Caffi, C. (2007). *Mitigation*. Amsterdam: Elsevier.

Channell, J. (1994). *Vague language*. Oxford: Oxford University Press.

Clemen, G. (1997). "The concept of hedging: Origins, approaches and definitions", in R. Markkanen and H. Schröder (eds.), 1997.

Fraser, B. (1975). "Hedged performatives", in P. Cole and J. L. Morgan (eds.), *Syntax and Semantics. Vol. 3*. New York: Academic Press, 187–210.

Fraser, B. (1980). "Conversational mitigation". *Journal of Pragmatics* **4**: 341–350.

Grice, H. P. (1975). "Logic and conversation", in P. Cole and J. L. Morgan (eds.), *Syntax and semantics. Vol. 3. Speech acts*. New York: Academic Press, 41–58.

Hübler, A. (1983). *Understatements and hedges in English*. Amsterdam: John Benjamins.

Jucker, A., S. Smith and T. Lüdge (2003). "Interactive aspects of vagueness in conversation". *Journal of Pragmatics* **35**: 1737–1769.

Kay, P. (1984). "The *kind of/sort of* construction", *Proceedings of the 10th Annual Meeting o the Berkeley Linguistic Society.*

Lakoff, G. (1972). "Hedges: A study in meaning criteria and the logic of fuzzy concepts", *Papers from the Eighth Regional Meeting of the Chicago Linguistic Society*, 183–228. Reprinted in *Journal of Philosophical Logic*, 1973, **2**: 4, 458–508, and in D. Hockney *et al.* (eds.). *Contemporary research in philosophical logic and linguistic semantics*. Dodrecht: Fortis, 221–271.

Partington, A. (2003). *The linguistics of political argument: The spin-doctor and the wolf-pack at the white house*. New York: Routledge.

Prince, E., J. Frader and C. Bosk (1982). "On hedging in physician-physician discourse", in R. J. Di Pietro (ed.), *Linguistics and the professions. Proceedings of the second annual delaware symposium on language studies*. Norwood, NJ: Ablex, 83–97.

Rosch, E. (1973). "Natural categories". *Cognitive Psychology* **4**: 328–350.

Salager-Meyer, F. (1995). "I think that perhaps you should: A study of hedges in written scientific discourse", in T. Miller (ed.), *Functional approaches to written texts: Classroom applications. Vol. I.* (*The Journal of TESOL France*, 1995, **2** (**2**)), pp. 127–143.

Schneider, S. (2007). *Reduced parenthetical clauses as mitigators. A corpus study of spoken French, Italian and Spanish. Studies in Corpus Linguistics 27*. Amsterdam: John Benjamins Publishing Company.

Schröder, H. and D. Zimmer (1997). "Hedging research in pragmatics; A bibliographical research guide to hedging", in R. Markkanen and H. Schröder (eds.), *Hedging and discourse. Approaches to the analysis of a pragmatic phenomenon in academic texts*. Berlin: Walter de Gruyter, 249–271.

Weinreich, U. (1966). "On the semantic structure of English", in J. H. Greenberg (ed.), *Universals of language. 2nd Edition*. Cambridge, MA: MIT Press, 142–217.

Zadeh, L. (1965). "Fuzzy sets". *Information and Control* **8**: 338–353.

New Approaches to Hedging
Edited by Gunther Kaltenböck, Wiltrud Mihatsch and Stefan Schneider


# 2

# A Contrastive Approach to Vague Nouns

*Gisle Andersen*

## Abstract

A very general way of denoting vagueness in language is by means of nouns with a maximally unspecific meaning, such as *thing*. In modern Norwegian, there is a range of nouns that can fill this function, notably *ting*, *sak* and *greie*, all of which may to some degree correspond to English *thing*. This chapter investigates recent trends in the use of such unspecific nouns, showing how they contribute to overall vagueness and non-commitment in language. Five different corpora of spoken Norwegian form the empirical basis of the investigation. In addition to their general use as place-holders, these nouns serve a range of different functions, as part of the set-marking tags, in presentative constructions and in what appears to be more specialised formulaic uses. The pattern of a possessive determiner followed by the singular form of a vague noun forms a common use in which the noun may take on more specific meanings, often with habitual connotations, in the direction of 'interest', or 'speciality'.

## 1. Introduction

Vagueness is an essential property of much, if not all, human communication. Vague features of language are used by speakers for a variety of purposes. Choosing a vague expression instead of a more precise one may have several motivations and does not necessarily entail any uncertainty on the part of the speaker. A speaker may, for example, opt for a vague description as part of a cooperative strategy to avoid providing more information than is required in a communicative situation. This can be seen as a way of reducing the processing costs of the utterance and as an economical strategy beneficial to both the speaker and the hearer. Vague items may also be used as part of a politeness strategy in which the speaker avoids sounding superior or pedantic. Therefore, use of vague expressions, in whatever form, is to be expected in naturally occurring conversation.

One way of being vague is by means of nouns whose meaning is maximally unspecific, that is to say, they are essentially void of lexical features but can be used to refer to any object or phenomenon, examples being *thing* in English or *ting* in Norwegian.[1] The aim of this chapter is to present the use and function of a set of such vague nouns in Norwegian, with reference to their English counterparts. The background for the interest in this topic is the observation that many languages have several nouns that denote vagueness in similar ways, an observation which begs the question – to what extent are vague nouns comparable across languages, and to what extent are vague nouns interchangeable within one language? Are their meanings and functions stable or subject to diachronic change? These are issues that I want to address in this chapter.

Vague nouns can be illustrated by the following examples.

(1) det er en av de **tingene** jeg husker (NoTa:004)
'that is one of the **things** I remember'

(2) baksnakking er jo mest typisk jente**ting** (UNO)
'slander is most typically a girl's **thing**'

(3) **tingen** er at vi må snakke mer (UNO)
'**the thing** is that we must talk more'

(4) skikkelig sånn tett med bilder og **ting** (UNO)
'really packed with pictures and **things**'

The examples show that a Norwegian vague noun like *thing* can be used for a variety of purposes, to be described in more detail in the following section. But Norwegian users also have other vague nouns at their disposal.

(5) for vi skal flytte og da har vi fått masse sånne **greier** fra internett (UNO)
'cos we're moving and we have got lots of **stuff** from the internet'

(6) 'ja det betyr at du får ikke lenger disse herre **sakene** i posthyllene dine (NoTa:123)
yes that means that you no longer get these kind of **things** in your pigeonhole'

(7) men jeg hadde **tingene mine** og sånt her i juni liksom (NoTa:026)
'but I had **my things** and stuff here in June'

[1] These are sometimes also referred to as 'placeholder words' (Channell, 1994) or 'general nouns' (Halliday and Hasan, 1976; Johansson, 2007). Strictly speaking, a noun like *thing* is not in itself vague, but semantically generic. I use the term 'vague noun' as shorthand for maximally generic nouns that contribute to the vagueness of utterances.

The chapter investigates both the functional variability of single items, as shown in examples (1–4), as well as lexical variability, as shown in examples (5–7). The use and functions of vague nouns can be studied from several perspectives. From a *cross-linguistic perspective*, the aim is to compare Norwegian and English pairs like *ting/thing* and address the issue of whether the use as vague nouns reflects language borrowing or parallel developments. From a *diachronic perspective*, the aim is to briefly outline the etymological origin of vague nouns, and to survey more recent developments on the basis of recent spoken corpus data. Finally, from a *synchronic perspective*, the study also aims to compare structural features and pragmatic functions of Norwegian vague nouns as evidenced by contemporary corpus data. This approach will hopefully shed light on the following research questions:

- To what degree are vague nouns comparable across languages?
- Are pairs like *ting/thing* characterised by functional equivalence or false friendships?
- Are available lexical items interchangeable within specific languages?
- Are their meanings and functions stable over time, or are they subject to change?

The aims and perspectives listed above are intended to show the general direction of a research programme and require more space than the scope of a single paper allows for. This is a recently initiated research project, and at the current stage only preliminary findings can be reported. I draw on data from various corpora, primarily Norwegian corpora representing speech. The Norwegian items are the investigational starting point, while English is used for reference and comparison. The intention here is not to provide a fully comprehensive survey of their use, but to sketch some ideas for how these items could and should be studied from a pragmatic and sociolinguistic point of view.

## 2. Formal Characteristics

This study deals specifically with four lexical items used as vague nouns in Norwegian; *ting*, *sak*, *greie* and *stoff*. What the four items have common is that, in at least in one nominal sense, they are maximally vague in meaning and denote 'an entity of any kind' or 'matter of an unspecified kind' (cf. OED –http://dictionary.oed.com/, *thing*). The lexical set consists of three countable nouns and one mass noun, namely *stoff*. Hence, in many instances the first three items translate to English *thing*, while *stoff* would generally translate to English *stuff*.

Other common features are that the four lexemes are relatively frequent items, they occur especially in informal settings and relaxed styles, and they are relatively more common in speech than in writing. Their use may be subject to stylistic or sociolinguistic variation. Impressionistically, English *stuff* would for instance appear less formal than *thing*, while Norwegian *greie* would appear less formal than the stylistically neutral noun *ting*.

From the outset, three functionally distinct types of use have been identified, the place-holder, the set-marking tag and the discourse marker, as illustrated by examples (8–10), respectively.

(8) hun hadde på seg **en sånn skikkelig vid greie** og så plutselig så bare datt puppen hennes ut (UNO)
'she was wearing **a really wide thing** and then suddenly her tit came out'

(9) det huset står der ennå med tårn **og greier** (TAUS:a49)
'the house is still standing there with towers **and things**'

(10) **tingen er** jeg vil ikke ha hustelefon (NoTa:026)
**'the thing is** I don't want to have a house phone'

In example (8), *greie* is the head of a noun phrase and functions as a conceptual place-holder, replacing a more specific item which the speaker has in mind (top, blouse, sweater, or the like). The vague noun contributes to the proposition expressed by the utterance and could not have been removed from it without affecting the grammatical integrity of the sentence/proposition; hence it is not a discourse marker. As place-holders these nouns provide a schema that guides the hearer towards a non-specific reading, signalling that the utterance is in need of pragmatic enrichment in order to be optimally relevant to the hearer.

In example (9), the plural form *greier* is part of the phrase *og greier*. This is a set-marking tag (Dines, 1980) whose function is to signal that the noun phrase refers to a semantically open collection of things, including the item explicitly mentioned (*towers*). Specifically to this case, the explicit noun is an illustrative example and the tag serves to indicate the impressive nature of the house talked about. The tag has a procedural function and is external to the proposition expressed by the utterance.

In example (10), *ting* appears as part of the more or less fixed phrase 'the thing is (that) . . . ', on a par with example (3) above. Here too, the vague noun is external to the proposition expressed by the utterance. It is part of a presentational strategy and has a textual, discourse-structuring function. It signals that the impending proposition can be interpreted as explanation and elaboration of previous discourse, potentially also adding weight to the impending proposition.

Note also that, as a propositional item, the vague nouns can constitute either heads of noun phrases as in examples (11–13) or the rightmost component of nominal compounds as in examples (14–16).

(11) så hadde de fra- f- blitt frastjålet **alle tingene** også (NoTa:007)
'and they had been robbed of **all (their) things** too'

(12) ja men drit i å melde deg på **den greia der** liksom (NoTa:031)
'yeah but don't bother to sign up for **that thing there** like'

(13) du skal hjelpe meg med å hente **noe saker** (NoTa:108)
'you will help me collect **some stuff**'

(14) en sånn **samuraiting** (NoTa:147)
'a (such) **samurai thing**'

(15) vi spiste de **baguettgreiene** før vi dro (NoTa:027, sic)
'we ate those **baguette things** before we left'

(16) det var en sånn liten **bokseksjonssak** (TAUS:c04)
'it was one of those **book shelf things'**

The examples give an impression of the structural variability with which the vague nouns occur. Note that all the three countable vague nouns can have either structural role (NP head of compound component). As regards functional properties, it will become evident that vague nouns are also characterised by great variability, and that different vague senses are associated with different structures. This is dealt with more extensively in Section 4.

## 3. Diachrony/Etymology

Given the obvious similarity of cognates like *ting* vs. *thing*, and *stoff* vs. *stuff*, it is of interest to study the diachrony of the individual items, with a view to tracing their common etymological origins. Norwegian and English are closely related languages, belonging to the northern and western branches of Germanic, respectively. Oxford English Dictionary provides valuable insights that are relevant for both English and Norwegian. Table 2.1 shows how the four Norwegian–English word pairs stem from common lexical sources.

**Table 2.1.** Etymological survey of Norwegian and English vague nouns

| Norwegian | English | Etymological origin[a] | Attested use as vague noun |
|---|---|---|---|
| *ting* | *thing* | OS *thing*/ON *þing*: assembly for judicial or deliberative purposes | ENG: c888 – present (K. ÆLFRED *Boeth.*) NOR: yes |
| *sak* | *sake* | OE. *sacu*, ON *so?k*: crime, accusation, lawsuit | ENG: not attested NOR: yes |
| *greie* | *graith* | Obs. (exc. Sc.), ON *greiðe*: trappings, equipage | ENG: 1513 – 1790 (DOUGLAS *Æneis*) NOR: yes |
| *stoff* | *stuff* | OF. *estoffe*: material, furniture; Sp.,Pg. *estofa*, cloth, textile fabric | ENG: 1580 – present (*Act 23 Eliz. c. 9 Preamb.*) NOR: yes |

[a]OS: Old Saxon; ON: Old Norse; OE: Old English; Obs.: Obsolete; OF: Old French, Sp.: Spanish, Pg.: Portugese.

An etymological description specific for Norwegian which is equally detailed as OED is unfortunately not available, although two (Dano-)Norwegian etymological dictionaries were consulted (Falch and Torp, 1992; Bjorvand and Lindeman, 2000). Therefore, the attested Norwegian use as vague nouns is not supplied with information about date or textual source in Table 2.1. The historical use of vague nouns needs further investigation based on historical text sources.

Several observations can be drawn from this survey. Etymologically related items are used as vagueness markers across languages. Table 2.1 is restricted to a bilingual survey, but it can be noted that the identical Germanic sources of vague nouns are found in German (*Ding*, *Sache*), Swedish, (*ting*, *grej*, *sak*), Danish (*ting*, *sag*), etc. Moreover, the vague nouns tend to derive from concrete, physical senses denoting either tangible objects like 'equipage' and 'textile fabric' or constitutional procedures like 'assembly' or 'lawsuit'. Through the processes of lexical change (bleaching) the forms have undergone loss of specific features and have acquired the maximally vague sense of '*matter of an unspecified kind*', '*an entity of any kind*'. The use as discourse markers and set-marking tags must be conjectured as later routinisations, as illustrated by the following trajectory:

$$\text{physical object} \rightarrow \text{vagueness} \rightarrow \text{discourse marker/set-marking tag}$$

Consequently, the developmental path of vague nouns parallels the development of items which undergo grammaticalisation from lexical items to discourse markers (Hopper and Traugott, 1993).

## 4. Pragmatic Functions

The empirical basis for the current study consists of five different corpora of spoken Norwegian. The corpora are available for research purposes from the Universities of Bergen and Oslo. Table 2.2 shows more detailed information about the corpora used.

**Table 2.2.** Spoken Norwegian corpora used in the study

| Corpus | Date | Location/dialect | Speakers |
|---|---|---|---|
| TAUS | 1971–1973 | Oslo | All generations |
| Norsk dialektkorpus (NDK) | 1970 | Bergen, Voss, Tromøya | All generations |
| UNO | 1997–1998 | Oslo | Teenage speakers |
| Big Brother corpus (BBc) | 2001 | Oslo (and other dialects) | Young adults |
| Norsk talespråkskorpus (NoTa) | 2005 | Oslo | All generations |

The availability of these corpora enables a description of recent developments and a comparison of the language of young speakers in three different periods, the 1970s, the late 1990s and the 2000s. In Section 5, I describe the distribution of the various types of use in different corpora.

### 4.1. Vague or not?

The most basic type of use of the items considered is the general use as a vague noun meaning 'an entity of any kind' or 'unspecified matter', as shown in examples (11–16) above. Looking at actual use in the five corpora investigated, it becomes clear that the four members of this lexical set show great differences with respect to the degree to which they are used with maximally vague meanings.

The noun *greie* is exclusively used with the vague sense similar to English *thing*. No specific senses were identified in any of the corpora of contemporary Norwegian.

The noun *ting* is virtually always used with the same vague sense, but the specific meaning of legal and judicial assembly also occurs, as in the name of the Norwegian parliament, *Stortinget.*

The noun *sak* is only occasionally used as a vague noun, and it has many other more specific meanings. These include 'court case', 'political issue' and 'controversy'.

Finally, the noun *stoff* turns out never to be used vaguely as place-holder in the corpora investigated. Unlike its English cognate *stuff*, no traces of use as a general vagueness marker were found. It is always used with more specific meanings that include 'textile fabric', 'narcotics', 'reading material', etc. As mentioned, this member of the set is also not syntactically interchangeable with the other three, being an uncountable mass noun. A more thorough investigation of historical and other text sources may reveal a different result.

### 4.2. Vague in what sense?

The most common structural realisation of vague nouns is as the head of a noun phrase or as the rightmost part of a compound. Functionally, these types of use are similar in that the noun is a lexically void substitute for a more specific referent. The vague nouns provide an incentive for the hearer to semantically enrich the proposition in order to arrive at the intended meaning of the utterance. The speaker has reason to assume that the hearer is able to make sense of the utterance containing a lexically unspecific item.

The referent may be recovered cotextually, contextually or situationally. For example, the referent may be a physical object that is visible to both the speaker and the hearer, as in example (17), where *thing* refers to the recording device (situational reference).

(17) ikke snakk med **den tingen** (UNO)
'don't speak with **that thing**'

Another typical reference for vague nouns is the preceding and, especially, the imminent discourse topic (cotext), as in examples (18–19).

(18) I går så ble det sagt **mye dumme ting**, av oss begge. (BB/BB01/22)
Lit.: 'Yesterday it was said **much stupid things** by both of us.'

(19) jeg skal si deg **en ting** jeg at e de siste fra femteklasse # hadde vi en som het (TAUS:a12)
'I'll tell you **one thing** I that eh the last from fifth grade we had one who was called ... '

Often, however, the exact referent is far less salient. Potentially different vague senses can be distinguished, and ambiguities commonly occur. I wish to argue that vague expressions generally can be used in a variety of communicative contexts, including (but not necessarily limited to) the following:

- The speaker does not know or wish to specify the exact nature of the concept.
- The speaker knows the exact nature of the concept but does not know or remember the term.
- The speaker knows both the nature of the concept and the term, but nevertheless chooses an inexact rendering of it. In such cases, the vagueness marker may act as a means of marking a psychological distance to a linguistic expression.

The ambiguity can be exemplified by nominal compounds consisting of a vague noun preceded by a specific one. Arguably, the phrase

(20) en sånn **samuraiting** (NoTa:147) / 'a (such) **samurai thing**'

can at least be interpreted in three different ways, as (1) a samurai, (2) an unspecified object belonging to or associated with a samurai or (3) a "samurai", in the sense of one of those things that people refer to as a "samurai". The difference between interpretations (1) and (3) may be subtle. Conceptually, both interpretations are construed as cases where the intended referent is the concept of a samurai. Unlike (1), interpretation (3) involves an added marking of a psychological distance to and non-incorporation of the word samurai in the speaker's vocabulary. That is to say, the vagueness marker has a **metalinguistic** function of indicating that samurai represents unfamiliar or exotic vocabulary. In fact, it functions much in the same way as the pragmatic marker *like* with a metalinguistic function, as described in Andersen (2001).

This metalinguistic interpretation does not seem right in an example like (21).

(21) et eller annet sånn **kjøttgreie** (TAUS:c09) / 'some sort of **meat thing**'

Here, the referent is an object made by meat, but its precise name and/or characteristics are unfamiliar to the speaker. In other words, the example involves both a vague term and concept. In example (22), on the other hand,

(22) de **baguettgreiene** (NoTa:027, sic) / 'those **baguette things**'

the vague noun phrase can be interpreted as (1) 'the baguettes', (2) 'the things resembling baguettes' ('the baguette-like items') or (3) 'the "baguettes"' with the metalinguistic function described above. This interpretation does not seem unlikely if the exact reference is situationally or cotextually salient and known to the speaker and the hearer.

Arguably, then, vague nouns have a potential of marking either conceptual vagueness or psychological distance towards a chosen term. The psychological distance or lack of conceptual specificity may be reinforced by other pragmatic phenomena.

(23) han har disse herre # har noe sånn **steingreier** skjønner du (NoTa:071)
'he has these here # has some kind of **stone things** you see'

(24) så gjorde jeg masse andre ting gikk på sånn **teatergreier** og sånn (NoTa:116)
'and then I did lots of other things and went to sort of **theatre things** and stuff'

Examples (23–24) show how vague expressions co-occur with pauses and discourse markers, providing a stronger signal of the psychological distance or non-incorporation. Such co-occurrence is highly common in colloquial speech.

### 4.3. The set-marking tag

Use of the set-marking tag can be illustrated by the following examples.

(25) noen breer **og noe greier** (UNO)
'some glaciers **and some stuff** '

(26) det huset står der ennå med tårn **og greier** (TAUS:a49)
'the house is still standing there with towers **and things'**

(27) men også litt alvorlige episoder med slagsmål **og saker og ting** (TAUS:a45)
'but also quite serious incidents with fights **and stuff and things**'

(28) så jeg får sette på noe varmeelementer **og greier og greier** (NoTa:108)
'then I have to put on some heat elements **and things and things**'

From the examples it can be noted that all the three countable vague nouns, *greie*, *sak* and *ting*, can be used as set-marking tags. Moreover, the vague nouns are always plural when used in this context. Several pragmatic functions can be associated with this usage. In example (25), the tag indicates a wider semantic scope and a loose interpretation of the nominal phrase. Moreover, the tag can be used to emphasise the impressive nature of the concept talked about, as in example (26). Sometimes the set-marking tag is combinatory, consisting of more than one noun. This is the case in example (27), which involves the combination of *saker* and *ting*. Combinatory set-marking tags always involve these two nouns and in that particular order; no other combinations were found in the corpus data. Finally, the plural form of *greie* can be used as a duplicate set-marking tag, as in *og greier og greier* in example (28).

### 4.4. The textual discourse marker

The textual discourse marker can be further illustrated by the following examples.

(29) **tingen er at** vi må snakke mer (UNO)
'**the thing is that** we need to talk more'

(30) **det som er greia er at** det samme skjer med når han # selv blir el- gammel vet du (NoTa:036)
'**that which is the thing is that** the same happens with when he himself becomes old you know'

(31) **saken var nemlig den at** vi mistet huset under krigen # på Filipstadulykken (TAUS:a25)
'**the thing was namely that** we lost our house during the War in the Filipstad disaster'

Johansson (2007) provides evidence of the structure in example (29) in the Oslo Multilingual Corpus, labelling it as 'utterance launcher' (*ibid.* 73). In the current spoken data, we note that all three countable vague nouns, *ting*, *sak* and *greie*, are used with this presentative function. There is considerable structural variation, and the patterns include not only a straightforward S-V-*that* pattern, but also a cleft construction, as in example (30), which literally translates to 'that which is the thing is that . . . .' The textual function of these constructions is to indicate how to interpret the following proposition in relation to the previous discourse, as an explanation or further elaboration of it, as well as adding focus to this proposition.

From a cognitive perspective, Schmid (2000) refers to nouns like *thing* as representative of a larger category of 'shell nouns', whose function is to cast complex, proposition-like chunks of information temporarily into nominal concepts. The choice of lexical item used for this purpose in the Norwegian data – *ting, sak* or *greie* – is likely to be affected by stylistic level and whether the speaker is young or old, *greie* being the least formal and *sak* the most formal of the three alternatives. For example, the construction *det som er greia er at* is restricted to the speech of men and women in their early twenties in the data investigated. Similar usage differences are further demonstrated by the survey of use presented in Section 5.

### 4.5. Extended use: 'interest', 'speciality'

The corpus examples reveal another type of use which seems to represent a linguistic innovation. This is the use of *greie* after a possessive pronoun in what seems to be a semi-fixed structure denoting 'interest field' or 'speciality'.

(32) men e # ja de atletiske tingene var liksom ikke **min greie** (NoTa:005)
'but eh # yeah those athletic things were like not **my thing**'

(33) å krangle er ikke **min greie** i det hele tatt (NoTa:141)
'arguing is not **my thing** at all'

(34) TV er **deres greie**. (NNC:DB990227)[2]
'TV is **their thing**.'

The meaning of poss. + *greie* seems to be comparable to the archaic expression *my cup of tea* or to *my thing* in contemporary English, which appears to be used with the same connotations. Sometimes, utterances with this construction are held in a euphemistic or ironic tone, where it is clear from the context that something is certainly not "her thing", without this being stated explicitly. Other times, emphasis may be explicitly given, as in 'not my thing at all' in example (33).

Note that it is only *greie* which is used with these connotations – alternatives like *min ting* or *min sak* would not yield this interpretation. In fact *min sak* might often imply 'my business' (and no business of yours), as would German *meine Sache*.[3] Usually the pattern poss. + *greie* appears in negative contexts, as in examples (32) and (33), describing something which is not the interest or skill of the subject. Occasionally, however, the construction may be used positively, as in example (34). The construction virtually always has a pronominal subject.

## 5. Survey of Usage

Having described the main types of use of vague nouns that occur in the five corpora, I now present a survey showing which types of use occur in which corpora. This survey is given in Table 2.3. The five different functions are listed and exemplified in the leftmost column. The sign "+" before the vague noun indicates occurrence in the corpus, while a "–" sign indicates non-occurrence of that particular noun. (See Table 2.2 for a more detailed description of the corpora.)

We note that the general use as place-holders, either as head of NP or rightmost compound component, is found in all the five corpora investigated. All three countable vague nouns occur in all corpora, with the exception of *ting* as head of NP, which was not found in The Norwegian Dialect Corpus (NDC), and *sak* as a compound component, which was not found in the Big Brother corpus (BBc). This non-occurrence is seen as a result of limited corpus size rather than as a reflection of any significant sociolinguistic difference.

As regards the use as a textual discourse marker (*the thing is that*), some interesting differences can be observed. Judging by these data, the use of *greie* for this purpose is clearly an innovation, as it only occurs in the most recent corpus, namely, the one collected in 2005 (Norsk talespråkskorpus; NoTa). It is the young speakers in the corpus who use this item with this

[2] I had to consult a large, written corpus, namely the Norwegian Newspaper Corpus (NNC), in order to find tokens with a different pronominal subject than first person.

[3] Thanks to one of the anonymous reviewers for pointing out this meaning of *Sache* in German.

**Table 2.3.** Survey of usage in the different corpora

| | TAUS | NDC | UNO | BBc | NoTa |
|---|---|---|---|---|---|
| | **Oslo** | **Bergen** | **Oslo** | **Oslo** | **Oslo** |
| | **1970s** | **1970s** | **1990s** | **2001** | **2005** |
| **Place-holder, head of NP** *forskjellige ting (different things)* | + ting | – ting | + ting | + ting | + ting |
| | + greie | + greie | + greie | + greie | + greie |
| | + sak | + sak | + sak | + sak | + sak |
| **Place-holder, compound component** *kjøttgreie (meat thing)* | + ting | – ting | + ting | + ting | + ting |
| | + greie | + greie | + greie | + greie | + greie |
| | + sak | + sak | + sak | – sak | + sak |
| **Textual discourse marker** *the thing is that … (tingen er at … )* | – ting | – ting | + ting | + ting | + ting |
| | – greie | – greie | – greie | – greie | + greie |
| | + sak | – sak | + sak | – sak | + sak |
| **Set-marking tag …** *og greier (… and stuff)* | – ting | – ting | + ting | – ting | + ting |
| | + greie | + greie | + greie | + greie | + greie |
| | + sak | + sak | – sak | – sak | – sak |
| **Extended use: interest, speciality** *ikke akkurat min greie (not exactly my thing)* | – ting | – ting | – ting | – ting | – ting |
| | – greie | – greie | – greie | + greie | + greie |
| | – sak | – sak | – sak | – sak | – sak |

particular function. It also seems that *ting* used as textual discourse marker is an innovation, although an earlier one, as *ting* occurs consistently in the three most recent corpora and not in the two corpora from the 1970s. As regards the noun *sak* used with the discourse marker function, this represents traditional usage which occurs in all corpora except for BBc.

The use of vague nouns as set-marking tags shows a different pattern with respect to choice of lexical item. Here, it is the noun *greie* which is used persistently in all the periods investigated, as it is recorded in all five corpora. The noun *ting* as a set-marking tag does not occur in the corpora from the 1970s, suggesting that this new function may be an innovation. On the other hand, *sak* is used as a set-marking tag only in the 1970s corpora and is consistently non-occurring in the three most recent corpora.

Finally, as mentioned, *greie* is the only vague noun which has the extended use after possessive pronouns, denoting the sense of 'interest' or 'speciality'. As seen from Table 2.3, this pattern occurs only in the two most recent corpora.

## 6. Summary of Findings

The most important findings of this chapter can be summarised as follows. Unlike its English cognate, the uncountable noun *stoff* turns out not to be used in a maximally vague sense as placeholder in the corpora investigated. It is only used in more specific senses such as 'drugs', 'textile fabric', etc.

The three countable nouns *ting*, *sak* and *greie* are all used as vague nouns in a variety of contexts, operating either as a propositional element as an obligatory head of NP or rightmost compound component, or at the discourse level, functioning as set-marking tag or textual discourse marker. Considering the development from the 1970s to the present, the number of functions of *ting* and *greie* has been extended, while the number of functions of *sak* has been reduced. In the most recent corpora, *greie* is used with all functions listed in Table 2.3, including the poss. + *greie* context, where it denotes 'interest' or 'speciality'. The noun *ting* has gained two new functions from the 1970s to the present, namely those of textual discourse marker and set-marking tag. On the other hand, *sak* appears to be losing ground, as its previous function as a set-marking tag is not found in the most recent corpora.

All in all, the study has outlined what seem to be recent trends in the use of vague nouns. The presentational strategies *tingen/greia er at* appear to be innovations of the past decade. Similarly, the pervasive *ikke (helt) min greie* seems to be a very recent innovation with a clear parallel in its English counterpart *not (exactly) my thing*, suggesting that it may be a borrowing from English.

The use of vague nouns in speech certainly merits further investigation. It is of interest to identify other possible semi-fixed expressions containing vague nouns, one candidate being *Hva er greia (med X)?* (lit. 'What is the thing (with X)?'). This not found in corpora but seems to be common in blogs, etc. Also, one should consult historical text sources to pinpoint more exactly the historical occurrence of vague uses of the nouns, an issue which has only briefly been addressed in this chapter. And finally, a much more thorough account of sociolinguistic variation is needed, focusing on gender and age as obvious factors that should be investigated.

## References

Andersen, G. (2001). *Pragmatic markers and sociolinguistic variation.* Amsterdam: John Benjamins.

Bjorvand, H. and F. O. Lindeman (2000). *Våre arveord – Etymologisk ordbok.* Oslo: Novus.

Channell, J. (1994). *Vague language*. Oxford: Oxford University Press.

Dines, E. (1980). "Variation in discourse – 'and stuff like that'". *Language in Society* **9**: 13–31.

Falch, H. and A. Torp (1992[1903–1906]). *Etymologisk ordbog over det norske og det danske sprog*. Oslo: Bjørn Ringstrøms Antikvariat.

Halliday, M. A. K. and R. Hasan (1976). *Cohesion in English*. London: Longman.

Hopper, P. J. and E. C. Traugott (1993). *Grammaticalization*. Cambridge: Cambridge University Press.

Johansson, S. (2007). *Seeing through multilingual corpora: On the use of corpora in contrastive studies*. Amsterdam: John Benjamins.

Schmid, H.-J. (2000). *English abstract nouns as conceptual shells: From corpus to cognition*. Berlin/New York: Mouton de Gruyter.

New Approaches to Hedging
Edited by Gunther Kaltenböck, Wiltrud Mihatsch and Stefan Schneider


# 3

# HEDGES IN CONTEXT: FORM AND FUNCTION OF *SORT OF* AND *KIND OF*

*Anita Fetzer*

## ABSTRACT

This chapter investigates the form, function and scope of the classical hedges *sort of* and *kind of* in the context of political discourse accounting for their particularities in the dialogical discourse genre of political interview and in the monological genre of political speech. The methodological framework employed is an integrated one: it combines quantitatively oriented corpus analysis with qualitatively oriented sociopragmatics, thus supplementing the fundamental cognitive-linguistics-anchored premise of prototypicality with the pragmatic premise of intentionality of communicative action. In the extended frame of reference, a hedge signifies whether the speaker intends her/his communicative contribution or one of its constituents to count as a more prototypical case of representation or whether s/he intends it to count as a less prototypical case of representation.

The introduction sets the stage, and the second section examines the theory and practice of the hedges *sort of* and *kind of*. Section 3 argues for *sort of* and *kind of* to be assigned the status of a contextualization cue. Section 4 introduces the data, and Section 5 presents a genre-specific analysis of *sort of* and *kind of* in political speeches and interviews accounting for distribution, collocation and scope. Section 6 examines their more-fuzzy-making and less-fuzzy-making function in the context of politics, and the final section summarizes the results obtained and concludes.

## 1. Introduction

Hedges have become a prevailing topic of research in linguistics, pragmatics, discourse analysis and corpus linguistics. Discourse analysis and corpus linguistics focus their investigations on the distribution and function of linguistic forms, which have been classified as hedges, such as *sort of, kind of, like* or *something like*. The former is more qualitatively oriented and the latter is quantitative in nature, thus shedding light on their frequency, distribution and collocations on the one hand, and on their sequential status and preferred uses in discourse genres and social contexts on the other (e.g. Brinton, 1996; Andersen, 2000; Aijmer, 2002; Coates, 2003; Mauranen, 2004).

The connectedness between the form and function of a hedge is at the heart of investigation in pragmatics, combining a hedge's distribution, form and semantics with its function. Here, the implicit assumption that a linguistic form classified as a hedge counts as a hedge in any context does not hold any longer. Rather, a bidirectional perspective between form and function, and between function and form, is adopted considering both synchronic and diachronic perspectives. The analysis of different corpora allows for the identification of preferred usage, language change, grammaticalization and pragmaticalization, as, for instance in Aijmer's analysis of *I think* (Aijmer, 1997) or in Traugott and Dasher's examination of *actually, indeed, in fact* or *well* (Traugott and Dasher, 2002).

In synchronic-linguistics-based grammars of English, hedges are examined under the header of adverbs and adverbials. In *A Grammar of Contemporary English* (Quirk *et al.*, 1985), they are allocated to the category of subjunct with narrow scope, which is defined as having 'a subordinate ( . . . ) role in comparison with adjuncts; they lack the grammatical parity with other sentence elements' (Greenbaum and Quirk, 1990: 176). In the heterogeneous class of subjunct, hedges are attributed to the subcategory of intensifier as downtoner with a compromiser function. Compromisers have only a slight lowering effect on the predication and tend to call in question the appropriateness of the verb concerned. In a grammar-for-communication scenario, compromisers refer to the appropriateness conditions of an utterance signalling that they 'reach out towards an assumed norm but at the same time reduce the force of the verb' (Quirk *et al.*, 1985: 455). In a similar vein, Ungerer (1988) differentiates between propositional adverbials and scope adverbials. The former are a constitutive part of the proposition, and for this reason truth-conditional, while the latter are metalinguistic. Propositional adverbials are process adverbials and adverbials of time, for instance, and scope adverbials are hedges and comment clauses, for example. Depending on their position in the sentence, scope adverbials have narrow-scope and wide-scope interpretations.

In the *Longman Grammar of Spoken and Written English* (Biber *et al.*, 1999), hedges are attributed to the class of stance adverbs, which are defined as 'adverbials that overtly mark a speaker's or writer's attitude to a clause or comment about its content. They can be divided in three categories: epistemic, attitude and style' (Biber *et al.*, 1999: 382). Stance adverbs have six major areas of meaning, namely, (1) certainty and doubt, (2) actuality and reality, (3) source of knowledge, (4) limitation, (5) viewpoints or perspective and (6) imprecision. Relevant to our investigation of the form, function and distribution of hedges are those stance adverbs, which signify imprecision. They tend to focus on a particular element in the clause, suggesting that the proposition (or part of it) is imprecise.

In cognitive linguistics, hedges are defined with respect to their semantics and pragmatics in the framework of prototypicality conditions, or to use Lakoff's own words in his original definition of hedges as 'words whose meaning implicitly involves fuzziness-words whose job is to make things fuzzier or less fuzzy' (Lakoff, 1975: 234). Hedges may thus be differentiated into more-fuzzy hedges and less-fuzzy hedges (Fetzer, 1994, 2004): the former anchor the object, constituent or clause, over which they have scope, closer to the periphery of the prototype to which they refer, while the latter anchor it closer to its core.

The research tradition of hedges has primarily focussed on the more-fuzzy definition, refining the original definition and subcategorizing hedges as *adaptors* (Prince *et al.*, 1982), *adjusters* (Aijmer, 2002) and *epistemic modal forms* (Coates, 2003), for instance. Most of the investigations have, however, not explicitly accommodated the fact that fuzziness is a scalar concept, anchoring 'the object', over which a hedge has scope, to a singled-out area on a scale. By referring to a particular area and by anchoring the object at hand to the area, the object is bounded by more fuzziness on the one side of the scale and by less fuzziness on the other side of the scale. Looked upon from a reasoning and accessibility-of-information perspective, for something to be classified as more fuzzy, for example for an interview to be classified as ***a sort of*** *interview* or for asking questions to be classified as ***sort of*** *asking questions*, the interview or the activity of asking questions needs to have been contrasted with its less-fuzzy counterpart, that is, with *an interview* ***par excellence*** or with *asking questions* ***as it is usually done***. The anchoring of the object at hand to the scale is not arbitrary but depends on the semantics of the hedge. The higher degree of indeterminateness the linguistic device used as a hedge expresses, for instance ***some sort of*** *interview* or ***something like*** *sort of asking questions*, the closer the object is anchored to the periphery. The higher degree of determinateness the linguistic devices used as a hedge express, for example ***this sort of*** *interview* or ***what sort of*** *asking questions*, the closer the object is anchored to the core.

In line with Bolinger's seminal work on degree words (Bolinger, 1972), hedges may both identify and intensify. Depending on their collocations, they signal how a sentence or constituent is to be interpreted, specifying whether the sentence or constituent refers to a more prototypical case, as is the case with the collocation 'demonstrative + *sort of*', or to a less prototypical case, as is the case with 'indeterminate quantifier + *sort of*' or 'hedge + *sort of*'.

Linguistics- and cognitive-science-based investigations of hedges account for their form and function. While there is generally no controversy about their function of making things, that is objects, constituents or clauses, over which they have scope more fuzzy, the forms employed to achieve that goal may vary. Hedging can be performed through the employment of adverbs and adverbials, whose semantics entail vagueness, through comment clauses, whose semantics entail epistemic modality or through a particular phonological realization, such as stress or rising intonation in English. In spite of the inherent complexity and context dependence of the matter, the frame of investigation has so far been primarily restricted to the unit of a sentence.

The goal of this chapter is to investigate the form, function and scope of the classical hedges *sort of* and *kind of* in the context of political discourse accounting for their particularities in the dialogical discourse genre of political interview and in the monological genre of political speech. The methodological framework employed is an integrated one: it combines quantitatively oriented corpus analysis with qualitatively oriented sociopragmatics, thus supplementing the fundamental cognitive-linguistics-anchored premise of prototypicality with the pragmatic premise of intentionality of communicative action (Fetzer, 2002). In the extended frame of reference, a hedge signifies whether the speaker intends her/his communicative contribution or one of its constituents to count as a more prototypical case of representation or whether s/he intends it to count as a less prototypical case of representation.

The following section examines the theory and practice of the hedges *sort of* and *kind of.* Section 3 argues for *sort of* and *kind of* to be conceived as contextualization cues. Section 4 introduces the data, and Section 5 presents an analysis of *sort of* and *kind of* in political speeches and interviews accounting for distribution, collocation and scope. Section 6 examines their more-fuzzy-making and less-fuzzy-making function in political discourse, and the final section provides a concludes.

## 2. *Sort of/Kind of*: Theory and Practice

The original definition of hedges as 'words whose meaning implicitly involves fuzziness – words whose job is to make things fuzzier or less fuzzy' (Lakoff, 1975: 234) is anchored to the research paradigm of cognitive semantics and to its premise that semantic meaning is best represented by prototypes defined by prototypicality conditions specifying whether the object at hand is anchored to the periphery or to the core of a prototype. Against this background, hedges target the act of reference by contextualizing it and particularizing its conditions of use. They signify the contextual conditions under which an act of reference is felicitous thus making explicit the connectedness between extra-linguistic object, cognitive object and linguistic expression. For this reason, hedges convey relational meaning, relating extra-linguistic object, linguistic expression and cognitive prototype. Moreover, they signify an instruction-of-interpretation about how the nature of the connectedness between extra-linguistic object, cognitive prototype and linguistic expression is speaker-intended and how the speaker intends the hearer to interpret that connectedness.

In the following section, the most prominent analyses of *sort of* and *kind of* are presented and particular reference is given to the question of how that tripartite connectedness is accounted for.

### 2.1. Adaptor

The discrepancy between the conventional meaning of an expression and its use has been at the heart of almost all investigations of the form and function of hedges. Prince *et al.* (1982) examine the function of *adaptors*, a subclass of more-fuzzy hedges, for instance *roughly speaking*, *in a way*, *or something like that*, *rather*, *like*, *kind of* and *sort of*. Like classical hedges, adaptors are multi-functional. Regarding the felicity of an act of reference, they restrict the application of the object, over which the adaptor has scope, to a more particularized and thus less general context signifying that the speaker has selected an approximative lexical item, which may be negotiated. Furthermore, adaptors indicate that the speaker does not have enough evidence to present a clear-cut case of classification and therefore may provide a rough classification only, or that in her/his production of utterances s/he cannot – at that particular stage of composing her/his utterance – find the intended linguistic expression amongst the number of activated terms. Alternatively, the adaptor may also activate a number of semantically related objects on the hearer's side when s/he processes the utterance at hand.

All of the communicative functions listed above are based on the premise that adaptors and their inherent evidential or epistemic meaning signal an approximative lexical choice. As discussed in the previous section, approximation is a scalar concept, which connects an extra-linguistic object, a linguistic expression and a cognitive prototype. Calculating the nature of the connectedness amongst the three entities is performed by anchoring them to a scale. Similarity between the extra-linguistic object, linguistic expression and cognitive prototype results in anchoring the object to the core of the prototype thus referring to it as a less-fuzzy concept, for instance with the construction 'determinate DET + linguistic expression' or 'linguistic expression *par excellence*', while less similarity, if not contrast, between the extra-linguistic object, linguistic expression and cognitive prototype results in anchoring the object to the periphery of the prototype, thus referring to it as a more-fuzzy concept, for instance as a *sort of* or *kind of* object.

### 2.2. Modifier and boosted modifier

In his examination of *sort of*, Andersen (2000) also differentiates between the two different meanings of *sort of*, but explains them along different lines: the more-fuzzy *sort of* is classified as a modifier signalling loose interpretation of a vague and less well defined entity, and the less-fuzzy *sort of* is analysed as the head of a noun phrase with a postmodifier and seen as equivalent to 'type of' indicating category membership (cf. Andersen, 2000: 48).

The signalling of a loose interpretation is paraphrased by Kay (1984) as 'what you might call'. According to him, it is not possible to intensify the hedging function of *sort of* with the booster *very*, for instance. A corpus analysis of the phrases *very sort of* and *very kind of* in the British National Corpus (BNC) disconfirms that claim. This might be due to more recent changes in English and thus to the high degree of grammaticalization and the ongoing process of pragmaticalization of *sort of/kind of* as a more-fuzzy hedge. The boosted hedge *very sort of* is more frequent than the boosted hedge *very kind of*, which is due to the polyvalence of *very kind of*, in which *kind* can be an adjective, for example *that is very kind of you*. The linguistic contexts of the boosted more-fuzzy hedge generally display signals of impromptu use of language, such as further expressions of indeterminateness and vagueness, that is *if you like* in example (1), *one way nor the other* and *I don't know* in example (3), *sort of* in example (4), *quite* in example (5) and *like* in example (6). Additionally, the boosted more-fuzzy-hedge co-occurs with self-corrections and hesitation devices, as in examples (1), (2) and (5):

(1) Did you not find that *er* the work then became ***very sort of*** *com compartmentalized if you like*, very specific people were doing bits of jobs rather than a feeling that you were all part of a much larger thing?

(2) *You are, you, you were* ***very sort of*** standard-wise

(3) I don't know, I'm not ***very sort of*** convinced *one way nor the other*

(4) Yes, every now and then the temptation to do something *sort of* very cool and ***very sort of*** ten point

(5) I always remember him he was alright *bu* but *hi* his mum was ***very sort of*** *quite* lenient, and he was really strict.

(6) *cos* I haven't, *like* she perceived that I was ***very kind of*** lost *really*.

The boosted more-fuzzy hedge *sort of* does not only modify verbal phrases (examples 1, 3) but also adjectives and adverbs (examples 2, 4, 5). The collocation *very* with more-fuzzy hedge *kind of* only occurs with verbal phrases (example 6).

### 2.3. Adjuster

In her analysis of discourse particles, Aijmer (2002) pays particular attention to the functions of discourse particles accommodating both interpersonal and interactional domains of discourse. What is of relevance to this examination of hedges is the subclass of *adjusters*. A classical representative of adjusters is *sort of*, whose core meaning is metalinguistic and thus procedural, signalling 'that the hearer will be able [to] figure out the meaning of what is said even if it [is] only approximate' (Aijmer, 2002: 209). Since discourse particles are multi-functional, *sort of* may express evidential meaning, in particular imprecision, and for this reason, affect the truth value of the proposition. Regarding its discursive function, *sort of* signifies self-repair. On the interpersonal plane of communication, it is assigned the status of an affective marker hedging strong opinions by toning down the impact of the communicative contribution, thus reducing its imposition and at the same time establishing common ground. This is also reflected in Brown and Levinson's research on politeness (Brown and Levinson, 1987), in which hedges refer indexically to the Gricean maxims (Grice, 1975), thus triggering a conversational implicature in order to signify interpersonal meaning, for instance positive politeness (or solidarity) and negative politeness (or respect).

The adaptor or adjuster *sort of* has undergone some important development from a narrow-scope modifier of an object or constituent to a wide-scope, metalinguistic modifier and procedural device anchored to the force of a communicative contribution. In other words, the scope of a hedge is extended from phrasal scope to clausal scope, while the function of a fuzzy maker is extended from narrow-scope adaptor to wide-scope shield (Prince *et al.*, 1982). The development is not unidirectional, however, as the wide scope attributed to shields may be narrowed down and shields may fulfil the function of approximators, as is the case with the comment clause *I think*, for example (cf. Aijmer, 1997).

The extension of scope as well as the narrowing down of scope are closely connected with the expression of the speaker's attitude. Following Fraser in his analyses of hedged performatives (Fraser, 1987) and discourse markers (Fraser, 1999), these linguistic devices make explicit a connection between a communicative contribution and the linguistic and non-linguistic context, expressing relational meaning. They signal aspects of the speaker's intention with respect to her/his position vis-à-vis the hearer or preceding context. For instance, they may express the speaker's distancing her/himself from the communicative contribution.

### 2.4. Discourse connective

The interpersonal dimension of hedges is also stressed by Le Lan (2007) in her examination of connectives, which is used as a cover term referring to discourse markers, hedges, comment clauses and particles. Not only are connectives indexical by definition and therefore dynamic and multifunctional but they also signify some mental movement from the speaker's to the hearer's point of view, and vice versa, regulating and organizing the fundamental triad of speaker, hearer and discourse. Le Lan comes to the conclusion that the function of indicating intersubjective positioning assigns these linguistic devices a metacommunicative, rather than a metalinguistic function. This also holds for the more- and less-fuzzy hedges *sort of* and *kind of*, which from a linguistic perspective make phrases and clauses more or less fuzzy, or to use her own words: 'Hedges enable the speaker to qualify the illocutionary force of his/her utterance by making things clearer or more obscure' (Le Lan, 2007: 109). Thus, their primary goal lies in the regulation and organization of discourse.

In his examination of constructions of intersubjectivity, Verhagen (2005) goes even further. According to him, language has a primarily intersubjective function, which he spells out as mutual management of cognitive states. Conventions are mutually shared rules, and 'grammatical elements and syntactic constructions have systematic, conventional functions in the dimension of intersubjective coordination'(Verhagen, 2005: 9). The question now is whether this also holds for the more- and less-fuzzy hedges *sort of* and *kind of*. In the introductory section, these hedges are looked upon as words, which can identify and intensify. In their identifying function, *sort of/kind of* make the object, constituent or clause, over which they have scope, less fuzzy, and in their intensifying function, they make it more fuzzy.

To summarize and conclude, the communicative function of the hedges *sort of* and *kind of* to express relational meaning, relating extra-linguistic objects (or entities), cognitive prototypes and linguistic expressions is a context-dependent endeavour par excellence. In the research paradigm of interactional sociolinguistics, it is the job of a contextualization cue to express that type of meaning, as is examined below.

## 3. *Sort of/Kind of*: A Contextualization Cue Par Excellence

In his original definition of contextualization cue, Gumperz defines the linguistic (or extra-linguistic) device as 'any aspect of *surface* form of utterances, which when mapped onto message content, can be shown to be *functional* in the *signaling of interpretation frames*' (Gumperz, 1977: 199). Not only are contextualization cues anchored to the metalinguistic, if not metacommunicative domain of communication, signalling procedural meaning, but they are also allocated to the interface of cognitive linguistics and functional linguistics.

Interactional sociolinguistics provides a truly dialectical frame of reference accommodating both the examination of parts, such as objects, constituents and clauses, and the examination of wholes, that is, discourse, thus connecting explicitly the cognitive operation of inference with the sociocultural activity of conversation. In his more recent works, Gumperz (1991: 232) refines the original definition of contextualization cue, stressing the relational nature of the concept:

> They serve to highlight, foreground or make salient certain phonological or lexical strings *vis-à-vis* other similar units, that is they function relationally and cannot be assigned context-independent, stable, core lexical meanings. Foregrounding processes, moreover, do not rest on any one single cue. Rather, assessments depend on cooccurrence judgments ( . . . ) that simultaneously evaluate a variety of different cues. When interpreted with reference to lexical and grammatical knowledge, structural position within a clause or sequential location within a stretch of discourse, foregrounding becomes an input to implicatures, yielding situated interpretations.

In the analysis of the theory and practice of hedges, *sort of* and *kind of* have been defined as expressing relational meaning, relating extra-linguistic objects, cognitive prototypes and linguistic expressions. Assigning these hedges, the status of contextualization cue has the consequence that the linguistic forms *sort of/kind of* cannot per se fulfil the function of making things more fuzzy. Rather, their local linguistic contexts and collocations need to be interpreted '*vis-à-vis* other similar units', that is, the objects, constituents, clauses or communicative contributions over which they have scope. Furthermore, the connectedness between *sort of/kind of* and their collocations needs to be evaluated because the 'assessments depend on cooccurrence judgments ( ... ) that simultaneously evaluate a variety of different cues'. Only then can they instruct the hearer about possible speaker intentions, that is, whether the communicative contribution (or one or more of its constitutive parts) is intended to be allocated closer to the core of the prototype or prototypical scenario and thus is intended to be less fuzzy, or whether it is intended to be allocated closer to the periphery and thus is intended to be more fuzzy.

In the following sections, the distribution, collocation, scope and function of *sort of* and *kind of* are examined within the social context of political discourse. In the following section, the data are presented.

## 4. The Data

The dyadic data investigated comprise 22 full-length dyadic political interviews recorded and transcribed between 1990 and 2003. The 1990-data were recorded from the program *On the record* (BBC1); the 1997 and 2001 data comprise interviews with the leaders of the leading British parties (BBC/ITV). The 2003 interview is about the war in Iraq. The data are systematized in Table 3.1:

**Table 3.1.** The political interviews

| Date | Interviewee + interviewer |
|---|---|
| 2003 | Tony Blair (Labour PM) + J. Paxman |
| 2001 general election | Tony Blair (Labour PM) + D. Dimbleby |
| 2001 general election | Tony Blair (Labour PM) + J. Dimbleby |
| 2001 general election | William Hague (Conservative Opposition) + D. Dimbleby |
| 2001 general election | William Hague (Conservative Opposition) + J. Dimbleby |
| 2001 general election | Charles Kennedy (Liberal Democrats) + D. Dimbleby |
| 2001 general election | Charles Kennedy (Liberal Democrats) + J. Dimbleby |
| 1997 general election | John Major (Conservative PM) + D. Dimbleby |
| 1997 general election | John Major (Conservative PM) + J. Dimbleby |

**Table 3.1.** (*Continued*)

| Date | Interviewee + interviewer |
|---|---|
| 1997 general election | John Major (Conservative PM) + J. Paxman |
| 1997 general election | Tony Blair (Labour Opposition) + D. Dimbleby |
| 1997 general election | Tony Blair (Labour Opposition) + J. Dimbleby |
| 1997 general election | Tony Blair (Labour Opposition) + D. Frost |
| 1997 general election | Tony Blair (Labour Opposition) + J. Paxman |
| 1997 general election | Paddy Ashdown (Liberal Democrats) + D. Dimbleby |
| 1997 general election | Paddy Ashdown (Liberal Democrats) + J. Dimbleby |
| 1997 general election | Paddy Ashdown (Liberal Democrats) + D. Frost |
| 1997 general election | Paddy Ashdown (Liberal Democrats) + J. Paxman |
| 1990 On the record | Michael Heseltine (Conservative) + J. Dimbleby |
| 1990 On the record | John Prescott (Labour Opposition) + J. Dimbleby |
| 1990 On the record | Tony Blair (Labour Opposition) + J. Dimbleby |
| 1990 On the record | John Gummer (Conservative Minister) + J. Dimbleby |

The monological data comprise 10 political speeches delivered by leading British politicians at the Conservative, Labour and Liberal Party conferences. They are systematized in Table 3.2:

**Table 3.2.** The political speeches

| Date | Politician |
|---|---|
| 2006 | Brown – speech at Labour Party Conference |
| 2006 | Cameron – speech at Conservative Party Conference |
| 2006 | Campell – speech at Liberal Party Conference |
| 2005 | Cameron – speech at Conservative Party Conference |
| 2005 | Davis – speech at Conservative Party Conference |
| 2005 | Fox – speech at Conservative Party Conference |
| 2005 | Kennedy – speech at Liberal Democrat Party Conference |

**Table 3.2.** (*Continued*)

| Date | Politician |
|---|---|
| 2005 | Rifkind – speech at Conservative Party Conference |
| 2004 | Blair – speech at Labour Party Conference |
| 2004 | Howard – speech at Conservative Party Conference |

The 22 political interviews comprise 150,044 words with 52 tokens of *sort of/kind of* and the speeches contain 35,844 words with 12 tokens of *sort of/kind of*. The genre-specific distribution of the token confirms the research carried out on *sort of/kind of* as a marker of spoken dialogical language (Biber, 1988; Biber *et al.*, 1999; Andersen, 2000; Aijmer, 2002) rather than as a marker of a written-to-be-spoken format.

In the following sections, the distribution, collocation, scope and function of *sort of/kind of* are examined more closely in their local linguistic contexts.

## 5. Distribution, Collocation and Scope

In the political interviews and speeches, *sort of/kind of* occurs with a number of different collocational patterns. Table 3.3 summarizes the distribution of *sort of/kind of* in the dialogical

**Table 3.3.** Collocations and distribution of *sort of/kind of* in the interviews

| Collocations of *sort of* | Collocations of *kind of* |
|---|---|
| A sort of NP (7) | A kind of NP (6) |
| The sort of NP (5) | The kind of NP (9) |
| Sort of NPs (1) | |
| This sort of NP (2) | This kind of NP (2) |
| That sort of NP (2) | That kind of NP (2) |
| What sort of NP (2) | |
| | Any kind of NP (1) |
| Some sort of NP (2) | Some kind of NP (2) |
| Sort of VP (9) | |

**Table 3.4.** Collocations and distribution of *sort of/kind of* in the speeches

| **Collocations of *sort of*** | **Collocations of *kind of*** |
|---|---|
| | Kind of VP (1) |
| What sort of NP (1) | What kind of NP (5) |
| | The kind of NP (2) |
| This sort of NP (1) | |
| That sort of NP (1) | That kind of NP (1) |

data, and Table 3.4 summarizes their distribution in the monological data. The absolute frequency of the tokens is given in brackets:

There is an almost even distribution of *sort of* and *kind of* in the collocation [indefinite article + *sort of/kind of* + NP], which suggests that the two forms are interchangeable. This also holds for the collocations [demonstrative + *sort of/kind of* + NP] and [indeterminate quantifier + *sort of/kind of* + NP] with two tokens each. With the other collocations, however, there seem to be context-specific preferences. There is a distinct preference for *the kind of NP* with the collocation [definite article + *sort of/kind of* + NP], which is almost twice as frequent as its *sort of*–anchored counterpart. Pluralized NPs, which occur just once, only co-occur with *sort of.* This also holds for VPs. The determinate collocation *what sort of NP* is only used with *sort of*, and the indeterminate collocation *any kind of NP* is just used with *kind of.*

In the monological genre of political speech only 12 tokens of *sort of/kind of* occur and they are distributed amongst the following collocations, in which, as in the table above, the absolute frequency is given in brackets.

Unlike the distribution of *sort of/kind of* in the dialogical genre of interview, the distribution of *sort of* and *kind of* is more scattered. There is only one token of the collocation [*kind of* + VP] in the political speeches, and there is no such token in the interviews, where the VP is only modified by *sort of.* Collocations of *kind of* and *sort of* with NPs also show preferences for one of the two modifiers. The collocation [demonstrative + *sort of/kind of* + NP] occurs once with the distal form and thus seems to be interchangeable. Its proximity-indicating counterpart [demonstrative + *sort of* + NP] only occurs with *sort of.* The collocation [definite article + *sort of/kind of* + NP] occurs twice, but only with *kind of.* The most frequent collocation is *what kind of NP*, which occurs five times, while its *sort-of*-based counterpart occurs just once.

### 5.1. [*sort of/kind of* + NP]

In the interview data, 43 of the 52 *sort of/kind of*-tokens are anchored to a NP. Within that scenario, there are 3 instances, in which the determiner co-occurs with an adjective,

[DET + ADJ + *sort of/kind of* + NP]: two of the three examples with an indefinite DET and *sort of* are produced by the interviewer (IR), and the other with a demonstrative and *kind of* is produced by the interviewee (IE):

(7) IR you're ***a*** **straightforward** *kind of* guy

(8) IR ... and under those circumstance, I'm asking you, what would you do? Will you share that, as ***a*** **straight** *kind of* guy?

(9) IE ... look they can carry on trumpeting ***that*** **old** *sort of* ***erm*** music hall tune from fifty, sixty years ago but no one believes that that is the Labour Party I'm leading today.

In examples (7) and (8), *kind of* is realized within an NP as an attributive modifier (De Smedt *et al.*, 2007). The attribute comprises both ADJ and *kind of* and occurs right before the noun *guy*, over which it has scope thus modifying it accordingly. Because of that it is not the appropriateness conditions of the adjectives *straightforward* and *straight*, which are indexed, but rather the appropriateness conditions of the reference to the IR's direct communication partner with the colloquial term *guy*. In example (9), the NP is introduced with the distal demonstrative *that* and the adjective *old*, thus signifying the NP's high degree of determinateness. Within that sequence, *sort of* would be very likely to be assigned the status of a head of an NP, which is premodified by DET and ADJ. However, that high degree of determinateness resulting from the determinate DET, the ADJ and the head of the NP *sort* requires to be analysed within its local linguistic context, accommodating the results obtained from our examination of the interactional-sociolinguistic concept of contextualization cue and its co-occurrence patterns. In example (9), the local linguistic context of the NP is characterized by a high degree of determinateness on the one hand, and the hesitation device *erm* realized right before the postmodifier *music hall tune from fifty, sixty years ago*. Consequently, *sort of* can no longer be assigned the status of head, but rather that of a hedge with scope over the NP *music hall tune from fifty, sixty years ago*, thus making the NP more fuzzy by signifying that the speaker has some reservations about the appropriateness conditions of *music hall tune from fifty, sixty years ago*.

The other 40 tokens of *kind of/sort of* anchored to a NP co-occur with a determiner and with a quantifier in the interview data. In the indeterminate-determiner scenario, for example in examples (10) and (11), assigning the token the status of head of a NP seems plausible from a form-based angle. This is also the case with the determinate-determiner scenario in example (12) from the interview data:

(10) IR Jonathan can we now just stop this. ***I mean*** this is just carrying ***the thing*** on and on .... ***And quite frankly***, there is ***a*** *sort of* feeding process, you only have to change a comma ....

(11) IE when I left the government I was not for a moment of the view that there was ***a*** *sort of* return ticket and I haven't changed my mind ... .I see no point in trying to ***if you like*** create ***another*** *sort of* media story. It's not gonna happen ...

(12) IE ***well I think*** that politics is a tough trade ***I mean*** heaven forfend that ***erm*** exchanges should get personal ***that*** *sort of* thing, thank goodness, has never happened to me ***but of course*** . . . .

In all of the examples, *sort of* could be analysed as a head plus postmodifier configuration with *sort* as its head. This is because *sort* collocates with an indeterminate DET. The postmodifiers would be *feeding process* in example (10), *media story* in example (11) and *thing* in example (12).

Analogously to the analysis of example (9), the local context of the tokens needs to be considered closely. In example (10), there is the indeterminate reference *thing*, referring to their prior discussion, and the style disjunct *quite frankly* (Greenbaum and Quirk, 1990) introducing forthcoming criticism. The postmodifier of the head configuration would be *feeding process*, which is used with a metaphorical reading in that case. Consequently, *sort of* is assigned the status of a hedge with scope over *feeding process* indexing the appropriateness conditions of the metaphorically used term. An almost identical argumentation holds for the analysis of example (11). From a form-based angle and because of the determiners *a* and *another*, *sort* is more than likely to be assigned the status of a head of the NPs *a sort of return ticket* and *another sort of media story*. In the first instance, *sort of* co-occurs with a noun used metaphorically, viz. *return ticket*, referring to the politician's decision. Consequently, it is assigned the status of a hedge with scope over *return ticket* whose appropriateness conditions are indexed. In the second instance, *sort of* co-occurs with the hedge *if you like* and with the general noun *media story*. Like in the previous instance, *media story* is used metaphorically in the context of political discourse, which needs to be based on facts and not on stories. Consequently, *sort of* is assigned the status of a hedge with scope over media story indexing its appropriateness conditions.

Example (12) is different from the one analysed so far. Here, *sort* is the head of the NP *that sort of thing*. The high degree of determinateness results from the demonstrative DET *that* and the anaphoric reference of the head *sort* and its postmodifier *thing*. The head refers to the sequential topic *politics is a tough trade* and the postmodifier refers to the subtopic *political attacks can get personal*. The high degree of determinateness – due to its anaphoric reference – is never at stake in spite of the indeterminateness manifest in the modality marker *I think* and in the vague semantics of the postmodifier *thing*.

In the monological data, there are only 12 tokens of *sort of/kind of*. All but one is anchored to a NP. Within that scenario, there are 6 instances, in which the NP is premodified by a *wh*-word, namely, *what sort of/kind of* NP (one collocating with *sort of* and 5 collocating with *kind of*), there are two examples with a determinate DET collocating with *kind of*, one example with the proximity-indicating demonstrative collocating with *sort of* and two instances with the distal demonstrative, as in examples (13), (14), (15), (16) and (17):

(13) The government says 'but we all know what we are talking about'. ***What*** *kind of* complacency is that? That is no way to make laws . . .

(14) Because ***just what*** *kind of* democracy was it that delivered back in May? A democracy which returns an outright majority government on little more than a third of the popular vote

(15) We are***n't the*** *kind of* people to be broken by terror. We won't appease it. And together, as one nation, we will confront it.

(16) I would not dare to say that Gordon Brown is psychologically flawed. I leave ***that*** *sort of* thing to No 10. I do say that Mr. Brown is a team player – who believes in a team of one.

(17) ***This*** *sort of* description, with only marginal differences, could have come from Darfur today, the Balkans in the 1990s, Nicaragua in the 1980s or Cambodia in the 1970s.

In examples (13) and (14), *sort of* collocates with the pronoun *what* and the nouns *complacency* and *democracy*, thus assigning it the status of a premodified head with the postmodifiers *complacency* and *democracy*. The nouns are used with their literal meanings, and their semantics is characterized by a high degree of abstractness. Consequently, the *wh*-question word premodifying the head is assigned the function of a less-fuzzy contextualization cues specifying their degree of abstractness. This is reinforced by the adverb *just* in example (14). In example (15), *kind of* is under the scope of negation. Again, it is assigned the status of a head premodified by a determinate DET and postmodified by the noun *people*. The determinate DET collocating with wide-scope negation (Fetzer, 2007b) narrows down the domain of reference of the general noun *people*. In examples (16) and (17), *sort of* collocates with the demonstratives *this* and *that* signifying determinate meaning. Again, *sort of* is assigned the status of head premodified by demonstratives with anaphoric reference in example (16) and cataphoric reference in example (17), and postmodified by a general noun, that is *thing*, in example (16) and *description* in example (17).

In the data investigated only the indeterminate quantifiers, *some* and *any* occur in *sort of/kind of*-anchored collocations composed of a quantifier and a noun phrase. *Some* collocates with *kind of* and *sort of*, but *any* only with *kind of*. Of the 52 token, 5 co-occur with an indeterminate quantifier in a NP-anchored cluster, and they are used by the IR, IE and audience member (AM) with the role of an IE, as is the case with examples (18) and (19):

(18) IE no no no for many people this in not an issue. You're trying to make it an issue because you hope then that you will get ***some*** *sort of* story because I've moved a subclause ***somewhere*** that there is a significance which I shall not

(19) AM … is there ***any chance whatsoever*** of happening to form an intelligent debate prior to ***any*** *kind of* informed referendum on the subject, because what you've had for the past few years is nothing but nonsense … .

From a form-based angle, the indeterminate quantifier *some* premodifies the noun *sort* in example (18), and within that cluster *story* is assigned the status of a postmodifier. From a function-based perspective, it is not the type of story, which is at the heart of the interaction, but rather the fabricated nature of the information. Assessing this co-occurrence pattern, *sort of* is assigned the status of a hedge with scope over story, which is made more fuzzy. This is supported by the indeterminate adverbial *somewhere* in the directly adjacent utterance, adding a further layer of fuzziness. In example (19), the inherently negative quantifier *any* premodifies the noun *kind*, which is assigned the status of head with its postmodifier-*informed referendum on the subject*. Unlike example (18), where the form and function of *sort of* clashes and where *sort of* is assigned the status of a hedge, the form and function of *kind of* do not clash. This is supported by the less-fuzzy adverbial *any chance whatsoever* and the negative context *what you've had for the past few years is nothing but nonsense*, narrowing down the utterance's domain of reference.

Depending on its linguistic context, the collocation [*sort of/kind of*+NP] can be hedge, making things more fuzzy, or head of NP, making things less fuzzy. Can *sort of/kind of* also fulfil that dual function in VP-anchored collocations?

### 5.2. [*Sort of/kind of*+VP]

In the dialogical data, there are 9 tokens of *sort of*, and in the monological data there is only one token of *kind of* (example 24). In the research literature examined above, *sort of/kind of* collocating with a VP is assigned the status of a hedge, making the VP, over which it has scope, more fuzzy. In all of the examples analysed, *sort of* fulfils that function. In example (20), it has scope over the underlined VP 'spun against', indexing the appropriateness conditions of the IE's word play, which is further elaborated on in her/his contribution. This is introduced by the reformulatory device *in the sense*. In example (21), *sort of* has scope over the VP *consider the enormity*, indexing its appropriateness conditions thus making it more fuzzy and more acceptable for the communication partner. The same line of argumentation holds for the analysis of examples (22), (23) and (24), in which it has scope over the VP indexing its appropriateness conditions, thus making it more fuzzy:

(20) IE well, I I ***sometimes*** think we're more *sort of* <u>spun against</u> than spinning, ***in the sense*** that people have this huge thing about it ...

(21) IE well Jonathan let's *sort of* <u>consider the enormity</u> of what you've just said ...

(22) IE and I'm not prepared to be taken down ***some road*** that you've carefully worked out in order to try and *sort of* <u>change</u> the emphasis

(23) IR but so when he says there will be no further cuts, Michael Portillo says there will be f f further cuts, he <u>is</u> ***erm*** *sort of* <u>whistling</u> in the wind?

(24) The city of the Olympic Games for Britain in 2012. Let me tell you what won that bid. Yes, we had a magnificent team led by Seb Coe, a great London Mayor who backed it to the hilt, a country behind us [*applause*] *kind of* <u>gets better</u> every year that line actually [*laughter*] but what won it was London itself.

What is of relevance to this investigation of hedges is the observation that *sort of/kind of* used as a more-fuzzy hedge tends to co-occur with other markers of indeterminacy and vagueness as well as with hesitation devices, as is the case with the examples (9), (10), (11), (18) and all of the VP-anchored collocations. In its function as a head with a postmodifier, it tends to co-occur with markers of determinacy and certainty, as is the case with the examples (12), (13), (14), (15), (17) and (19). These co-occurrence patterns make *sort of/kind of* a prime candidate for the interactional-sociolinguistic concept of contextualization cue.

## 6. Function

An investigation of the form and function of hedges in context does not only need to account for their collocations in local linguistic contexts but also for the social context in which the interaction takes place. This prerequisite has been accommodated to some extent by explicitly accounting for their genre-specific distribution. To account for the fine-graded interplay between their communicative function of expressing assertiveness or certainty on the one hand and tentativeness or responsiveness on the other (Simon-Vandenbergen, 1996, 2000), both the social context in which the monological and dialogical interactions take place and the co-occurrence of *sort of/kind of* with other linguistic devices conveying responsiveness and certainty need to be considered. The frame of reference, which seems most promising for that endeavour, as has been argued for above, is the research paradigm of interactional sociolinguistics with its key concept of contextualization cue (Gumperz, 1991).

In more recent approaches to political discourse analysis, political discourse is conceptualized as *politics as text and talk*, or to use ethnomethodological terminology, political discourse is looked upon as *doing politics* (Chilton and Schäffner, 2002). That is to say, politicians and other agents within the field of politics interactionally organize their social and interactional roles by using language and other semiotic codes in a strategic manner, accommodating their heterogeneous audience's face wants and information wants (Brown and Levinson, 1987). Depending on their communicative intentions and at the stage, at which their communicative contributions occur (Grice, 1975), they may make them more responsive or more certain. But how do they accomplish that task?

Feeding on the interactional-sociolinguistics premise of indexicality of communicative action, communicators use indexicals in an intentional and strategic manner to make their communicative contribution more fuzzy and thereby more responsive, or less fuzzy and thereby more certain. To achieve that goal, they can use different kinds of discourse connectives, thus indexing the appropriateness conditions implicitly, or they can use explicitly realized references to the appropriateness conditions (Celle and Huart, 2007; Fetzer, 2007a).

In the data investigated, *sort of/kind of* tend to co-occur with discourse markers, such as *well, now, first, second* or *look.* These indexicals signal how the speaker intends her/his audience to interpret her/his communicative contribution and its underlying argumentation. *Sort of/kind of* co-occur also with other hedges, for instance *more or less*, *in the sense*, *somehow* or *almost*, thus intensifying the communicative contribution's degree of fuzziness, and *sort of/kind of* co-occur with the communicative strategy of understatement based on double negation (Fetzer, 2007b), reducing the degree of speaker commitment to the validity of her/his contribution. Furthermore, *sort of/kind of* co-occur with interpersonal markers, such as *you know, if you like, I mean* or *to my best knowledge*, assigning the communicative contribution the status of intersubjectivity, and *sort of/kind of* co-occur with question tags. If realized with falling intonation contour, the tag makes the contribution more certain, and if realized with rising contour, it makes the contribution more responsive (Leech and Svartvik, 1994: 127).

*Sort of/kind of* also co-occur with expressions of epistemic modality: probability and possibility express tentativeness, and logical necessity expresses certainty. Frequently, the modal verbs *can/could, must, shall/should* and *will/would* co-occur with modal adverbs, in particular with *perhaps, possibly, probably* and *obviously*, thus intensifying the speaker's degree of commitment to her/his communicative contribution. Furthermore, *sort of/kind of* co-occur with cognitive verbs used as parentheticals, such as *I mean*, *I know*, *I think*, *I believe*, *I feel* and *it seems*, assigning the communicative contribution some degree of intersubjectivity. Depending on the semantics of the verb, they may boost the degree of speaker commitment expressed, as is the case with *I believe* and *I know* in political discourse, or they may weaken it, as is the case with *I think* and *it seems*. This also holds for *sort of/kind of* co-occurring with verbs of communication, for instance *talk* and *suggest*, attributing a lower degree of speaker commitment to the communicative contribution.

In the following sections, the prototypical co-occurrence pattern of *sort of/kind of*, which assigns them the status of a more-fuzzy hedge and a less-fuzzy hedge, is examined more closely.

### 6.1. S*ort of/kind of* with its more-fuzzy function

Whenever *sort of/kind of* are anchored to the collocation [*sort of/kind of* + VP], their default function is to make the VP more fuzzy. The results obtained from the extensive research on the 'standard hedge' (cf. Sections 1 and 2) have been corroborated by this corpus-based investigation of political interviews and speeches. What is of relevance, however, is the fact that the VP-anchored collocation is less frequent than their NP-anchored counterpart. But why is the more-fuzzy-making function assigned the status of default?

From a lexical-semantics perspective, *sort of/kind of* denote the category of a type, but not the concrete object, entity or situation as such. *Sort of/kind* can be paraphrased by *a type of* x, but not 'x' itself. For this reason, they are intrinsically indeterminate. The degree of fuzziness expressed by the two devices can be intensified by the adverb *very*, making the object, entity or situation, over which they have scope, even more fuzzy. This might be due to an ongoing process of semantic bleaching, that is, to say the expression of fuzziness has become conventionalized to such an extent that speakers feel *sort of/kind of* not to express 'genuine fuzziness' any longer. Another interesting observation is that in the majority of cases, in which *sort of/kind of* is assigned a more-fuzzy-making function, its local linguistic context contains other expressions of vagueness, such as hedges, understatements, interpersonal markers, question tags and expressions of epistemic modality. As has been pointed out above, these co-occurrence patterns may intensify the degree of fuzziness expressed if *sort of/kind of* collocate with a VP. However, in contexts in which *sort of/kind of* co-occur with a NP, these contextualization cues are of prime importance, as they guide the communication partners how the speaker intends her/his communicative contribution to be taken and how they are intended to interpret it.

Another important cue for assigning *sort of/kind* the status of a more- or less-fuzzy hedge is anchored to the literal or non-literal use of the NP. If the noun anchored to *sort of/kind of* is used in a metaphorical manner, the function expressed by *sort of/kind of* is to make the NP more fuzzy, and if the noun is used in its literal sense, *sort of/kind* make the noun less-fuzzy.

### 6.2. *Sort of/kind of* with its less-fuzzy function

As has already surfaced in the discussion above, *sort of/kind of* do not per se realize the function of making things more fuzzy. While the fuzzy-making function is conventionalized with VPs, with NPs it is context dependent.

In linguistic contexts, in which the NP collocating with *sort of/kind of* is fronted, *sort of/kind of* is more likely to be assigned the function of making things less fuzzy. The same holds for the collocation [*sort of/kind of* + NP] co-occurring with relative clauses, where *sort of/kind of* are more likely to be assigned the function of making things less fuzzy. Other factors which have an impact on the communicative function of *sort of/kind of* are (1) the semantics of the noun realized in the postmodifier slot and (2) the discursive reference realized by the devices. If the noun anchored to *sort of/kind of* is used non-metaphorically and if *sort of/kind of* realize anaphoric or cataphoric reference, *sort of/kind of* do not realize their default function of making things more fuzzy but rather their non-default, identifying function thus making things less fuzzy, as is the case with the following examples:

(25) AM ... Ok. The penny on the income tax will be more than enough to pay for your education, you say, that but it'll only raise about three billion. ***The sort of*** spending you're planning, with the health service, with ***the other bits and pieces***, you're going to need ***a vast amount more*** ...

IE well

AM Which are ***the other bits*** that you will put up, the hard working tax payers will have to pay for?

(26) IR … I understand it therefore that ***in your view*** it is ***extremely important*** that ***the*** *kind of* reforms that you have advocated are put in place?

(27) IE … and on most of the issues you and I have been discussing Labour has got ***no policies*** and ***no spending commitments whatsoever nor indeed*** any tax commitments of ***any sort now if that's the*** *kind of* politics ***you want***, fine …

(28) IE ***I'm s- I am sure*** that if we let teachers get on with their jobs and made ***the*** *sort of* changes that I am talking about, we would retain people in the profession

(29) IE ***I mean*** this – ***I mean***, you put your finger really on the centre of the dilemma here. It is a role model, and in something as almost instantaneous, so there's no time for advice, planning, thinking through your reactions or response, whatever it might be, ***and this*** *kind of* incident happens. ***I think*** …

(30) IE …. and we preserved this country's future in Europe ***now that's the*** *kind of* co-operation I'm interested in.

In example (25), ***the*** *sort of* has a referring function indexing some prior discourse. For this reason, it is assigned an identifying function, making things less fuzzy. This interpretation is not unambiguously supported by the local linguistic context, in which we find more-fuzzy cues, that is *other bits and pieces* as well as less-fuzzy cues, namely, *a vast amount more*. In the follow-up questions, however, the AM with IR function makes her/his communicative intention to obtain less-fuzzy information unambiguously clear: s/he asks the politician to name the other bits. In examples (26), (27), (28) and (30), the collocation [DET + *kind of/sort of* + NP] is directly followed by a relative clause thus making the NPs *the kind of reforms*, *the kind of politics*, *the sort of changes* and *the kind of cooperation* less fuzzy. Another indicator for the less-fuzzy function is a demonstrative used as a premodifier with anaphoric reference in example (29).

The local linguistic context and co-occurrence patterns support the less-fuzzy-making function of *sort of/kind of*: in example (25), the semantics of the rather general term *spending* is specified by signifying its domains of reference. In example (26), there are further boosters, namely, *extremely important* and the specification *in your view* contributing to the less-fuzzy function; in example (27), there is a negative context (*no spending … no commitments … of any sort*) and the other-reference realized with the verb of intention, that is, *you want*, which make the context less fuzzy; in example (28), there is the expression of the epistemic modality of certainty *I am sure* and in example (30), the discourse marker *now*, focussing the audience's attention, thus supporting the less-fuzzy function. Example (29) is more ambiguous because of the use of parentheticals (*I mean*, *I think*), which generally favour a more-fuzzy reading. Due to its anaphoric reference, however, *sort of* is assigned a less-fuzzy-making function.

## 7. Conclusion

The examination of the form and function of *sort of/kind of* in political discourse has shown that the two devices can be assigned the status of a contextualization cue par excellence. When collocating with a VP, they make the VP over which they have scope more fuzzy, and when collocating with a NP, they can make the NP more fuzzy and less fuzzy – depending on position, co-occurrence and sequential status.

In the social context of political discourse, *sort of/kind of* are less frequent than in ordinary mundane everyday talk. Moreover, while their VP-anchored more-fuzzy function is more frequent in ordinary talk, it is the NP-anchored collocation, which is more frequent in political discourse. Because of its semantics, the more-fuzzy-making function is the default for both VP- and NP-anchored collocations in political discourse, where they signify particularized contextual frames, for instance a negotiation-of-meaning sequence, in which the communicative status of particularized discourse topics, particularized questions or answers is at stake. Regarding their perlocutionary effects in the social context of doing politics, the more-fuzzy-making function allows the communicators to keep their communicative intentions diplomatically vague and at the same time signify solidarity and responsiveness. The less-fuzzy-making function, by contrast, allows the communicators to attribute clarity to their communicative intentions, thus signifying certainty and assertiveness. In the discourse of politics, it is not the either more- or less-fuzzy-making function of the two devices, but rather their fine-graded interplay and their interaction with other linguistic devices expressing certainty and vagueness, which contribute to the inherent persuasiveness of the genre.

## Acknowledgments

I am grateful to the two anonymous reviewers and the editors of this volume for helpful comments on the first version of this contribution. I would like to thank Peter Bull (University of York, UK) for sharing some of his data with me.

## References

Aijmer, K. (1997). "I think – An English modal particle", in T. Swan and O. Jansen (eds.), *Modality in Germanic languages. Historical and comparative perspectives*. Berlin: de Gruyter, 1–47.

Aijmer, K. (2002). *English discourse particles: Evidence from a corpus*. Amsterdam: Benjamins.

Andersen, G. (2000). *Pragmatic markers and sociolinguistic variation: A relevance-theoretic approach to the language of adolescents*. Amsterdam: Benjamins.

Biber, D. (1988). *Variation across speech and writing*. Cambridge: Cambridge University Press.

Biber, D., S. Johansson, G. Leech, S. Conrad and E. Finegan (1999). *Longman grammar of spoken and written English*. London: Longman.

Bolinger, D. (1972). *Degree words*. The Hague: Mouton.

Brinton, L. (1996). *Pragmatic markers in English: Grammaticalization and discourse functions*. Berlin: de Gruyter.

Brown, P. and S. Levinson (1987). *Politeness. Some universals in language usage*. Cambridge: Cambridge University Press.

Celle, A. and R. Huart (eds.) (2007). *Connectives as discourse landmarks*. Amsterdam: Benjamins.

Chilton, P. and C. Schäffner (2002). in P. Chilton and C. Schäffner (eds.), *Politics as text and talk: Analytical approaches to political discourse*. Amsterdam: Benjamins, 1–41.

Coates, J. (2003). "The role of epistemic modality in women's talk", in R. Facchinetti, M. Krug and F. Palmer (eds.), *Modality in contemporary English*. Berlin: de Gruyter, 331–348.

De Smedt, L., L. Brems and K. Davidse (2007). "NP-internal functions and extended uses of the 'type' nouns kind, sort, and type: Towards a comprehensive, corpus-based description", in R. Facchinetti (ed.), *Corpus linguistics 25 years on*. Amsterdam: Rodopi, 225–255.

Fetzer, A. (1994). *Negative Interaktionen: kommunikative Strategien im britischen Englisch und interkulturelle Inferenzen*. Frankfurt: Lang.

Fetzer, A. (2002). "Communicative intentions in context", in A. Fetzer and C. Meierkord (eds.), *Rethinking sequentiality: Linguistics meets conversational interaction*. Amsterdam: Benjamins, 37–69.

Fetzer, A. (2004). *Recontextualizing context: Grammaticality meets appropriateness*. Amsterdam: Benjamins.

Fetzer, A. (2007a). "Context, contexts and appropriateness", in A. Fetzer (ed.), *Context and appropriateness: Micro meets macro*. Amsterdam: Benjamins, 3–27.

Fetzer, A. (2007b). "Non-acceptances in context". *Intercultural Pragmatics* **4 (4)**: 493–520.

Fraser, B. (1987). "Pragmatic formatives", in J. Verschueren and M. Bertuccelli-Papi (eds.), *The pragmatic perspective*. Amsterdam: Benjamins, 179–194.

Fraser, B. (1999). "What are discourse markers? *Journal of Pragmatics* **31**: 931–952.

Greenbaum, S. and R. Quirk (1990). *A student's grammar of the English language*. London: Longman.

Grice, H. P. (1975). "Logic and conversation", in P. Cole and J. L. Morgan (eds.), *Syntax and Semantics*. New York: Academic Press, 41–58.

Gumperz, J. (1977). "Sociocultural knowledge in conversational inference", in M. Saville-Troike (ed.), *Linguistics and anthropology*. Washington: Georgetown University Press, 191–211.

Gumperz, J. J. (1991). "Contextualization and understanding", in A. Duranti and C. Goodwin (eds.), *Rethinking context: Language as an interactive phenomenon*. Cambridge: Cambridge University Press, 229–252.

Kay, P. (1984). "The kind of/sort of construction". *Berkeley Linguistics Society* **10**: 128–137.

Lakoff, G. (1975). "Hedges: A study in meaning criteria and the logic of fuzzy concepts", in D. Hockney, et al. (eds.), *Contemporary research in philosophical logic and linguistic semantics*. Dodrecht: Fortis, 221–271.

Leech, G. and J. Svartvik (1994). *A communicative grammar of English*. London: Longman.

Le Lan, B. (2007). "Orchestrating conversation: The multifunctionality of *well* and *you know* in the joint construction of a verbal interaction", in A. Celle and R. Huart (eds.), *Connectives as discourse landmarks*. Amsterdam: Benjamins, 103–116.

Mauranen, A. (2004). "There's a little bit different. Observations on hedges in academic talk", in K. Aijmer and A. B. Stenström (eds.), *Discourse patterns in spoken and written corpora*. Amsterdam: Benjamins, 173–197.

Prince, E., J. Frader and C. Bosk (1982). "On hedging in physician-physician discourse", in R. J. Di Pietro (ed.), *Linguistics and the profession*. Norwood: Ablex, 83–97.

Quirk, R., S. Greenbaum, G. Leech and J. Svartvik (1985). *A grammar of contemporary English*. London: Longman.

Simon-Vandenbergen, A. M. (1996). "Image-building through modality: The case of political interviews". *Discourse & Society* 7: 389–415.

Simon-Vandenbergen, A. M. (2000). "The functions of *I think* in political discourse". *International Journal of Applied Linguistics* **10 (1)**: 41–63.

Traugott, E. and R. Dasher (2002). *Regularity in semantic change*. Cambridge: Cambridge University Press.

Ungerer, F. (1988). *Syntax der englischen Adverbialien*. Tübingen: Niemeyer.

Verhagen, A. (2005). *Constructions of intersubjectivity*. Oxford: Oxford University Press.

New Approaches to Hedging
Edited by Gunther Kaltenböck, Wiltrud Mihatsch and Stefan Schneider


# 4

# Mitigating and Being Vague in Interpreter-Mediated Discourse

*Bernd Meyer and Birte Pawlack*

> Pretty much anything we can say in one language can be translated into any other
>
> Ray Jackendoff

## Abstract

In this chapter, we show how interpreters intervene in the communication process by adding mitigators and vague expressions, despite the lack of any linguistic triggers in the source-text. The objects of study are *bushes* that, according to Caffi (2007), affect mainly the propositional content. Furthermore, we analyze the use and the rendition of proper names.

The examined corpus (CoSi) contains three performances of one and the same talk on socio-political matters held in Brazilian Portuguese, translated into German by five different interpreters (approximately 35.000 words). Analyzing the source–target correspondence, we discovered that all interpreters added mitigators although no triggers were given in the source text. Examples for such items are *eine Art* ("a sort of"), *der ein oder andere* ("one or other of"), *eigentlich* and *praktisch* ("practically"/"basically speaking"). Where interpreters add mitigators to the original statements, the propositional content changes and the validity of the utterance is constrained, so that the interpreter gives his or her subjective tone to the discourse. With regard to proper names, the subjects in this study show a general tendency to substitute them or to combine them with generic expressions in the target discourse.

## 1. Introduction

Considering the fact that interpreters in the 1950s still claimed to be working "as faithfully as sound-amplification" (Glémet, 1958, cited from Pöchhacker, 2004: 141), it is impressive how standard concepts, the self-perceptions of the practitioners and their research agendas, have changed over the past 40 years. Although a layperson may still be fond of the idea that interpreters simply render a previously uttered statement, most researchers and providers of interpreting services either implicitly or explicitly acknowledge that a mismatch between source- and target-text/discourse is unavoidable – and in some cases even desirable. This view of translators and interpreters as "intervenient beings" (Maier, 2007) is backed by the insight that acts of translation are based on choices and that "each choice, reflected upon or not, represents an intervention" (Munday, 2007: xiv). Thus, the notion of "intervention" directly points to the questions of linguistic equivalence, cultural filtering, and cultural action in oral and written translation (House, 1981; House and Rehbein, 2004; Rehbein, 2006).

However, what is considered to be an intervention varies to a large extent: although Moeketsi (2007) calls for organizational interventions in interpreter training and institutional language policies to enhance the quality of court interpreting in post-apartheid South Africa, other authors understand interventions in translation as related to linguistic features of discourse such as dialogue coordination and different types of renditions (Müller, 1989; Wadensjö, 1998), adaptation strategies (Kohn and Kalina, 1996), the speaking out of implicit information (Mason, 2006) or divergent intonational patterns (Nafá Waasaf, 2003; Ahrens, 2004). All these studies and many others not mentioned here provide examples for the active involvement of interpreters.

In addition to the influence of context, the issues of processing constraints and workload seem to play a major role when studying the frequency and types of interventions in different modes of interpreting. When an interpreter is working in the simultaneous mode, less time is available to handle differences in mutual knowledge or culture if they occur. Therefore, Setton (2006: 382) maintains that, in theory, renditions should provide all necessary communicative clues that allow for a correct interpretation, but that "in practice, the simultaneity constraints scramble the discourse, so that it becomes difficult to establish any more than occasional, indirect correspondences between communicative clues in the product and linguistic properties of the original."

Although it is widely acknowledged that a mismatch between source and target discourse is often unavoidable in oral translation due to processing problems and time constraints, written translation is often perceived as reproducing the writer's intentions and even the concrete linguistic formats used in the original message more faithfully. Nevertheless, certain shifts of source–target correspondence can be found even in written translation. As the Housian notions "covert translation" and "cultural filtering" suggest (cf. House, 2006), translators often, deliberately or not, adapt the target text to the stylistic preferences and communicative conventions of the target language community. House (2006: 344) emphasizes that such adaptations are necessary to establish a relationship of equivalence between source and target text. Equivalence, however, is a relative concept. It does not mean identity: "absolute equivalence would in fact be a *contradictio in adiecto*" (*ibid.*). Thus, mismatches between source and target text may be the result of linguistic and contextual factors such as structural linguistic constraints, preferences of the interpreter, and/or the target language community, cultural conventions, or differences in knowledge. House proposes a "cultural filter" as "a means of capturing cognitive and socio-cultural differences in expectation norms and discourse conventions between source and target linguistic-cultural communities." The cultural filter leads translators to account for certain cross-cultural differences and guides their choices with regard to specific linguistic features of text. Focusing especially on differences between English and German academic prose and popular scientific texts, House shows in various studies that translations between German and English differ systematically along certain continua such as directness versus indirectness, explicitness versus implicitness, etc.

The normative concept of correspondence between source and target discourse is still considered to be the "'ideal standard' for the interpreters' translational product" (Pöchhacker, 2004: 141), with this standard being captured (and sometimes even measured) by terms such as accuracy, fidelity, and completeness. However, analyses of interpreter performance have shown that this normative concept is misleading. Owing to the complex demands of the interpreting task such as role conflicts, cultural differences, linguistic constraints, processing problems, etc., strict source–target correspondence, even on the level of functional equivalence, often cannot be achieved. The question, therefore, is not whether a rendition is accurate and complete. Rather, one should ask in which respect a rendition deviates from the original and what effects this mismatch has on the message and the interaction as a whole.

In this chapter, we investigate this issue with regard to the addition of mitigators and vague expressions by interpreters. We focus our analyses on lexical categories that were originally neither mitigated nor used vaguely in the source language discourse. Examples include the rendition of proper names by class names or indefinite pronouns and the use of certain mitigators such as German *eigentlich, praktisch* and *im Grunde genommen* ("practically" or "basically speaking"). Such additions of mitigators and substitutions of originally precise expressions may result in renditions that, in certain respects, differ from the original versions. The examples discussed are *bushes* according to Caffi's (2007) classification, that is, they allow the speaker to express a lower commitment regarding the truth or the validity of the statement. Although some similarities exist to the stylistic phenomena discussed by Juliane House and her collaborators – for example, the directness/indirectness distinction – the differences between source and target discourse observed in our data are not the result of cultural filtering (House, 1998). A non-mitigated or precise version of the same utterance or section of talk would have been grammatically possible and stylistically completely appropriate. Mitigating and vague language may therefore be due to processing problems, memory constraints or lack of knowledge of the interpreters.

Furthermore, knowledge differences between the speaker and the audience may play an important role. With regard to mitigating, our data suggest that interpreters mitigate statements especially when the original, source version is a strong claim by the speaker, containing information that is presumably novel or uncommon for the audience. In this sense, the addition of certain mitigators such as *eigentlich* seems to be triggered by the interpreter's attempting to make these statements more acceptable for the audience. In this case, the use of certain mitigators may be seen as a caveat, based on the assumption that the addressee(s) are less likely to reject a mitigated statement. This strategy can also be observed in academic discourse (Graefen, 2000). Our assumption is similar regarding the substitution of proper names: although scholars in translation and interpreting studies usually claim that names are easy to render, there is some evidence that interpreters adapt names according to the assumed knowledge of the audience. The substitution or expansion of names reflects this evaluation of the different stores of knowledge of speaker and audience.

The corpus, though relatively small (35,000 words), is composed of three largely convergent talks given by a Brazilian rainforest activist to a German audience. In two cases, interpreting was conducted in the consecutive mode, whereas in one case two teams of interpreters worked in the simultaneous mode. This systematic variation allows us to compare the source–target correspondence in different modes of interpreting.

## 2. The CoSi-Corpus

The CoSi-corpus consists of comparable performances of five consecutive and simultaneous interpreters. We opted for a constellation in which a foreign language–speaking expert speaks to a non-expert audience in a public setting in Germany. For this purpose, we cooperated with the German nongovernmental organization (NGO) "KOBRA" (*Koordination Brasilien*), a network of rainforest and third world activists. As part of their regular activities, the NGO organized the visit of a Brazilian speaker involved in campaigns against the use of genetically modified crops (soy) and the plantation of soy in the Amazon basin.

The speaker came to Germany in May 2006 for a series of three lectures on the same topic. The lectures were given in Berlin, Hamburg, and Heidelberg. Two of these lectures were rendered in the consecutive mode, whereas in one case (Heidelberg), simultaneous interpreting was provided. The event took place at the Department for Translation and Interpreting of the University of Heidelberg. We were able to use the available professional system for conference interpreter training including booths, headsets for the audience, etc. This enabled us to have two teams, each with two simultaneous interpreters working side by side, in different booths, on the same speech.

The audience was similar in each case: German rainforest activists, concerned citizens who wanted to know more about genetically modified food, and people with a general interest in Brazilian politics or environmental issues. In Heidelberg, however, there was also a considerable number of university students present, as the talk was part of the "regional studies" program offered by the department.

Professional interpreters were hired through an interpreting agency that had already cooperated with the NGO on several previous occasions. To prepare themselves, the interpreters received written material on the topic of genetically modified crops, as well as the manuscript of the speech, which was available one day before the events took place. The manuscript was the same for all three lectures but the speaker frequently deviated from it. Thus, the speech was largely spontaneous and therefore not always text-based. Rather, the manuscript served mainly as an *aide-mémoire* for the speaker. The interpreters were all native speakers of German with Portuguese as their B-Language. All of them had good professional records and earned their livings with translation and interpreting, although one was an autodidact with no formal training. Three of the interpreters were more familiar with European Portuguese, whereas two reported that they mainly work with Brazilian Portuguese. Although four members of the group worked in various contexts (media, conferences, court), one mainly worked for the European Parliament. The consecutive interpreter in Hamburg ("Hans") also participated in the Heidelberg lecture as a simultaneous interpreter (Figure 4.1).

**Hamburg**

- Interpreter: "Hans"
- B-Language: Brazilian Portuguese
- Formal training: no
- Professional experience: conferences, court, media

**Berlin**

- Interpreter: "Petra"
- B-Language: European Portuguese
- Formal training: university degree in conference interpreting
- Professional experience: conferences, court, media

**Heidelberg, Booth 09**

| "Hans" | "Maria" |
|---|---|
| B-Language: Brazilian Portuguese | B-Language: European Portuguese |
| No formal training | University degree |
| conferences, court, media | conferences, court, media |

**Heidelberg, Booth 10**

| "Sabine" | "Franz" |
|---|---|
| B-Language: Brazilian Portuguese | B-Language: European Portuguese |
| University degree | University degree |
| conferences, court, media | European Parliament |

**Figure 4.1.** Interpreters participating in the study.

Two weeks after the conferences, all five interpreters answered a questionnaire on their professional experience, their second language acquisition, what they like and dislike regarding different types of interpreting and different conference settings and their thoughts on the particular lectures on rainforest issues and genetically modified crops.

The three talks were recorded and transcribed using the EXMARaLDA transcription editor (www.exmaralda.org). In the case of the consecutive mode, the transcripts contained both the original speech and the subsequent renditions. In Heidelberg, however, where simultaneous interpreting was provided, we transcribed the original speech and the two audio streams from the booths separately (Figure 4.2). Nevertheless, the temporal relations between source and target

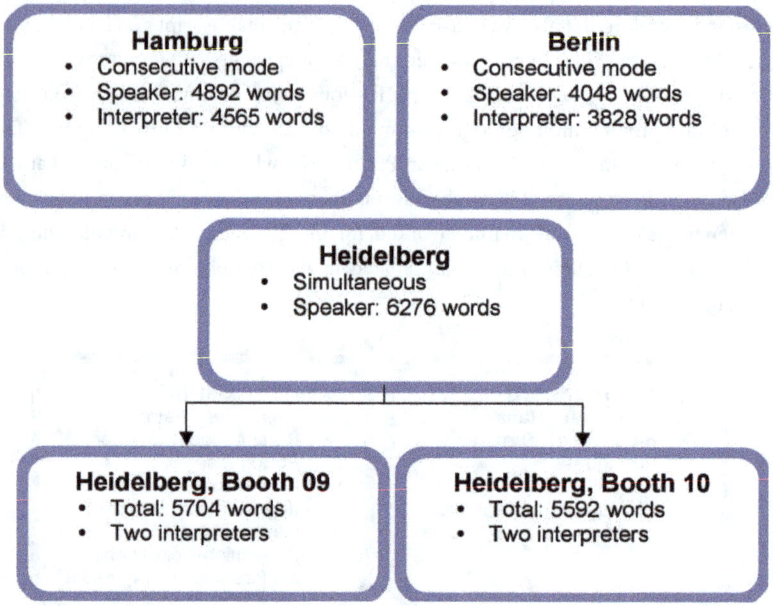


**Figure 4.2.** Features of the transcripts.

discourse (time-lag) were documented by annotating the time at which each statement began. This was necessary because the temporal extension of speech and the spatial extension of writing diverged to an extent that could not be included in the transcript. A detailed analysis of the temporal relations in smaller segments of discourse was only possible by referring to the sound-file.

This set of data varies systematically on one hand and is semi-controlled on the other. The setting and working conditions for the interpreters were authentic with regard to preparation time, preparation material, and payment. The interpreters rated the speakers' performance (argumentative style and articulation) as "normal" or "typically Brazilian." The content was nearly the same in all lectures, although the formulations were often not entirely identical. With regard to the argumentative structure of her talk, the speaker used a presentational, assertive style. She always began with descriptive sections in which she gave a *tour d'horizon* on the topic and ended with presented political measures that need to be taken and political demands to which the audience should adhere. Thus, the data were uniform in the sense that there was a high degree of convergence between each individual lecture with regard to parameters that are important for interpreters. The one parameter that varied systematically was the difference between consecutive interpreting in Berlin and Hamburg and simultaneous interpreting in Heidelberg. Furthermore, the B-language of the interpreters (European or Brazilian Portuguese) varied, with the subjects representing both of these options for each mode of interpreting. Nevertheless, all subjects worked from their B-language into their A-language (German). One subject, "Hans," was present both in Hamburg and Heidelberg and thus interpreted the same speaker and the same speech for a second time one day after doing so in the consecutive mode in Hamburg, allowing for an analysis of individual variation in interpreter performance. CoSi can be accessed free of charge at http://exmaralda.org/en_sfb_k6.html (password-protected).

## 3. Vague Names and Mitigated Statements

In this section, we discuss in more detail how proper names and certain statements are rendered and which role generic expressions and mitigators play in this regard. We begin with an example from our data. The example (1) "Chico Mendes-HD" is taken from booths 09 and 10 in Heidelberg, where the interpreters are "Hans" and "Franz." In the excerpt, the Brazilian speaker is talking about possible solutions to the social and ecological problems in the Amazon basin. More specifically, she speaks of so-called extractive reserves (*reservas extrativistas*): areas under legal protection that, at the same time, could be economically used by rubber tappers and other small businesses on a sustainable basis to preserve the ecological foundations of the rainforest. In this context, the speaker quotes a former Brazilian politician, *Chico Mendes*.

(1) Example "Chico Mendes-Heidelberg"

| Speaker (48m:17s) | "Hans" (48m:23s) | "Franz" (48m:22s) |
|---|---|---|
| *Eh Chico Mendes que foi um grande líder • • amazônico, dizia que a reserva extrativista é a reforma agrária do povo amazônico.* | *((1,5s)) Einer der großen Anführer dieser Bewegung im Amazonasgebiet hat immer gesagt, Schutzgebiete sind eigentlich die Agrarreform des Amazonasgebietes.* | *((4s)) Es hat • einmal • • jemand • • gesagt, • • • das ist eigentlich schon fast schon eine Art Agrarreform bei uns.* |
| Uh Chico Mendes who was a great Amazonian leader said that the extractive reserve is the land reform of the Amazonian people. | One of the great leaders of this movement in the Amazon region always said that protected areas are actually the land reform of the Amazon region. | Someone once said that this is actually almost a type of land reform for us. |

Mendes was the leader of the trade union of rubber tappers in the Brazilian federal state of Acre. Gunmen, presumably hired by *fazendeiros* (big landlords), murdered him in 1988. Mendes is seen as a martyr of the social and ecological movements in Brazil. His struggle received international attention even by the UN, who stopped funding certain programmes when Mendes and his unionists proved that these programmes, instead of protecting the rainforest, fostered intensive agribusinesses in the area. For Brazilian activists, it is normal to refer to Mendes in discussions about developmental policies and the rainforest. Among the German audience, however, he is probably not as well known. The quote is an absolute ( = non-mitigated) statement: *a reserva extrativista é a reforma agrária do povo amazônico*, "the extractive reserve is the land reform of the Amazonian people." The Brazilian speaker in our data explicitly indicates that the statement is a quote, names Mendes as the original author, and characterizes him as a "great Amazonian leader." Thus, she anticipates that the name is not familiar for the audience.

The interpreters start their utterances with a time lag of 4 and 5 seconds. Thus, they are still finishing their previous section of talk when the speaker begins the new quote. However, while "Hans" pauses only for a second and a half before he starts his rendition, "Franz" starts to render the section of talk after a pause of 4 seconds. Although both interpreters remain close behind the speaker, they both avoid the use of the name *Chico Mendes*. Although "Hans" omits the name and uses only the generic "one of the great leaders," "Franz" goes one step further and simply uses the German indefinite pronoun *jemand* "someone." Hence, both interpreters substitute the speaker's reference to the person *Chico Mendes*, who is an authority on rainforest issues. The speaker's argument in favor of extractive reserves and the fact that they could significantly change the economics of the area is backed by her reference to this authority. By omitting this indication of authorship, both interpreters change the weight of the argument (Johnen and Meyer, 2007). Particularly in the rendition by "Franz" ("Someone once said…"), the argument is no longer embedded in the political discourse of the Brazilian social movement. Furthermore, both interpreters add mitigators to the quoted statement, although the source version contained no such mitigators. Although "Hans" uses *eigentlich* (loosely translated by "actually" in the English gloss), "Franz" combines different mitigators (*eigentlich schon*, *fast schon*, and *eine Art* "a sort of"). Thus, the interpreters transformed a strong political claim, a rallying cry, into a relatively cautious statement.

Of course we cannot exactly know what triggered the substitution/omission of the name *Chico Mendes* and the addition of mitigators. However, the interpreter "Hans" indirectly justified them when answering our questionnaire two weeks after the events. He made the general remark that Brazilian speakers usually assume too much when talking to a non-Brazilian audience. The conclusion, therefore, would be that the name *Chico Mendes* and the statement about extractive reserves and the *reforma agrária* refer to realities that are not common for the German audience and thus might be difficult to process for interpreters. Considering that "Hans" frequently works with Brazilian NGO's, whereas "Franz" mainly works in the European Parliament and has European Portuguese as his B-language, we may assume that "Hans" changed the message deliberately, whereas the mitigated version of "Franz" simply occurred due to perceptual difficulties or lack of knowledge on his part.

In the following sections, we present quantitative data concerning the rendition of names and the addition of mitigators and discuss why certain linguistic expressions are frequently used to mitigate absolute statements.

### 3.1. Proper names and vague expressions

By using proper names, speakers may anchor or back-up information in specific ways, allude to common knowledge and shared experiences, or present themselves as standing in a certain relation to others. Although it is unlikely that one would object to these observations, conflicting views regarding proper names can be found in interpreting studies. Seleskovitch (1962) maintains that names require linguistic "transcoding" rather than interpreting. She proposes a triangular process model of interpreting as a heuristic mental activity and transcoding as a simple, mechanistic conversion of signs into other signs (Pöchhacker, 2004: 97). Unlike Seleskovitch, Gile stresses names as potential problems for interpreters, especially when the interpreter is not familiar with a particular name or its pronunciation in the target language (Gile, 1995: 173f). However, Gile focuses more on the form than on the function of names, whereas Vianna (2005: 181f) maintains that, "if speaker and interpreter share contextual assumptions not accessible to the audience" (as it may occur in the case of proper names), interpreters are forced to provide information that is not explicitly encoded in the source-language discourse.

In our data, we were able to identify four types of proper names, namely persons (*Lula, Chico Mendes*), institutions (*IDEC, Congresso Nacional*), places (*Amazônia, Pará*), and products (*soja Roundup-Ready*). The frequencies ranged between 1% and 2% of the total number of words spoken by the speaker. We compared each token in its context with the target language version to identify different types of renditions. In the case of proper names, we identified five types of renditions:

- A name is rendered as a name, sometimes with minimal (phonetic) adaptations ("N – N")
- A name is omitted, with no rendition at all ("N – Ø")
- A name is rendered by a pronoun referring to previous occurrences in the local context of the target language discourse ("N – Pro")
- A name is rendered by a generic characterization, i.e. a class or common noun ("N – Gen")
- A name is rendered as a name and additional characterizations are provided, which enhance the accessibility for the German audience ("N – N+")

In example (1) we provided an example of the substitution of a name by a generic lexical item (N – Gen) or by a pronoun (N – Pro). In the following we present an example of the rendition type "N – N+," that is, the expansion of a name. In example (2) "Congresso Nacional" the name of an institution (*congresso nacional*, "National Congress") is repeated and the interpreter provides additional information regarding this name. Although one may argue that the audience in this case probably did not need the information that the National Congress in example (2) refers to the *Brazilian* National Congress and not any other, the example counts as a case of a proper name being expanded and in which implicit or presupposed knowledge is thus explicitly verbalized.

(2) Example "Congresso Nacional"

| **Speaker** | **Interpreter "Hans" (consecutive)** |
|---|---|
| People in wheelchairs occupied the National Congress for several days (. . .) | People in wheelchairs beleaguered the National Congress of Brazil for several days (. . .) |

The identified rendition types accounted for all occurrences in our data. The number of borderline or unclear cases was small. Most occurrences clearly fit with one of the categories we established. Thus, all occurrences of proper names in our corpus were captured, so that we were able to compare different interpreters as well as their performance in different modes of interpreting with regard to this linguistic phenomenon.

The percentages of different rendition types in different modes of interpreting (Table 4.1) show that in most cases, the majority of names are rendered as names (47–74%). Zero renditions range between 4% and 12%, pronominal reproduction between 2% and 7%. Most pronominal renditions are demonstratives or deictic expressions; indefinites are used only in a few cases. Generic reproductions (N – Gen) and expansions of names (N – N+) are together the second most common type of name reproduction.

**Table 4.1.** Frequencies of different rendition types in our data

| | **N** | **Ø** | **Pro** | **Gen** | **N+** |
|---|---|---|---|---|---|
| Heidelberg 09 ($n = 81$) | 38 | 10 | 6 | 10 | 17 |
| | (47%) | (12%) | (7%) | (12%) | (21%) |
| Heidelberg 10 ($n = 81$) | 60 | 3 | 6 | 4 | 8 |
| | (74%) | (4%) | (7%) | (5%) | (10%) |
| Hamburg ($n = 63$) | 33 | 5 | 3 | 5 | 17 |
| | (52%) | (8%) | (5%) | (8%) | (27%) |
| Berlin ($n = 57$) | 34 | 4 | 1 | 5 | 13 |
| | (60%) | (7%) | (2%) | (9%) | (23%) |

Although these findings confirm the observation that names may indeed be sources of trouble for the listener and/or the interpreter, the percentage values did not show clear differences between consecutive and simultaneous interpreting. Our initial assumption was that consecutive and simultaneous interpreting would constrain interpreter performance in different ways and that this would have an impact on how names are rendered and how much time and effort is spent, for example, on expanded renditions of names (the N+-type). We thought that consecutive interpreting, compared to simultaneous interpreting, would allow for more variation on the part of the interpreter, thus triggering an increase in renditions other than N-to-N. This was not the case, however, as the interpreters varied individually. The most obvious example of this phenomenon is the comparison of the two teams of simultaneous interpreters in Heidelberg who simultaneously worked with the same speech. Here, the input is virtually the same but the output differs to a large extent. Although only 47% of names in booth 09 were rendered as names, the neighboring booth 10 decided to render 74% of the names as they were. Accordingly, the number of N+-renditions (combination of names and additional information) is low in booth 10 (10%), whereas more than twice as many names in booth 09 were combined with additional information (21%).

The consecutive performances (Hamburg and Berlin), however, were comparable to one another. In these events, N-to-N-renditions range between 52% and 60%, the percentages of zero-renditions and generic renditions are low, and the N+-renditions range between 23% (Berlin) and 27% (Hamburg). Thus, it becomes clear that there are three settings in which interpreters acted quite similarly (Hamburg, Berlin, Heidelberg 09), with one setting (Heidelberg 10) posing an exception. Therefore, the contrast found in the data seems to be more a difference between individuals and not between modes of interpreting.

The picture becomes even more interesting when we look at the triggers of N – Gen and N – N+ renditions. Table 4.2 shows how often each interpreter or interpreter team reproduced different name types as N+ or as generic renditions. As shown in Table 4.2, the percentages of generic or expanded renditions are high for persons and places and slightly lower for institutions, with the exception of the Berlin lecture. Mostly names of institutions containing regional terms such as *Centro Universitário do Pará* "University Centre of Pará" or acronyms such as *CTNbio*

**Table 4.2.** Generic characterizations or expanded renditions per name type

| | Places (%) | Persons (%) | Institutions (%) | Products (%) |
|---|---|---|---|---|
| Heidelberg, booth 09 | 41 | 50 | 20 | 16 |
| Heidelberg, booth 10 | 19 | 14 | 13 | 16 |
| Hamburg | 38 | 44 | 25 | 40 |
| Berlin | 33 | 33 | 31 | 25 |

"National Commission for Bio-Security" were replaced or received further elaboration, so that they could be made more accessible for the German audience. This shows that interpreters considered the lecture to be difficult (for themselves and/or for the audience) mainly with regard to Brazil's political personnel and geographic landscape. In the case of institutional names, however, only minor changes are necessary to increase accessibility, as are in most cases these names already composed of class nouns. They are proper names built based on class nouns, sometimes in combination with place names. Thus, their level of accessibility is already high.

The quantitative results show that the substitution or expansion of names is applied more frequently to specific name types (such as place or person names) and that some interpreters use this strategy more often than others. As a consequence, one should be careful with straightforward explanations for this phenomenon. Although N+ and generic renditions usually make names more accessible for the audience, this might not be the reason why the interpreters use this strategy. Nevertheless, these rendition types have an impact on the quality of interpreting, as they camouflage the fact that the original speaker used a linguistic item that was not accessible, or less so than in the original context. Thus, it appears as if the speaker has anticipated a knowledge deficit of the audience with regard to these names, while in fact she did not – at least not in all cases.

### 3.2. Mitigating statements: *Eigentlich*, *im Grunde genommen*, *praktisch*

In interpreting studies, mitigating is mainly dealt with in the context of politeness and face (Pöchhacker, 2004: 144). However, Mason and Stewart (2001), who analyze data from police interrogations and court interpreting (the O. J. Simpson trial), also observed that a literal style of interpreting "tends to dissuade interpreters from adding, for example, hedges or particles to convey pragmatic implicature" (*ibid.*: 58). This may result in a rendition that is, in some illocutionary sense, weaker than the original. The authors suggest, for example, that "the marked use of the present tense in Spanish [in the sense of a *presente de anticipación*, M. & P.] may find its equivalent in hedging in English" (*ibid.*: 68). A statement such as *Mañana me voy* [lit.: 'Tomorrow I (will) leave'] might then be best translated as "Tomorrow I will surely/certainly/definitely leave."

Hence, the addition or omission of hedges is seen as a means of rendering communicative dimensions that are either implicitly dealt with in the source discourse or that cannot be reproduced directly in the target language. Such analyses, however, are related to settings in which the addition of hedges enhances the accuracy of the rendition. By adding hedges, certain aspects of discourse are encoded explicitly and will thus be expressed in the target version. In our data, however, we observed the opposite: by mitigating, the interpreter brings in a dimension that was not dealt with in the source version – neither implicitly nor explicitly. Although the original speaker makes a clear and direct statement, the interpreters avoid such clarity.

The following two examples ("Chico Mendes-Berlin" and "Chico Mendes-Hamburg") illustrate that the phenomenon observed in example (1) is not an exception. All the interpreters mitigate and modify this stretch of talk regardless of the mode of interpreting and the fact that the speaker's statement is very similar in all lectures. Although the interpreter repeats the name (*Chico Mendes*) in example (3) (Berlin), the interpreter in example (4) (Hamburg) uses an indefinite pronoun (*man*). Both consecutive interpreters substitute (as in Berlin) or explain (as in Hamburg) the term *reserva extrativista*.

(3) Example "Chico Mendes-Berlin"

| **Speaker** | **Interpreter "Petra" (consecutive)** |
|---|---|
| *Chico Mendes, antes de morrer, dizia que as reservas extrativistas são a reforma agrária do povo da floresta.* | *((1s)) Chico Mendes hat mal gesagt, dass diese traditionelle Bewirtschaftung im Grunde genommen die Agrarreform für das Amazonasgebiet darstellt.* |
| Chico Mendes, before he died, said that the extractive reserves are the land reform for the people of the forest. | Chico Mendes once said that, basically speaking, this traditional cultivation represents the land reform for the Amazon region. |

(4) Example "Chico Mendes-Hamburg"

| **Speaker** | **Interpreter "Hans"(consecutive)** |
|---|---|
| *((1s)) Chico Mendes dizia, alguns meses antes de morrer, • • que a reserva extrativista é a reforma agrária do povo da Amazônia.* | *((4,5s)) Man sagt bei uns in der Gegend, dass Sammelreservate — also solche Gebiete extensiver Waldnutzung, ((1s)) in deren/ in denen Produkte des Waldes gesammelt werden, also nicht abgebaut, sondern gesammelt werden — eigentlich die Agrarreform • • der Menschen in Amazonien ist.* |
| Chico Mendes said, some months before he died, that the extractive reserve is the land reform of the people of Amazônia. | In our area, there is a saying that extractive reserves – that is to say, areas of intensive use in which products of the forest can be collected, and not cultivated, but collected – is [sic] actually the land reform of the people in Amazônia. |

Furthermore, both interpreters mitigate the speaker's statement with *im Grunde genommen* ("basically speaking") or *eigentlich* ("actually"). Thus, examples (3) and (4) provide further evidence for the addition of mitigators in contexts where they are not required for stylistic or grammatical reasons. Moreover, the mitigated versions contradict the intentions of the speaker, who is obviously making a political claim she strongly believes in. As the context of additional mitigating is similar in all three cases, we are able to identify the features these sections have in common:

- Reference to a person the audience is unfamiliar with (*Chico Mendes*)
- Use of specialized language (*reserva extrativista, reforma agrária*)
- The underlying claim that environmental policies and social reforms go hand in hand – an idea that was common among German environmentalists in the early eighties, but might not be taken for granted today

Thus, the substitution or omission of proper names, the explanation of specialized terms and the addition of mitigators occur within a context of propositional elements and ideological patterns that the audience is not familiar with. Examining the data, we searched for contexts where interpreters add mitigators without being forced to do so for grammatical or stylistic reasons. We found 42 cases in which interpreters mitigated statements that were originally absolute and not restricted. In Table 4.3, we present a survey of the expressions used by different interpreters.

**Table 4.3.** Survey of additional mitigating in our data

| Interpreter | Location | Mode | Additional mitigating |
|---|---|---|---|
| "Petra" | Berlin | Consecutive | 1 × *eigentlich* "actually," 5 × *im Grunde genommen* "basically speaking," 1 × *im Grunde* "basically," 1 × *mal* "sometimes" |
| "Hans" | Hamburg | Consecutive | 6 × *eigentlich* "actually," 1 × *vielleicht* "maybe," 2 × *manchmal* "sometimes," 2 × *oft* "often," 1 × *fast* "almost" |
| | Heidelberg | Simultaneous | 3 × *eigentlich* "actually," 1 × *etwas* "a bit," 1 × *wirklich* "really" |
| "Maria" | Heidelberg | Simultaneous | 6 × *praktisch* "practically" |
| "Sabine" | Heidelberg | Simultaneous | – |
| "Franz" | Heidelberg | Simultaneous | 7 × *eigentlich* "actually," 1 × *ein bisschen* "a bit," 1 × *etwas* "a bit," 2 × *schon fast* "almost" |

As Table 4.3 shows, the interpreters in our data did not add mitigators to the same extent but rather differed individually. Although "Maria" (booth 9 in Heidelberg) uses *praktisch* "practically" six times, her colleague "Sabine" from the neighboring booth did not add any mitigators, even though she worked parallel to "Maria." Furthermore, the types of expressions used for mitigating are found in different frequencies. Although both *praktisch* and *im Grunde genommen* are used six times, *eigentlich* is used seventeen times. Table 4.4 gives an overview of the expressions and their possible classifications. The expressions found are all predicative, that is, adverbials or particles. Although the most frequent mitigators (*eigentlich*, *im Grunde genommen*, *praktisch*) constrain the validity of a statement and thereby mitigate the assertion, the second group (*manchmal*, *fast*, *oft*, *etwas*, *ein bisschen*) expresses a matter of degree, with the isolated *vielleicht* expressing guessing or probability.

**Table 4.4.** Types, tokens, and functions of additional mitigators

| Type | Number | Function |
|---|---|---|
| *Eigentlich* "actually" | 17 | Predicative, restrictive |
| *Im Grunde [genommen]* "basically speaking" | 6 | Predicative, restrictive |
| *Praktisch* "practically" | 6 | Predicative, restrictive |
| *Wirklich* "really" | 1 | Predicative, restrictive |
| *[manch]mal* "sometimes" | 3 | Predicative, matter of degree |
| *[schon] fast* "almost" | 3 | Predicative, matter of degree |
| *Oft* "often" | 2 | Predicative, matter of degree |
| *Etwas* "a bit" | 2 | Predicative, matter of degree |
| *ein bisschen* "a bit" | 1 | Predicative, matter of degree |
| *Vielleicht* "maybe" | 1 | Predicative, expression of probability or guessing |
| **Total** | 42 | |

To understand the reasons for the use of these expressions, we need to analyze how and the contexts in which they are used in more detail. In each case, we focus the analysis on the most frequently used item, that is, *eigentlich* in assertive utterances.

As with many particles, the meaning of *eigentlich* is not easy to grasp. Albrecht (1977: 26) claims that it restricts the validity (*Gültigkeit*) of a sentence and thus weakens the assertion.

The particle exhibits a strong affinity to adversative (*eigentlich*..., *aber*... "actually..., but...") and conditional sentences (*wenn*..., *eigentlich*... "if/while/when..., actually..."). Especially the use with adversative "but" triggers a contrastive reading distinguishing between a basic, primary proposition and a secondary proposition that restricts the first one: *Eigentlich trinke ich keinen Wein, aber heute mache ich eine Ausnahme*, "Usually I do not drink wine, but today I make an exception." The primary proposition therefore concerns the normal state or initial thought, whereas the secondary proposition brings in a new, unusual, or initially not foreseen aspect. *Eigentlich*, then, characterizes the first proposition as being valid only under certain circumstances: it is valid "with reservations." Thus, although the lexical classification of *eigentlich* as a particle or a modal adverb is controversial (Kohrt, 1987), its seems clear that *eigentlich* in assertive utterances always signals a contrast between different layers of knowledge: an overt, "foregrounded" or common sense proposition is presented as standing in contrast to another, as of yet unknown, uncommon or covert proposition (Harden, 1983; May 2000). The function of contrasting these two thoughts or alluding to implicit, secondary layers of knowledge is also a common feature of *eigentlich*, *praktisch*, and *im Grunde genommen*. In many (but not all) cases, theses expressions can be used interchangeably without causing any major difference in their interpretation [example (5)].

(5) Example "No time"

*Ich habe praktisch/ eigentlich/ im Grunde genommen keine Zeit, aber...*
"I have practically/ actually/ basically speaking no time, but ..."

Thus, the addition of these expressions allows interpreters to allude to another proposition that does not need to be mentioned explicitly. The interpreter weakens the absolute statement of the speaker by suggesting that the strong claim is of conditional validity and needs to be seen in relation to some other proposition. This proposition, however, which the speaker has not dealt with at this point in time, may remain covert in the rendition or it may be presented in the following local context. In this way, the mitigator invites the listener to make inferences about the background of the allusion. As a result, the direct, partly aggressive, or provocative style of presentation, which is probably a typical feature of political speeches in general, is locally transformed into a more deliberative and balanced talk, even when the propositional content itself is easy to understand and not controversial. This can be illustrated by example (6) "consumer protection." In this example, the Brazilian speaker states quite frankly that, in the context of the cultivation of transgenic soy, norms of consumer protection were not observed. The excerpt is from the Heidelberg lecture.

(6) Example "Consumer protection"

| Speaker | Interpreter "Hans" (simultaneous) |
|---|---|
| *((1s)) Ahn • nenhuma norma de proteç ão ao consumidor foi respeitada.* | *Also es gibt eigentlich keinerlei Verbraucherschutzrichtlinie, die wirklich beachtet • • • worden wäre.* |
| Um none of the norms for consumer protection were observed. | So there is actually no consumer protection directive that would have been really observed. |

The Brazilian statement is quite clear. Particularly, it does not leave room for interpretation or exceptions: all norms of consumer protection were violated (in the case she is talking about). This statement is tough and presents Brazil as a country where the government disrespects laws and the health of consumers plays no role in the decisions of its officials – a typical banana republic. As the German audience is probably not surprised by this message, we have to ask why the interpreter adds *eigentlich* and *wirklich*. Our – admittedly interpretative – answer is that this addition is not linked to some anticipated knowledge deficit of the audience or conflicting views on Brazilian internal policy. Rather, the interpreter simply enhances the acceptability of an absolute statement by opening space for interpretations by restricting the validity: according to the rendition, there might have been some consumer protection directive that was observed, but that was not *wirklich* "really" observed. These mitigators facilitate approval and thus make the statement more palatable and smooth. In this way, mitigating may be related to the handling of knowledge differences (as in the *Chico Mendes* examples), or it may simply be an attempt to prevent audience misunderstanding or doubt.

## 4. Conclusion

In a critique of the lopsided concept of hedging as a means of protecting the speaker against possible criticism (especially with regard to academic discourse), Graefen (2000) argues that discourse in academia is often based on insecure knowledge bases that require hedging not for reasons of face, but rather because the speaker cannot be always fully accountable for the knowledge she or he is talking about. Thus, the metaphors used in the context of hedging and mitigation (*shields*, *hedges*, *bushes*, etc.) are partly misleading. Protection is not the only reason why speakers mitigate statements or use vague language. Factors other than face such as the availability of knowledge or processing costs (Jucker *et al.*, 2003) may be equally important.

In this chapter, we looked at modifications interpreters carried out when rendering original discourse into another language. We focused our analysis on the rendition of proper names and the rendition of absolute or bare statements, that is, elements of discourse that are originally neither vague nor mitigated. Initially, we expected to observe some relationship between the mode of interpreting (simultaneous or consecutive) and the types and frequencies of such modifications. However, the empirical facts convinced us that such modifications do not depend on time constraints but rather seem to vary individually. Although most of our interpreters mitigated bare statements, there was one subject who never did so. The same thing happened when we looked at the rendition of proper names: although some interpreters worked quite freely with these expressions, others rarely substituted or expanded a proper name (see also Meyer 2008).

Nevertheless, our study revealed a general tendency among the subjects to enhance the intelligibility of discourse by mitigating or being vague. The substitution or expansion of proper names, as well as the use of mitigators in contexts where they are neither required nor triggered by the source discourse does not seem to be merely coincidental. By analyzing the occurrences in detail, it became clear that the rendition of non-vague and non-mitigated parts of discourse is related to certain types of names and statements. It is especially in the contexts with unfamiliar names, technical terms, or new and uncommon thoughts that interpreters modify the original version. However, some acts of mitigation seem to be triggered by the mere fact that the speaker made a statement that was direct and absolute. Such directness, one may presume, is difficult to render if the interpreter does not share the subjective and epistemological basis from which the original statement was borne. In this sense, the botanic and martial metaphors used in mitigation research may indeed be adequate. It is the interpreter who protects his or her product against possible lack of understanding – even though this may lead to a non-faithful or inaccurate rendition.

## References


Ahrens, B. (2004). *Prosodie beim Simultandolmetschen*. Frankfurt/Main: Peter Lang.

Albrecht, J. (1977). "Wie übersetzt man eigentlich "eigentlich"? in H. Weydt (ed.), *Aspekte der Modalpartikeln*. Tübingen: Niemeyer, 19–37.

Caffi, C. (2007). *Mitigation*. Amsterdam: Elsevier.

Gile, D. (1995). *Basic concepts and models for interpreter and translator training*. Amsterdam: Benjamins.

Glémet, R. (1958). "Conference interpreting", in A. D. Booth and A. H. Smith (eds.), *Aspects of translation*. London: Secker & Warburg, 105–122.

Graefen, G. (2000). "*Hedging als neue Kategorie? Ein Beitrag zur Diskussion*". Available at http://www.kuwi.euv-frankfurt-o.de/de/lehrstuhl/sw/sw2/forschung/hedging/hedging_als_neue_kategorie/index.html. Retrieved on December 9, 2008.

Harden, T. (1983). *An analysis of the semantic field of the German particles überhaupt and eigentlich*. Tübingen: Narr.

House, J. (1981). *Translation quality assessment*. Tübingen: Narr.

House, J. (2006). "Text and context in translation". *Journal of Pragmatics* **38**: 338–358.

House, J. and J. Rehbein (eds.) (2004). *Multilingual communication*. Amsterdam: Benjamins.

Johnen, T. and B. Meyer (2007). "Between connectivity and modality: Reported speech in interpreter-mediated doctor-patient communication", in J. Rehbein, C. Hohenstein and L. Pietsch (eds.), *Connectivity in grammar and discourse*. Amsterdam: Benjamins, 395–417.

Jucker, A., S. W. Smith and T. Lüdge (2003). "Vagueness in interaction". *Journal of Pragmatics* **35**: 1737–1769.

Kohn, K. and S. Kalina (1996). "The strategic dimension of interpreting". *Meta* **41** (**1**): 118–138.

Kohrt, M. (1987). "Eigentlich, das "Eigentliche" und das "NichtEigentliche". Zum Gebrauch einer so genannten Abtönungspartikel". *Münstersches Logbuch zur Linguistik* **10**: 1–44.

Maier, C. (2007). "The translator as an intervenient being", in J. Munday (ed.), *Translation as intervention*. London: Continuum, 1–17.

Mason, I. (2006). "On mutual accessibility of contextual assumptions in dialogue interpreting". *Journal of Pragmatics* **38**: 359–373.

Mason, I. and M. Stewart (2001). "Interactional pragmatics, face, and the dialogue interpreter", in I. Mason (ed.), *Triadic exchanges. Studies in dialogue interpreting*. Manchester: St. Jerome, 51–70.

May, C. (2000). *Die deutschen Modalpartikeln*. Frankfurt/Main: Lang.

Meyer, B. (2008). "Interpreting proper names: Different interventions in consecutive and simultaneous interpreting?", in J. House (ed.), *Beyond intervention: Universals in translation processes*. *Transkom* 1/1 (special issue), 105–122 (www.trans-kom.eu).

Moeketsi, R. M. H. (2007). "Intervention in court interpreting: South Africa", in J. Munday (ed.), *Translation as intervention*. London: Continuum, 97–117.

Munday, J. (ed.) (2007). *Translation as intervention*. London: Continuum.

Müller, F. E. (1989). "Translation in bilingual conversation: Pragmatic aspects of translatory interaction". *Journal of Pragmatics* **13**: 713–739.

Nafá Waasaf, M. L. (2003). "La variacíon acústica de los correlates entonacionales en interpretación simultánea ingles-español". *Miscelánea: A Journal of English and American Studies* **27**: 55–186.

Pöchhacker, F. (2004). *Introducing interpreting studies*. London: Routledge.

Rehbein, J. (2006). "The cultural apparatus. Thoughts on the relationship between language, culture, and society", in K. Bührig and J. D. ten Thije (eds.), *Beyond misunderstanding. Linguistic analyses of intercultural communication*. Amsterdam: Benjamins, 43–96.

Seleskovitch, D. (1962). "L'interprétation de conférence". *Babel* **8** (**1**): 13–18.

Setton, R. (2006). "Context in simultaneous interpretation". *Journal of Pragmatics* **38**: 374–389.

Vianna, B. (2005). "Simultaneous interpreting: A relevance-theoretic approach". *Intercultural Pragmatics* **2** (**2**): 169–190.

Wadensjö, C. (1998). *Interpreting as interaction*. London, New York: Longman.

New Approaches to Hedging
Edited by Gunther Kaltenböck, Wiltrud Mihatsch and Stefan Schneider


# 5

# The Diachrony of Rounders and Adaptors: Approximation and Unidirectional Change

*Wiltrud Mihatsch*

## Abstract

Approximation markers blur the category boundaries of lexical items and thus affect the propositional content of an utterance. According to Prince *et al.* (1982), within the category of approximators two basic types have to be distinguished: adaptors such as *kind of* and *sort of*, which affect lexical meaning, and rounders such as *around* and *about*, which flag numerical imprecision. Based on data from French, Italian, Portuguese and Spanish as well as German and English, this chapter will analyse the communicative and cognitive foundations of this distinction, and try to explain why adaptors can become rounders, as in the case of *like*, but not vice versa. The ultimate aim of this chapter is to establish a cross-linguistic semantic map of approximation.

## 1. Introduction: Adaptors and Rounders

The profusion of terms in the domain of hedging is to a large part due to the multifunctionality (or polysemy) of hedging expressions and the difficulty to distinguish between similar functions, which are often diachronically related. It is therefore crucial to part from a sound classification of the different subtypes of hedging. I will here adopt the taxonomy established by Prince *et al.* (1982), who distinguished between approximators and shields.[1]

[1] See Caffi (2007) for a similar classification that distinguishes between bushes (approximators in Prince et al.'s terminology) and hedges (as well as shields), which roughly correspond to Prince et al.'s shields.

The difference between approximators and shields is based on the semantic impact of the former and the lack of such an impact of the latter, thus reflecting a fundamental difference as to the linguistic level they operate on. Approximators thus modify the semantics of a proposition as in (1), whereas shields operate on pragmatic aspects such as the illocutionary force of an utterance or speaker attitudes as in (2), but not the propositional content of an utterance (also see Briz Gómez, 1995 for the distinction between semantic and pragmatic mitigation):

(1) His feet were *sort of* blue
(2) *I think* his feet were blue (Prince *et al.*, 1982: 85)

Although this distinction is fundamental, many markers show ambiguous uses, and quite often approximator functions can arise as implicatures of shields and vice versa, as Kaltenböck (this volume) shows.

Within the category of approximators Prince *et al.* (1982) distinguish between adaptors and rounders. The difference between adaptors and rounders is based on the expressions modified – lexical conceptual meaning in the case of adaptors such *kind of* and *sort of* as in *I suppose a parish priest is a kind of social worker* (Cruse, 1986: 138) and numerical values in the case of rounders like *about* or *around* as in *about fifty.*[2]

However, it is not clear whether it is justified to postulate two different categories. From a semantic point of view it might be descriptively sounder to just subsume both uses under one category, since the semantic effect can be generally described as widening the extension of a modified item. If lexical meaning is affected by approximation, the category boundaries are loosened by eliminating parts of the intension and widening the extension. If numerical values (and chronological scales) are concerned, the same effect arises, just on a numerical scale. Furthermore, many markers can be used both as rounders and as adaptors, such as Spanish *como*, English *like* or French *genre*.

However, the distinction may indeed have a cognitive and/or functional basis, since many markers are restricted to just one function. This is the case of all preposition-based rounders such

[2] Both quantificational approximation (such as *almost fifty*) and the approximation of adjectives and telic concepts (such as *rather intelligent, near completion*) can be scalar, depending on the marker and on the modified constituent. This important aspect of approximation will not be considered here. Instead, I will concentrate on non-scalar approximation such as *about fifty* or *a kind of cactus*. Quirk *et al.* (1985: 597–602) distinguish four types of downtoners, i.e. scalar and non-scalar approximators in Prince *et al.*'s terminology. According to Quirk *et al.*, compromisers such as *quite, more or less, sort of* and *rather* question the appropriateness of an expression and are weaker downtoners than "diminishers" such as *slightly.* Furthermore, the directionality may vary, "approximators" (in Quirk *et al.*'s terminology scalar markers such as *almost* and *nearly*), which also question the use of an expression, move towards a point, whereas so-called minimizers such as *barely* or *hardly* indicate a deviation from a value (also see Ducrot's important publications (e.g. 1972) on French *presque* and *à peine*).

as French *vers* or English *about*, and also the adaptors Spanish *especie de* and French *espèce de*. And, as the diachronic analysis will show, for most markers the two functions develop separately and can only converge as a consequence of further functional changes.

The aim of this chapter will be to investigate both the foundations of this distinction and the possible zones of transition. In addition to a synchronic analysis[3] diachronic data will allow important insights into the dynamics of change disclosing striking asymmetries between the two categories.

A first step towards this distinction will be the study of the subtle differences between the synchronic cognitive and communicative functions of rounders and adaptors.

## 2. Rounders vs. Adaptors

### 2.1. Cognitive mechanisms

From a cognitive perspective, quantificational approximation is much simpler than lexical approximation. Rounders operate on a unidimensional scale and open up a zone above and below a value on a scale in the case of non-scalar rounders. The scope of approximation largely depends on the size of the numeral and on the context (also see Lavric, this volume). A survey done by Devos *et al.* (1998: 171) shows that on the level of seconds approximation generates an interval of about 5 seconds, an interval of 5 minutes on the level of minutes and half an hour and hours for hours. Rounders affecting days allow a slack of seven days, months allow for two weeks, and years allow for a variation depending on the number. An expression like *around 4000 B.C.* allows for 50–500 years, and *around 1974* allows for two years. The intervals are symmetrical for non-scalar markers, if round numbers do not interfere as in *around 10h57*, where the interval is situated between the closest round numbers, thus between 10:55 and 11:00. Another important factor contributing to the interpretation of rounders is the extralinguistic situation. In everyday situations may be more flexible than in a laboratory setting or in other special domains.

Adaptors are less predictable and cognitively more complex, since they operate in a multidimensional space – metaphorically speaking. The marker itself just indicates that the modified lexeme has a wider extension than without the marker. Only contextual or extralinguistic knowledge determine which semantic features have to be eliminated or loosened and, perhaps more importantly, which features are maintained. Sometimes they just indicate a slight deviation

---

3 The most important data source of this analysis is C-ORAL-ROM, an oral corpus containing comparable subcorpora of French, Italian, Portuguese and Spanish. For better readability I have eliminated all the intonation marks, emphasis mine.

which cannot be further specified, perhaps even just a deviation from a prototype and not strictly speaking approximation:

(3) et euh autour euh il y a **comme** un petit liseré bleu en zigzag là tu vois ? [C-ORAL-ROM ffamcv05]
'and uh around uh there is **like** a small blue zigzag braid you see?'

(4) . . . . a uno de los que iban, le quitaron el dinero no sabes que llevaban aquí **como** una cartera en la cintura . . . ' [CREA, 1998, ORAL]
'and one of them who went, they stole him his money don't you know they wore here **like** a purse around the waist'

In many cases, modified concrete nouns maintain the specification of shape as in (5) and (6), in which a speaker describes a sculpture (and which show that adaptors can be stacked), or maintain the function, frequently related to shape, as in (7):

(5) quand on regarde de près on a **comme des espèces de** petits poils qui ressortent [C-ORAL-ROM fpubmn02]
'if you have a closer look you have **like sort of** little hairs popping out'

(6) puisqu'on voit **comme une sorte de** gros nid [C-ORAL-ROM fpubmn02]
'since you can see **like a sort of** big nest'

(7) le radiateur il était percé alors je sais pas il a pris des une boîte de de pellicule photos il a fait **un espèce de** bouchon enfin un truc et il a réussi à la démarrer.[C-ORAL-ROM ffammn14]
'the radiator was pierced so I don't know he took a film box he made **a kind of** cork well a thingy and he managed to get it started'

However, quite often the semantic relations are utterly unpredictable, especially with abstract nouns, adjectives and verbs.

Unlike rounders, which do not exclude the value modified by the marker, but rather refer to a zone including the marked value (but see Sadock, 1977 and the discussion in Wierzbicka, 1991: 356), adaptors are only used to designate referents that are not usually referred to by the unmarked lexical item.

### 2.2. Discourse functions of rounders and adaptors

Closely related to the semantic effects of approximation markers are the motivations of speakers to use them (also see Crystal and Davy, 1975 in Channell, 1994: 8; Hyland, 1998).

Rounders are often used when speakers have to make informed guesses as to quantities, especially if more specific information would be expected than a speaker is able to give. In other cases a speaker may well be informed about rather exact values, which, however, would be too pedantic in certain situations. In these cases the maxim of quantity demands an approximate quantification (Channell, 1994: 173, 178–192), which can thus be flagged. Yet another reason may be the reduction of the speaker's responsibility, for instance in scientific or political contexts, here rounders render assertions less prone to critique (also see Andersen, this volume).

Interestingly, many motives for adaptor uses resemble the uses of rounders, for instance the avoidance of overly specific assertions or exaggerated terminological exactness (cf. Hyland, 1998), as well as a lack of knowledge about the exact classification of a referent or concept.

However, the minimization of precision following the maxim of quantity in certain contexts, for instance in order to avoid overly specific, technical sounding designations by marking too specific lexical items by approximation markers, tends to be marginal for lexical items. When speakers select a lexical expression they may vary the level of generalization and use less technical or more generic terms or just use placeholders (see Mihatsch, 2006; Andersen, this volume). Retrieving unusually specific, pragmatically marked but semantically adequate expressions modified by an explicit approximation marker is quite costly and therefore avoided. One example given by Channell (1994) is *kind of pina* [sic] *colada* in a situation where the expression is appropriate, but the speaker does not want to show off (Channell, 1994: 190–192). Here the adaptor reduces the distance between speaker and hearer and thus operates on an intersubjective level (see Channell, 1994: 190–192; Vigara Tauste, 1996: 16, 28f.; Aijmer, 2002: 191–193).

Remarkably, a series of important uses are restricted to adaptors. In many situations, the correspondence between referents or concepts and lexemes is rather loose, for instance in the case of lexical gaps, and also with new, rare or highly abstract referents or concepts demanding ad hoc classification. Furthermore, unlike the highly frequent numerals and other quantificational expressions many lexemes are not very frequent and therefore likely to be affected by word-finding problems. Here speakers may be perfectly informed about a concept or referent, but momentarily or permanently lacking the correct term. Therefore, adaptors are used in situations with word-finding problems, where a flexibilized, semantically similar, but more current item is used to replace a more appropriate but (momentarily) unavailable expression. This use is very common, which explains why speakers often use adaptors even before they have access to a substitute:

(8) MAR: ouais voilà on a fait **une espèce de** c' est **un genre de**
SOP: de ?
MAR: comment ça s' appelle c'est un
[C-ORAL-ROM ffamdl04]

'MAR: yeah well we did **a kind of** it's **a sort of**
SOP: of?
MAR: how do you call it it's a'

Word-finding problems do not affect numerals and common quantifiers, which are highly frequent, early-acquired expressions.

Thus in the case of adaptors, the specific problems of speech production play an important role. These markers are particularly useful in spontaneous spoken language due to the specific time-sensitive conditions of oral speech production processes and their low degree of planning (see Koch and Oesterreicher, 1990), while rounders do not show this correlation with informal spoken language (see the corpus analyses in Mihatsch, 2010a).

## 3. Origins

Both the cognitive and communicative characteristics of adaptors and rounders determine the distinct paths which lead to their emergence out of other linguistic expressions. For instance, spatial prepositions indicating a rough position on a numerical scale may become rounders or comparative markers such as *like*, which may express some degree of similarity between a concept or referent and the semantics of a lexical expression, may become adaptors. This also explains why rounders and adaptors tend to be systematically realized by different expressions (exceptions will be discussed below in Section 3.3). In the following sections I will analyse some of the most strongly entrenched markers.

### 3.1. Rounders and spatial metaphors

Numerical approximation can be achieved by a variety of linguistic means such as suffixes like French *-aine,* restricted to 12 and multiples of 10. The same is true for Italian *-ina*, Portuguese *-ena*, Spanish *-ena*, which all go back to Latin *-ēnus* (DRAE, s.v. *ena*), used for distributive numerals, especially collective numerals designating intervals of time (Pharies, 2002).

Romance languages also have a specific suffix deriving approximations of thousand, such as French *-ier* (*millier*) and Portuguese *-ar* (*milhar*) and *-eiro* (*milheiro*) (Hundertmark-Santos Martins, 1998: 59), Italian *-aio* (*migliaio*, and also *centinaio*) (Dardano and Trifone, 1997: 226f.). These suffixes originally served to create relational adjectives (cf. DRAE, s.v. *-ar*).

Another specific way of indicating approximative numerical values is the use of round numbers (see Lavric, this volume), which emerge as a consequence of the greater formal simplicity of reference points in numeral systems such as the multiples of 5 and 10 in the decimal system (Krifka, 2007). The greater complexity of other numbers (compare *twenty* and *twenty-one*) usually implicates a more precise reading. Remarkably, all rounders tend to combine with round numbers (see Mihatsch, 2010a).

Straightforward rounders are the learned expressions French *approximativement*, *d'une façon approximative*, Spanish and Portuguese *aproximadamente*, Italian *approssimativo, -amente* from Latin *aproximare* 'bring close', originally a spatial metaphor.

Yet another spatial source is the use of distal spatial deictics metaphorically indicating a rough zone around a number on a scale (see Mihatsch, 2010b) frequent in Portuguese:

(9) **Lá/ali/aí** pelas 4 da tarde (Gärtner, 1998:149)
'approximately [lit: 'there'] at about 4 p.m.'

(10) Sua biblioteca tem **aí** uma centena de livros (ADLP, s.v. aí)
'His library contains about [lit. 'there'] a hundred books'

In all the Romance languages analysed here distal spatial deictics can be used as rounders in combination with an approximative spatial preposition such as French *par*:

(11) et c' est des des requins qui doivent faire un mètre vingt un mètre cinquante **par là** [C-ORAL-ROM ffammn01]
'and they are sharks that must be one meter one meter twenty long, more or less [lit.: 'around there']

However, the most important (i.e. frequent, productive and cross-linguistically relevant) group of rounders go back to spatial prepositions, for instance French *vers*, English *around* or *about*, Spanish *hacia*, even rounders in non-Indo-European languages follow this pattern (Hagège, 1982: 36–37, 44).

As discussed above, rounders are cognitively unidimensional since they create a boundaryless zone on a quantificational scale. Scales of course are a metaphorical way of dealing with numbers – certainly a primary metaphor, i.e. in Grady's sense a metaphor arising very early on in ontogenesis due to a strong association of experiences from different domains as in 'more is up' (Grady, 1997). The more individuals a heap contains, the higher it gets. Scales are related to our cognitive access to counting. Number sequences are a fundamental way of learning to count. Numbers beyond the domain of "subitizing", the direct recognition of quantities, i.e. numbers above 3 or 4, are learned by children as linguistic routines as part of a sequence of number words (Hurford, 1987: 114–146, 194; Wiese, 2003: 133). Number sequences can be easily imagined metaphorically as spatial scales, probably vertical scales as many metaphors show, for instance *up to a hundred*, *below zero*, *high and low numbers*, *rising prices*, etc., related to the primary metaphor 'more is up'.

A large and varied group of rounders in many languages are thus derived from spatial prepositions. Many of them are dynamic, i.e. imply movement. Sometimes fictive motion (Talmy, 2000) is involved, i.e. the visualization of static situations in terms of movement. In the domain of approximation goal-oriented prepositions containing the idea of fictive motion can create local approximation:

(12) Elle habite **vers** la Porte de Pantin. (Lang, 1991: 329)
'She lives **toward** Porte de Pantin'

(13) **Hacia** los montes, la compacta humareda de un incendio alza sus redondas nubes negras (Platero 61, in Morera Pérez, 1988: 224)
'**Toward** the mountains, the compact smoke of a fire raises its round black clouds'

This approximative use of fictive motion can be metaphorically transferred to the realm of quantification and thus reflect the cognitive process of estimating quantities:

(14) j' ai dû y aller **vers** le vingt-trois vingt-quatre [C-ORAL-COM ffamcv07]
'I must have gone there **toward** the twenty-third twenty-fourth'

Some uses even contain verbs of movement, a possible bridge from the spatial preposition to the rounder function, since here the whole utterance is metaphorical, the preposition by itself can still be interpreted as a spatial preposition:

(15) Elle **marchait sur** ses vingt ans (Henriot Aricie, in Brun III,2, in Grevisse and Goosse, 1993: 1526)
'She approached her twenties' (literally: 'She **walked toward** her twenty years')

Such an intermediate step seems plausible, since this would make the metaphorical leap smoother. However, diachronic corpus analysis does not bring up evidence in favour of this assumption – neither for this group of rounders, nor for the other rounders derived from spatial prepositions, since the earliest attestations of spatial prepositions used as rounders do not show a preference for expressions containing verbs of movement (Mihatsch, 2010a). Even the first occurrences as rounders are not bound to such complex metaphors.

Prepositions expressing a (fictive or real) movement towards a landmark are an important source for rounders in many languages, for instance French *vers*, Italian *verso*, Spanish *hacia*, English *towards*. This sense is also the source of the German rounder *gegen*, today rather expressing an opposition than an approaching movement, Spanish and Portuguese *para*, and French *sur*, Italian *su*, Portuguese *sobre* and Spanish *sobre*, whose prevailing sense today is 'on' ( López, 1972: 173; Bruyne, 1993: 693; Fagard, 2006: 242). However, diachronic corpus analysis shows that the older sense 'towards' in hostile movements must be the source of the rounders (Mihatsch, 2010a).

Now linear approaching movement suggests a unidirectional and therefore scalar approximation,[4] but surprisingly, these markers now tend to be non-scalar, as becomes clear in examples where they modify already approximative expressions:

(16) plutôt le matin **vers** neuf heures neuf heures et demie pour euh même un peu plus tôt [C-ORAL-COM ffammn07]
'rather in the morning **toward** nine o'clock, half past nine for um even a bit earlier'

---

[4] Scalar rounders based on these prepositions have an upper boundary, since the progression from lower to higher numerals is determined by the ontogenetic directionality of number sequences.

According to Marcq (1980: 134) German *gegen* is scalar, according to Plank (2004: 171) it can also be used as a non-scalar rounder. Corpus data from C-ORAL-ROM (see footnote 3 for a short description) as well as dictionaries (see ZVI for Italian *verso*) and grammars also point to prevailing non-scalar senses of this group, for instance Italian *su* + article, *verso* (Dardano and Trifone, 1997: 138, 359, ZVI, GEUI), Spanish *hacia*, *sobre* (López, 1972: 194; Esbozo, 1973: 443; Bruyne, 1993: 693;Vera Morales, 2004: 464,), Portuguese *sobre* (ADLP), Latin *sub*, *ad* (Menge, 2005: 253, 275).

Scalar readings rather seem to arise from the interaction with certain linguistic expressions such as French *fin* 'end', implying an endpoint:

(17) **Vers la fin** de la première scène on connaît déjà les péripéties. (Bat-Zeev Shyldkrot, 2005: 215)
'**Toward the end** of the first scene you already know all the ups and downs'

Another group of rounders derives from prepositions expressing circular movement, such as French *autour de*, *environ*; Italian *intorno a*, *attorno a*, *all'incirca*, *circa*; Portuguese *à volta de*, *à roda de*, *ao redor*, *em torno de/a*, *em derredor de*; Spanish *alrededor de*, *en torno a*; and also English *around*, *round*, *about* and German *um (die)*. Like Italian *circa* many cognates in other European languages like German *zirka*, French *circa* or English *circa* are Latinisms (GDW, Grevisse and Goosse, 1993: 1477, OED) derived from Latin *circa* meaning 'around' and also 'approximately' (Menge, 2005: 255). This clearly points to the importance of rounders in formal registers. Due to their source these are all non-scalar and cannot be combined with telic elements as in **around the end of the play*.

Another, less productive group is derived from dynamic prepositions meaning 'through', such as French *par*, Italian *per*, Portuguese *por* and Spanish *por*. Here the hedging force goes back to a movement possibly crossing points or zones of a scale (also see Lang, 1991: 432f.). In C-ORAL-ROM the rounder function is very rare, we rather observe spatial approximation (Cannesson and Saint-Dizier, 2002) based on fictive motion for this group. Since the source expresses a passing movement possibly crossing all boundaries, both upper and lower limits, these rounders are all non-scalar (Luque Durán, 1976: 113) as in Portuguese *pelas cinco da tarde* 'at around five p.m.'

Other rounders are derived from static prepositions indicating spatial closeness, such as French *dans les parages de*, *dans la zone de*, *du côté de*, *aux alentours de*, *aux environs de*, *près de*, *à peu près*, *proche(s) (de)*; Italian *vicino a*, *nei pressi di*, *cerca de*; Portuguese *perto de*; Spanish *cerca de*, *en los alrededores de*. Those referring to an extended zone such as French *dans les parages de*, *dans la zone de*, *du côté de*, *aux alentours de*, *aux environs de* and the equivalents in the other Romance languages lead to non-scalar rounders, while those used to situate points in relation to a landmark rather lead to scalar rounders, for instance French *près de*, often interchangeable with and etymologically related to *presque* 'almost':

(18) on arrive déjà très rapidement à **près de vingt** minutes de passage d' un de d' exercice de syntaxe on **presque vingt oui** on arrive à presque vingt-cinq minutes même [C-ORAL-ROM ffammn03]

'you arrive already very easily at **close to** twenty minutes of working on a syntax exercise you almost twenty yes you arrive even at almost twenty-five minutes'

The same is true for Spanish *cerca de*, glossed 'almost' in MOL. According to ADLP and Gärtner (1998: 149) as well as C-ORAL-ROM Portuguese *cerca de* is not scalar, while *perto de* is, although according to ADLP it is not.

This group acquires the idea of scalarity on the basis of the inherent directionality of numerical scales in combination with the position of one point in relation to another, while prepositions referring to extended neighbouring zones in relation to a place lead to non-scalar rounders (Mihatsch, 2010c).

Similarly German *an die* also has a scalar reading (although WDW postulates a purely non-scalar meaning), just like English *by* (Quirk *et al.*, 1985: 692, OED).

In all languages studied here, prepositional constructions referring to intervals can also become rounders, for instance French *de x à y*. Intervals as such are not approximative, but are a good starting point since intervals comprise a series of numerical values and can thus be used to give a choice of alternative values:

(19) je pense que nous étions si mes souvenirs sont exacts euh **entre quinze et vingt personnes** [C-ORAL-ROM ffammn20]
'I think we were if I remember correctly uh **between fifteen and twenty** people.'

Here the process of approximation is more complex since speakers have to give two numerical values, which of course enlarges the approximated zone, but demands a greater cognitive and communicative effort.

Also related to intervals but only observed in French is the rounder *dans (les)* 'in the' (Melis, 2003: 244; Vaguer, 2003), probably derived from uses with time spans often containing an event and following a reference event as in *dans les cinq ou six premiers mois* 'within the five or six first months', linked to a preceding explicit or implicit moment in time, a use also observed in the other languages analysed here. There is a rather small step from a time span giving a range of possible dates for an event to approximation as in French *dans les*. Perhaps round numbers used for age indications span a bridge from intervals to approximation, since round numbers here are often used for time spans, too, cf. the English translation 'in his fifties':

(20) c'est un grand, gros homme, **dans les cinquante** ans, ... (Frantext, Sue, Eugène (1843): *Les Mystères de Paris*)
'He is a tall big man, **in his** fifties, ... '

French *dans les* has furthermore developed unambiguous rounder uses:

(21) ça doit vous coûter **dans les** cent balles [C-ORAL-ROM ffammn22]
'that should cost you about [literally 'in the'] a hundred quid.'

Syntactically, most rounders tend to lose their prepositional properties (this is also true for local (or spatial) postpositions, depending on the language type. Plank thus refers to the generic term 'adposition') as they get entrenched:

> When local adpositions, whatever their own sources, are metaphorically extended to the domain of numerical approximation (as in 'around five bottles'), as they not uncommonly are, and when such expressions are then admitted to grammatical relations otherwise reserved for noun phrases, such as subject and direct object, as is only natural, a conflict is bound to arise: the internal structure of such expressions is that of an adpositional phrase, headed by the ex-local adposition, but their external distribution is that of a noun phrase. Plank (2004: 166)

However, the syntactic changes are often partial in nature and many of these rounders are syntactically hybrid, since they can occupy both slots of prepositions as in (22) and modifiers as in (23):

(22) They returned to their quarters **about** three o'clock. (OED s.v. *about*, 1882 Daily News 22 Mar.)
(23) That cost **about** a hundred quid.

As the comparative analysis has shown rounders derived from spatial prepositions are particularly widespread and productive, although other rounder types also go back to spatial metaphors, certainly due to the importance of the notion of scalarity for counting.

### 3.2. Adaptors and the notion of similarity

Well-known adaptors are English *like*, *sort of*, *kind of* and equivalent adaptors in other languages such as French *comme*, *espèce de*, Spanish *como*, *especie de*, German *Art*, and the superficially similar expressions French *genre* and Spanish *tipo* as well as the cross-linguistically less common adaptors of deictic origin Portuguese *assim*, Dutch *zo* and German *so*. These markers all have in common a source based on the notion of global resemblance. This is most obvious in the case of the adaptors English *like* as well as French *comme,* Portuguese *como* and Spanish *como* (marginally German *wie*, see Mihatsch, 2010a) going back to markers of similative comparison that serve to compare two entities (Haspelmath and Buchholz, 1998: 278, 313), either globally or by comparing activities of different individuals:

(24) He is like his grandfather.
(25) A house like a palace.
(26) She behaves like a child.

Like the preposition-based rounders these adaptors derive from a preposition. However, the semantic mechanism is different since it is not based on a spatial metaphor, but on the idea of a global comparison, which usually implies only a partial resemblance and thus an approximation (Haspelmath and Buchholz, 1998: 278). These markers become adaptors as they lose their syntactic and semantic relationality and become modifiers of noun phrases:

(27) on voit **comme** une sorte de gros nid [C-ORAL-ROM, fpubmn02]
'you can see **like** a sort of big nest'

This mechanism is restricted to lexical approximation, where an intended referent or concept is designated via a semantically similar lexical item, with which it shares a number of semantic properties. Similarity is not an appropriate mechanism for numerical approximation, where the contiguity of values on a scale is crucial.

Less common but semantically very similar is the emergence of adaptors from qualitative deictics (see Mihatsch, 2010b), which give rise to adaptors in Portuguese (cf. Bittencourt, 2000: 264; Pereira Lima-Hernandes, 2005), German (Lovik, 1990) and Dutch (Corver and Zwarts, 2006). The deictics English *such*, *like that*, German *so*, French *comme ça*, *tel*, Italian *così*, *tale,* Portuguese *assim, tal* and Spanish *así, tal* establish a relation of similarity between a target and a unit provided by situational deixis or anaphorical relations to a preceding or following unit – or referring to common knowledge of speaker and hearer. Thus the deictic can intervene in situations where naming is difficult and where it is necessary to fall back on contextual information, perhaps accompanied by a gesture or pointing to an object:

(28) J'aimerais une robe **comme** ça.
'I'd like a dress like that'

Now Portuguese *assim*, German *so* and Dutch *zo* have developed an approximative meaning indicating a lack of information or imperfect categorization, often in contexts of word-finding problems (also see Brauer-Figueiredo, 1999: 122) – without the deictic component. The following example is ambiguous. In a bakery shop a customer asks for some kind of pastry. One reading is deictic, here we could imagine a pointing gesture:

(29) Geben Sie mir **so'n** Streuselapfel (Lovik, 1990: 123)
'Give me **such a** crumbly apple/a crumbly apple like that'

However, the recorded answer 'we haven't got that right now' shows that the purely approximative reading is relevant here, not the deictic interpretation.

Utterances with abstract nouns are clearly approximative, here the adaptor just shows that the linguistic description is incomplete and based on semantic similarity with the target:

(30) ah hhh mas havia **assim** uma aura que o envolvia
[C-ORAL-ROM pfamdl17]
'ah but there was like (literally 'such') an aura that surrounded him'

Although the step from a qualitative deictic to adaptor uses seems rather small, this path does not seem to be as widespread as the one leading from taxonomic nouns to adaptors (see Mihatsch 2007 for a comparative study). Superficially the taxonomic nouns underlying many adaptors such as English *sort of* and *kind of* (see Lakoff, 1972; Channell, 1994; Kay, 1997; Aijmer, 2002), French *espèce de*, *genre de*, *sorte de* (Rouget, 1997; Fleischman and Yaguello, 2004), and also Italian *specie di*, *tipo di,* Portuguese *espécie de*, *tipo de*, *gênero de*, Spanish *especie de*, *tipo de*, and some rather marginal adaptors are both semantically and syntactically very different from the similative marker or the qualitative deictic. These markers are all based on nouns expressing taxonomic class inclusion, which establish thus very clear-cut category boundaries (also see Fetzer, this volume), so the question is what the link between class inclusion and semantic approximation might be. All these nouns go back to Graeco-Latin learned influence, and all of them have come to mean '(sub)category' at some point. However, like similative markers taxonomic nouns are relational, since they are usually employed to classify a noun with respect to another, usually superordinate noun. In most uses they are the semantic and syntactic heads of *N1 of N2-constructions*:

x is a kind of y
= x is a subclass of y

Such constructions are common in definitions of scientific terms. However, in everyday use, where most lexical items are acquired rather ostensively and, in the case of concrete nouns at least, have a holistic perceptual basis, explicit categorization is rather marginal and restricted to very specific situations and concepts. Explicit definitions in everyday language are useful when new concepts have to be categorized, or when speakers have to explain marginal rare concepts. For instance, according to Wierzbicka, "an apple is an apple", but "I think of *paw-paws* as of, 'some kind of (tropical) fruit'" (Wierzbicka, 1985: 217). These uses are quite entrenched for taxonomic nouns in everyday language, and are even mentioned in good dictionaries, i.e. in OED (s.v. *sort*): "denoting that some thing, person, quality, etc., is, or may be, included in the specified class, although not typical of it or possessing all its characteristics." The last phrase shows how a taxonomic noun becomes an adaptor. Frequent uses of taxonomic nouns in everyday situations where classification criteria or properties of marginal items are not usually well known or well established may lead to a reinterpretation as markers signalling messy spontaneous classification easily reinterpreted as a vague comparison rather than subclassification, in particular with abstract nouns (see Mihatsch 2007):

(31) PER: dans dans sa vie et dans tous les les livres je trouve qu' il y a vachement tu sais **un espèce de retour cyclique**
[C-ORAL-ROM ffamcv09]
'PER: in in his life and in all the the books I find that there is loads of you know **a kind of circular movement**'

So sloppy categorization may lead to a reinterpretation of hyponymy or class inclusion as cohyponymy or resemblance, which is cognitively more primitive than hyponymy (for an overview see Mihatsch, 2006: ch. 2). Since marginal lexemes tend to be specific rather than generic, taxonomic nouns meaning 'species', 'subcategory' pointing to subcategorization are more frequent sources than taxonomic nouns situated on more generic levels such as French *genre* 'genus', which is traditionally the superordinate counterpart of 'species'.

In all the languages analysed, this source is very productive, we find strongly entrenched adaptors such as English *kind of* and *sort of*, French *un genre de*, *une espèce de*, *une sorte de*, Italian *una specie di*, *una sorta di*, Portuguese *uma espécie de*, *uma sorte de*, Spanish *una especie de*, German *eine Art*. Most adaptors of this type are most frequent in spontaneous, informal spoken language (see Mihatsch, 2010a) – unlike the rounders discussed above.

Now many nouns meaning 'genus' as well as semantically similar nouns meaning 'type' or 'style' also become adaptors in Romance languages, however, in syntactically different constructions, for instance French *genre*, and also Italian, Portuguese and Spanish *tipo* and a couple of others:

(32) fai **tipo** un ragno ma molto più geometrico capito ?
[C-ORAL-ROM ifamcv28]
'you make like [literally 'type'] a spider, but a lot more geometrical, you understand?

These markers go back to another source construction. Unlike the source of adaptors such as *kind of*, based on subcategorization, here the underlying construction situates two expressions within one and the same superordinate category:

(33) ce connaisseur émérite que redoutaient toutes les femmes **du genre de** Mme Schontz
(FRANTEXT, Balzac, Honoré de (1845): *Béatrix*)
'that eminent connoisseur whom all the women **of the kind of** Mrs Schontz feared'

Taxonomic nouns meaning 'species' are not used in these constructions:[5]

(34) *toutes les femmes de l'espèce de Mme Schontz
'all the women of the species of Mrs Schontz'

These expressions often appear in examples or explanations (Rosier, 2000: 212, 216; Pereira Lima-Hernandes, 2005: 70f.), where the first noun tends to be less specific than the following noun (cf. Danon-Boileau and Morel, 1997: 196f.; Vincent, 2005: 190). The classification of two NPs belonging to one implicit superordinate category can be easily reinterpreted as a direct comparison, thus resemblance, and therefore the taxonomic noun can usually be replaced by a similative marker

[5] English *kind* and *sort* are indeterminate as to the distinction between genus and species.

without affecting the meaning of the utterance. Syntactically this construction tends to get reduced in Romance languages (Danon-Boileau and Morel, 1997: 194f.), as can be seen in (35):

(35) c'est dans des entreprises euh à moitié euh enfin pas vraiment privées d**es entreprises publiques genre SNCF** euh [ELICOP Corpus Tours, file faf01gb6.txt]
'that's in companies uh half uh well not really private public companies like (literally 'kind') SNCF uh'

*Genre* is here a similative preposition like *comme* 'like', which, just as *like,* can become an adaptor when the syntactic relationality is lost and the preposition becomes a modifier as in (32). In C-ORAL-ROM we can observe the following adaptors based on this construction: French *genre, style,* Italian *stile, tipo,* Portuguese *género, tipo, estilo,* Spanish *tipo.* These adaptors are quite frequent items in the analysed Romance languages, but non-existent in English and German.

Other more marginal and more specialized means of lexical approximation are certain suffixes usually derived from denominal suffixes originally creating relational adjectives ( Rainer, 1999: 4612–4625; Lüdtke, 2005: 218–222), so there must be a special connection leading from relational adjectives to adaptors. Relational adjectives derived from nouns reduce the lexical meaning of the base nouns, since adjectives usually pick out single typical (not always necessary) properties. Coseriu calls this phenomenon "deconcentration" (Coseriu, 1968: 14). Thus *childish* means 'behaving like a typical child, but not necessarily possessing all properties' (as for the variety of uses of *–ish* see Albrespit, 2005). Many of these suffixes become adaptor suffixes, typically with colour adjectives as in *reddish*, *bluish*, German *rötlich*. Even these highly specialized adaptors are thus ultimately linked to the concept of resemblance. Similar suffixes can be observed in Romance languages, *-âtre* in French (Molinier, 2005; vgl. Noailly, 2005: 271), going back to Latin *-aster*, already expressing a relation of similarity as in *līliaster* from *līlium*, and also in *nigraster* 'blackish' (Pharies, 2002: 112f.). In the other Romance languages suffixes deriving colours are a lot more varied and usually derived from suffixes creating denominal adjectives, (some of them participles), as in Italian *azzurrino, grigiolino, rossiccio* (Mutz, 2000: 28), *biancastro bianchiccio, verdognolo* (Lüdtke, 2005: 353); Portuguese *enegrecido, avermelhado, azulado, verdoengo, esverdeado, amarelado, esbranquicado*; Spanish *blanquecino, azulenco azulado, amarillento, amarillejo, verdoso, verdusco, negruzco* (Lüdtke, 2005: 354).

### 3.3. All-purpose approximators

Despite the cognitive and communicative differences between rounders and adaptors, they also share certain properties. Both announce a discrepancy between the conventional meaning of a linguistic expression and its meaning in a concrete utterance and widen the extension of the modified expression, be it a lexical unit or a quantified expression. In both cases the choice of the expression is less than perfect.

This is the basis of a number of approximators not restricted to either of the two types. One basic mechanism of such markers is the strategy of opening up a paradigm and thereby showing that other neighbouring expressions would be equally possible, neighbouring points on a numerical or chronological scale as well as semantically related lexical items. In such a situation speakers often give more than one possible solution, thus open up the paradigmatic axis within the syntagmatic axis when they are not sure which expression to use (cf. Blanche-Benveniste, 1997: 17):

(36) y entonces/vamos mi marido y yo a una **casita** que tenemos en el campo/bueno/**a una casita/a una casaza/a una especie de balneario** (M-A-58, Cortés Rodríguez, 1991: 33)
'and then my husband and I go to a **cottage** we have in the countryside well **a cottage a little house a kind of spa'**

(37) Il a déjà commis chais pas **trois quat(re) cinq** fautes (Gülich, 1994: 44)
'He has already committed I don't know **three four five** mistakes'

This strategy is also visible in the approximative uses of certain disjunctive set tags formally closing open lists (Dubois, 1992; Channell, 1994):

(38) j' avais euh quatorze ans **ou quelque chose comme ça** [C-ORAL-ROM ffamcv03]
'I was fourteen years old **or something like that**'

(39) habría que construir una especie de cómo le diría yo ? como de cobertizo **o algo así** [C-ORAL-ROM epubdl04]
'One should build a kind of how shall I say like a shed **or something like that**'

Another way of signalling an open list of possible candidates is the use of exemplification markers such as French *par exemple* 'for example', *disons* 'say', *mettons* 'let's put' (cf. Dostie, 2004: chap. 7; Rossari, 2000) and equivalent expressions in the other Romance languages. Examples specify an abstract or very generic expression by giving a more concrete or more specific item out of a set of equally illustrative items (Manzotti, 1998: 121; Rossari and Jayez, 1999: 461). Examples are therefore arbitrary choices, since the selected item is just one of a number of possible other examples. Exemplification markers are metacommunicative devices commenting on the choice of an expression (cf. Gülich and Kotschi, 1996: 74 for a discussion of such commenting devices).

(40) Você precisa de uma cultura literária geral, que não deve ser feita duma vez só, mas dentro de um programa que pode durar **ponhamos** seis anos. (http://zemauriciorocha.blogspot.com/2006_12_01_archive.html, 7.3.2007)
'you need a general literary culture that must not be done just once, but within a programme that may go on for **let's put** six years'

(41) de cinq cents mètres à treize cents à **disons** entre onze cents et treize cents mètres [C-ORAL-ROM ffamdl17]

'from five hundred meters to thirteen hundred to say between eleven and thirteen hundred meters'

Most of these markers are also used as approximators except for explicit learned markers such as French *par exemple*. I suspect that here the exemplification is too transparent and explicit to be backgrounded in approximator uses.

Another strategy apt for all kinds of approximation is the use of shields in Prince *et al.*'s (1982) terminology, hedges and shields in Caffi's (2007) terminology. Many shields are reduced parentheticals as discussed by Schneider (2007, this volume) and Kaltenböck (this volume) signalling metapragmatic awareness. Both epistemicity-based plausibility shields such as *I think* or French *chais pas moi,* Spanish *qué sé yo*, German (*ich habe*) *keine Ahnung,* Spanish *a lo mejor* 'perhaps', and attribution shields based on evidential mechanisms by attributing an information to a source other than the speaker, i.e. by using expressions like *presumably* or *according to x* (Prince *et al.*, 1982: 89–93) or French *entre guillemets* (Gülich and Kotschi, 1996: 68; Blanche-Benveniste, 1997: 11) comment on the problematic use of an expression by pointing to the act of speaking and the speaker's somewhat arbitrary choice of an expression (thus a strategy sharing some properties with exemplification):

(42) conseguían decir **a lo mejor dos tres** palabras muy sencillas pero nada más [C-ORAL-ROM enatco01]
'they managed to say perhaps two three very simple words but nothing else'

Shields express speaker attitudes and modify the illocutionary force of utterances, however, they do not conventionally modify the truth conditions of a proposition. However, approximation can arise as an implicature (see Kaltenböck, this volume, on *I think*) and represent thus a link between pragmatic and semantic approximation – also see Ran (this volume) for an analogous development of the Mandarin mood marker *ba* to rounder uses. The basic functions of shields not related to any specific semantic or syntactic units do not restrict their use to either rounder or adaptor readings.

## 4. From Adaptor to Rounder: A One-Way Path?

The different sources and their semantic properties have shown that at least in the case of the most strongly entrenched approximators discussed in Sections 3.1 and 3.2 either rounders or adaptors emerge, i.e. at least in a first step some of the most common approximators are clearly separated. However, some of these approximators such as Spanish *como* fulfil both adaptor and rounder functions. So the question is how and when such a second step leading to rounder uses may take place.

If we look at the rounders derived from prepositions analysed in Section 3.1 it is striking to see that they do not develop any further functions at all, except for certain very rare uses of spatial prepositional expressions used as scalar adaptors with lexical items:

(43) VAL: c' est **proche de** l' obsession quoi
BET: ouais mais c' est beaucoup plus euh l' obsession euh c' est c' est pareil sauf que l' obsession tu te rends compte que c' est une obsession [C-ORAL-ROM ffamcv08]

'VAL: it is **close to** obsession you know
BET: yeah but it's a lot more uh obsession uh that's the same thing except that with an obsession you realize it's an obsession'

Similarly English *about* is also used to modify qualities as in *I am about tired of this. Is your work about finished? Near about* (all examples from OED, s.v. *about*). *About* is deintensifying with gradable adjectives, expressing near achievement with telic verbs, which thus takes up the idea of a scale underlying the spatial metaphors creating rounders. This also explains certain rounder uses with colours as in *Une robe dans les bleus* 'a dress in the blues', which Vaguer paraphrases as *dans la gamme des bleus* 'within the range of blue colours' (Vaguer, 2003: 136), or Italian *un colore vicino al verde* (ZVI) 'a colour close to green', suggesting colour scales.

Apart from these rather isolated uses still showing the spatial metaphor neither preposition-based rounders nor other rounders ever develop typical adaptor uses expressing a global semantic approximation of lexical items, at least in the languages analysed here.

The panorama of adaptors is quite different. Here subsequent changes are very productive, and, as will be shown, related to informal oral speech and specific problems thereof, such as word-finding difficulties or other formulation problems.

As for the Romance adaptors equivalent to *like*, my own corpus analysis (Mihatsch, 2010a) has shown that historically they are not limited to informal registers, but frequent in literary texts, religious treatises, etc. (also see Rees, 1971: 28). However, according to Sundheim (in Montes, 1980/1981: 672) these uses of Spanish *como* were drastically reduced after the Siglo de Oro, towards the end of the 17th century. Today Spanish *como* is rather restricted to informal spoken language, where it has gained a new impetus and developed new functions often based on problematic situations in speech production. This is also true for the other languages analysed here, where these adaptors are particularly frequent in informal spoken language today, often even serving as hesitation markers:

(44) e quindi lì bisogna sempre inventarsi he un qualche qualche cosa in più anche **come** non so **come** una un eh mi sono incartata [C-ORAL-ROM imedin04]
'and therefore it is always necessary to invent oneself, something more also **like** I don't know **like** a a uh I have lost track'

Other new functions just signal figurative speech – a function derived from the semantic approximative use with metaphors. Just like lexical approximation, metaphors are based on similarity, although across two conceptual domains (see Authier-Revuz (1995) discussed by Caffi, this volume; Rees, 1971: 28). Adaptors may thus signal metaphorical readings:

(45) i francesi hanno voluto **come** pagare un debito verso il loro poverissimo ciclismo [C-ORAL-ROM imedsp01]
'The French wanted to **like** pay a dept toward their poor cyclism'

From there it is a small step to a marker just signalling the inappropriateness of a term not necessarily due to semantic deviations, but rather stylistic clashes or changes in register and other diasystematic violations. In (46) the generic term *something for the nerves* is semantically correct, but obviously the speaker feels that a more specific established term such as *tranquilizer* might be more adequate:

(46) me dieron el azahar un **como** una cosa para los nervios y tal
[C-ORAL-ROM efammn08]
'they gave me the orange blossoms a **like** something for the nerves and so on '

In (47) Italian *come* is used to indicate a phonetic resemblance of an expression with the target the speaker does not remember:

(47) lo diceva in un a una giornalista lì lui era alla manifestazione ora **come** Bordonne si chiam [ava] [C-ORAL-ROM, ifamcv23]
'he said that to a journalist he was at the demonstration now his name was **like** Bordonne.'

Just like the Romance equivalents, even more so, English *like* serves to signal marked expressions, such as figurative speech, and also stylistic discrepancies (Andersen, 1998: 158, 2000: 20, 25). All these uses are derived from semantic approximation via the flagging of figurative metaphoric expressions, which also explains why rounders do not develop such uses. Rounders just affect the numerical values referred to, there is no possible transition to flag stylistically marked expressions in the case of numerals.

Another derived function is the use as a shield used for pragmatic mitigation as in *Y'a comme un problème* 'there is like a problem' (Moline, 1996: 265; Mihatsch, 2009), softening an assertion, or mitigating a piece of advice as in (48) and thus sounding less patronizing:

(48) donc ce qui n' est pas négligeable non plus pour le rangement toujours bien mettre les deux bouchons emboîtés l' un dans l' autre c' est **comme beaucoup plus pratique** et je vous conseille de pas la ranger dans ce sens-ci mais dans l' autre sens...
[C-ORAL-ROM fnatbu02]

'so what is equally not negligible for cleaning up always put well the two lids one in the other that's **like much more convenient** and I advise you not to put it in this sense but in the other sense'

Shield uses derived from adaptors are not specified for a particular type of shield, i.e. plausibility or attribution in Prince *et al.*'s (1982) classification, but mitigate an illocution in an unspecified way.

In Spanish in particular, these uses are strongly entrenched, especially with the intensifier *muy* (Moreno Ayora, 1991: 42) – so obviously semantic approximation cannot be involved, rather the negative evaluation is softened:

(49) (...) es un rollo o sea todo muy mecánico venga esto no lo reconoce lo meto en el diccionario esto no sé qué esto hhh sabes? **como muy monótono** [C-ORAL-ROM efamdl35]
'it's a hassle, that is, everything is very mechanical. Come on, it does not recognize this one, I put it into the dictionary, that one whatever, that one you know? **Like, very monotonous**'

In Spanish, Portuguese (and English) these adaptors have also developed a new rounder use:

(50) Haverá na cidade **como** dous mil judeus. (ADLP, s.v. *como*)
'In the city there must be **like** two thousand Jews'

(51) me parece que solo podían ir **como** cuatro familiares por cada estudiante [C-ORAL-ROM efammn06]
'I think that only **like** four family members per student were allowed to come.'

Such uses are impossible in French, Italian and German:

(52) *Il est **comme** huit heures (Moline, 1996: 268)
'It is **like** eight o'clock'

In French and Italian numbers can be modified, however, if an indefinite pronoun precedes the similative marker:

(53) alors quelquefois je connaissais je connais pas tous les bouquins comprenez j' en ai **quelque chose comme** quatre mille là-bas (ELICOP, Corpus Auvergne file faf19bk8.tv)'
'so sometimes I knew I don't know all the books you see I have **something like** four thousand over there

(54) Avevo collezionato per **qualcosa come** 25 anni Espressi e Panorama.. (http://www.forumtime.it/Forum/index.php, 08/02/2009)
'I had collected for **something like** 25 years Espressi and Panorama'

Marginally, this is also possible in German:

(55) und es dauerte **sowas wie** zehn Stunden bis wir wieder Strom hatten (http://de.nntp2http.com/sci/physik/2005/08/b8a39127ee7592e3d06695a2fd70aaa7.html, 08/02/2009)
'and it took **something like** ten hours until we got the electricity back.'

According to the data discussed in Siegel (2002: 55) the rounder *like* seems less of a semantic approximator than a pragmatic mitigator (although I believe (57) is possible):

(56) He has about six sisters.
(57) ? Yes, he has exactly six.
(58) He has, like, six sisters.
(59) Yes, he has exactly six.
(60) Yes, he has about six.

How does the transition of the adaptor towards the rounder function come about? I would like to argue that we have to assume an intermediate step of adaptor uses as shields signalling some communicative inadequacy or deviation, for instance diasystematic markedness, of an expression. The entrenchment of this use may then lead to further uses of this new shield with quantifying expressions. According to my corpus analysis, the French and Italian adaptors derived from a marker of comparison (and which cannot be used as rounders) do not show a well-established shield function, even less so German, where the adaptor *wie* is very marginal, which points indeed to a necessary intermediate step as a shield before rounders can emerge.[6] However, neither has Portuguese well entrenched shield uses according to my data – so perhaps the rounder function of Portuguese *como* might be influenced by Spanish – or in analogy with the rounder *assim* going back to a similar adaptor. Interestingly the emergence of shield uses also leads to a subsequent syntactic flexibilization, as can be observed in the cases of Spanish *como* and English *like* (see Mihatsch, 2009, 2010a).

Similarly the deixis-based adaptors Portuguese *assim*, German *so* and Dutch *zo* have also developed a series of further functions, for instance as indefinite articles:

(61) Ich mache mir auch ständig Gedanken, wie **so ne** Uni von innen aussieht und wie **so eine** Vorlesung abläuft,...
(www.medi-learn.de/medizinstudium/foren/archive/t-23353.html, 15/08/2007)
'I keep thinking how a [literally '**such a'**] university looks like from inside and how a [literally '**such a'**] lecture works...'

[6] Rounders may also occasionally act as shields when used to diminish the risks of the speaker making quantitative statements, for instance in academic texts (Hübler, 1983; also see Markkanen and Schröder, 1997; Prince *et al.*, 1982).

(62) portanto normalmente ponho **assim** uma frasezita qualquer
[C-ORAL-ROM pfamcv12]
'Usually I put like some little phrase [literally '**such a** little phrase']'

They also show clearly entrenched shield functions, for instance mitigating requests:

(63) traga **assim** algumas páginas suas para eu sentir o seu estilo. (Houaiss, s.v. assim)
'Bring **like** a couple of pages of yours so that I can get an impression of your style.'

(64) Wenn du es dir installierst, kannst du mal **so** deinen Ersteindruck Beschreiben? (http://www.computerbase.de/news/software/betriebssysteme/windows/2005/januar/auch_window, 10/02/2008)
'When you get it installed, can you **like** describe your first impression?'

Furthermore, in all three languages these adaptors have developed rounder functions:

(65) Moosbrugger leerte **so** (seine) fünf Flaschen (Plank, 2004: 169)
'Moosbrugger emptied **like** five bottles'

(66) vocês ainda se encontram **assim** vinte trinta pessoas ?
[C-ORAL-ROM pfamdl11]
'You still get together, **like** twenty thirty people?'

(67) Het concert duurde [**zo'n** veerig minuten] (Corver and Zwarts, 2006)
'The concert took **like** forty minutes'

Again we observe a co-occurrence of shield and rounder functions springing from an adaptor, plausibly the shield function coming first.

Interestingly a similar transition can be observed for an adaptor suffix, namely English *-ish*, going back to a denonimal suffix forming adjectives, which is now also used as a rounder ( Quirk *et al.*, 1985: 395; Channell, 1994: 68):

(68) I'll be there by eight**ish** (Quirk *et al.*, 1985: 395)

Here I would like to argue that the rounder does not develop from a shield function, but perhaps the adjectival use of the suffix and thus frequent derivations of approximative colour adjectives such as *blueish* are already close to the scalarity of rounders.

Similar arrays of new functions can be observed for French *genre* and related expressions in the other Romance languages analysed here, for instance Italian *tipo*, which can indicate word-finding problems:

(69) JOX: (. . .) perché praticamente c' era da mettere dei prodotti era di geografia me lo ricordo ancora c'era da mettere dei prodotti in base alla collina pianura no ?
VER: eh ? ah ah **tipo**
JOX: no eran **tipo**

VER: cereali birra...
JOX: sì eran **tipo**...
VER: luppolo... [C-ORAL-ROM ifamcv03]
JOX: ...because really you had to put crops it was geography I can still remember that you had to put crops at the foot of the hill plain no?
VER: eh? uh uh **like**
JOX: they were not **like**...
VER: cereals, beer
JOX yes they were **like**
VER: hop

Many uses also serve pragmatic mitigation:

(70) ALE: perché non provi nel **tipo** nelle pagine gialle...?
[C-ORAL-ROM ifamcv15]
'Why don't you check in like in the yellow pages?
(71) What about **like** «demon»? (Fleischman 1998: 38)

All these expressions are syntactically quite flexible and can modify a variety of constituent types and just like *kind of* and *sort of* these adaptors were originally restricted to NPs.

Again, the uses are not any longer linked to semantic approximation, and also indicate some metacommunicative distance, perhaps also supported by the exemplification function of the source. In the four Romance languages they can also modify numerals:

(72) Il saute **genre** 1 m 30 sans peine. (Yaguello, 1998: 18)
'he jumps **like** 1 m 30 without an effort'
(73) enfin je rentrais &euh **style** à six heures du matin quoi
[C-ORAL-ROM ffamdl03]
'Well I returned uh **like** at six o'clock in the morning'
(74) cioè o spendere **tipo** un' ottanttina di mila lire
[C-ORAL-ROM ifamcv02]
'thus or spend **like** eighty thousand lire'
(75) acho que havia **tipo** sessenta pessoas a ver o concerto
[C-ORAL-ROM, pfamcv05]
'I think there were **like** sixty people watching the concert'

Recently, at least in informal language, (especially Brazilian) Portuguese *tipo* (Bittencourt, 2000: 264; Pereira Lima-Hernandes, 2005) and French *genre* (Fleischman, 1998: 20) have become highly frequent discourse markers with A structuring function, comparable to English *like*.

The only important group of adaptors in Romance languages not used as rounders are French *espèce de* and the equivalents. So one might suspect that these adaptors do not offer a possible bridge towards rounders. However, English *sort of* and *kind of* occur with numerals, albeit very marginally (also see Aijmer, 2002: 196):

(76) c'mon !!! read a little bit !!! **kinda hundred** people already said that ! (www.gamingring.com/forum/archive/index.php/t-144-p-2.html, 22/02/2008)
(77) No further than **sorta twenty** mins by bus, work starts too early in the morning. (blog.myspace.com/index.cfm?fuseaction = blog.view&friendID, 22/02/2008)

So why is the rounder function rather marginal with these expressions? Perhaps because the necessary preliminary emergence of pragmatic shield functions lacks here. Now these adaptors have also developed additional functions – namely markers flagging figurative speech via the signalling of semantic deviance of metaphors (Aijmer, 2002: 178f., 194). As with the other adaptors certain uses with metaphors show that semantic approximation is backgrounded, flagging foregrounded, since here the marker is necessary in order to announce an unusual metaphor and in order to prevent a semantic clash between the literal reading of the source lexeme and the human attributes of the metaphor:

(78) il y en avait que deux qui étaient là depuis cinq ans pour préparer Normale Sup au Saint-Cloud et il y avait dans le fond **une espèce de sanglier** aux ongles noirs avec les cheveux longs [C-ORAL-ROM ffamdl05]
'there were only two who had been there for five years in order to prepare Normale Sup in Saint-Cloud and in the back there was **sort of** a wild boar with black nails and with long hair'

As other adaptors these are frequently observed as markers flagging formulation problems:

(79) MAR: ouais voilà on a fait une **espèce** de c' est **un genre de**
SOP: de ?
MAR: comment ça s' appelle c'est un
[C-ORAL-ROM ffamdl04]

'MAR: yeah well we did **a kind of** it's **a sort of**
SOP: of?
MAR: how do you call it it's a'

However, unlike other adaptors the Romance equivalents of *kind of* do not show any entrenched uses as shields, while the English expressions do have established uses as shields (also see Fetzer, this volume), a necessary intermediate step towards rounder uses:

(80) ^it was . ((a !little)) **sort of** 'rather un:pl\easant in the /end# [...] (Aijmer, 2002: 200)
(81) ^can't we **sort of**'leave a'Belgium and :Luxembourg
(Aijmer, 2002: 200)
(82) (...) could we **sort of** meet or something. (Channell, 1994: 135)

English *kind of* and *sort of* are also syntactically more flexible and often phonetically reduced (Aijmer, 2002: 183), while the Romance adaptors only occur prenominally and apart from some changes pointing to a loss of nominal features such as gender and number (see Mihatsch, 2007, 2010a) they preserve the syntactic structure of the complex NP. Perhaps both the lack of entrenched shield uses and the co-existence and formal identity with the older taxonomic 'N1tax *de* N2'-construction block further functional and syntactic reanalyses of the Romance expressions leading to shields and rounders.

## 5. Conclusion: A Semantic Map

If we draw a semantic map[7] (see Haspelmath, 2003) of approximators and synchronically (via polysemy) and diachronically (via semantic change) related functions, we can immediately see that in this domain unidirectionality is the rule, bidirectionality the exception (Figure 5.1).

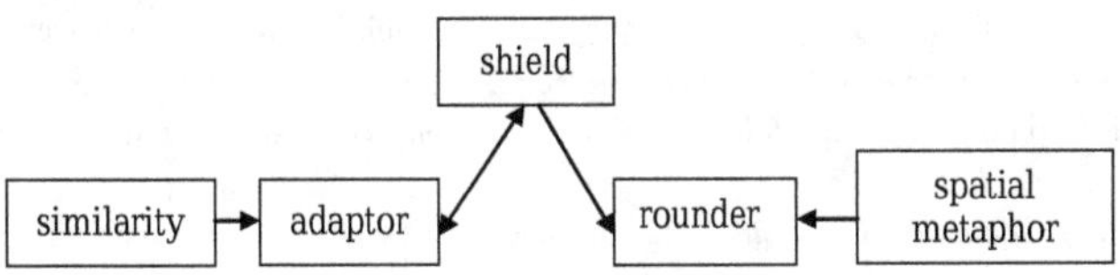


**Figure 5.1.** A simplified semantic map of approximation.

While adaptors as well as shields are productive sources for further functions, rounders seem to be an endpoint, and, related to this observation, adaptors can become rounders, not vice versa. The data suggest furthermore that only adaptors that have gone through an intermediate stage as shields may become rounders. The high frequency of adaptors in spoken informal language and their particular functions in situations with formulation problems are a good basis for further innovations and a greater variety of discourse functions, which may then lead to new uses as shields. As Fetzer (this volume) and Kaltenböck (this volume) point out and as my data from Romance languages have shown, the changes between adaptors and shields are bidirectional, and indeed, both are highly useful (although not restricted to) spoken informal language.

---

[7] Semantic maps give a visual representation of cross-linguistic-related functions, either synchronically linked by polysemy and/or diachronically linked via semantic changes, and thus facilitate the discovery of directional changes.

## References

ADLP = Buarque de Holanda Ferreira, A. (1999). *Novo Aurélio Século XXI. o dicionário da língua portuguesa. 3rd Edition*. Rio de Janeiro: Nova Fronteira.

Aijmer, K. (2002). *English discourse particles: Evidence from a corpus*. Amsterdam: John Benjamins. (Studies in Corpus linguistics, v.10).

Albrespit, J. (2005). "Le suffixe *-ish* en anglais: Comparaison par approximation". *Travaux de linguistique du CERLICO* **(18)** Intensité, comparaison, degree, pp. 80–97.

Andersen, G. (1998). "The pragmatic marker *like* from a relevance-theoretic perspective", in A. H. Jucker and Y. Ziv (eds.), *Discourse markers: Descriptions and theory*. Amsterdam: John Benjamins, 147–170.

Andersen, G. (2000). "The role of the pragmatic marker *like* in utterance interpretation", in G. Andersen and T. Fretheim (eds.), *Pragmatic markers and propositional attitude*. Amsterdam: John Benjamins, 17–38 (Pragmatics and beyond 79).

Bat-Zeev Shyldkrot, H. (2005). "Grammaticalisation, changements semantiques et polysemie: le cas de *vers* et *envers*", in O. Soutet (ed.), *La polysémie*. Paris: Presses de l'université Paris Sorbonne, 203–230.

Bittencourt, V. de Oliveira. (2000). "Tipo (Assim) como Delimitador de 'Unidades de Informação'". *Estudos Lingüísticos* **29**: 264–269.

Blanche-Benveniste, C. (1997). *Approches de la langue parlée en français*. Gap/ Paris: Ophrys.

Brauer-Figueiredo, M. (1999). *Gesprochenes Portugiesisch*. Frankfurt/Main: Teo Ferrer de Mesquita.

Briz Gómez, A. (1995). "La atenuación en la conversación coloquial. Una categoría pragmática", in L. Cortés (ed.), *El español coloquial. Actas del I Simposio sobre análisis del discurso oral*. Almería: Servicio e Publicaciones, 103–122.

Bruyne, J. de. (1993). *Spanische Grammatik*. (Translated by *D.-J. Gütschow*), Tübingen: Niemeyer.

Caffi, C. (2007). *Mitigation*. Amsterdam: Elsevier.

Cannesson E. and P. Saint-Dizier (2002). "Defining and representing preposition senses: A preliminary analysis". Paper presented at the ACL WSD workshop, Philadelphia.

Channell, J. (1994). *Vague language*. Oxford: Oxford University Press.

C-ORAL-ROM = Cresti, E., Moneglia, M. (Eds.) (2005). *C-ORAL-ROM: Integrated reference corpora for spoken Romance languages*. CD-ROM. Amsterdam/ Philadelphia: Benjamins (Studies in Corpus Linguistics 15).

Cortés Rodríguez, L. (ed.) (1991). *Sobre conectores, expletivos y muletillas en el espanol hablado*. Málaga: Editorial Librería Àgora.

Corver, N. and J. Zwarts (2006). "Prepositional numerals". *Lingua* **116 (6)**: 811–835.

Coseriu, E. (1968). "Les structures lexématiques", in T. Elwert (ed.), *Probleme der Semantik*. Wiesbaden (ZFSL, Beiheft, N.F. 1), 3–16.

CREA = Real Academia Española, *Corpus de Referencia del Español Actual* (http://www.rae.es/NIVEL1/CREA.HTM).

Cruse, D. A. (1986). *Lexical semantics*. Cambridge: CUP. Cambridge Textbooks in Linguistics.

Danon-Boileau, L. and M. Morel (1997). "*Question, point de vue, genre, style*… : les noms prépositionnels en français contemporain". *Faits de Langues* **9**. La préposition: une catégorie accessoire? Paris: Ophrys. pp. 193–200.

Dardano, M. and P. Trifone (1997). *La nuova grammatica della lingua italiana*. Bologna: Zanichelli.

Devos, Filip, P. Maesfranck and G. De Tré (1998). "Granularity in the interpretation of *around* in approximative lexical time indications". *Journal of Quantitative Linguistics* **5 (3)**: 167–173.

Dostie, G. (2004). *Pragmaticalisation et marqueurs discursifs: analyse sémantique et traitement lexicographique*. Louvain-la-Neuve: De Boeck-Duculot.

DRAE = Real Academia Española (1989). *Diccionario Manual e Ilustrado de la Lengua Española. 4th Edition*. Madrid: Espasa Calpe.

Dubois, S. (1992). "Extension particles, etc". *Language Variation and Change* **4 (2)**: 179–205.

Ducrot, Oswald (1972). *Dire et ne pas dire*. Paris: Hermann.

ELICOP = Brosens, V., et al. (1997–2000). *Etude linguistique de la communication parlée,* Katolieke Universiteit Leuven. [http://bach.arts.kuleuven.ac.be/elicop].

Esbozo = Real Academia Española (1973). *Esbozo de una nueva gramática de la lengua española*. Madrid: Espasa Calpe.

Fagard, B. (2006). "Evolution semantique des prépositions dans les languaes romanes". Thèse de doctorat.

Fleischman, Suzanne. (1998). "Des jumeaux du discours: *genre* et *like*". *La linguistique* **34 (2)**: 31–47.

Fleischman, S. and M. Yaguello (2004). "Discourse markers across languages? Evidence from English and French", in C. L. Moder and A. Martinovic-Zic (eds.), *Discourse analysis across languages and cultures*. Amsterdam/Philadelphia: Benjamins, 129–147.

FRANTEXT = Base textuelle *FRANTEXT* (http://zeus.inalf.cnrs.fr/)

Gärtner, E. (1998). *Grammatik der portugiesischen Sprache*. Tübingen: Niemeyer.

GDW = Grimm, J. and W. Grimm (1854–1893). *Deutsches Wörterbuch. Vol. 16*. Leipzig: Hirzel.

GEUI = Giacoma, L. and S. Kolb (eds.) (2001). *Großwörterbuch für Experten und Universität. Italienisch–Deutsch, Deutsch–Italienisch*. Bologna/Stuttgart: Zanichelli/Klett.

Grady, J. (1997). "A typology of motivation for conceptual metaphor. Correlation vs. resemblance", in R. W. Gibbs and G. J. Steen (eds.), *Metaphor in cognitive linguistics*. Amsterdam/Philadelphia: Benjamins, 79–100.

Grevisse, M. and A. Goosse (1993). *Le Bon Usage. Grammaire française. 13th Edition*. Paris/Louvain-La-Neuve: Duculot.

Gülich, E. (1994). "Commentaires métadiscursifs et "mise en scène" de l'élaboration du discours". *CALaP* **12**: 29–51.

Gülich, E. and T. Kotschi (1996). "Textherstellungsverfahren in mündlicher Kommunikation. Ein Beitrag am Beispiel des Französischen", in W. Motsch (ed.), *Ebenen der Textstruktur. Sprachliche und kommunikative Prinzipien*. Tübingen: Niemeyer, 37–80.

Hagège, C. (1982). *La structure des langues*. Paris: PUF.

Haspelmath, M. (2003). "The geometry of grammatical meaning: Semantic maps and cross-linguistic comparison", in M. Tomasello (ed.), *The new psychology of language II*. Mahwah, New Jersey: Lawrence Erlbaum, 211–242.

Haspelmath, M. and O. Buchholz (1998). "Equative and similative constructions in the languages of Europe", in J. van der Auwera (ed.), *Adverbial constructions in the languages of Europe*. Berlin/New York: Mouton de Gruyter, 277–334.

Houaiss, A. (2001). *Dicionário Houaiss da língua portuguesa*. Rio de Janeiro: Objetiva.

Hübler, A. (1983). *Understatements and hedges in English*. Amsterdam: John Benjamins.

Hundertmark-Santos Martins, M. T. (1998). *Portugiesische Grammatik. 2nd Edition*. Tübingen: Niemeyer.

Hurford, J. R. (1987). *Language and number. The emergence of a cognitive system*. Oxford/New York: Blackwell. (To the three graces of the magic 14).

Hyland, K. (1998). *Hedging in scientific research articles*. Amsterdam: John Benjamins.

Kay, P. (1997). *Words and the grammar of context*. Stanford: Center for the study of language and information. (CSLI lecture notes 40).

Koch, P. and W. Oesterreicher (1990). *Gesprochene Sprache in der Romania: Französisch, Italienisch, Spanisch.* Tübingen: Niemeyer. (Romanistische Arbeitshefte 31).

Krifka, M. (2007). "Approximate interpretations of number words: A case for strategic communication", in G. Bouma, I. Kräer and J. Zwarts (eds.), *Cognitive foundations of interpretation.* Amsterdam: Koninklijke Nederlandse Akademie van Wetenschapen, 111–126.

Lakoff, G. (1972). "Hedges: A study in meaning criteria and the logic of fuzzy concepts". *Papers from the Eighth Regional Meeting of the Chicago Linguistic Society*, Chicago, pp. 183–228.

Lang, J. (1991). *Die französischen Präpositionen. Funktion und Bedeutung.* Heidelberg: Winter. (Reihe Siegen 95).

López, M. L. (1972). *Problemas y métodos en el análisis de preposiciones.* Madrid: Gredos. (Biblioteca románica hispánica 2; 143).

Lovik, T. A. (1990). "Geben Sie mir so'n Streuselapfel: Hedging in Authentic Speech". *Die Unterrichtspraxis/Teaching German* **23** (**2**): 121–128.

Lüdtke, J. (2005). *Romanische Wortbildung: inhaltlich, diachronisch, synchronisch.* Tübingen: Stauffenburg. (Stauffenburg-Handbücher).

Luque Durán, J. (1976). *Las Preposiciones. Vol. 2.* Madrid: Soc. Gen. Española de Libreria. (Coleccion 'Problemas básicos del español').

Manzotti, E. (1998). "L'esempio. Natura, definizioni, problemi". *Cuadernos de Filologìa Italiana* **5**: 99–123.

Marcq, P. A. (1980). "Histoire de *gegen*". *Etudes germaniques* **2**: 133–144.

Markkanen, R. and H. Schröder (eds.) (1997). *Hedging and discourse. Approaches to the analysis of a pragmatic phenomenon in academic texts.* Berlin/New York: De Gruyter.

Melis, L. (2003). "Le groupe prépositif comme déterminant du nom", in P. Haderman, A. Van Slijcke and M. Berré (eds.), *La syntaxe raisonnée.* Bruxelles: De Boeck & Larcier, 235–250.

Menge, H. (2005). *Lehrbuch der lateinischen Syntax und Semantik.* New ed. by T. Burkard and M. Schauer. *2nd Edition.* Darmstadt: Wiss. Buchges.

Mihatsch, W. (2006). "*Machin, truc, chose*: La naissance de marqueurs pragmatiques", in M. Drescher and B. Job (eds.), *Les marqueurs discursifs dans les langues romanes: approches théoriques et méthodologiques.* Frankfurt: Peter Lang, 153–172.

Mihatsch, W. (2007). "The construction of vagueness: *Sort of* expressions in Romance languages", in G. Radden, K.-M. Koepcke, T. Berg and P. Siemund (eds.), *Aspects of meaning constructing meaning: From concepts to utterances.* Amsterdam/Philadelphia: Benjamins, 225–245.

Mihatsch, W. (2009). "The approximators French *comme*, Italian *come*, Portuguese *como* and Spanish *como* from a grammaticalization perspective", in C. Rossari, C. Ricci and A. Spiridon (eds.), *Grammaticalization and pragmatics: Facts, approaches, theoretical issues.* Bingley: Emerald, 65–91. (Studies in Pragmatics 5).

Mihatsch, W. (2010a). "*Wird man von Hustensaft wie so ne art bekifft?*" Approximationsmarker in romanischen Sprachen. Frankfurt am Main, Klostermann (Analecta Romanica 75).

Mihatsch, W. (2010b). "Von der Deixis zur Approximation", in C. Maaß and A. Schrott (eds.), *Wenn Deiktika nicht zeigen: Deiktische Formen als Satzkonnektoren und Marker. Deixis, Pragmatik und Grammatikalisierung.* Münster et al.: LIT Verlag, 261–281.

Mihatsch, W. (2010c). "Les approximateurs quantitatifs entre *scalarité* et non-*scalarité*". *Langue française* **165**: 125–153.

MOL = Moliner, M. (1998). *Diccionario de uso del español. (3rd Edition, Vols. 2.* Madrid: Gredos.

Moline, E. (1996). "Y'a comme un problème: un emploi métalinguistique de comme? *Champ du signe*: 249–277.

Molinier, C. (2005). "Sur la forme et le statut des adjectives de couleur formés par dérivation". *Le français moderne* **73**: 145–156.

Montes, J. J. (1980/1981). "Sobre el *como* de atenuación". *Boletín de Filología de la Universidad de Chile* **XXXI**: 667–675.

Moreno Ayora, A. (1991). *Sintaxis y semántica de como*. Málaga: Ágora.

Morera Pérez, M. (1988). *Estructura semántica del sistema preposicional del español moderno y sus campos de usos*. Puerto del Rosario.

Mutz, K. (2000). *Die italienischen Modifikationssuffixe*. Frankfurt am Main et al.: Lang.

Noailly, M. (2005). "L'intensité de la couleur: remarques sur l'emploi de très devant bleu, rouge, vert, jaune", in I. Choï-Jonin, M. Bras, A. Dagnac and M. Rouquier (eds.), *Questions de classification en linguistique: Méthodes et descriptions*. Bern: Peter Lang.

OED = Simpson, J. and E. Weiner (eds.) (1989). *The Oxford English dictionary. OED online. 2nd Edition.* The Oxford University Press. (http://dictionary.oed.com)

Pereira Lima-Hernandes, M. C. (2005). "*A Interface Sociolingüística/Gramaticalização: estratificação de usos de tipo, feito, igual e como, sincronia e diacronia*". Tese doct. do Instituto de Estudos da linguagem Unicamp.

Pharies, D. (2002). *Diccionario etimológico de los sufijos españoles y de otros elementos finales*. Madrid: Gredos. (Biblioteca Románica Hispánica 5, Diccionarios, 25).

Plank, F. (2004). "Inevitable reanalysis. From local adpositions to approximative adnumerals, in German and wherever". *Studies in Language* **28 (1)**: 165–201.

Prince, E., C. Bosk and J. Frader (1982). "On Hedging in physician-physician discourse", in J. di Pietro (ed.), *Linguistics and the professions*. Norwood/New Jersey: Ablex, 83–97.

Quirk, R., et al. (1985). *A comprehensive grammar of the English language*. London: Longman.

Rainer, F. (1999). "La derivación adjectival", in I. Bosque and V. Demonte (eds.), *Gramática descriptiva de la lengua española Vol. 3*. Madrid: Real Academia Española/Espasa Calpe, 4595–4643.

Rees, G. O. (1971). "*Comme* dans les phrases du type *Il était comme fou*". *Neuphilologische Mitteilungen* **72**: 20–29.

Rosier, L. (2000). "Les petits *rapporteurs* de discours". *Travaux linguistique du Cerlico* **13**: 209–229.

Rossari, C. and J. Jayez (1999). "*Par exemple*: une procédure d'exemplification par la preuve", in B. Combettes, C. Schnedecker and A. Theissen (eds.), *Ordre et distinction dans la langue et le discours*. Paris: Champion, 461–478.

Rossari, C. (2000). "Les emplois de *disons* de la langue au discours", in G. Martel (ed.), *Autour de l'argumentation*. Québec: Nota bene, 107–125.

Rouget, C. (1997). "*Espèce de, genre de, sorte de*: Approximatifs ou sous-catégorisateurs? in P. Carvalho and O. Soutet (eds.), *Psychomécanique du langage. Problèmes et perspectives. Actes du 7e Colloque International de Psychomécanique du langage (Cordoue, 2–4 juin 1994)*. Paris: Champion, 289–298. (Champion varia 11).

Sadock, J. M. (1977). "Truth and approximations". *Proceedings of the Third Annual Meeting of the Berkeley Linguistics Society*: 430–439.

Schneider, S. (2007). *Reduced parenthetical clauses as mitigators. A corpus study of spoken French, Italian, and Spanish.* Amsterdam/Philadelphia: Benjamins. (Studies in Corpus Linguistics 27).

Siegel, M. E. A. (2002). "*Like*: The discourse particle and semantics". *Journal of Semantics* **19**: 35–71.

Talmy, L. (2000). *Toward a cognitive semantics. Vol. 1: Concept structuring systems.* Cambridge, MA/ London, UK: The MIT Press. (Language, speech and communication).

Vaguer, C. (2003). "La préposition *dans*: vecteur d'approximation?". *Revue de Sémantique et Pragmatique* **14**: 135–155.

Vera Morales, J. (2004). *Spanische Grammatik. 4th Edition*. München/Wien: Oldenbourg.

Vigara Tauste, A. M. (1996). "Español coloquial: Expresión del sentido por aproximación", in T. Kotschi, W. Oesterreicher and K. Zimmermann (eds.), *El español hablado y la cultura oral en España e Hispanoamérica*. Frankfurt am Main, Vervuert; Madrid: Iberoamericana, 15–44.

Vincent, D. (2005). "The journey of non-standard discourse markers in Quebec French: Networks based on exemplification", in M.-B. Mosegaard Hansen and C. Rossari (eds.), *The evolution of pragmatic markers*. Special issue of *Journal of Historical Pragmatics*, **6(2)**: 188–210

WDW = Wahrig, G. (2000). *Deutsches Wörterbuch*. new ed. by R. Wahrig-Burfeind. *7th Edition*. Gütersloh/München: Bertelsmann.

Wierzbicka, A. (1991). *Cross cultural pragmatics. The semantics of human interaction*. Berlin: Mouton de Gruyter.

Wierzbicka, A. (1985). *Lexicography and conceptual analysis*. Ann Arbor: Karoma.

Wiese, H. (2003). *Numbers, language, and the human mind*. Cambridge: Cambridge University Press.

Yaguello, M. (1998). *Petits faits de langue*. Paris: Editions du Seuil. (La couleur des idées).

ZVI = Zingarelli, N. (1999). in M. Dogliotti and L. Rosiello (eds.), *Lo Zingarelli. Vocabolario della lingua italiana12th Edition*. Bologna: Zanichelli.

New Approaches to Hedging
Edited by Gunther Kaltenböck, Wiltrud Mihatsch and Stefan Schneider


# 6

# Hyperbolic Approximative Numerals in Cross-Cultural Comparison

*Eva Lavric*

## Abstract

Examples like Sp. *dos pasos* (two steps), *cuatro gotas* (four drops), *mil veces* (a thousand times), etc. show that there are some applications of numerals in which exact numbers are used systematically to denote indefinite numbers. Such uses are linked to certain very specific numerals, either rather low ones (2, 3, 4, 5), or high but 'round' ones (100, 1,000). They are hyperbolic in the sense that the number indicated cannot be true, and that several variants of one expression (with 100, 1,000, 10,000, etc.) often coexist. Such approximative numerals are linked to – at least partly – similar substantive nuclei across several languages, and they show a high degree of idiomaticity. But the idiomatic expressions differ from one language to another: Sp. *dos pasos* (two steps) corresponds to Ger. *drei Schritte* (three steps), Sp. *cuatro gotas* (four drops) to Ger. *drei Tropfen* (three drops).

This chapter collects and analyses hyperbolic approximative numerals in French, English, Italian, German and Spanish, and describes them through formulae using ***n*** for minimization and ***N*** for maximization (ex.: **0** = ¬ **1*n*** *there is not one single* ... ). The contribution addresses the following questions:

1) What are hyperbolic approximative (uses of) numerals?
2) How do listeners recognize them?
3) What is their function in discourse?
4) What types of nouns are concerned?
5) Which numbers are concerned?
6) What is the cognitive basis of approximative uses?

7) What are the discursive mechanisms that surround them?
8) How are hyperbolic numerals treated in conversation?

## 1. Introduction

There is a well-known animal whose name in German is *Tausendfüßler*, in French *mille-pattes*, in Spanish *ciempiés*, in Italian *millepiedi* and in English *centipede*. Actually, there seems to be some dissent among the languages as to the number of legs this animal has, although all languages agree on the fact that it has many of them. Zoologists on the other hand assure us that the number of feet is by no means a round one, and that it differs from subspecies to subspecies.[1] So why does none of the languages give an exact, non-round number, depending on the morphology of the local subspecies? Or why don't they simply call it *manyfeet*?

In fact, all languages **do** give an exact number, but it differs from culture to culture. And they all give an exact and **round** number, a power of 10. Rather surprisingly but understandably, I suppose that nobody actually thinks that this exact and round number corresponds to reality.

This zoological example[2] shows a few very interesting things:

- It is possible to say an exact number and mean an approximative one.
- This works with round numbers like *a hundred* and *a thousand.*
- In such uses, *a hundred* and *a thousand* seem to be interchangeable.
- The hearer does not tend to think that the number is meant literally.

Such non-literal or approximative uses are restricted to certain numerals. If the animal in question were called, e.g. *the 88-feet*, or *the 2,432-feet* in a language, we would probably think that the number was accurate.

This phenomenon has hardly been studied so far. The only studies I know are a subchapter in Channell (1994: 89–90) and a short article by Luján Martínez (1994), who shows the existence of the phenomenon for high round numbers in a variety of cultures. But in fact, it is not restricted to those. An earlier paper I wrote about approximative numerals in French (Lavric, 2007), was entitled: "Comment se fait-il que *sept minutes* soient toujours exactement sept minutes, mais que *cinq minutes* puissent parfois être beaucoup plus?" (How come *seven minutes* are always exactly seven minutes, but *five minutes* can sometimes be much more?) It seems thus that a similar program exists for small numbers.

---

[1] Between 18 and 120, but not more than 70 for the European species, says a zoologist friend of mine.

[2] Many thanks to Josef Weidacher for suggesting me this example.

Let us start here with a series of examples (mixed English and French):

(1) **one** minute, please!
(2) **a** drop **or two**, but no real rain;
(3) - À moi, comte, **deux** mots!
'-Come here, count, for two words!'[3]
(4) c'est à **trois** pas d'ici
'that's three steps from here'
(5) I'll call you back in **five** minutes
(6) il n'y a pas **trente-six** façons de voir la chose
(literally: 'there aren't thirty six ways of seeing the thing ... ')
(7) I can give you **a hundred** reasons for it;
(8) parmi les **mille et une** manières de faire l'amour ...
'among the 1,001 ways of making love ... '
(9) tu n'es encore pour moi qu'un petit garçon semblable à **cent mille** petits garçons
'you are still to me nothing more than a little boy similar to 100,000 little boys'
(10) it happens **a million** times a day.[4]

From these examples we can conclude that there are some applications of numerals in which exact numbers are used systematically to denote approximative numbers; i.e. the cardinal corresponds pragmatically to an indefinite quantifier (*a few, many*).[5] We can see that these expressions have a certain degree of idiomaticity, which makes them subject to cross-linguistic variation and valuable for cross-cultural comparisons.

My study will be about French, English, German, Spanish and Italian, but these languages do not have equivalent status in the study: in fact, French acts as a sort of reference language, as for this language I can rely on the corpus constituted by Pierre Rézeau's (1993) "Petit dictionnaire des chiffres en toutes lettres", a complete collection of idiomatic expressions related to numbers, which is based on the systematic analysis of a series of novels in colloquial French.[6] For the other

[3] In all examples, the interlinear translation is intended to be word by word and not idiomatic.

[4] Here the French examples come from Rézeau (1993), the English ones from my English informants; example 9 is of course taken from Saint-Exupéry's "The Little Prince".

[5] The meaning-in-use is the same (*a thousand* ⇔ *many*), but the form and the literal meaning are of course different, as *a thousand* literally always means $999+1$. Even the predominance of approximative uses for certain very prominent numerals (100, 1,000) does not mean one should alter their basic semantic description (see Lavric, 2007).

[6] This analysis was done initially for Bernet and Rézeau's (1989) dictionary of colloquial French, but it turned out that the numerical expressions were so important that they filled a small volume of their own. In Rézeau's dictionary, the numbers come in mathematical order, and within each number chapter, the expressions related to that special number come in alphabetical order. I thank my colleague Peter Handler for not only indicating, but even offering me this very valuable source book.

languages I simply turned to native speakers, one or two for each of them, and conducted an extended interview with them about the subject.[7] This means that the collection for French is exhaustive, and that it gave me the overall structure of my own corpus (see Table 6.1); while the interviews about the other languages basically followed this structure, thus revealing a number of very interesting convergences and divergences.

This contribution will try to answer the following questions:

1) What are hyperbolic approximative (uses of) numerals?
2) How do listeners recognize them?
3) What is their function in discourse?
4) What types of nouns are concerned?[8]
5) Which numbers are concerned?[9]
6) What is the cognitive basis of approximative uses?
7) What are the discursive mechanisms that surround them?
8) How are hyperbolic numerals treated in conversation?

## 2. What are Hyperbolic Approximative (uses of) Numerals?

For this definition we can draw upon the observations we have already made. Our basic definition is that an approximative (use of a) numeral is a (use of a) numeral where an exact number is meant to express a non-exact number. However, according to Channell (1994: 78–90), there are two types of approximative numerals, "plain" ones and hyperbolic ones. "Plain" approximative numerals[10] (Channell, 1994: 79–89) are those "where the precise number given acts as an indicator for a vague interval which is symmetrical about the number given" (p. 89), i.e. when the population of a city is said to be one million, or when a person is said to be six feet tall.[11]

---

[7] Many thanks to Andrew Skinner, Tom Rankin, Martha Lavric, Alfonso Merello-Astigarraga and Angelo Pagliardini for being my informants. For the French examples, the numbers following them in the table refer to the page in Rézeau's dictionary. They are all authentic and taken from Rézeau's novel corpus; see there for further references. Many thanks to Carmen Konzett and Philip Herdina for correcting my English.

[8] In examining questions 4 and 5, we shall pay special attention to cross-cultural similarities and differences.

[9] My hypothesis being that the program applies to low numbers on the one hand, and to high and round numbers on the other.

[10] This term is not from Channell, but was coined by us.

[11] For such plain approximative or 'approximate' uses, see also Krifka (2007).

The second type according to Channell (1994: 89–90) are approximative numerals used for exaggeration, i.e. hyperbolic approximative numerals, and this is the type we are interested in.

Following a suggestion by Philip Herdina, we might introduce a terminological distinction between "approximate" uses, i.e. Channel's "plain" approximative uses, where the real number is situated within a rather small interval that surrounds the round number given, and approximative, i.e. hyperbolic, numerals, which are related to the real number of referents in the form of an exaggeration.

Here are some characteristics that may help recognize the latter:

a) The commutability with indefinite quantifiers and with other approximative numerals:[12] whether I speak of *un petit garçon semblable à mille, à dix mille, à cent mille* or *à de nombreux, à bien des, à une infinité d'autres petits garçons* ('a little boy similar to a thousand, ten thousand, one hundred thousand or many, numerous, an infinity of other little boys'), the meaning is always the same, the only thing that varies is the degree of exaggeration, of intensification.

b) The fact that not all numerals are concerned:[13] I might say that I'll come back in *two minutes*, in *five minutes*, in *ten minutes*, in *a minute or two*, and all these expressions correspond more or less to the same vague period of time; but if I say that it starts in *seven minutes*, in *eighteen minutes* or that it lasts *thirty-seven minutes*, *eighty-eight minutes* or *one hundred and forty-one minutes*, I must be aware of the fact that these numbers will be taken literally.[14] This means that we are dealing with a norm phenomenon in the Coseriu sense (see Coseriu, 1979; Lavric, 2005), while the basic, mathematical sense of the numerals is part of the language system (see footnote 5).

c) The idiomaticity of the expressions concerned, and hence, their cross-cultural variation, which makes the inter-language comparison very interesting. For example, for rain, and also for drops of milk in a coffee, or for amounts of alcohol, etc., we have the following cross-language correspondences:[15] English *a drop or two*, French *deux gouttes*, Italian *due gocce*, German *drei Tropfen*, Spanish *cuatro gotas*; for a small walking distance, French uses *deux pas* or *trois pas*, German *drei* or *fünf Schritte*, Spanish *dos pasos* and Italian *due passi* (note the correspondence between Spanish and Italian); and if there is really a very small audience at an event or an assembly, the Spanish and the Italian speak of *quattro*

---

[12] See Luján Martínez (1994: 161).

[13] This characteristic actually also holds for "plain" approximative or 'approximate' numerals. Krifka (2007) explains why this is the case, i.e. why approximative uses concern mainly 'round' numbers, which are reference points on more coarse-grained scales. Devos *et al.* (1998) relate the probability of an exact interpretation to the fine-grainedness of the scale a number belongs to.

[14] Bultinck (2005: 299) develops a similar reasoning concerning a stick either 1 m long or 1.03 m long.

[15] For a systematic overview and classification of all our examples, see Table 6.1.

*gatti, cuatro gatos* (literally'four cats'), the German of *fünf Maxeln* ('five little men'), the French of *quatre pelés et un tondu.* ('four peeled ones and one sheared one').[16]

## 3. How do Listeners Recognize Them?

Channell (1994: 79, 87–88) asks how approximative uses are identified, and her answer is that it is context and world knowledge together with the 'roundness' of the number that trigger the approximative reading. This is a correct, but rather too general, explanation. Furthermore, we have seen that approximativeness does not only concern round numbers.

As far as hyperbolic approximative numerals are concerned, they can be seen as an excellent example of Grice's conversational implicatures (see Grice, 1975/1989).[17] Listeners conclude that they must be dealing with a hyperbolic approximative use if the following conditions are fulfilled:

a) the speaker cannot possibly know the number,

and

b) the number cannot be true.[18]

When somebody uses expressions like Fr. *deux secondes, deux enjambées* (two seconds, two strides), It. *due minuti, due parole* (two minutes, two words), Sp. *te lo he dicho mil veces* (I told you a thousand times), Ger. *auf ein Wort!* ([come] for one word), it is very improbable that he has actually counted the number of steps separating him from a certain place, the number of words he is going to say, or the number of times he has repeated the same information, and it is equally improbable that he will only need two seconds to fulfil a certain task, or two minutes to be back from a certain place, or that one word will suffice to explain his query.

In a normal type of conversation, in which both partners assume that the cooperative principle is valid, the hearer will thus conclude that the numeral is to be understood in a non-literal way, that it is an instance of exaggeration, of hyperbole. He might protest about it and say, e.g. "you are exaggerating", but in general this will not be the case and he will accept it as a very common type of language game and tend not to give it a second thought.

---

[16] But French also has the expression *il n'y avait pas un chat* ('there was not even a cat').

[17] Channell (1994: 18) speaks of "vagueness by implicature".

[18] McCarthy and Carter (2004: 152–153) see impossibility or counterfactuality as an important test for hyperbole. One important point in this context is the extreme improbability of the very roundness of the numbers concerned.

## 4. What is their Function in Discourse?

Approximative numerals, and especially their idiomatic or semi-idiomatic variants, are normally hyperbolic numerals.[19] They can be hyperbolic in both senses, making a small thing, a small amount, seem even smaller, which in traditional rhetoric is called "meiosis", and they can amplify a big thing, a big number or amount, which would in turn be called "auxesis" (see McCarthy and Carter, 2004: 151).

The goal is always the same: hyperbolic language in general is all about expressivity, concretization, intensification, which is the real point in the use of hyperbolic approximative numerals.[20] The quantification itself might in some cases be utterly redundant: *envoyer quelqu'un aux cinq cents diables, aux cent mille diables, aux quatre cent mille diables* does not mean anything different from *envoyer quelqu'un au diable.*[21]

Here I would like to introduce a symbol for the two possible functions of hyperbolic approximative numerals, i.e. minimizing, which will be represented by the variable ***n***, and maximizing, which will be designated by ***N***; i.e. ***n*** is a general formula for small numbers used for meiosis, ***N*** for big (and round) numbers used for auxesis. *I'll come back in a second* would be an instance of *n*, *I told you a hundred times* would be an instance of *N*.[22] (Based on this, we will be able to give short formulae for a series of derived programs, like $1/n$ or $N+1$, which we will see later.)

Starting from the assertion that approximative numerals are very often hyperbolic numerals, a certain number of points have to be made:

- It has been stated that approximation is something that applies only to certain numbers and not to others. In fact, this is only true for its idiomatic side; but there is also a

[19] Approximative numerals in their non-idiomatic variant, i.e. plain approximative or in our new terminology 'approximate' numerals, are usually approximations of specific quantities, e.g. *forty-five minutes* to denote a time interval of three-quarters of an hour plus/minus five or ten minutes (see Krifka, 2007).

[20] The use of the numeral ten in German for expressivity purposes was studied in a short article by Langner (1989).

[21] French for: 'to send someone to 500 devils, to 100,000 devils, to 400,000 devils or simply to the devil'.

[22] And one might be tempted to introduce something like a super-mega-***N*** on the one hand and a super-mini-***n*** on the other, to account for the fact that the degree of exaggeration of approximative numeral expressions may vary from small to huge, as one and the same time span might, e.g., be designated by *two minutes* or by *one second.*

creative aspect to it.[23] In fact, I might perfectly well say: *I've told you three hundred and forty-five thousand six hundred sixty-six times not to do this!* and listeners would certainly not be tempted to take this literally, as the same mechanism of implicature as described above would apply (I cannot know the number, the number cannot be true). I shall call this type of phenomenon "pseudo-approximative uses", and it is clear that it can apply to any number whatsoever. However, this will only lead to some singular, idiosyncratic example of a nonce use here and there, and not to new idioms adopted by the whole language community.

- Approximative numerals are very often hyperbolic numerals, but not all hyperbolic numerals are approximative numerals in the sense described. For instance, there are hyperbolic numerals that do not use exact numbers, but instead expressions such as *dozens*, *hundreds*, *thousands*, etc., which are quite frequent means of expressing numerical hyperbole in different languages.[24] They do not correspond to my definition of approximative numerals and have thus not been included in the present study. But they could be included in further studies, as the two phenomena are actually quite similar.[25]
- What I have already included (see Table 6.1) are expressions for empty sets and for totality, as many of them work with exact numerals (ex. *not a penny*, *vingt-quatre heures sur vingt-quatre*, 24/24 hours) and as they show the same features of hyperbolicity as the core integral number expressions.[26]

Before moving on to the numbers and the types of nouns concerned, let us touch on the question of idiomaticity. What is striking about hyperbolic approximative numerals is the number of variants that exist for most expressions, which means that their idiomaticity has to be seen as a

[23] McCarthy and Carter (2004: 150–151) show that hyperbolic expressions in general are subject to a dichotomy between conventionalized, "dead" uses and new, creative, idiosyncratic findings that resemble very much the one that is known to hold for metaphors.

[24] See their study (for English) in Channell (1994: 90–91), as well as in McCarthy and Carter (2004). Note that in French there is a special type of expressions: *une dizaine* (about 10), *une douzaine* (about 12), *une quinzaine* (about 15), *une vingtaine* (about 20), *une trentaine* (about 30), *une quarantaine* (about 40), *une cinquantaine* (about 50), *une soixantaine* (about 60), *une centaine* (about 100), *un millier* (about 1,000), which is an approximation, but not a hyperbole program (see Channell, 1994: 93–94, based on Grevisse, 1975).

[25] This could lead to the inclusion of expressions such as *tons*, *light years*, *centuries*, *aeons* (see McCarthy and Carter, 2004: 176), i.e. plural forms of very big counting units. But then we would be leaving the field of numerical expressions.

[26] This again is an aspect of hyperbolicity that could be related to other quantitative expressions with a strong percentage of hyperbolic uses like *all* or *none*, but this would definitely lead us too far. However, the specialized literature about such expressions can be very helpful when studying our approximative numerals (e.g. Stempel, 1980, 1983).

relative one, an idiomaticity that allows for several variants, although excluding many others.[27] See the following examples:

(11) Fr. *à cent à l'heure* = *à deux cents à l'heure* = *à trois cents à l'heure* = *à mille à l'heure* = *à cent mille à l'heure*[28]
'at 100/200/300/1,000/100,000 [kilometers] per hour'

(12) Sp. *cien veces* = *quinientas veces* = *mil veces* = *cien mil veces*
'100/500/1,000/100,000 times'

(13) It. *cento volte* = *mille volte* = *un milione di volte*
'100/1.000/1,000,000 times'

(14) Fr. *cent fois* = *mille fois* = *dix mille fois* = *trente-six mille fois*
'100/1,000/10,000/36,000 times'

(15) Ger. *Es steht eins zu hundert* = *eins zu tausend* = *eins zu einer Million*
'the probability is 1: 100, 1: 1,000, 1: 1,000,000'

(16) Engl. *a moment* = *a second* = *a minute* = *a tick* = *two ticks* = *two seconds* = *two minutes* = *a minute or two*

There are of course completely idiomatic expressions with numbers, like Fr. *être/se mettre sur son trente-et-un* (to be/to put oneself on one's thirty-one) (to be very well dressed, to dress sumptuously) or *haut comme trois pommes*, (three apples high, referring to a person's height) which have been included at the end of Table 6.1 – because they might be interesting to see and to compare across languages – but are not really the focal point of the present study.[29]

## 5. What Types of Nouns are Concerned?

The types of nouns concerned by approximative numeral uses can be seen in the columns of Table 6.1. They are quite similar in the five languages I have studied. Not very surprisingly, a

---

[27] For French, Rézeau's (1993) dictionary is an extremely valuable source, as it gives precise information about the relative frequency of the expressions concerned. We have taken into account this frequency in our overall table by printing in **bold the most frequent**, i.e. the standard, **variants**, leaving in plain text the less frequent expressions (e.g. *à/en deux enjambées* [in two strides] is more frequent than *à/en trois/quatre enjambées* [in 3/4 strides], *trois fois rien* [three times nothing] is standard compared to *six foix rien* [six times nothing], etc.). This kind of distinction could of course only be introduced for French, as our methodology for the other languages does not allow frequency counts.

[28] See also It.: *alla velocità della luce*, 'at light speed'.

[29] A good collection of these idiomatic expressions with numbers in French is the book by Bologne (1994). Rézeau (1993) has also collected a great number of these expressions. We take them into account, for all our languages, by adding an annex to our overall table (see part 6 of Table 6.1).

large majority of these represent measuring units[30] of different types, namely:

- Iteration, Repetition: *times*
- Probability: *chances*
- Distance(s): *steps*, *meters*, *miles*
- Time: *seconds*, *minutes*, *hours*, *days*, *years*
- Money: *pennies*, *cents*, *dollars*

Apart from this, there are a few "special programs" which are smaller, but recurrent in several languages (see the last column of Table 6.1). These include drops, words and persons present (see above, section 2).

What is striking, however, is the very concrete possibility to use many of the approximative numerals with a vast range of different noun types, virtually with any type of countable noun (see column (a) of Table 6.1). The following collection of examples is only in French, as I have extracted them from Rézeau's (1993) dictionary in order to ensure authentic contexts.[31] (Similar examples could certainly be found in other languages, which could be one of the aims of further studies in the field.)

(17) Elle passa entre les meubles qui encombraient son chemin en **deux** tours de hanche. Le mouvement était souple et preste, et mou en même temps.
'She passed between the furniture that stood in her way in two turns of [her] hips. The movement was elastic and quick, and soft at the same time.'

(18) – Vous en faites bien des histoires, pour **trois** brins de lavande!
'What a fuss you are making of three blades of lavender!'

(19) ... un pastis double troublé de **trois** gouttes d'eau
'a double 'pastis' troubled by three drops of water'

(20) Des petits films pathétiques qui sortaient dans **trois** salles.
'Small pathetical films that were shown in three cinemas'

(21) ... être le point de mire de **cent** yeux malveillants et sévères.
'to be the focus point of a hundred ill-willing and strict eyes'

(22) Ténèbres et silence ne me valaient rien. Si je m'aventurais, l'effroi m'arrivait au galop. **Cent** démons se donnaient rendez-vous dans ma chambre.

---

[30] Eschenbach (1995) studies these measuring units, and she distinguishes among them two categories: "*abstract measuring units*" ("abstrakte Maßeinheiten", 1995: 55) like *meters, kilograms* and *hectares*, and "*concrete measuring units*" ("konkrete Maßeinheiten") based on parts of the human body, like *steps*, *fingers*, *stone-throws*, etc. It seems that the latter should be especially frequent with approximative numerals, as they belong to the same order of things, see the "distance" section (column c) of Table 6.1. As for the "money" section (column e), it is interesting to note the number of old currencies represented, while there seems to be not a single expression related to the euro.

[31] Remember that Rézeau is working on a large corpus of novels in colloquial French.

'Darkness and silence did not help me. Did I step forward, panic would come galloping on me. A hundred daemons would come together in my bedroom.'

These examples show that approximative uses have to be considered as a possibility inherent in certain numerals, independent of their combination with specific noun types. This is true for small as well as for big numbers, for ***n*** and for ***N***.

## 6. Which Numbers are Concerned?

My first hypothesis was that the numbers concerned should be of two types: low numbers on the one hand, and high round numbers on the other, corresponding to the two basic hyperbolic functions of minimizing and maximizing (meiosis and auxesis). But in fact, there is also a certain range of "middle" numbers, from 7 to 20 or 40, which can be used approximately to designate considerable amounts, considerable numbers. In fact, in these middle numbers more than in others, approximativity depends on the context, and they are more likely to have a high percentage of non-approximative uses. What also depends on the context is the choice between meiosis and auxesis, between minimizing and maximizing. Fr. *parler à quelqu'un à trois pas* 'to speak to somebody at [a distance of] three steps' seems to correspond to a considerable number in comparison with our habits, while It. *a cento passi di qui* 'a hundred steps from here' minimizes the distance to be covered. In fact, *a hundred* is the highest numeral to be used either as *n* or as *N* (see Table 6.1).[32]

For my reference language French, where my corpus, based on Rézeau (1993), can claim to be representative, I have tried to establish an overview of approximative numerals weighted by their importance (Figure 6.1). I have included only integral numbers and represented the relative

0 1 2 3 4 5 7

10 12 15 20 36 99 100

999 1000 1001 9 999 10 000 99 999 100 000

1 000 000 1 000 000 000

**Figure 6.1.** Overview of French approximative numerals (only integral numbers, weighted by importance).

[32] While French *trente-six* '36' is invariably associated with maximizing.

importance of the numeral as an approximator by its size in the graphic. Of course this is only impressionistic, but it can give a first overview of the numbers we shall have to deal with.[33]

Figure 6.1 shows the importance of each numeral in the totality of approximative uses in a given text corpus. What could be done to complete this, would be to include the percentage of approximative uses of each numeral in comparison to its total number of uses and thus to its non-approximative uses.[34]

In my comments about the different approximative numbers, I shall follow this overview for the integral numbers, distinguishing between low, middle and high numbers. But the whole list in fact starts with zero, and that is why the first category will be the ways to express the empty set. This order is also in accordance with the plurilingual Table 6.1. What is added in Table 6.1 are the non-integral numbers, i.e. fractions and percentages, which will be treated here as the last category. Of course, fractions and percentages also have minimizing and maximizing variants, and they especially include expressions of totality – which will result for this part of the contribution in a movement from empty set to totality, and even to more-than-totality, as we shall see.

### 6.1. Empty set (see 1. in Table 6.1)

The main program for expressing the empty set can be rendered as **0** = ¬ **1*n***. In all the languages I have studied, the notion of "nothing" can be expressed through the negation of one, plus a very small counting unit.[35] (I am here giving a series of examples for each type of numerical expression I describe. For a more complete collection see Table 6.1).

(23) Fr. *n'avoir pas un sou/pas un kopeck, être sans un, sans un centime/radis*
'not to have one sou/one kopeck, to be without one, without a cent/a radish'
It. *non avere un soldo/una lira/un centesimo*
'not to have a coin, a lira, a cent'
Sp. *no tener ni un duro/ni un céntimo*
'not to have a five-pesetas-coin/not to have a cent'
Ger. *nicht einen (einzigen) Groschen haben, keinen roten Heller wert sein*
'not to have a (single) cent, not to be worth a red small coin'
Engl. *I haven't got a cent* = *I haven't got a single penny*

---

[33] And it could in a further step be compared with similar overviews for English, German, Italian and Spanish, which would, I think, reveal a great similarity but also certain significant differences.

[34] Such a study was done by McCarthy and Carter (2004: 179–180) for certain English hyperbolic quantitative expressions.

[35] Note that in this case **n** does not represent the number (as the number is *one* in all such expressions), but that it represents a very small counting unit.

In English, very interestingly, there is a similar program but with two instead of one: $\mathbf{0} = \neg\, \mathbf{2n}$: *I havent't got tuppence* = *I haven't got two d.* But the richest language for this kind of expressions seems to be Italian, since we have: *non capisco un'acca, non ho un cavolo, non vedo un fico secco*, and in general *non ... un cazzo/un cavolo* with different verbs.[36]

### 6.2. Low numbers (see 2. in Table 6.1)

In the domain of low numbers (ranging basically from one to five) most languages operate preferably with *two* and *three* (see the extensive collection of examples in Table 6.1),[37] but here English has got a special idiosyncrasy, as its preference clearly goes towards *one or two, a ... or two* (in the sense of a few).[38] This is very interesting, as this program of coordination or juxtaposition of two consecutive (or near) numbers to express approximation also exists in other languages, but with a different effect. If we take French examples like *deux ou trois, trois ou quatre, quatre ou cinq*, or in the juxtaposition variant *deux trois, trois quatre, quatre cinq*, and also similar expressions with "middle" numbers like *sept ou huit, dix ou douze, douze ou vingt, trente ou quarante*, the effect in all these cases is approximation, but never hyperbole. In all these cases the real number cannot be very far from the range that is being indicated. With English *one or two*, however, we have an expression that is clearly used with a minimizing, hyperbolically exaggerating purpose.

### 6.3. "Middle" numbers (see 3. in Table 6.1)

"Middle" numbers, i.e. the ones ranging more or less from seven to anything beyond a hundred, are used to express hyperbolically a considerable number in cases where the expected number would be very low, often only one.

For instance, very recently, I witnessed a discussion (in German) where the president of our faculty's curriculum committee complained about having received **seven** different proposals for curricula from department X (while of course it should be normal that a department first agrees on a single common curriculum proposal before sending it to the committee). One participant then asked a question that several of us were asking themselves, i.e. whether "seven" had been meant literally or as a pleasant exaggeration (knowing department X, one could actually not be so

[36] 'I don't understand an "h", I don't have a cabbage, I don't see a dry fig, not a ... penis, not a ... cabbage.'

[37] Five is important too, but only because of its combination with minutes.

[38] For a discussion of this expression as an approximator, see Bultinck (2005: 293–294, 298–299). Bultinck considers the possibility that *a/one ( ... ) or two* might even denote four or more, but he considers it less likely than a reference corresponding to the literal meaning of the expression.

sure . . . ). And it turned out that the latter had been the case, in fact they had sent in two or three proposals, still far too many. This episode is an interesting example of a metalinguistic negotiation about the approximativeness of a numeral, and it showed that seven can actually be used in a non-literal way, but that it is a less current number for approximation and might give rise to misunderstanding.

This possibility with seven might be due to the fact that it is seen as the perfect number (see biblical and religious traditions), which shows in the following French example:

(24) *elle avait [ . . . ] l'élégance de* ***sept*** *Grace Kelly . . .* (Rézeau, 1993: 140)
'She had the elegance of seven Grace Kellys'

Other "middle" numbers to be used approximatively are 10, 15 and 20, which shows that in the middle range roundness is already an important criterion. One more important number is 12, which is prominent because it is the basis of earlier counting systems (so it **was** round in its time).[39]

But above all, the middle numbers host a very curious French idiosyncrasy, which is the use of thirty-six (*trente-six*) as an approximator, in expressions like our ex. (6): *Il n'y a pas trente-six façons de voir la chose* ('there aren't thirty-six ways of looking at the thing'). This is a very common way of expression in French, so common that it has spread to affect other numbers, since we also find 36,000, and even 46,000 and 56,000 used in a similar way.

The formula for it would be: $\neg\,\mathbf{36} = \neg\,\boldsymbol{N} = \mathbf{1}$. The existence of 36 ( = many) variants or reasons of, or ways of seeing, something is negated, which means, there is only one variant, or one reason, or one way of seeing the thing in question.

Why thirty-six is idiomatically used for this kind of assertion, is a mystery that still has to be solved. Thirty-six is not a round number, but it is three dozen. It is the number of cases of roulette (leaving out the zero). Maybe it is only a codification of a pseudo-exact use, but maybe further research will show us a clear explanation. Be it what it be, this explanation must go back to before 1306, since this is the year of the first written record (in *Joinville, St. Louis*) of the expression according to the 1994 edition of the "Trésor de la langue française".[40]

[39] Channell (1994: 84) points out "the importance of 12 in Western European cultures", and she goes as far as writing (1994: 94): "12 and 15 count as round in the French system"; probably because of the existence of expressions like Fr. *une douzaine* ('about 12'), *une quinzaine* ('about 15').

[40] By the way, there might be more such mysteries, as some Spanish informants assert that in Spanish, 'twenty-seven' (*veintisiete*) and 'eighty' (*ochenta*) might have systematic approximative uses. I am still looking for confirmation of this fact.

## 6.4. High round numbers (see 4. in Table 6.1)

For middle numbers, and for high numbers even more, the major criterion for the possibility of approximative uses is roundness. Therefore, we have to ask what a round number is. The simplest answer would of course be: a round number is a power of 10.[41] But this is true only with our counting systems, where 10 is the basis. In other counting systems, there are other round numbers, always depending on the basis of the system.[42] We do not have to go very far in order to see an example of this, as our own measuring system for time does not function on the basis of 10, but on the basis of 60 (and 12, and 24, etc.). And consequently, for temporal units, *5*, *10*, *15*, *30* and *60* (and *a quarter* and *a half*) are rounder than *a hundred*, *a thousand* or *ten thousand* and thus more prone to approximative uses.[43]

A special program for maximizing even more would be the multiplication of two high numbers (**$N \times N'$**), which produces expressions like Fr. *voir trente-six mille chandelles* (to see 36,000 candles), *envoyer quelqu'un aux quatre cent mille diables* (to send someone to the 400,000 devils).

The importance of *a hundred, a thousand, ten thousand, a hundred thousand, a million* and *a billion* for numeric hyperbole is a constant in all five languages I have studied, and certainly in many more. It seems, however, that in English this program is more restricted than in other languages: following my informants it works normally with *times*, but much less with distances, money, etc. – see Table 6.1, where English expressions are lacking in the corresponding columns.

A further aspect that has to be pointed out in the context of high round numbers, is two derived programs that exist in several languages and that can be described as **$N - 1$** and **$N + 1$**. The most

---

[41] Sigurd (1988) is a very interesting linguistic contribution entitled: "Round numbers". Sigurd cooperated with a mathematician when writing it, and he is able to give a rather complicated formula that accounts for the fact that, e.g., 150 is rounder than 175. This is interesting, but not really relevant to approximative numerals, as we do not find any of these intermediate cases among them, no 125 or 250, but only simple and clear cut powers of 10. Channell (1994: 81–83) quotes Rosch (1975) to say that round numbers, i.e. multiples of 10, serve as cognitive referent points in the context of the numerical system, in relation to which other numbers are positioned: "in a natural category such as numbers, not all members are equivalent. Certain members of the category serve as reference points to which other members are related" (Channell, 1994: 83). Krifka (2007) explains degrees of salience – and thus of roundness – in numbers by the granularity of the scales they are part of, i.e. 100 is part of a more coarse-grained scale than 150 and must thus be rounder.

[42] See Luján Martínez (1994); see also Channell (1994: 84), based on Menninger (1969). She points out that "six feet is a RPN [reference point number] quantity in Britain and North America, when talking about people's heights" (1994: 84).

[43] For a study about approximative time expressions (but only with the approximator *around*) see Devos *et al.* (1998).

common one is $N-1$, which gives rise to approximators such as 99, 999, 9,999, and also 99.9 and 99.99 (which, strictly speaking, would be $N-0.1$ and $N-0.01$, i.e. subtracting one from the last digit from the right), very prominent with percentages and chances (see below). $N+1$ is a smaller program with one variant in French: *mille et une* (clearly related to the book, as it is much more frequent in the feminine and is generally used with *et*, whereas the normal form in counting would be *mille un*),[44] and two variants in English, *a hundred and one* and *a million and one* – all these expressions being used above all to refer to a great variety.

## 6.5. Non-integral numbers (fractions and percentages) (see 5. in Table 6.1)

Approximation is not restricted to integral numbers. Fractions and percentages, too, offer important and interesting possibilities for hyperbolic uses of exact numbers. As for integral numbers, fraction approximators can work in both directions, minimizing and maximizing. A third program that is often expressed through fractions is totality and more-than-totality. All these variants can be described by mathematical formulae with $\boldsymbol{n}$ and $\boldsymbol{N}$.

*6.5.1. Minimizing.* The basic formula for minimizing through fractions is $\mathbf{1/N = n}$. A very small number or quantity can be expressed by a fraction with the numerator 1 and a high and round denominator. See the following examples from French and Spanish: Fr. *le quart* ('1/4'), *le dixième* ('1/10'), *le centième* ('1/100'), *le millième* ('1/1,000'), *le millionième* ('1/1,000,000'); Sp. *la millonésima parte* ('1/1,000,000'), *la milésima parte* ('1/1,000'), *la centésima parte* ('1/100'), *la décima parte* ('1/10'), *la cuarta parte* ('1/4').

A related program would be the expression of nothing through the negation of such a fraction; i.e. one variant of $\mathbf{0} = \neg \boldsymbol{n}$ is $\mathbf{0} = \neg\ \mathbf{1/N}$. In French, e.g. *pas un* ('not a ... ') can be intensified to become *pas le millionième d'un* ('not 1/1,000,000 of a ... '). This amounts to reasoning "a fortiori": if I haven't seen even the smallest part of a policeman, I haven't seen a policeman either. And if I haven't got a cent, I haven't got a euro or a pound either. This is a way of presenting unpleasant things ironically, making them seem less unpleasant through wit and humour.

If we remember the special maximizing program $\boldsymbol{N \times N'}$, it is not surprising that there is a special minimizing program through fractions that corresponds to the formula $1/\boldsymbol{N} \times \mathbf{1/N'}$, featuring in French expressions like *le quart de la moitié* ('1/4 of 1/2'), *le quart du quart* ('1/4 of 1/4'), *le quart du centième* ('1/4 of 1/100'), *un quart de millième de seconde* ('1/4 of 1/1,000 of a second'), *un millième de millième de seconde* ('1/1,000 of 1/1,000 of a second').

---

[44] Here are the results of a Google research: *mille et une* 121,000, *mille et un* 74,000, *mille une* 635, *mille un* 4,510.

*6.5.2. Maximizing.* Maximizing through fractions is something that is most often related to the $N-1$ program we have already described in the "high and round numbers" section. The fraction variant of it would be $\mathbf{N-1/N}$, and it is common in many languages: see Fr. *neuf fois sur dix* ('nine times out of ten'), *neuf chances sur dix* ('nine chances out of ten'); Ger. *in neun von zehn Fällen* ('in nine cases out of ten'); Engl. *ninety-nine point nine percent certain*; Sp. *el noventa y nueve por ciento* ('99 %').

*6.5.3. Totality and more-than-totality.* One very important function of fractions in hyperbole is the expression of totality, as totality can be expressed in a very concrete, striking way through formulae of the $\mathbf{N/N}$ type. Here different languages share similar, but not completely identical idiomatic expressions like Fr. *vingt-quatre heures sur vingt-quatre, sept jours sur sept, douze mois sur douze, trois cent soixante-cinq jours par an* ('24 hours out of 24, 7 days out of 7, 12 months out of 12, 365 days a year') and Sp. *veinticuatro horas al día, siete días a la semana, cincuenta y dos semanas al año* ('24 hours a day, 7 days a week, 52 weeks a year').

This kind of expression also allows a kind of absurd climax, in expressions like Fr. *vingt-cinq heures sur vingt-quatre* ('twenty-five hours out of twenty-four'), which corresponds to a formula $\mathbf{N+1/N}$ and thus expresses more-than-totality. These expressions are typical exponents of the absurd, humoristic side of hyperbole; e.g. Fr. *avoir onze doigts de pied dans la tombe, le mouton à cinq pattes* ('to have eleven toes in the tomb', 'the five-legged sheep'). Even a further climax cannot be ruled out; see Engl. *thirty-six hours a day*, It. *quarantotto ore su ventiquattro* ('fourty-eight hours out of twenty-four').

Before going on to the cognitive, discursive and conversational implications of approximative numerals, let us mention a special program that exists in all five languages: it is the replacement of a numeral by a letter, like a variable in mathematics, see Fr. *X fois, pour la énième fois, à la vitesse grand V* ('*X* times', 'for the *n*th time', 'at speed *V*'), Sp. *equis veces, equis* ('*X* times', '*X*'), Ger. *zig, X, zigmal, X Mal, zum X. Mal* ('-ty', '*X*', '-ty times', '*X* times', 'for the *X*th time'), It. *per l'ennesima volta* ('for the *n*th time'), and Engl. (a little bit different, but related) *umpteen*, *umpteen times* and *zillions*. Although it goes beyond what I have defined as approximative uses of exact numbers, it is related to them especially through the use of hyperbole and shows very clearly the complicated patterns of similarities and differences between languages we can find in this highly idiomatic area.[45]

Of course, the lists I have given of hyperbolic approximative numerals in French, German, English, Spanish and Italian can only be tentative. A lot of work remains to be done to complete these lists first for the languages mentioned, and then for more and other languages

---

[45] Rézeau dedicates one whole chapter of his dictionary to this phenomenon (1993: 225–239).

and cultures.[46] It would also be very interesting to carry out a quantitative study measuring the quantitative importance of the phenomenon. Actually, hyperbolic approximative use might well be the most frequent type for certain numerals, which might in turn be the most frequently used numbers.[47]

One could also ask whether there are other linguistic items that are preferred in a hyperbolic variant, as was done in a contribution by Landheer (2007).

And finally, one could ask whether the existence of approximative, hyperbolic uses should affect the semantic description of the numerals concerned. I have discussed and answered this question (negatively) in an earlier paper (Lavric, 2007) and shall not go into any more detail here (see footnote 5).

What is still to be done here is to provide an exploration of the cognitive basis of approximative uses, a discussion of the discursive mechanisms that surround them and finally of the way they are treated in conversation. For this part of my contribution, fortunately, I shall be able to draw on a small amount of existing specialized literature in the fields to be presented.

## 7. What is the Cognitive Basis of Approximative uses?

When talking about the cognitive bases of approximative uses, one core question might be the nature of the numbers concerned. Why is it that certain types of numbers are prone to hyperbolic

---

[46] Here are a few Turkish examples of hyperbolic approximative numerals that my colleague Manfred Kienpointner has established with the help of one of his Turkish students (Yüksel Güsel; many thanks to both!):

- *iki adém*: 'two steps'
- *üç beş kere/üç dört kere*: 'three five times'/'three four times' (' = two or three times')
- *bir dakika*: 'one minute';
- *beş kuruşum kalmadı*: 'I haven't got five kurusch' ( = small unit of old money)
- *Sana bin kere söyledim*: 'I told you a thousand times'
- *Sana yüz kere sordum*: 'I have asked you a hundred times'
- *Ikide bir soru soruyorsun*: 'you are asking two questions in one' (' = ask something many times')
- *yirmi dört saat boyunca uyumadım*: I haven't slept for twenty-four hours

There is no direct equivalent in Turkish for Ger. *es ist fünf vor zwölf* ('it is five to twelve') and Fr. *aller aux quatre cent diables* ('to go to the four hundred devils').

[47] Meninger (1969) (quoted in Channell, 1994: 83–86) describes how "some numbers seem almost to lose their literal meaning (Meninger says the meaning 'fades') when they are frequently used to designate a vague quantity [ . . . ].[ . . . ] the exact number meaning 'fades', leaving the signification 'a few' or, more often 'many'" (Channell, 1994: 85–86).

approximative uses, and others are not? In order to find out, we shall have to examine the concept of "low number" and the concept of "round number", as they are seen by cognitive psychology.

On low numbers, one interesting study is the one by Pannain (1997), who claims that *one*, *two*, *three* and maybe *four* are learned and represented differently with respect to the other numbers. Children first acquire the concepts of *one*, *two*, *three* and *many*, long before they learn the counting operation that is the basis for all other numbers (see Hurford, 1987: 141). These first numeric concepts are thus learned by experience and not by counting.

For round numbers, I can refer to Rosch's (1975) study (quoted in Channell, 1994: 81–83), who found that round numbers are cognitively more salient than others; actually they are reference point numbers and such

> reference point numbers [...] [are] more 'easily' accessible, and [...] faster to interpret [...]. [They] require less processing than other numbers, and, therefore, [are] suitable for use in approximations. (Channell, 1994: 83).

Moreover, all parents I've spoken to agree that their children acquired the round numbers 100 and 1,000 long before being able to count as high as that. Of course, they used them not as exact numeric designations, but as approximative expressions to denote high quantities. So it seems that the approximative meaning comes first in language acquisition, and that big round numbers might be represented differently from other, "ordinary" numbers. They might be, just like small numbers, part of the empirically learned and represented numerical system which precedes the operation of counting and is independent of it.[48] In effect,

> [According to] research [...] concerning the concept of number in human cognition [...] evidence is forthcoming that our sense of numbers rests on two distinct cognitive systems: First, a nonsymbolic system of quantity estimation, addition and subtraction that can also be found with animals and infants, and secondly, a symbolic system resting on counting that appears to be genuinely human [...]. The first system is inherently approximative, and it mostly shows up with larger numbers. [...] The two systems are related to each other, but they fulfil separate roles, and we cannot say that one – say, the approximative one of quantity estimation – is to be preferred over the other. (Krifka, 2007: 114–115)

---

[48] Here are some more cognitive-psychological studies on numerals, which are discussed in detail in Lavric (2007) and will therefore only be touched upon here:

- Brown (1979) studied the numbers from 0 to 9 with the method of the semantic differential and he shows that numbers have a strong connotative meaning.
- Bromme (1990) shows that there are even numbers that are seen as more even, and odd numbers that are seen as more odd than others.
- Both studies show that numbers convey information that is not purely numerical in the mathematical sense.

## 8. What are the Discursive Mechanisms that Surround Them?

Another important question concerning approximative numerals is the ultimate "raison d'être" of this kind of mechanism. Why are we using all these hyperboles? Why can't we simply stick to the bare facts? And why do listeners accept without protesting when someone assures them that the shop is *à deux pas d'ici* ('two steps from here'), or that s/he has repeated the same gesture *a thousand times*? One important reason for the use of hyperbolic numerals might be politeness, which tells us, e.g. to minimize the size of imposition and to maximize praise of others and profit for others (see Leech, 1983).

But an interesting answer to the why of hyperbole is given by Stempel (1983) in his article entitled"Zur Rolle der Hyperbolik in der Alltagsrhetorik" (The Role of Hyperbole in Everyday Rhetoric). He explains the use of hyperbole by the co-construction of identities in conversation. All participants collaboratively negotiate their "faces", the presentation of their self, which is very often done through narratives and which definitely requires a certain amount of exaggeration (see also Stempel, 1980). This does not mean that participants are deliberately boasting, but that they are trying to make themselves seem interesting. This can be done through positive, and also through negative exaggeration. Actually, we are ready to present ourselves as a complete failure, rather than admitting that we are just normal and average.[49] Being average or just like everybody else would not be something worth telling or worth talking about. In fact, there are two aspects to it: we want to be interesting as a person, and we want to be perceived as a good narrator. So the narrator sometimes exaggerates at the expense of the character. The listeners will know anyway that it is just a story. That is why we embellish and exaggerate, the main point being that the story should not be banal. The realities we thus construct may not correspond 100% to "objective" reality, but they correspond to our subjective reality, to the way we have lived the facts, and it is this subjective reality that will assure the empathy and the sympathy of our interlocutors.[50]

One important point in it is also the complicity of the listeners: when interpreting a hyperbole, they switch to another mode of understanding, another mode of reception which might be compared to that of readers of fiction.[51] This leads us to our last point, the way in which hyperbolic numerals are treated in conversation.

---

[49] Stempel (1980) is a comment on the example of a narrator who very cleverly presents himself as a complete loser ("the eternal second" in his area of specialty), maybe fishing for pity, or trying to appear interesting, while "outside the narration" he seems to be rather happy with himself (in fact he is a local champion).

[50] See McCarthy and Carter (2004: 156) reporting Norrick (1982): "the speaker [...] [produces] the hyperbole as a personal, affectively involved, overstated simulacrum of reality."

[51] See McCarthy and Carter (2004: 152): "hyperbole is not heard as an act of lying."

## 9. How are Hyperbolic Numerals Treated in Conversation?

Further research about the topic of hyperbolic approximative numerals in several languages and cultures could go into the direction pre-figured by McCarthy and Carter's article (2004) entitled: "'There's millions of them': hyperbole in everyday conversation". The study combines a theoretical overview of hyperbole studies in pragmatics with an empirical analysis of a series of conversational episodes; a large part of the hyperboles analysed are numerical in nature. They are partly of the *hundreds/thousands*-type and partly of our own approximative numerals-type. Moreover, McCarthy and Carter (2004) is the only study I know of[52] that acknowledges both the auxesis and the meiosis type of numeric hyperbole and gives examples of both.[53]

So what can be asked and what can be seen when looking at conversational episodes with hyperbolic numerals? McCarthy and Carter (2004), e.g., carefully analyse listener responses. They show that the literal and the hyperbolic meaning of the expression are both present and that the tension between them creates a complicity, a game, a kind of collaborative fiction (see also Stempel, 1980) between interlocutors. Listeners usually signal their uptake through laughing or other signals, and they may even enter the language game and play it, too, or they may comment on it metalinguistically.

> [...] hyperbolic expressions usually pass without challenge by listeners, who accept them as creative intensifications for evaluative or affective purposes such as humour and irony, and who make their own supportive contributions to the figure of speech (McCarthy and Carter, 2004:150).

This makes the hyperbolic exchange a kind of conversational island, for which a shift in footing usually occurs (from serious to playful or non-literal conversation), which can be shown through various signals uttered by the speaker (*though*, *d'you know*, *erm* ... ).

In conclusion, we can quote McCarthy and Carter's statement (2004: 153) that

> any full account of hyperbole must have an interactive dimension. [...] hyperbole is validated in interaction and can only be described adequately by including the listener's contributions to the emergent act.

---

[52] Apart from a small remark and one single example of meiosis in Channell (1994: 90).

[53] Their examples are quoted and commented on later by Norrick (2004), whose study is less relevant for our subject, as it concentrates on extreme case formulations – and the vast majority of approximative numerals are hyperboles, but not extreme cases. In fact extreme cases have received more attention in hyperbole research than other types of hyperbole that are seen as less strong (see e.g. Schemann, 1994). Maybe approximative numerals are a good counterexample to this assertion, as they can reach very high degrees of exaggeration without being confined to an extreme.

Another relevant point in McCarthy and Carter's work is the fact that it is a corpus study. They draw on the CANCODE corpus of everyday English conversation they themselves have compiled, and try to show how corpus linguistics can help in conversation analysis. They choose a series of linguistic items that seem hyperbole-prone (*dozens of, millions of, a hundred, a thousand, masses of, heaps of, hours, years, endless, gigantic* and the like, a total of 36 expressions, of which five are approximative numerals) and look up the occurrences they find in their corpus. This allows them to give a statistical overview of the proportion of hyperbolic uses in total uses of a certain form, which goes from 100% (*dozens of, zillions of* ) to 30% for *a million*, 5% for *a thousand* and 3% for *a hundred*.

This could give rise to a further research program: the expressions presented here, with maybe the additional category of approximators such as *hundreds, thousands*, etc., may serve as an input to a conversational corpus study in languages other than English: French, Spanish, Italian, German.[54] The first thing to do would be to provide the statistical overview for each expression, to see how much it tends to approximative usages and how many of its uses are still exact ones. And finally, one could have a close look at a series of conversational episodes to see how the hyperbolic uses of numerals are integrated in the interaction.

One point that seems to me very promising is to look at their interaction with other markers of quantitative approximation, e.g. rounders[55] like *about, or so* and others, which often occur together with hyperbolical numerals. I shall illustrate what I mean with an example from McCarthy and Carter (2004: 170, ex. 8):

(25) < $1 > I live in Nottingham now cos I came here to study at the university.
**Been here for about a thousand years.**
< $2 > [laughs]
< $1 > Em. or it feels like it.

Why does the speaker add *about* to his/her approximative numeral? And why does it create a comical effect? My interpretation would be that the rounder *about* generates the expectation that the speaker will really be as exact as he can in the quantitative information he is about to give, i.e. that he/she would use an 'approximate', but not a hyperbolical numerical expression (see footnote 19). The completely absurd and exaggerated number that follows gives rise to a discrepancy which is perceived as a punch line. Thus, the rounder introducing the hyperbolic numeral helps to reinforce the humorous effect, which is shown by the laughter. As the same happens in another of

---

[54] English can be said to have been done already by McCarthy and Carter (2004).

[55] This term was introduced by Prince *et al.* (1982), see Mihatsch's contribution in this volume. Channell calls them "vague additives" (1994: 18) or "approximators" (1994: 44–45). The latter term is also used by Devos *et al.* (1998).

McCarthy and Carter's examples (p. 170, ex. 14), it would be worthwhile to see whether there is a general pattern behind it and whether this also holds for other languages and cultures.

## 10. Conclusion

Approximative numerals are very often hyperbolic numerals. They basically come in two types, small numbers and high round numbers, and they are idiomatic only to a certain point – though these idiomaticities can give rise to interesting comparisons between languages. They have preferences for certain types of nouns, but they can basically occur with any countable noun. They follow certain rhetoric schemes that can be described by formulae like $\mathbf{0} = \neg\, \mathbf{1}\boldsymbol{n}$, $\mathbf{1}/\boldsymbol{N} \times \mathbf{1}/\boldsymbol{N}'$ or $\boldsymbol{N} + \mathbf{1}/\boldsymbol{N}$, and they do this cross-linguistically, but with some idiosyncrasies, like French *trente-six* (36). They generally use numbers that are represented differently than others and are learnt by children through experience and not through counting. They are used by speakers for exaggeration and intensification, with the aim of making their speech and themselves seem more interesting to their interlocutors. And, they are co-constructed in conversation as a special kind of non-literal footing, whose micro-effects in conversation still have to be studied in greater detail.

## References


Bernet, C. and P. Rézeau (1989). *Dictionnaire du français parlé. Le monde des expressions familières.* Paris: Seuil.

Bologne, J.-C. (1994). Les Sept merveilles. Les *expressions* chiffrées: *Jamais deux sans trois, les neuf Muses, faire la une….* Paris: Larousse.

Bromme, R. (1990). "Prototypikalität bei exakt definierten Begriffen: Das Beispiel der geraden und ungeraden Zahlen". *Sprache & Kognition* **3**: 155–167.

Brown, A. S. (1979). "Implicit semantic structuring of numbers". *American Journal of Psychology* **4**: 669–679.

Bultinck, B., 2005. *Numerous meanings. The meaning of English cardinals and the legacy of Paul Grice.* Amsterdam: Elsevier (Current Research in the Semantics/Pragmatics Interface 15).

Channell, J. (1994). *Vague language.* Oxford University Press: Oxford (Describing English language).

Coseriu, E. (1979). System, Norm und 'Rede', in: Coseriu, E., *Sprache – Strukturen und Funktionen. XII Aufsätze zur allgemeinen und romanischen Sprachwissenschaft*, In Zsarb. mit Hansbert Bertsch u. Gisela Köhler hrsg. von Uwe Petersen (Tübinger Beiträge zur Linguistik 2) (3rd edition). Tübingen: Narr, 45–60.

Devos, F., P. Maesfranckx and G. De Tré (1998). "Granularity in the interpretation of *around* in approximative lexical time indications". *Journal of Quantitative Linguistics* **5**: 167–173.

Eschenbach, C. (1995). *Zählangaben – Maßangaben. Bedeutung und konzeptuelle Interpretation von Numeralia.* Wiesbaden: Deutscher Universitäts-Verlag (Studien zur Kognitionswissenschaft).

Grevisse, M. (1975). *Le bon usage.* 10th Edition. Gembloux: Duculot.

Grice, H. P. (1975/1989). "Logic and conversation", in D. Davidson and G. Harman (eds.), *The logic of grammar.* Encino/Belmont, CA: Dickenson; 64–75. again in: Cole, P. and J. L. Morgan (eds.) (1975). *Syntax and semantics 3: Speech acts.* New York: Academic Press; 41–58. and in Grice, H. P. (ed.) (1989). *Studies in the way of words.* Cambridge, MA: Harvard University Press, 22–40.

Hurford, J. R. (1987). *Language and number. The emergence of a cognitive system.* Cambridge, MA: Basil Blackwell.

Krifka, M. (2007). "Approximate interpretations of number words: A case for strategic communication", in G. Bouma, I. Krämer and J. Zwarts (eds.), *Cognitive foundations of interpretation.* Amsterdam: Koninklijke Nederlandse Akademie van Wetenschapen, 111–126.

Landheer, R. (2007). "La polysémie due à l'emploi hyperbolique", in D. Trotter (ed.), *Actes du XXIV^e Congrès International de Linguistique et de Philologie Romanes, Aberystwyth 2004. Vol. IV.* Tübingen: Niemeyer, 129–137.

Langner, H. (1989). "Das Zahlwort 'zehn' und seine Beziehungen zu semantisch verwandten Wörtern". *Sprachpflege* **38** (**3**): 29–31.

Lavric, E. (2005). "Sistema, norma y habla en la semántica de los determinantes nominales españoles", in G. Wotjak and J. Cuartero Otal (eds.), *Entre semántica léxica, teoría del léxico y sintaxis.* Frankfurt a.M. e.a.: Peter Lang, 29–39 (Studien zur romanischen Sprachwissenschaft und interkulturellen Kommunikation 22).

Lavric, E. (2007). "Les numéraux approximatifs, ou : comment se fait-il que *sept minutes* soient toujours exactement sept minutes, mais que *cinq minutes* puissent parfois être beaucoup plus ?", in D. Trotter (ed.), *Actes du XXIV^e Congrès International de Linguistique et de Philologie Romanes, Aberystwyth 2004. Vol. IV.* Tübingen: Niemeyer, 139–153.

Leech, G. N. (1983). *Principles of Pragmatics.* London/New York: Longman.

Luján Martínez, E. R. (1994). "El uso de los numerales como cuantificadores indefinidos". *Lingüística (ALFAL)* **6**: 159–166.

McCarthy, M. and R. Carter (2004). "'There's millions of them': Hyperbole in everyday conversation". *Journal of Pragmatics* **36**: 149–184.

Menninger, K. (1969). *Number words and number symbols.* Cambridge, MA: MIT Press.

Norrick, N. R. (1982). "On the semantics of overstatement", in K. Detering, J. Schmidt-Radefeldt and W. Sucharowski (eds.), *Akten des 16. Linguistischen Kolloquiums Kiel, 1981. Vol. II: Sprache erkennen und verstehen.* Tübingen: Niemeyer, 168–176.

Norrick, N. R. (2004). "Hyperbole, extreme case formulation". *Journal of Pragmatics* **36**: 1727–1739.

Pannain, R. (1997). "Pertinenze linguistiche e cognitive nello studio della categoria lessicale dei numerali", in M. Carapezza, D. Gambarara and F. Lo Piparo (eds.), *Linguaggio e cognizione. Atti del XXVIII Congresso della Società di linguistica italiana, Palermo, 27–29 ottobre 1994.* Roma: Bulzoni, 265–284.

Prince, E. F., J. Frader and J. C. Bosk (1982). "On hedging in physician-physician discourse", in R. J. Di Pietro (ed.), *Linguistics and the Professions.* Norwood, NJ: Ablex, 83–97.

Rézeau, P. (1993). *Petit Dictionnaire des chiffres en toutes lettres.* Paris: Seuil.

Rosch, E. (1975). "Cognitive reference points". *Cognitive Psychology* **7**: 532–547.

Schemann, H. (1994). "Hyperbel und Grenzwert", in A. Sabban and C. Schmitt (eds.), *Sprachlicher Alltag. Linguistik – Rhetorik – Literaturwissenschaft. Festschrift für Wolf-Dieter Stempel 7. Juli 1994.* Tübingen: Max Niemeyer, 499–502.

Sigurd, B. (1988). "Round numbers". *Language in Society* **17**: 243–252.

Stempel, W.-D. (1980). Alltagsfiktion. In: Ehlich, K. (ed.), *Erzählen im Alltag.* Frankfurt a.M., Suhrkamp (Suhrkamp Taschenbuch Wissenschaft 323), 385–402.

Stempel, W.-D. (1983). "Ich vergesse alles'. Bemerkungen zur Hyperbolik in der Alltagsrhetorik", in M. Faust, et al. (eds.), *Allgemeine Sprachwissenschaft, Sprachtypologie und Textlinguistik.* Tübingen: Narr, 87–98.

**Table 6.1.** (Hyperbolic) Approximative Numerals in French, Italian, Spanish, German and English Syntagmatic and Paradigmatic Typology.

(Very frequent expressions are printed in bold letters, in comparison with others which can also be found, but less frequently. French examples are followed by numbers which refer to Rézeau's *Dictionnaire*; for the other languages, my thanks go to Angelo Pagliardini, Alfonso Merello Astigarraga, Martha Lavric, Andrew Skinner and Tom Rankin)

| **Quantitiy/ number** | **Types of nouns** | | | | |
|---|---|---|---|---|---|
| | **(a) (Countable) Noun of any type:** ***(or small subcategories words, rain, persons present)*** | **(b) Iteration/ repetition, probability:** ***times, chances*** | **(c) Distance(s):** ***steps, meters, miles*** | **(d) Time:** ***seconds, minutes, hours, days, years*** | **(e) Money:** ***pennies, cents, dollars*** |
| **1. Empty set**[a] (often negation + one unit, or negation + very small quantity) | | | | | |
| | ***Fr*** ... **à zéro** (16–19) pas pour un sou/deux sous de ... (68)<br>***It* non ... un cavolo/un fico secco/un cazzo**<br>**zero spaccato** ( = niente niente)<br>***Sp* cero**<br>**no ... uno**<br>***Ge* nicht der hunderste Teil**<br>***En* zero tolerance**<br><br>**Words**<br>***Fr*** pas un (seul) mot (37)<br>***Ge*** nicht ein (einziges) Wort<br><br>**Rain, drops**<br>***Ge*** nicht ein Tropfen = kein einziger Tropfen | ***Ge* nicht ein (einziges) Mal** = kein einziges Mal | ***Ge* nicht einen Schritt** | ***Ge* nicht eine Minute** haben | ***Fr* (n'avoir) pas/plus un sou** (42), pas un kopeck (42)<br>'être sans un (34), *elliptic for* sans un sou, centime, radis<br>deux fois rien (65)<br>**trois fois rien** (99)<br>six fois rien (138)<br><br>***It* non avere un soldo/ una lira/un centesimo**<br><br>***Sp* no tener ni un duro/ ni un céntimo**<br><br>***Ge* nicht einen (einzigen) Groschen** |

**Table 6.1.** (*Continued*)

| **Quantitiy/ number** | **Types of nouns** | | | | |
|---|---|---|---|---|---|
| | **(a) (Countable) Noun of any type:** (*or small subcategories words, rain, persons present)* | **(b) Iteration/ repetition, probability:** *times, chances* | **(c) Distance(s):** *steps, meters, miles* | **(d) Time:** *seconds, minutes, hours, days, years* | **(e) Money:** *pennies, cents, dollars* |
| | **Persons present**<br>***It*** **non** . . . **un cane/ un'anima**<br>***Ge*** (kein Schwein)<br>***Fr*** (il n'y avait) **pas un chat** | | | | haben = keinen Groschen haben<br>**keinen roten Heller** wert sein<br><br>***En*** **not a cent**<br>**not a single penny**<br>**I haven't got a penny**<br>**I haven't got tuppence**<br>**I haven't got two d.** (*old currency*) |
| **2. Small quantity/amount** | | | | | |
| **2.1. Cardinal number** | ***Fr*** **un(e) ou deux** (45)<br>**deux** (57)<br>**deux (ou) trois** (57, 66)<br>**trois** (91)<br>**trois (ou) quatre** (100)<br>**quatre** (106)<br>quatre (ou) cinq (121)<br>cinq (ou) six (132)<br>six (ou) sept (139)<br>cinq à sept (141)<br>sept (ou) huit (142)<br>**dix** (e.g. gouttes) (151)<br>quatorze (165) | ***Fr*** **une ou deux fois/une fois ou deux** (45)<br>**deux (ou) trois fois** (66)<br>**trois fois** (99)<br>**trois (ou) quatre fois** (101)<br>quatre ou cinq fois (121)<br>cinq ou six fois (132)<br>**pas trente-six** (façons de)<br>***Sp*** tres o cuatro veces<br>***Ge*** warte **einmal** (*Austrian*) | ***Fr*** **à deux pas** (57, 59)<br>**à trois pas** (92)<br>à quatre pas (106)<br>à cinq pas (129)<br>à six pas (137)<br>**à dix pas** (152)<br>**à cent mètres** (197)<br>**à/en deux enjambées** (58)<br>à/en trois enjambées (94)<br>en quatre enjambées (110) | ***Fr*** **une seconde** (45)<br>**deux secondes** (57)<br>**trois secondes** (101)<br>**cinq secondes** (133)<br>en cinq sec(s) (133)<br>**dix secondes** (157)<br>en quinze secondes (168)<br>**une minute** (44)<br>**deux minutes** (57, 65)<br>(en) **trois minutes** (94)<br>**cinq minutes** (131)<br>cinq (ou) six minutes | ***Fr*** **un sou, un rond, une thune** (42)<br>**(à) deux sous** (57, 67–68)<br>avoir pour deux sous/ pour dix centimes de . . . (68)<br>**(à) deux ronds** (67–68)<br>deux (ou) trois sous (67)<br>**(à/de) trois sous** (101)<br>(à /de) trois balles, trois kopecks (102)<br>**(à/de) quatre sous** (122) |

<table>
<tr>
<td></td>
<td>**_Sp_ dos**<br>**dos o tres**<br>**tres**<br>**tres o cuatro**<br>**cuatro**<br>cuatro o cinco<br>cinco o seis<br>seis o siete<br>siete u ocho<br>**diez**<br>**_Ge_** ein, zwei<br>**zwei, drei**<br>**drei**<br>**_En_ a couple of**<br>**one or two**<br>**a … or two**<br>two or three<br><br>**Words**<br>**_Fr_** dire/toucher un/deux/trois mot/s à qn. de qc. (32, 57, 68, 92)<br>en un/deux mot/s (comme en cent/mille) (32–33, 71)<br>**un mot**<br>**deux mots**<br>**_It_ due parole**<br>**due cose**<br>**_Sp_ dos palabras**<br>**_Ge_ auf ein Wort!**<br>**in/mit fünf Wörtern**<br>**in fünf Worten**<br>**in drei Sätzen**<br>**_En_ can I have a word**<br><br>**Persons present**<br>**_Fr_ quatre pelés et un tondu** (121–122)<br>**_It_ quattro gatti**</td>
<td>**ein-,** (oder) **zweimal**<br>**zwei-, dreimal**<br>drei-, viermal<br>vier-, fünfmal<br>fünf-, sechsmal<br>**_En_ two or three times**</td>
<td>(être) à deux doigts de (73)<br>*(only metaphorically)*<br>à deux tours de roue (59)<br>*but also:* être/habiter à deux minutes<br>**_It_ a due passi**<br>**fare quattro passi**<br>**fare quattro salti** ( = ballare un po')<br>**a un tiro di schioppo**<br>**_Sp_ dos pasos**<br>dar **cuatro pasos** (después de comer)<br>**a dos manzanas**<br>**a tres manzanas**<br>**_Ge_ einen Schritt**<br>**drei Schritt**<br>**fünf Schritt(e)**<br>zwei Schritt vor und drei zurück<br>**hundert Schritte tun**<br>**ein(en) Katzensprung**<br>**ein(en) Hupfer** enfernt<br>ein Hupferl *(Viennese)*<br>**ein(en) Sprung** entfernt<br>**_En_ a stone-throw** from here</td>
<td>cinq (ou) dix minutes<br>**dix minutes** (156)<br>le temps de compter jusqu'à quatre (106)<br><br>**_It_ un attimo**<br>**un secondo**<br>**due minuti**<br>**cinque minuti**<br>**dieci minuti**<br>**due o tre minuti**<br>**_Sp_ un momentito**<br>**un momento**<br>**un segundo**<br>**dos segundos**<br>**tres segundos**<br>**cinco segundos**<br>**diez segundos**<br>**un minuto**<br>**dos minutos**<br>**tres minutos**<br>**cinco minutos**<br>cinco o seis minutos<br>cinco o diez minutos<br>**diez minutos**<br>**_Ge_ einen Moment**<br>ein Momenterl<br>**einen Augenblick**<br>**eine Sekunde**<br>zwei Sekunden<br>**eine Minute**<br>zwei Minuten<br>drei Minuten<br>**fünf Minuten**<br>zehn Minuten<br>ich komm **auf einen Sprung** zu dir/vorbei *(indication of time!)*</td>
<td>à cinq sous (129)<br>**(à) dix sous** (152)<br>**(à) cent balles** (198)<br>**(à/de) cent sous** (201)<br>**trois fois rien** (99)<br>six fois rien, dix fois rien<br><br>**trois francs six sous** (100)<br>deux francs six sous, cinq francs six sous<br>**_It_ due lire quattro soldi**<br>**_Sp_ tres pesetas**<br>**cuatro perras**<br>**cinco duros**<br>**_Ge_ drei Groschen**<br>**_En_ a penny or two**</td>
</tr>
</table>

**Table 6.1.** (*Continued*)

| **Quantitiy/ number** | **Types of nouns** | | | | |
|---|---|---|---|---|---|
| | **(a) (Countable) Noun of any type:** ***(or small subcategories words, rain, persons present)*** | **(b) Iteration/ repetition, probability:** ***times, chances*** | **(c) Distance(s):** ***steps, meters, miles*** | **(d) Time:** ***seconds, minutes, hours, days, years*** | **(e) Money:** ***pennies, cents, dollars*** |
| | ***Sp*** **cuatro gatos**<br>ser/haber **cinco gatos y un tambor** (en las manifestaciones)<br>***Ge*** **fünf Maxeln**<br><br>**Rain, drops**<br>***Fr*** **deux gouttes**<br>**trois gouttes**<br>***It*** **due gocce**<br>***Sp*** **cuatro gotas**<br>***Ge*** **drei Tropfen**<br>***En*** **a drop or two** | | | ***En*** **a moment**<br>**a second**<br>**a minute**<br>**two minutes**<br>**a couple of minutes**<br>**a minute or two**<br>**five minutes**<br>**ten minutes** (or so)<br>**a tick**<br>**two ticks** | |
| **2.2. Iteration/ repetition** in time or distance | | ***Fr*** deux fois (par jour … ) (65) | ***Fr*** **tous les/toutes les dix** + *indication of time or distance* (159)<br>***Ge*** **alle fünf Schritt**<br>alle fünf Meter<br>**alle zehn Schritt**<br>**alle hundert Schritt**<br>alle hundert Meter | ***Fr*** **toutes les cinq secondes** (133)<br>**tous les/toutes les dix** + *indication of time or distance* (159)<br>**toutes les trente secondes** (180)<br>toutes les quarante secondes (190) | |

| | | | | | |
|---|---|---|---|---|---|
| | | | | **toutes les deux minutes** (66)<br>**toutes les cinq minutes** (132)<br><br>***Sp* cada cinco segundos**<br>**cada diez minutos**<br>***Ge*** alle drei Sekunden<br>alle drei Minuten<br>**alle fünf Minuten**<br>alle zwei, drei Jahre<br>***En* every five minutes** (or so) | |
| **2.3. Ordinal number** | | ***Fr* (c'est) la première et la dernière fois** (47)<br>***Ge* es ist das erste und das letzte Mal**<br>**zum ersten und zum letzten Mal**<br>***En* it's the first and the last time** | | ***Ge* in der ersten Minute**<br>**aud den ersten Blick**<br>**im ersten Moment** | |
| **3. (Relatively) Considerable amount/number**[b] | | | | | |
| **3.1. Cardinal number** | ***Fr* plus d'un(e)** (39)<br>cinq (ou) six (132)<br>six (ou) sept (139)<br>cinq à sept (141)<br>**sept** (140)<br>sept (ou) huit (142)<br>huit ou dix (147)<br>neuf ou dix (150)<br>**dix** (151)<br>dix ou douze (156)<br>**douze** (161) | ***Fr* pas qu'une fois** (44)<br>**sept fois** (140)<br>**dix fois** (151)<br>dix-douze fois (156)<br>quatorze fois (166)<br>quinze fois (168)<br>**vingt fois** (171)<br>vingt-cinq fois (179)<br>trente fois (180)<br>***It* più di una volta**<br>***Sp* más de una vez** | ***Fr*** (e.g.: parler à qn.)<br>**à trois pas** (92)<br>à cinq pas (129)<br>(e.g. reconnaître qn.)<br>**à dix pas** (152)<br>**à quinze pas** (167)<br>cent coudées (199)<br>**à cent pas** (197)<br>à deux cents pas (207) | ***Fr* (dans) six mois** (139)<br>**dix ans** (153)<br>**vingt ans** (171), (*seen also as a symbol of youth*)<br>**huit jours** (147)<br>**quinze jours** (168)<br>(*not always approximative*)<br>***It* quindici giorni** | |

**Table 6.1.** (*Continued*)

| **Quantitiy/ number** | **Types of nouns** | | | | |
|---|---|---|---|---|---|
| | **(a) (Countable) Noun of any type:** ***(or small subcategories words, rain, persons present)*** | **(b) Iteration/ repetition, probability:** ***times, chances*** | **(c) Distance(s):** ***steps, meters, miles*** | **(d) Time:** ***seconds, minutes, hours, days, years*** | **(e) Money:** ***pennies, cents, dollars*** |
| | douze ou vingt (161)<br>quatorze (165)<br>**quinze** (167)<br>quinze ou vingt (169)<br>**vingt** (170)<br>vingt-cinq (178)<br>trente (179)<br>trente ou quarante (180)<br>**(pas) trente-six** (184)<br>***Sp* más de uno**<br>cinco o seis<br>seis o siete<br>**diez**<br>**doce**<br>**quince**<br>**veinte**<br>cuarenta<br>***Ge* mehr als ein**<br>***En* fivish**<br>**ninish**<br>**tenish** | **veinte veces**<br>***Ge* mehr als einmal**<br>**fünfzig Mal**<br>***En* more than once**<br>**a dozen times** | être sous quatre pieds de terre (112), à six pieds sous terre (137)<br>***It* a cento passi**<br>***Ge* hundert Schirtt**<br>**hundert Meter** | ***Ge* acht Tage**<br>**vierzehn Tage**<br>(*not always approximative*)<br>**in zehn Jahren**<br>**in zwanzig Jahren**<br>***En* a fourtnight** | |
| **3.2. Ordinal number** | ***Fr* le/la dixième** (160)<br>le/la quatorzième (167)<br>**le/la vingtième** (175) | ***Fr*** (pour)<br>la huitième fois (148)<br>**la dixième fois** (160) | | | |

| | | | | | |
|---|---|---|---|---|---|
| | | la quinzième fois (169)<br>**la vingtième fois** (175)<br>la trentième fois (180)<br>***Sp* la décima vez**<br>**la vigésima vez** | | | |
| **4. Big/high quantity/amount/number** | | | | | |
| **Cardinal number** | ***Fr*** trente ou quarante (190)<br>quarante (188)<br>cinquante (191)<br>quatre-vingts ou cent (194)<br>**cent** (195–196)<br>deux cents (207), trois cents, six cents, huit cents<br>**mille** (211–212)<br>deux mille, trois mille, cinq mille, dix mille, douze mille, vingt-cinq mille, vingt-sept mille, trente mille, cinquante mille (220)<br>des mille et des cents (213)<br>**dix mille** (218)<br>onze mille (et des) (219)<br>**trente-six mille** (219)<br>quarante-six mille<br>cinquante-six mille<br>**cent mille** (220), trois cent mille (221)<br>**un million (de)** (222)<br>dix millions, cent millions,<br>cent cinquante millions,<br>trois cents millions, dix mille millions<br>**un milliard (de)** (223–224),<br>cent milliards, mille milliards | ***Fr* trente-six fois** (186)<br>quarante fois (189)<br>cinquante fois (192)<br>soixante fois (193)<br>**cent fois** (199–200)<br>deux cents fois (208)<br>**mille fois** (215–216)<br>**dix mille fois** (218)<br>**cinquante mille fois** (220)<br>**cent mille fois** (221)<br>des millions, des milliards de fois (223)<br>***It* cento volte**<br>**mille volte**<br>**un milione di volte**<br>***Sp* veintisiete veces**<br>**ochenta veces**<br>**cien veces**<br>**quinientas veces**<br>**mil veces**<br>**cien mil veces**<br>***Ge* hundert Mal**<br>tausend Mal<br>zehntausend Mal<br>**hunderttausend Mal**<br>***En* ten times** (a day)<br>**a hundred times** (a day)<br>**a thousand times** (a day)<br>ten thousand times | ***Fr* à cent mètres** (197)<br>**à cent pas** (197)<br>(être) à cent lieues (de) (197), à mille lieues de (214)<br>***Sp* a cien metros**<br>**a mil metros**<br>***Ge* hundert Schitt**<br>**hundert Meter** | ***Fr* soixante minutes** (193)<br>**cent ans** (198)<br>cent sept ans (206)<br>cent cinquante ans (207)<br>trois cents ans<br>***Sp* sesenta minutos**<br>**cien años**<br>***It* cent'anni**<br>è **un secolo** che ti aspetto<br>***Ge* in hundert Jahr(en)**<br>das tausendjährige Reich | ***Fr*** coûter/valoir/gagner des cents et des mille (201), des mille et des cents (213)<br>***Sp* quinientas pesetas**<br>**mil pesetas**<br>**diez mil pesetas**<br><br>**Other nouns**<br>***Sp* mil colorados,**<br>**mil azules** (pelota vasca)<br>***En* the sixty-four thousand dollar question**<br>***Ge* (Elferfrage)**<br>***En* you look a million dollars** |

**Table 6.1.** (*Continued*)

| Quantitiy/ number | Types of nouns | | | | |
|---|---|---|---|---|---|
| | **(a) (Countable) Noun of any type:** (*or small subcategories words, rain, persons present)* | **(b) Iteration/ repetition, probability:** *times, chances* | **(c) Distance(s):** *steps, meters, miles* | **(d) Time:** *seconds, minutes, hours, days, years* | **(e) Money:** *pennies, cents, dollars* |
| | **mille et un(e)** (217)<br>cent et un(e) (205)<br>*Sp* **cien**<br>**mil**<br>**diez mil**<br>**treinta mil**<br>**cien mil**<br>**un millón**<br>**un billón**<br>*En* **a hundred and one** ways of/to . . .<br>**a million and one** (reasons, uses . . . )<br><br>**Special program: letters**<br>*Fr* à la vitesse V<br>*Sp* **equis**<br>*Ge* **zig**<br>**X**<br>**der Tag X**<br>**le jour j**<br>*En* **umpteen**<br>**zillions**<br>**gazillions** | **a million times** (a day)<br>ten million times<br><br>**Special program: letters**<br>*Fr* x fois<br>*Sp* **equis veces**<br>*Ge* **X Mal**<br>**zigmal**<br>*En* **umpteen times** | | | |

| | | | | | |
|---|---|---|---|---|---|
| **Ordinal number** | *Fr* le/la soixantième (193)<br>**le/la centième** (205)<br>**le/la millième** (217)<br>**le/la mille et unième** (218)<br>**le/la dix millième** (218) | *Fr* (pour)<br>**la trente-sixième fois** (188)<br>la cinquantième fois (193)<br>la quatre-vingt-dix-neuvième fois (194)<br>**la centième fois** (205)<br>**la millième fois** (217)<br>**la mille et unième fois** (218)<br>**la cent millième fois** (221)<br>la onze cent millième fois (222), la millionième fois (223), la cent millionième fois (223)<br>**pour la enième fois**<br>*It* per **l'ennesima volta**<br>**la centesima volta**<br>*Ge* **zum hundersten Mal**<br>**zum tausendsten Mal**<br>**zum hundert-tausendsten Mal**<br>**zum X. Mal**<br>*En* **for the hundredth time**<br>**for the umpteenth time** | | | |
| **5. Fractions, percentages** | | | | | **Other Nouns** |
| **5.1. Small quantity/ amount** *(With numerator 1 and a high denominator)* | *Fr* **le/la millionième** (21)<br>**le/la millième** (21)<br>**la centième partie/le centième** (22)<br>**le dixième** (22) | *Fr* **une chance sur dix** (152)<br>**une chance sur mille** (213)<br>une chance sur un million (223) | *Fr* **un quart de millimètre** (24) | *Fr* **un quart de seconde** (45)<br>**un dixième de seconde** (45)<br>**un centième de seconde** (22) | |

Table 6.1. (*Continued*)

| Quantitiy/ number | Types of nouns | | | | |
|---|---|---|---|---|---|
| | **(a) (Countable) Noun of any type:** ***(or small subcategories words, rain, persons present)*** | **(b) Iteration/ repetition, probability:** ***times, chances*** | **(c) Distance(s):** ***steps, meters, miles*** | **(d) Time:** ***seconds, minutes, hours, days, years*** | **(e) Money:** ***pennies, cents, dollars*** |
| | **le quart** (22), le quart de la moitié, le quart du quart, le quart du centième<br>le tiers du quart (24)<br>***Sp*** **la millonésima parte**<br>**la milésima parte**<br>**la centésima parte**<br>**la décima parte**<br>**la cuarta parte**<br>***Ge*** **zu drei Viertel** | ***Sp*** **una oportunidad entre diez**<br>**una oportunidad entre mil**<br>***Ge*** **die Chance/Es steht eins zu hundert/ tausend /einer Million**<br>***En*** **a chance out of ten**<br>**a one-in-ten chance**<br>**a one-in-a-hundred chance**<br>**a one-in-a-thousand chance**<br>**a one-in-a-million chance**<br>**a one-in-a-million find** | | **un millième de seconde** (21), un quart de millième de seconde (46),<br>un millième de millième de seconde (46)<br>**un millionième de seconde** (21, 46)<br>un dix millionième de seconde (46)<br>**un quart d'heure** (23)<br>***It*** **mezzo minuto**<br>**mezz'ora**<br>***Sp*** **una décima de segundo**<br>**una centésima de segundo**<br>**una milésima de segundo**<br>**un cuarto de hora**<br>***Ge*** **ein Viertelstündchen**<br>**eine Viertelstunde**<br>***En*** **a split second** | |

| | | | | | |
|---|---|---|---|---|---|
| **5.2. (Realtively) considerable amount/ number** | ***Ge* jeder zehnte** | | | ***Fr*** *Iteration:* tous les quatre matins (125)<br>*Future moment:* un de ces quatre (matins) (126) | |
| **5.3. Half** | ***Sp* uno de cada dos**<br>***Ge* jedes zweite Wort**<br>**jeder zweite** | ***Fr* une fois sur deux** (44), deux fois sur quatre, cinq fois sur dix<br>***It* la metà delle volte**<br>***En* every other time** | | ***Fr* un jour sur deux** (45)<br>***Sp* cada dos por tres**<br>***Ge* jeden zweiten Tag**<br>**die Hälfte seines Lebens**<br>***En* every other day**<br>**every five minutes** | ***Fr* avoir un pied dans la tombe** (30)<br>n'y aller que d'une fesse (36)<br>ne bander que d'une (36)<br>ne bosser que d'une mirabelle (37)<br>**ne dormir que d'un œil** (37)<br>***It* avere un piede nella tomba**<br>**dormire con un'occhio solo**<br>***Ge* mit einem Fuß im Grab stehen**<br>**mit einem Fuß im Gefängnis stehen**<br>***En* to have one foot in the grave**<br>**to have a foot in the door, both feet in the door** |
| **5.4. Majority** | ***Fr* les/aux trois quarts** (25)<br>les quatre cinquièmes (26)<br>quatre-vingts pour cent (26)<br>**trois** (+ subst.) **sur quatre** (102)<br>**huit** (+ subst.) **sur dix** (147) | ***Fr* deux fois sur trois** (65)<br>**trois fois sur quatre** (102)<br>quatre-vingt-quinze fois sur cent (27) | | ***Fr*** deux jours sur trois (65)<br>les trois quarts du temps (25)<br>***Ge* drei Viertel der Zeit** | |

**Table 6.1.** (*Continued*)

| Quantitiy/ number | Types of nouns | | | | |
|---|---|---|---|---|---|
| | **(a) (Countable) Noun of any type:** ***(or small subcategories words, rain, persons present)*** | **(b) Iteration/ repetition, probability:** ***times, chances*** | **(c) Distance(s):** ***steps, meters, miles*** | **(d) Time:** ***seconds, minutes, hours, days, years*** | **(e) Money:** ***pennies, cents, dollars*** |
| | | **trois chances sur quatre** (102)<br>quatre-vingts chances pour/sur cent (26)<br>quatre-vingt-dix chances pour/sur cent (27) | | | |
| **5.5. Near-majority** | ***Fr*** **les neuf dixièmes** (26)<br>**neuf** (+ subst.) **sur dix** (149)<br>quatre-vingt-dix pour cent (27)<br>quatre-vingt-dix-neuf pour cent (27)<br>les neuf cent quatre-vingt-dix-neuf millièmes (28)<br>les/à 99,99% (27)<br>***It*** **il novanta percento**<br>**il novantanove percento**<br>***Sp*** **el noventa y nueve por ciento** | ***Fr*** quatre-vingt-dix-neuf chances pour/sur cent (27)<br>**neuf chances sur dix** (149)<br>**neuf fois sur dix** (149)<br>***Ge*** **in neun von zehn Fällen**<br>**zu 99%**<br>**du hast 99% Chancen, dass …**<br>***En*** **ninetynine percent certain**<br>**ninetynine point nine percent certain** | | ***Ge*** **es ist fünf vor zwölf** | |

| | | | | | |
|---|---|---|---|---|---|
| **5.6. Totality**[a] | ***Fr*** **(à) cent pour cent** (28)<br>Negation of a negative verb + one unit:<br>**n'en perdre pas une** (de parole) (36)<br>**n'en rater/louper pas une** (de sottise) (36)<br>***Sp*** **cien por cien** | ***Fr*** dix fois sur dix (149) | | ***Fr*** **vingt-quatre heures sur vingt-quatre** (177)<br>**sept jours sur sept** (142)<br>trois cent soixante-cinq jours (par an) (208)<br>vingt-quatre heures sur vingt-quatre, trois cent soixante cinq jours par an (178),<br>douze mois sur douze (162)<br>du premier janvier au trente et un décembre (49)<br>***It*** **lavora ventiquattro ore su ventiquattro**<br>***Sp*** **veinticuatro horas al día, siete días a la semana, cincuenta y dos semanas al año**<br>***Ge*** **vierundzwanzig Studen am Tag**<br>**365 Tage im Jahr**<br>**vierundzwanzig Studen am Tag, 365 Tage im Jahr**<br>***En*** (open) **twenty-four/seven** | ***Fr*** à/des deux mains (58, 64)<br>dormir sur ses deux oreilles (69)<br>***Ge*** **mit beiden Füßen im Kriminal stehen** |

**Table 6.1.** (*Continued*)

| **Quantitiy/ number** | **Types of nouns** | | | | |
|---|---|---|---|---|---|
| | **(a) (Countable) Noun of any type:** ***(or small subcategories words, rain, persons present)*** | **(b) Iteration/ repetition, probability:** ***times, chances*** | **(c) Distance(s):** ***steps, meters, miles*** | **(d) Time:** ***seconds, minutes, hours, days, years*** | **(e) Money:** ***pennies, cents, dollars*** |
| **5.7. More-than-totality**<br><br>**Fraction**<br>*or a number higher than a given standard/norm* | ***En* she speaks thirteen to the dozen** *( = non stop)* | ***Ge* hunderteinprozentig tausendprozentig** | | ***Fr*** vingt-cinq heures sur vingt-quatre (178), trente-six heures sur vingt-quatre (178)<br>trente-deux jours par mois (182)<br>***It*** lavora **quarantotto ore su ventiquattro**<br>***Ge* es ist fünf nach zwölf**<br>***En* twenty-five hours a day**<br>**thirty-six hours per day**<br>**eight days a week** | ***Fr*** avoir onze doigts de pied dans la tombe (30)<br>douze métiers, treize misères (162), treize métiers, quatorze misères (164)<br>j'ai (je n'ai) pas quatre bras (115)<br>la mouche à quatre culs (115), le mouton à cinq pattes (135) |
| **Special case: Inexistent date** (= *never*) | | | | ***Fr*** la vingt-cinquième heure (179)<br>tous les trente-six du mois (186)<br>le trente-deux décembre (182) | |

| | | | | | |
|---|---|---|---|---|---|
| | | | | la semaine des quatre jeudis (116)<br>(les calendes grecques)<br>***It*** (gli manca qualche lunedí)<br>(le calende greche)<br>***Ge* am 30. Februar**<br>***En* the ... of julember** | |

[a]Neither the empty set nor the totality , I must admit, are approximative numbers. I have included them in this overview because they complete the picture of hyperbolic categories. In fact, most of these empty sets or totalities are such only due to exaggeration, they are certainly not the fruit of an exact counting. Like the other approximative numerals they are part of a rhetoric of intensification through hyperbole; actually the empty set and the totality are the two extreme points of this very strategy. (Which means that in such uses one hundred percent are certainly not ninety-nine percent plus one, and even less 98% + 2 or 97% + 3.)

[b]The line between a considerable and a big amount is not so easy to draw; the one between a small and a considerable amount seems comparatively more clear.

## Appendix: More Nouns (Strongly Idiomatic, but not Completely Fixed Expressions)

### A.1. French

**mots:** ne pas connaître/comprendre un (seul) mot (37), dire/toucher un/deux/trois mot/s à qn. de qc. (32, 57, 68, 92), en un/deux mot/s (comme en cent/mille) (32-33, 71)

**km/h** (velocity) (*kilomètres* remains implicit): **à cent à l'heure** (196), à deux cents à l'heure (207), à trois cents à l'heure (208), à mille à l'heure (213), à cent mille à l'heure (221), **en quatrième (vitesse)** (127)

**coups:** en deux/trois/quatre coups de ... (cuiller à pot) (70,99-100), en deux coups les gros (71), en deux mouvements/temps (71), en deux temps (et) trois mouvements (21), en moins de deux (72), en cinq secs; **être aux/faire les cent coups** (202), cent dix-neuf coups (205), quatre cents coups (209), quatre cent dix-neuf coups (209)

**diables:** aller/courir/être aux **quatre/cinq cents diables** (209) envoyer qn. aux cinq cents diables (210), aux cent mille diables (221), aux quatre cent mille diables/perpètes (222)

**morceaux: en mille morceaux** (214), en trente-six mille morceaux (220)

**dieux** (curses): **vingt dieux** (172-173), cent dieux (199), mille dieux/mille dious (215), milliards de dieux (224);

**chandelles: voir trente-six chandelles** (187), voir trente-six mille chandelles (220)

**métiers, misères:** douze métiers, treize misères (162), treize métiers, quatorze misères (164), **trente-six métiers, trente-six misères** (187), cinquante métiers, cinquante misères (187), cent métiers cent misères (187)

**volontés: faire** (en passer par) **les quatre volontés de qn.**, passer ses quatre volontés à qn. (114), faire les trente-six volontés de qn. (186)

**taille: haut comme** deux/**trois pommes** (à genoux) (77, 95), gros comme trois liards de beurre (77)

**pelés et tondus: quatre pelés et un tondu** (un nombre dérisoire de personnes) (121-122), trois pelés et un tondu, trois pelés et deux tondus, trois pelés et quatre tondus, quatre pelés et trois tondus

**catégorie/ordre/classe/choix: de premier choix** (ordre, plan) (47), **de première classe** (bourre, catégorie, force, grandeur, qualité) (47): *as opposed to everything that is not first ('premier') and that is opposed not by the sense, but by the degree of exaggeration*: de deuxième division (86), de second choix (ordre, rang), de seconde zone (86), de troisième catégorie/classe/ordre/zone (102); de quatrième catégorie/ligne/ordre/rang/sous-sol, etc. (127); de sixième catégorie/ordre (139); deuxième couteau/second couteau (87), troisième couteau (103), quatorzième couteau (87), de second plan (90-91), de dixième ordre (160), de douzième ordre (163), de dix-septième ordre (170), de vingtième classe (174), de trente-sixième catégorie (188)

**comme n:** comme pas un(e) (31), **comme pas deux** (62), **pour deux** (83), **comme quatre** (109), **comme six** (137), comme dix (153), comme douze (109), comme trente (180), **comme trente-six** ( + nom) (185)

**n fois mieux/plus**: **dix/cent/mille fois mieux/pire, dix/cent fois plus/moins/trop** (199-200, 216)

**se mettre/se couper: se mettre**/couper **en quatre**/six (123-124)

**manquer: il (me, te) lui manque toujours cent sous pour faire cinq francs** (202), il (me, te) lui manque toujours dix-neuf sous pour faire un franc (170)

**âges:** de six à soixante-six ans (141), **de sept à soixante-dix-sept ans** (141)

**être sur son trente-et-un**

## A.2. Italian

**a cento all'ora**, alla velocità della luce
**avere sette vite come i gatti**
**sudare sette camicie** (= faticare molto)
gli vengono **i suoi cinque minuti** (= uno scatto d'ira)
mille volte? – mille? **millanta**! (Boccaccio, ital. antico)
**non capisce un'acca, non ho un cavolo, no vedo un fico secco, non capisce un cavolo**
**un dito di vino, due dita di vino**
**avere un piede su due staffe** (= Ger. zwischen zwei Stühlen sitzen)
**decalogo** (Moisé): regole, anche se non sono dieci

## A.3. Spanish

**cuatro pelos**
**un millón de gracias**
**mil besos**
**dos dedos** (cortar pelo)
**en el quinto demonio**
**cuatro casas** (pueblo pequeño)
**buscarle tres pies al gato** (de una situación que es obvia, buscar cosas raras ... )
**tener siete vidas**
**mil razones**
**de tres cojones** (muy bueno)
**cero patatero** (no tiene valor)
**a las mil maravillas**
**no me importa un pimiento**

**a millares**
**centenares**
**tres eran tres las hijas de Elena y ninguna era buena** (serie televisiva) (alguien que es pícaro, no muy malo ... )

### A.4. German

**17 Euro und ein paar zerquetschte**
**zwischen zwei Stühlen sitzen**
**im siebenten Himmel sein**
**sieben Leben haben wie eine Katze**
**Siebenmeilenstiefel**
**fünfe grade sein lassen**
**das fünfte Rad am Wagen**
**jemanden buckelfünferln** (Viennese)
**ein Potschochter sein** (Viennese)
**einen Achter haben** (bicycle)

### A.5. English

**it's five past three/it's five minutes past three** – but: **it's seven minutes past three** (always with "minutes")
**If I've told you once, I've told you more than once**
**If I've told you once, I've told you a hundred/a thousand/a million times**
**I feel like I ran a mile**
Bible: maximum age (German: 70) Engl.: three score years and ten (score = 20)
**a score = 20scores of** volunteers ...
**give or take a mile; give or take five minutes**

New Approaches to Hedging
Edited by Gunther Kaltenböck, Wiltrud Mihatsch and Stefan Schneider


# 7

# Approximative Expressions and their Loose Uses in Chinese ☆

*Yongping Ran*

## Abstract

This chapter investigates the uses of approximative numerals and numerical expressions in Chinese. Approximative numerical expressions are classified into two main types: one with the discourse marker *ba* and the other without an explicit marker. This chapter then discusses cultural connotations of numerical expressions in well-known sayings and ancient poems, and elaborates on the approximative uses of numerical expressions and their communicative effects in different contexts.

## 1. Introduction

Looseness is one of the pervasive features of language use, which can be observed with lexical expressions, including vague collectives (*bags of*, *crowds of*), dummy nouns (*thing*, *stuff*), numerical approximations (*about 40 students*, *two hours or so*) and so on (Channell, 1994; Cutting, 2007). These expressions have been approached in various ways with the discussions focusing on different aspects of vagueness, fuzziness, ambiguity, uncertainty, indeterminacy, approximation etc., all of which are non-literal or loose uses of language, or particular ways of

☆ The main ideas of this chapter were presented at the 10th International Pragmatics Conference, Sweden, in July, 2007.

speaking loosely (Bach, 2001). Vague language has been described, for instance, as words or phrases 'which deliberately refer to people and things in a non-specific, imprecise way' (Cutting, 2007: 6), such as *whatever, sort of or anything.* Approximations, however, are considered vague expressions with numbers or quantities, as in *ten minutes or so*, *around eight* or just vague approximators (Koester, 2007). Lakoff (1972), Wachtel (1980), Franken (1997), Nerlich *et al.* (2001) have provided enlightening insights into their contextual uses and functions from the perspective of both semantics and pragmatics.

Furthermore, in recent years discourse markers and particles have been given considerable attention from a discourse perspective (Schiffrin, 1987; Luke, 1988; Miracle, 1991; Lenk, 1998), a pragmatic perspective (Brinton, 1996; Erman, 2001) and a discourse-pragmatic perspective (Li, 2000). These findings have shown that communication is not merely a simple process of encoding and decoding lexical information but also that expressions are often used loosely and thus cannot be interpreted in a literal way. Typical examples are the approximative uses of an utterance, or the approximation triggered by a numeral or numerical expression.

Just as in English, expressions which have a clearly specified semantics but are flexible in their interpretation can also be found in Mandarin Chinese. There are hedging expressions, such as *dayue/dagai* (about/approximately), *shang xia/zuo you* (around), *cha bu duo* (almost) and *jie jin yu* (nearly/approximately), which are used whenever the addresser intends to express approximation in an explicit way. However, there are also structures containing a numeral whose semantic meaning is precise but which function loosely in context. Such types of words or expressions can be seen as approximators whose function consists in triggering a loose interpretation of other linguistic expressions. This frequently happens in connection with the utterance-final discourse markers, such as *ba*, *ma* and *ya*, whose function is pragmatic, i.e., to guide the interpretation of other expressions on the level of discourse. Moreover, there are also numerical expressions which are interpreted as approximate despite their definite semantics because of certain contextual constraints and their conventionalized uses. Such approximative expressions and numerals are frequently found in both contemporary Mandarin Chinese and Ancient Chinese, such as poetry from the Tang Dynasty (618–907) and the Song Dynasty (960–1279).

This chapter first provides a classification of types of approximative numerical expressions (in Section 2) and then discusses cultural connotations and conventionalized implicatures of numerical expressions (in Section 3). Section 4, finally, identifies three very specific contextual uses of approximative numerals.

## 2. Classification of Approximative Numerical Expressions

This section provides a classification of approximative uses of numerals in Mandarin Chinese. Section 2.1 first gives an overview of findings for the discourse marker *ba*, which serves as a basis for the discussion of its uses in connection with numerals in the following sections. As will become clear, the study of *ba* has to be extended to an investigation of how the discourse marker interacts with the utterance to which it is appended. One question is how we can talk of approximation even though the semantic meaning of the utterance appears to be precise and the numerical information is at face value. Section 2.2 then explores cases where *ba* is appended to an utterance containing a numeral. Section 2.3, finally, examines how approximative readings are achieved in context without explicit markers. This question will also be further pursued in the remainder of the chapter.

### 2.1. Introduction: Pragmatic functions of the discourse marker *ba*[1]

Unlike other discourse markers in Chinese, the discourse marker *ba* can be used to show the addresser's uncertainty about what is conveyed. Thus, it is more likely to appear with an approximative expression, or an expression with indeterminate meaning. It has long been considered a function word in Mandarin Chinese grammar (Ma, 2000) since it does not encode distinct lexical or independent semantic meaning. Yet it carries a very rich pragmatic load, such as indicating the attitude of the addresser towards the content of his/her utterance, or reducing his/her commitment to what has been presented in context (Han, 1995). It has therefore been referred to as a discourse particle, discourse marker or interactional particle (Chu, 2002, 2006; Ran, 2004).

Han (1995: 100) has categorized the relevant studies into two groups: (1) those treating *ba* as an interrogative mood marker and (2) those treating *ba* as an imperative mood marker. There is, however, also a more comprehensive analysis of *ba* as a final particle in *Hanyu Da Cidian* (Luo, 1994: 250), which identifies five functions: (1) to show that the addresser intends to negotiate something with the addressee, proposes advice or makes a request; (2) to express the addressee's agreement or approval; (3) to express the addresser's uncertainty, without requiring the addressee to make a response; (4) to indicate a pause of the addressee's speech while in a dilemma; (5) to show that the addresser has doubts or is making some conjecture. These uses clearly illustrate its pragmatic flexibility.

Let me add one further use to the above list, which is that of *ba* being used with a greeting which states the obvious, as in example (1). Here, it has interpersonal function which consists in engaging the addressee and starting a conversation in an initiative move.

(1) 买东西吧?
Mai dongxi *ba*?
buy things BA
Doing some shopping?

[1] *ba* (吧) is one of the utterance-final particles with no specified semantic meaning, such as *ne* (呢), *a* (啊), and *ya* (呀); however, it can perform different functions in context; it has thus been considered a discourse marker, or simply a function word.

Following Li and Thompson (1991), Han (1995) has argued that from a pragmatic perspective the function of *ba* is to weaken the addresser's commitment to the proposition of an utterance which is either declarative or imperative in structure. In other words, *ba* can add some mitigation to the utterance. This mitigation function of *ba* has been found to be pervasive in Chinese conversational interaction. It can help to soften the face-threatening force of an utterance or a speech act by showing the addresser's uncertainty, or to improve the intended persuasion effect, as illustrated in examples (2) and (3), respectively.

(2) 那不是这样的吧。
Na bu shi zheyang de *ba*.
that not be so DE BA
Maybe it is not so.

(3) 算了 吧，他还很 年轻。
Suan le *ba*, ta hai hen nianqin.
let it be LE BA he still very young
Let it be, he is still very young.

In example (2), because of the use of *ba* and the uncertainty it expresses, the force of negating or disagreeing is much reduced, i.e., mitigated. Hence, the addressee's positive face can be saved. In contrast, the negation without *ba* (viz. *na bu shi zheyang de* 'it is not so') would be considered quite a face-threat to the addressee. In example (3), the Chinese expressions *suan le* and *suan le ba* both have the aim of achieving a persuasion effect, but the latter would be considered more acceptable because of the mitigation function of the discourse marker *ba*. The use of *ba* is thus motivated pragmatically, with reference to its context, since communication necessarily involves a complicated dynamic process, which is the result of a concerted effort of the participants. Participants in a conversation do not merely express what they have in mind or what they believe to be true but also wait passively for automatic interpretation by the addressee (Li, 2000: 86). They also have to engage themselves in an appeal to the addressee for negotiation, as shown here by the use of *ba* at the end of an utterance. *Ba* also indicates the addresser's readiness for negotiation.

Furthermore, Chu (1998) and Shie (1991) have found that the basic contextual function of *ba* in Chinese conversational interaction is to express the addresser's uncertainty. In other words, its appearance shows that the addresser is not quite sure about what has been said because of his/her lack of sufficient evidence, or it shows that the conveyed information is indeterminate or approximate. Thus, in certain contexts, the implicit pragmatic force of *ba* is to express that the addresser requires relevant information for confirmation from the addressee.

## 2.2. Approximative numerical expressions with *ba*

Having outlined the general pragmatic functions of *ba* above, let me now turn to its appearance in numerical expressions. For these uses, it is possible to distinguish the following three cases of loose uses with approximative numerals.

A. A numerical expression (without approximator) + *ba* in final position, as in example (4):

(4) 四个小时吧，那个时候已经昏迷了，什么 都没说……
*Si ge xiaoshi ba*, na ge shihou yijing hunmi le, shenme dou mei shuo, ...
four CL[2] hour BA that CL time already coma LE what all not say, ...
For about four hours, I had been in coma during that period, so said nothing at all, ...

B. An approximator (e.g. *cha bu duo/dayue/dagai* 'about/almost/approximately') + a numerical expression + *ba*, as in example (5):

(5) 项目投资差不多四千万港币吧。
Xiangmu touzi *cha bu duo si qian wan gangbi ba.*
project investment almost forty million Hong Kong dollar BA
About forty million Hong Kong dollars have been invested into the project.

The above underlined numerical expression with the approximator *cha bu duo* is used to present the target information in an approximative way. The discourse marker *ba* helps to additionally highlight the approximative nature of the numerical.

C. A numerical expression + an approximator + ( . . . ) + *ba*, i.e., a numerical expression and an approximator followed by *ba*. The approximator includes *zuoyou* (about) and *qianhou* (about/around). Here, *ba* does not immediately follow the approximator but is preceded by a verb, as illustrated in examples (6) and (7):

(6) 他 三点左右来 吧。
Ta *san dian zuoyou* lai *ba.*
he three o'clock or so come BA
He will come at about three.

(7) 我们下午六点前后集中吧。
Women xiawu *liu dian qianhou* jizhong *ba.*
we afternoon six o'clock before after gather BA
We're going to get together at about six o'clock in the afternoon.

Let me briefly look at the functions of *ba* in each of the above examples. In example (4), although there is no explicit approximator, the approximation arises through the use of *ba*, which conveys the addresser's uncertainty or indeterminacy. Without *ba*, viz. *si ge xiaoshi* ('for four hours') would most likely be interpreted in a precise way. This is why the English equivalent of example (4) has to be rendered as *for about four hours*, although there is no approximator, for instance,

[2] CL (classifier) is a measure word in Chinese. A measure word is required whenever one is talking about numbers and quantities; it is placed between the numeral and the noun or verb. These counters serve to describe the thing which is being counted. Chinese grammar demands a measure word for just about everything which can be counted, and such a word can be different if different types of nouns or verbs are involved.

*dayue/zuoyou/chabuduo* ('about'), in the Chinese expression. In examples (5), (6) and (7), however, which contain an approximator before or after the numerical expression, *ba* marks the approximative character of those utterances and highlights it at the same time. Here, the addresser's uncertainty about the numerical information is explicitly indicated by *ba*. Besides, in contexts where different types of speech act functions are involved, such as predicting, guessing, suggesting, warning and threatening, *ba* helps to mitigate the illocutionary forces of those speech acts, or weaken the addresser's certainty.

It is through *ba* that the approximation of the utterances becomes highlighted. If *ba* is removed, the degree of approximation of the utterance is weakened as a consequence. This strengthens the addresser's certainty about what is expressed in the utterance and consequently precise information is conveyed or expected in most cases. Compare the following utterances with examples (4–7):

(4′) 四个小时，那个时候已经昏迷了，什么都没说，… …
*Si ge xiaoshi*, na ge shihou yijing hunmi le, shenme dou mei shuo, …
four CL hour that CL time already coma LE what all not say, …
For four hours, but I was in coma during that period, so said nothing at all, …

(5′) 项目投资差不多四千万港币。
Xiangmu touzi *cha bu duo si qian wan gangbi*.
project investment almost forty million Hong Kong dollar
About forty million Hong Kong dollars have been invested into the project.

(6′) 他三点左右来。
Ta *san dian zuoyou* lai.
He three CL or so come
He will come at about three.

(7′) 我们下午六点前后集中。
Women xiawu *liu dian qianhou* jizhong.
we afternoon six o'clock before after gather
We're going to get together at about six o'clock in the afternoon.

The deletion of *ba* in examples (4′–7′) does not change the semantics of these utterances, but the approximation in example (4′) disappears or becomes less explicit. This shows that *ba* expresses approximation in an utterance as in example (4) and also makes the approximative character of an utterance more explicit, as in examples (5)–(7), where the approximation is more highlighted than in examples (5′–7′). Both these uses can be seen as a result of the discourse function of *ba*, which indicates the addresser's uncertainty or indeterminacy about the meaning of the utterance.

### 2.3. Approximative uses without an explicit marker

Besides the above cases of approximative expressions with the discourse marker *ba,* there exist some idiomatic expressions or poetic structures, within which numerals are used in an approximate way, i.e., their contextual interpretation is loose despite their clearly specified semantics. This section explores approximation in those contexts, in particular how it arises and is interpreted.

The expressions in questions have to do with old sayings and ancient poems in Chinese. They are thus culturally loaded, which puts constraints on their interpretation. Compare, for instance, the following two examples.[3]

(8) 日照香炉生紫烟,
Rizhao xianglu sheng zi yan,
sunshine censer produce violet mist
The sunlit Censer peak exhales a wreath of cloud,
遥看瀑布挂前川。
Yao kan pubu gua qian chuan.
far watch fall hang front mount
Like an upended stream the cataract sounds loud.
飞流直下三千尺,
Fei liu zhi xia *san qian chi*, yi shi yinhe luo jiu tian,
fly straight down three thousand *chi*[4]
Its torrent dashes down three thousand feet from high,
疑是银河落九天。
Yi shi yinhe *luo jiu tian*.
as if the Silver River fall nine sky
As if the Silver River fell from azure sky.

(9) 仕女游人，络绎不绝，真不数"三十六家花酒店，七十二座管弦楼"。
Shinu youren, luo yi bu jue, shen bu shu '*san shi liu jia* hua jiudian, *qi shi er zuo* guanxian lou'.
maid tourist in an endless stream really 'thirty-six CL flower hotel seventy-two CL orchestral building'
Men and women stream by on pleasure bent to throng the countless taverns and music halls.

In example (8), the highlighted string *san qian chi* (three thousand feet) and *luo jiu tian* (fall nine sky – fall from azure sky) are both used loosely so as to achieve the figurative effect of immense height in a hyperbolical way. In example (9), we find a similar effect with *sanshiliu* (thirty-six) and *qishier* (seventy-two) expressing large quantities. The English equivalents of those numerical

[3] Example (8) is the poem *Wang Lushan Pubu* (Cataract on Mount Lu) written by Li Bai (701–762), one of the greatest romantic poets in the Tang Dynasty (618–907) in ancient China. The quoted English version is translated by the famous Chinese scholar Xu Yuanchong. Example (9) is an excerpt from *Rulin Washi* (The Scholar), a well-known realistic satiric novel written by Wu Jingxin (1701–1754), one of the greatest writers in the Qing Dynasty (1644–1912).

[4] *Chi*, a Chinese foot, it is a traditional unit of length, and equals to 33.33 cm.

expressions are therefore not translated literally. Even if *three thousand* is used in example (8), it cannot be interpreted as conveying exact information of the numerical expression since the expected figurative effect of the whole utterance is to express the scenic attractiveness of the mount with the help of a hyperbolic use of the numerical expression.

Further examples of this use are given in examples (10) and (11).

(10) 三十六计，走为上。
San shi liu ji, zou wei shang.
thirty-six strategies walk be best
Among various strategies, to sidestep is the best one.

(11) 俗话说, 女大十八变。
Suhua shuo, nu da *shiba bian.*
saying say girl old eighteen change
As the saying goes, a girl changes much before reaching her womanhood.

In example (10), *sanshiliu ji* (thirty-six strategies) does not mean there are merely thirty-six strategies to deal with things or solve problems but represents an approximate quantity of such strategies. Similarly, example (11) is used and interpreted loosely as ‘a girl changes much before reaching her womanhood’ rather than ‘a girl changes eighteen times before reaching her womanhood’. Such numerical expressions have become conventionalized. They do not convey literal information, although their semantics is explicit and specific enough. Therefore, those expressions cannot be translated into English in a literal way since their decoded meaning is not equivalent to the communicated information. The same can be found for other languages, such as Danish, where the number ‘117’ is used for an indefinite and large number, as in ‘there are 117 ways of doing this’, which has the meaning of ‘there are many different ways of doing this’.

Another example of this kind is the proper name 万里长城 (*wan li changcheng* – ‘the Great Wall’), which semantically means ‘the wall which is ten thousand miles in length’. Here, 万里 (*wan li*) cannot be interpreted literally as ten thousand miles although it encodes exact numerical information. Like *san qian chi* (three thousand feet) and *luo jiu tian* (fall nine sky – fall from azure sky) in example (8), such expressions have been used to emphasize the immense length of the great wall and are therefore loose uses of numerical expressions.

## 3. Cultural Connotations of Numerical Expressions

In Chinese, there are popular sayings and famous works including ancient poems, novels and stories, in which numerical expressions frequently appear with specified semantics but are meant to be interpreted in a loose way. What is characteristic of those expressions or the whole utterance they occur in is that they carry conventional implicatures, i.e., a kind of implicit meaning understood in a conventional way. They are used to achieve certain communicative effects, for instance, to increase the explanatory power of an utterance, show the vividness of what is being talked about or strengthen the persuasiveness of the speaker. The following examples illustrate this.

(12) 熟读唐诗三百首，不会作诗也会吟。
Shou du tangshi *san bai shou*, bu hui zuo shi ye hui yin.
frequently read Tang poem three hundred CL not able write poem also able chant
If you can recite three hundred poems of the Tang Dynasty, you will be able to chant poems, even if you are unable to write.

In the Tang dynasty (618–907) of ancient China, there appeared such well-known poets as Li Bai, Du Fu, Bai Juyi and so on, from who we have more than three hundred poems, although the exact number of these poems is unknown.[5] Whenever people talk about the poems of that period, these three hundred poems are usually mentioned. Example (12) is thus a typical case of approximation with numerical expressions, viz. *san bai shou*.

Examples (13) and (14) provide two more popular sayings whose implicit meanings are well understood among Chinese.

(13) 一个和尚挑水吃，两个和尚抬水吃，三个和尚没水吃。
*Yi ge* heshang tiao shui chi, *liang ge* heshang tai shui chi, *san ge* heshang mei shui chi.
one CL Buddhist monk fetch water with a pole two CL Buddhist monk carry water on a pole three CL Buddhist monk no water eat
One boy is a boy, two boys half boy, three boys no boy.

(14) 三个臭皮匠，合成一个诸葛亮。
*San ge* chou pi jiang, he cheng *yi ge* Zhuge Liang.
three CL cobblers combine one CL Zhuge Liang
Two heads are better than one.[6]

Example (13) is a well-known saying. Whenever it is quoted, the participants do not care much about the exact numerical information in the utterance, and it has long been considered a satirical warning against shirking responsibilities and avoiding joint efforts. The saying is conventionally used with the meaning that one monk carries two buckets of water on a pole, two monks carry one

[5] It is estimated that there are approximately 50 thousand poems, http://www.shiandci.net/ts.htm.

[6] The literal translation is 'Three cobblers with their wits combined equal Zhuge Liang'. Zhege Liang (181–234) is known as a statesman and strategist, prime minister of the Shu in the period of the Three Kingdoms (220–265). He is a mastermind whose name has long become a symbol of resourcefulness and wisdom in Chinese folklore.

bucket between them and three monks have no drinking water. The implication is that, if there is no joint effort or cooperation between people, success will not be achieved and more people do not always bring about the expected success. Similarly, in example (14) *san ge chou pi jiang* can be simply interpreted as 'two heads are better than one', which means people working together achieve more than people working individually. *San* (three) therefore is used loosely and contextually interpreted as *two*. In other words, the encoded numerical information is different from its loose interpretation and its expected communicative function since these utterances are used metaphorically. They cannot be interpreted literally because of the cultural conventions associated with such sayings.

Another example where an exact numeral is interpreted loosely by cultural convention is given in example (15).[7]

(15) 胡正卿心头十五个吊桶打水，七上八下。
Hu Zhengqing xin tou *shiwu ge diaotong dashui, qi shang ba xia.*
Hu Zhengqing mind fifteen CL bucket fetch water seven up eight down
Hu Zhengqing was much upset, thus quite unable to think straight.

The translation of the above utterance is loose enough. However, if its vividness and figurativeness are to be kept, those numerals might be interpreted literally as 'Hu Zhengqing was much upset, thus his heart was beating like fifteen buckets being hurriedly lowered into a well for water – eight going down while seven were coming up'. But in terms of the conventional implicit meaning of the popular saying *shiwu ge diaotong dashui, qi shang ba xia* in example (15), the whole utterance can simply be interpreted as 'Hu Zhengqing was much upset'.

There are also many expressions or set phrases from historical stories or old popular sayings, such as the numerical phrases *san gu mao lu* (三顾茅庐) from a famous historical story and its extended version *san guo qi men* (三过其门, as illustrated in examples (16) and (17), where the literal meaning of *three* does not figure in the translation.

(16) 经理三顾茅庐，真叫求贤若渴。
Jingli *san gu mao lu*, zhen jiao qiu xiao ruo ke.
manager three visit cottage really look for talent as if thirsty

[7] This is an excerpt from *Shui Hu Zhuan – Water Margin*, also called *Outlaws of the Marsh* or *All Men Are Brothers*, a popular story by Shi Nai'an (1296–1372). It is well known as one of the four greatest Chinese novels in history, together with *Journey to the West*, *Romance of the Three Kingdoms* and *Dream of the Red Mansions*. It tells stories of a group of heroes who stand for different classes of people daring to struggle against evil during the period 1119–1121. There are 105 men and 3 women in total, who are oppressed by the corrupt and unjust officials and then rise up.

The manager has visited the person for advice many times to seek a talent in such a way just like a thirsty person for water.

(17) 三过其门而不入
*San guo qi men* er bu ru.
three pass his door but not enter
Too busy to go home, even passing by one's own house.

The expression *san gu mao lu* in example (16), which means literally 'to visit the thatched cottage thrice in succession', comes from the story *Romance of the Three Kingdoms*, in which Liu Bei the founder and king of the kingdom Shu Han (221–263) called on Zhuge Liang (see footnote 9) three times with efforts in order to ask him to take up the important post of a statesman and strategist. After having been deeply moved by Liu Bei's visits and sincerity, Zhuge Liang finally accepted his request and became an important assistant. Nowadays, the expression *san gu mao lu* is used figuratively, which means calling on an important talent repeatedly to solicit his help, or to visit a place repeatedly to find a talented person. In this case, the numeral *san* (three) is not used in a strict sense and can only be interpreted loosely, as shown in the English translation in examples (16) and (17).

Some more loose uses of numerical expressions are provided in examples (18) and (19):

(18) 八仙过海，各显神通。
*Ba xiao guo hai, ge xian shen tong.*
eight immortal cross sea each show special prowess
Like the eight immortals crossing the sea, each one showing his special prowess.

(19) 他们大搞技术革新，真是八仙过海，各显神通。
Tamen da gao jishu gexin, zhen shi *ba xiao guo hai ge xian shen tong.*
they made great technical innovation really BE eight immortal cross sea each show special prowess
They have made great efforts in technical innovation and everyone of them has shown his own art and skill just like the eight immortals crossing the sea.

The above expression *ba xiao guo hai ge xian shen tong* is commonly quoted in situations where everyone tries to outshine everyone else, or have the chance to show their true worth or talent. It shows again that the numeral in such a saying or proverb tends to be used not in a strict sense. The addresser does not mean that there are merely eight people involved in the event.

Similar approximative uses of numerals can be found in Western languages, although maybe in different contexts. A centipede (literally 'hundred feet'), which is also called a 'thousand-leg' in Danish and a 'thousand-legger' in German, does *not* have a thousand legs, not even one hundred. The Greek translation of the (Hebrew and Aramaic) Old Testament is called 'the Septuagint' (often abbreviated with the Roman numeral LXX) because 70 scholars are supposed to have worked on it. In Danish, you can say that you are 'in seven minds' (*i syv sind*) if you cannot make up your mind. These are also cases of approximative uses of specific numerals (cf. also Lavric, this volume, for further examples).

## 4. Contextual Effects of Approximative Numerical Expressions

Apart from the larger cultural connotations discussed in Section 3, approximative numerals may also give rise to certain context-specific effects, which will be discussed below. I try to show how different contexts contribute to different interpretations of approximative numerals. In this context, it is useful to distinguish between descriptive (viz. dynamic, tranquility) effects and interpersonal (viz. mitigating) effects.

### 4.1. Dynamic effects

By dynamic effects, I mean the dynamic process or picture the addresser intends to create in descriptive texts. Such effects are typically found in poems in which numerical expressions have to be interpreted in an approximative or loose way. Typical examples are given in examples (20) and (21), where the numerals refer to birds flocking together and flying snowflakes, respectively.

(20) 一只一只复一只，五六七八九十只，凤凰何少鸟何多？[8]
*Yi zhi yi zhi fu yi zhi, wu liu qi ba jiu shi zhi*, fenghuang he shao niao he duo?
one CL one CL again one CL five six seven eight nine CL phoenix why few bird why many
One bird, two birds, birds flocking together, five, six, seven, eight, nine, ten birds, why are there more birds than phoenixes?

(21) 一片二片三四片，五片六片七八片，九片十片无数片，飞入芦花皆不见。[9]
*Yi pian er pian san si pian, wu pian liu pian qi ba pian, jiu pian shi pian wu shu pian*, fei ru lu hua jie bu jian.
one CL two CL three four CL five CL six CL seven eight CL nine CL ten CL countless CL fly into reed flower all not seen
One flake, two flakes, three and four flakes, five flakes, six flakes, seven and eight flakes, nine flakes, ten flakes and countless flakes (of snow), flying into the reed flowers and all disappear.

---

[8] This excerpt is taken from an ancient poem from the Tang Dynasty (618–907) entitled *Bai Niao Gui Chao* (*Hundreds of Birds Flying Back to their Nests*).

[9] This excerpt is taken from the ancient poem *Yong Xue* (*Ode to the Snow*) written by Zheng Banqiao (1693–1765) in the Qing Dynasty (1644–1912).

In examples (20) and (21), the numerical expressions are not intended to be interpreted literally but loosely, viz. the number of birds and snowflakes is countless. In addition, the enumeration creates a dynamic picture of flocking birds and flying snowflakes. In both examples, the intention is thus not so much to convey quantity information but to paint a dynamic picture, which results from the interplay of numeral expressions and contextual uses.

## 4.2. Tranquility effects

There are also cases where numerical expressions used approximately can create the impression of tranquility, for instance, in the poetic description of a place. Again, such effects can be seen as resulting from the interplay of numerical expressions and contextual uses, as in the following examples:

(22) 一花一柳一鱼矶，一抹斜阳一鸟飞；一山一水中一寺，一林黄叶一僧归。[10]
*Yi hua yi liu yi yu ji, yi mo xie yang yi niao fei; yi shan yi shui zhong yi si, yi lin huang ye yi seng gui.*
one flower one willow one fish rock one setting sun one bird fly one mountain one water among one temple one forest yellow leave one monk return
There are one flower, one willow, one rock projecting over the water, one setting sun, one bird flying; there are one mountain, one temple in a lake of water, one wood with yellow leaves, one monk returning home.

(23) 一山一水一洞天，一鸟一鱼一心齐。
*Yi shan yi shui yi dong tian, yi niao yi yu yi xin qi.*
one mountain one water one sky one bird one fish one mind together
One mountain centred in one lake of water, one bird flitting over with one fish swimming under.

In the above examples, the expressions with *one* are used in parallel to evoke a notion of tranquility or harmony of the places described, quite in contrast to the dynamic use described earlier. The numerals are still used in a loose way as there is not merely one flower, one willow, one bird and so on. Only such an interpretation can satisfy the expected relevance and achieve positive contextual effects of the numerical expressions in these contexts (cf. Sperber and Wilson, 1986/1995).

[10] This excerpt is taken from the poem *Shi Yi* (*Ten One*), written by He Peiyu in the Qing Dynasty.

### 4.3. Mitigation effects

As Lakoff (1972: 195) has pointed out, many expressions 'whose job is to make things fuzzier or less fuzzy', such as *more or less*, *roughly*, *approximately*, *about*, *somewhat*, are used as hedges. In interaction, they can serve as a communicative strategy to manage interpersonal relationships, for instance, to act as mitigating devices (cf. e.g. Caffi, 2007, Schneider, 2007).

In Chinese, there are similar expressions that are used for mitigation purposes. As mentioned in Section 2.2, approximative expressions with *ba* can reduce negative communicative effects. Similarly, the speaker may also use approximative expressions to hedge possible negative effects of what is being conveyed. For example,

(24) 经理: 我看会议不能邀请太多的与会者。
Jingli: Wo kan huiyi bu neng yaoqing tai duo de yuhuizhe.
manager I see meeting not can invite too many participant
Manager: In my opinion, we should not invite too many participants for the conference.
秘书：<u>大概需要三十个吧</u>。
Mishu: *Dagai xuyao sanshi ge ba.*
secretary about need thirty CL BA
Secretary: There should be about thirty participants.

(25) 王：这件事肯定会处理一批领导。
Wang: Zhe jian shi kending hui chuli yipi lingdao.
Wang this event certainly will punish lots of cadre
Wang: Lots of cadres involved in the event will be punished.
张：不会吧，<u>最多一两个</u>。
Zhang: Bu hui *ba*, *zuiduo yi liang ge.*
Zhang not BA at most one two CL
Zhang: Probably not, at most one or two.

In example (24), the secretary's response can be considered a suggestion for the conference participants. The function word *ba* and the approximative expression *dagai* (about) in the utterance help to achieve a mitigation effect since they reduce the force of her suggestion. Because of the unequal power relationship between the participants, an addressee of lower rank or status tends to adopt mitigating devices when presenting his/her viewpoint or stance to reduce possible unwanted effects.

Furthermore, approximative expressions used for mitigating purposes have a politeness function which can help to minimize disagreement between self and other, or maximize agreement between self and other in terms of Leech's (1983) agreement maxim in the Politeness Principle. This is illustrated in example (25), where *ba* reduces the addressee's certainty about what the addresser has said, and the approximative expression *zuiduo yi liang ge* mitigates his disagreement and allows the addresser to keep a positive face (cf. Brown and Levinson, 1987).

## 5. Concluding Remarks

In this chapter, I have discussed the loose uses of some Chinese approximative expressions. It has been found that in communication numerical expressions with definite semantics, i.e., conveying specified quantities, are often interpreted in a loose way, otherwise the expected meanings or intended effects of the whole utterance cannot be achieved. There are also numerical expressions which are used with explicit approximators. In either of these uses, the discourse marker *ba* may be added to highlight the approximative information of the utterance.

Approximative uses of numerical expressions have also been shown to be firmly rooted in cultural conventions, as illustrated by the common reading of numerals in well-known sayings and ancient poems. Moreover, the interpretation of numerals is highly context-dependent with different contexts giving rise to different contextual effects. I have tried to show that numerals can be used to create dynamic or tranquillity effects in descriptive texts but may also have an important mitigating effect in interpersonal relationships.

## Acknowledgment

I would like to thank the volume editors for their kind help and suggestions for the final version of my paper, and Professor Hartmut Haberland for his insightful comments. I am also very grateful for the support from the Key National Research Center for Linguistics and Applied Linguistics, Guangdong University of Foreign Studies, P.R. China.

## References

Bach, K. (2001). "Speaking loosely: Sentence nonliterality". *Midwest Studies in Philosophy* **25**: 249–263.

Brinton, L. J. (1996). *Pragmatic markers in English*. Berlin: Mouton de Gruyter.

Brown, P. and S. Levinson (1987). *Politeness: Some universals in language usage*. Cambridge: Cambridge University Press.

Caffi, C. (2007). *Mitigation*. Amsterdam: Elsevier.

Channell, J. (1994). *Vague language*. Oxford: Oxford University Press.

Chu, C. C. (1998). *A discourse grammar of Mandarin Chinese*. New York: Peter Lang Publishing.

Chu, C. C. (2002). "Relevance theory, discourse markers and the Mandarin utterance-final particle A/Ya". *Applied Linguistics and Acquisition* **37**: 1–42.

Chu, C. C. (2006). "A contrastive approach to discourse particles – A case study of the Mandarin UFP *Ne*". *Journal of Foreign Languages* (**3**): 7–29.

Cutting, J. (2007). *Vague language explored*. New York: Palgrave Macmillan.

Erman, B. (2001). "Pragmatic markers revisited with a focus on *you know* in adult and adolescent talk". *Journal of Pragmatics* **33**: 1337–1359.

Franken, N. (1997). "Vagueness and approximation in relevance theory". *Journal of Pragmatics* **28**: 135–151.

Han, Y. S. (1995). "A pragmatic analysis of the *ba* particle in Mandarin Chinese". *Journal of Chinese Linguistics* **23**: 99–128.

Koester, A. (2007). "'About twelve thousand or so': Vagueness in North American and UK offices", in J. Cutting (ed.), *Vague language expressed.* New York: Palgrave Macmillan, 40–61.

Lakoff, G. (1972). "Hedges: A study in meaning criteria and the logic of fuzzy concepts". *Papers from the Eighth Regional Meeting of the Chicago Linguistic Society*, University of Chicago, Chicago, IL, 8: 183–228.

Leech, G. (1983). *Principles of pragmatics*. London: Longman.

Lenk, U. (1998). "Discourse markers and global coherence in conversation". *Journal of Pragmatics* **30**: 245–257.

Li, I. C. (2000). *Utterance-final particles in Taiwanese: A discourse-pragmatic analysis*. Taibei: The Crane Publishing Co., Ltd.

Luke, K. K. (1988). "A conversation analysis approach to the study of utterance particles in Cantonese". Ph. D. dissertation. University of York, York.

Luo, Z. F. (1994). *Hanyu da cidian. [Comprehensive dictionary of Chinese]* Shanghai: Lexicography Press.

Ma, J. Z. (2000). *Ma shi wen tong*. Beijing: Commercial Press.

Miracle, C. (1991). "Discourse markers in Mandarin Chinese". Ph. D. dissertation. Ohio State University, Ohio.

Nerlich, B., V. Clarke and D. Clarke (2001). "Ambiguities we live by: Towards a pragmatics of polysemy". *Journal of Pragmatics* **33**: 1–20.

Ran, Y. P. (2004). "Pragmatic functions of the Chinese discourse marker *ba* and its contextual adaptability". *Modern Foreign Languages* **27**: 340–349.

Schiffrin, D. (1987). *Discourse markers*. Cambridge: Cambridge University Press.

Schneider, S. (2007). *Reduced parenthetical clauses as mitigators. A corpus study of spoken French, Italian and Spanish*. Amsterdam: Benjamins.

Shie, C. C. (1991). "A discourse-functional analysis of Mandarin sentence – final particles". M.A. thesis, National Chengchi University, Taipei.

Sperber, D. and D. Wilson (1986/1995). *Relevance: Communication and cognition*. Oxford: Blackwell.

Wachtel, T. (1980). "Pragmatic approximations". *Journal of Pragmatics* **4**: 201–211.

New Approaches to Hedging
Edited by Gunther Kaltenböck, Wiltrud Mihatsch and Stefan Schneider


# 8

# Weakening or Strengthening?: A Case of Enantiosemy in Plato's *Gorgias*☆

*Claudia Caffi*

## Abstract

The present chapter is grounded in the assumption that mitigation – and, within it, hedging operations – is ambivalent between weakening and strengthening functions. In a word, mitigation is a rhetorical phenomenon. As such, its study can benefit from the reflection on language use as it developed through the centuries in the field of rhetoric. Since rhetoric is viewed as the pragmatics of classical world, the chapter sets out to foreground some general connecting points between the two disciplines. The chapter presents an in-depth analysis of the use of the approximation marker "so to say," in a passage taken from Plato's dialogue *Gorgias*, which is also relevant in that it contains a definition of rhetoric. The contextualized analysis of the marker shows that it can be given two opposite interpretations: attenuating and reinforcing. In other words, the marker in question can be seen both as an approximator and an underscorer and illustrates a peculiar case of enantiosemy (Lepschy, 1981, 1982). The interpretation of the passage and the overall argumentative strategy followed by Plato to denigrate rhetoric radically changes according to the function assigned to this micro-stylistic choice, that is, weakening or strengthening. This kind of ambivalence can be described from a rhetorical viewpoint in terms of an antiphrastic tension, inherent in mitigation and, more in general, in stylistically modulated choices (Bally, 1970 [1909]) to which approximators belong.

☆Earlier Italian versions of this paper appeared in Caffi (2001: 142–165) and in G. L. Beccaria and Marello, C. (Eds.), 2002, *La parola al testo. Scritti per Bice Mortara Garavelli*, Edizioni dell'Orso, Alessandria, pp. 57–73.

## 1. Introduction

In the present chapter, I start from the assumption that pragmatics derives from classical rhetoric, rhetoric being the study of discourse and intentional communication aimed at specific purposes and implying the taking on of responsibility (cf. Hill and Irvine, 1993). Far from defining rhetoric as a "secondary grammar" opposed to the "primary grammar" of language (cf. Plett, 1985), this chapter calls for a comprehensive, integrated framework where rhetorical aspects are viewed as inherent in every linguistic level.

One of my starting assumptions in doing pragmatics is that pragmatics can be backed by other disciplines in the investigation of the multi-layered, multi-dimensional mechanisms of communication. The point is that this backing must be thought of not only synchronically but also diachronically. In particular, pragmatics should take rhetorical perspectives on language throughout the centuries into account and consider the stages of reflection on communication that rhetoric has gone through. One of the links between classical rhetoric and pragmatics is the fact that both disciplines do not deny the ambivalences that are part and parcel of communication. On the contrary, they both put them in the foreground. To substantiate the view of the deep-rooted link between rhetoric and pragmatics,[1] one could choose between two main lines of reasoning: either the discussion of some general theoretical stances of both disciplines or the in-depth analysis of a paradigmatic case which shows their convergence. In the following sections, the latter has been preferred. Therefore, after some general remarks on the similarities between rhetoric and pragmatics, I concentrate on a very specific example, taken from an author whose thoughts shaped Western culture, namely Plato. The analysis of a single phenomenon in a passage from one of Plato's dialogues allows me to illustrate how a discourse marker, apparently a mitigator, can be ambivalent in many subtle ways. I try to disentangle, from an integrated pragmatic perspective, the micro-paradox encapsulated by what seems to be an approximating marker that occurs in the definition of rhetoric given by Plato's character Gorgias in the dialogue that bears his name and is a milestone in the history of (anti-) rhetoric.

## 2. Pragmatics as *ἐμπειρία*

Among the main similarities between rhetoric and pragmatics, it is worthwhile mentioning here what the two disciplines share *ex negativo*, that is, the fact that they have been the object of the

[1] The first linguist to draw a systematic connection between pragmatics and rhetoric was Leech (1981), who opposed the two disciplines to grammar and particularly judgments of grammatical acceptability: "Semantics is rule-governed [grammatical]; pragmatics is principle-constrained [rhetorical]" (*ibid.*: 415). See also Leech (1983). A discussion of the links between the two disciplines is Venier (2008).

same kind of criticism. The paradigm of criticism against rhetoric can be found in Plato's dialogues, particularly in *Gorgias*, which I deal with in the sections below. In *Gorgias*, through the voice of his character Socrates, Plato makes the basic distinction between knowledge (which is at the core of science and cannot be false) and belief (which is at the core of opinion and may well be false) particularly explicit. Socrates, the archetypal philosopher, is opposed to Gorgias, the archetypal rhetorician, who, applauded and acclaimed by the public that is under his power, is presented at the climax of his career.

According to Plato (*Grg.* 455a 1), rhetoric is "a producer of persuasion [*πειθώ*] for belief, not for instruction in the matter of right and wrong." Rhetoric deals with any topic, even without knowing anything about it. Gorgias claims he can teach how to talk without actually knowing what one is talking about. Thus, rhetoric is *ἐμπειρία* rather than *τέχνη*; it is not a science but *ἐμπειρία καὶ τριβή*, a messy collection of extrinsic devices, "an empirical knack" (Dodds, 1985: 225), which neither presupposes nor generates knowledge.

Socrates argues in *Gorgias* that rhetoric is not an art but a practice:

> and I say it is not an art, but a habitude, since it has no account to give of the real nature of the things it applies, and so cannot tell the cause of any of them. (*Grg.* 465a 2–5, Plato, translated by Lamb, 1961: 319)

It should be noted, however, that although Plato attributes this statement to Socrates in this particular dialogue, he does not question the power of words elsewhere. In fact, as Dodds (1985: 10) points out, in another Platonic dialogue, *Phedrus*, the character Socrates describes rhetoric as a spoken word that can change the souls of people, a "*ψυχαγωγία τις διὰ λόγων*" (a fascination of the souls through speech) (*Phd.* 261a). This Plato regards as a dangerous ability for two main reasons, namely, (a) it is not scientific and relies on irrationality; and (b) it is ethically neutral.

Similarly, pragmatics has been regarded by some as a "wastebasket," a loose domain, or a messy field of heterogeneous studies that often yield no more than unscientific guesses or sketchy descriptions of data lacking stable evaluative criteria and a clear rationale. Paradoxically enough, the awareness of a need for new, flexible, epistemological paradigms capable of dealing with the complexity of discourse is stronger in well-established disciplines like natural sciences and physics than in fields like social sciences and linguistics, which are still deeply affected by the myth of objectivity.

Aristotle's *Rhetoric* (Aristotle, 1975) begins by explaining that rhetoric deals with discourse, an activity that is to some extent common to, and known by, all human beings. The same could be said of pragmatics, which has been seen as a chaotic mixture of studies focusing on knowledge shared by all people. This view is backed empirically and can even be vindicated theoretically, in that pragmatic and ethnomethodological approaches do tend to assume that all speakers of a given language are competent members of the group who share specific common knowledge of language and its use. The point, in fact, is to make this shared procedural knowledge explicit, and in this connection, pragmatics has repeatedly shown that there are no clear-cut distinctions between folk-theories and "scientific" theories.

The alleged triviality of the object of analysis in pragmatics has sometimes elicited patronizing attitudes on the part of scholars from other linguistic or philosophical fields. Clearly, disciplines that do not deal with the intricacies of real language praxis lend themselves more easily to formalization than pragmatics does. On the other hand, from a pragmatic standpoint, formal analyses of artificial examples and limited numbers of variables out of context are hardly interesting either. I do not embark here on a discussion of theoretical ideological trends in linguistics (including pragmatic linguistics) and philosophy of language. Nevertheless, it can be noted that the tendency today to contrast pragmatics against semantics, logic, and cognitive linguistics, is not at all unlike Plato's earlier opposition between rhetoric and science, truth, and ethics.

It cannot be denied, at any rate, that a pragmatic perspective, however imperfect its tools presently may be, makes it possible to tackle fundamental issues of language usage and contextualized interaction in all their multidimensionality. Although this may entail reductions of formalization that can lead to inconsistencies, it makes it possible to deal with complex, dynamic systems from a perspective that is not too distorted. Moreover, the theoretical flexibility of pragmatics and its various interfaces with other disciplines surely are strengths when we adopt an integrated systemic approach, which will allow us to envisage, rather than a specific structure (e.g., the sentence, the utterance, the speech act), a pattern, that is, an organization that is in turn based on different, intertwined dimensions (be they sociological, psychological, cognitive, emotive, etc.). From a general epistemological point of view, pragmatics is well aware that it can only provide partial and contextualized analyses within interpretative models that are culturally and historically determined. Similarly, and above all, pragmatics is aware that it is impossible in principle to avoid influences of analysts on their own analyses (cf. Caffi, 1994).

Plato's main argument against rhetoric is that the latter is not connected to a thorough knowledge of any specific field. Yet this argument can be reversed and employed to demonstrate the strength of rhetoric, and indeed, it can be attributed to a lack of understanding of the true nature of rhetoric, which is considerably more than simply the art of "well speaking" (*ars bene dicendi*). Actually, as Aristotle (*Rhet.* 1355b) explains, rhetoric is the study of discourse forms and organization:

> [i]t is thus evident that Rhetoric does not deal with any one definite class of subjects [...] and further, that its function is not so much to persuade, as to find out in each case the existing means of persuasion.

It is hence a type of *meta-theory* of discourse that investigates the conditions that make discourse coherent and effective and enables users to derive methods for building up effective texts. Traditionally, rhetoric dealt mainly prescriptively with discourse without providing a comprehensive description of what is constitutive of it or explaining how it functions. Indeed, the study of what makes up discourse is a pragmatic project that requires the contributions of a number of other disciplines as well. Such a study can only be achieved by integrating pragmatics with non-hegemonic approaches in other fields like psychology, sociology, semiotics, and cognitive science.

Plato's attacks on rhetoric could just as well have been aimed at pragmatics. Plato accused rhetoric of being *κολακεία*, that is, flattery, adulation, seduction appealing to the soul rather than generating knowledge (like philosophy); this was like his criticism of gastronomy for appealing to the body rather than contributing to the knowledge of it (like medicine) (cf. *Grg*. 464d–e). This kind of criticism was surely misleading and paradoxical, if only because it was expressed with astonishing (and seductive) rhetorical skill. In fact, the seductive power of discourse does not lie in rhetoric (or pragmatics) as such but in *λόγος*, or rather, in *enacted speech*. This power is reflected in the exploitation of the expressive resources of a language by someone for someone else, and in the clustering of these resources around a communicative project, where expressive and conative aspects are indexically intertwined. A non-idealistic theory of discourse must adopt this project, which is shaped by formal choices, and must account for it as part of a theory of communicative action (cf. Habermas, 1987).

## 3. A Pragmatic Analysis of a Passage from Plato's *Gorgias*

Antiphrasis sums up the pervasive ambivalence of communication in one paradoxical, aggressive move. An antiphrastic current also runs through mitigation, as every occurrence of mitigation implies that there is something to mitigate, thus switching on a warning light while at the same time trying to switch it off. In fact, ambivalence is so much at the very core of mitigation (cf. Caffi, 1999, 2001, 2007) that without the support of co-text, context, and shared knowledge, it is impossible to establish whether mitigation is part of a ritual – for example, a strategic form of caution, *sprezzatura*, or "studied unconcern" (cf. Castiglione 2002 [1528]; Ossola, 1987) – or something else.

The cues reflecting speakers' stances toward their utterances may be subtle and modulation may be microscopic; however, giving up considering such cues means losing sight of the connections between language and its users. In the integrated pragmatic approach adopted here, attenuating modulation, which is realized by grammatically and pragmatically heterogeneous means, is multi-layered and multi-dimensional. On the one hand, it involves choices centered around an instrumental pole related to the speaker's practical goals – particularly the minimization of risks linked to making recipients do or believe things. On the other hand, it involves choices centered around a relational pole related to the construction of identity (cf. Giles et al., 1979; Caffi, 1999, 2001, 2007). This latter pole has been neglected by pragmatic research thus far or has been seen restrictively as coinciding with politeness systems (Brown and Levinson, 1978, 1987).

Against this background, I concentrate on a specific attenuating phrase, that is, *ὡς ἔπος εἰπεῖν* ("so to say"), taken from the passage in Plato's dialogue *Gorgias* where Gorgias defines rhetoric (450b–c). I will observe how this phrase, apparently an approximator, contributes to the multi-dimensional construction of meaning and of the character of Gorgias by considering some pragmatic effects originating from the use of the phrase in that particular context.

Clearly, it is necessary to be cautious when applying procedures intended mainly for the analysis of everyday communication to the analysis of a literary work (Segre, 1985). This is particularly true for a text like *Gorgias*, which is semiotically highly complex, polysemic, and "hyper-rhetorical."[2] Characters in *Gorgias* are essentially textual devices that, in addition to their functions in the text's argumentative dialectics, gain independent existence and credibility thanks to a fine-grained dialogic mimesis. Dodds claims that the dialogue has a "peculiar emotional power" whose secret is "that its author felt the issue as a deeply personal one, and has communicated the resulting tension to his readers" (Dodds, 1985: 31). Given that rhetoric is depicted in the dialogue as the art of success, the question becomes: "by what standard shall we measure success?" (Dodds, 1985: 4). The personal tone of the dialogue and the author's involvement in the matter at stake (the opposition of two ways of life) make the dialogic mimesis strikingly brilliant. In what follows, I discuss a case of pragmatic micro-ambivalence that sheds some light on what makes the text hyper-rhetorical. This discussion shows that such an application lends itself easily to a critical analysis of Plato's works as well as other classics. Pragmatics may, in turn, get new insights from the texts themselves. The analysis proposed in the following sections is also meant to encourage the study of lexical polysemies in further detail and to start an in-depth examination of the multi-functionality of discourse markers beyond their use in face-to-face interaction. It can be read as an attempt of applying pragmatic tools to the fine-grained study of a literary text. The phrase *ὡς ἔπος εἰπεῖν*, which is the focus of the next few sections, can be defined as a case of "pragmatic enantiosemy" or "enantiopraxy" on an analogy to what Lepschy (1981: 153–166; 1982: 349–378) has called "enantiosemy" in discussing lexemes that have opposite meanings (e.g., "ferial," meaning both a feast day and a weekday).

## 4. A Cluster of Markers

The passage analyzed here (*Grg*. 450a–e) has the highest concentration of discourse markers in the whole text. This is partly explained by a subsequent shift from a dialogic structure to a monologic one characterized by long argumentative turns by Socrates. Other parts of the dialogue display a similar adjacency-pair structure (typically, question–answer), but the hammering

[2] *Gorgias* has been defined "hyper-rhetorical" by Joly (1990). See also Perelman (1955).

occurrence of modal cues at the beginning of both Socrates' and Gorgias' turns in this specific passage especially strikes the reader's attention.

The following list includes the attenuating modulations occurring in the passage, most of which are parenthetical formulae pertaining to the epistemic-doxastic modality (cf. Urmson, 1952; Venier, 1991; Schneider, 2007), whereas the remaining few are meta-linguistic comments: *ὡς ἔοικεν*, "it seems" (450a); *οἶμαι*, "I take it" (450c); *μοι δοκεῖς*, "I understand" (450d; 450e); *ὡς ἔπος εἰπεῖν*, "so to say" (450b); *ὀρθῶς λέγων*, "properly speaking" (450c); again, *ὡς ἔπος εἰπεῖν*, specularly uttered by Socrates (450d); *ὡς ἐγώ φημι*, "I maintain" (450c).

These markers are first of all highly functional to the mimesis of the dialogic discourse conveying Plato's thinking. At the same time, from a cognitive point of view, they reflect the dialogue construction process, particularly the encoding of thoughts, while expressing different degrees of commitment to particular propositions or utterances. Moreover, from an interactional perspective, they contribute to the fictional speakers' self-presentations, "face-work," and constructions of identity, in that the speakers use them to appear cautious, patiently searching for truth, willing to understand correctly, and cooperative. We may well hypothesize that the high number of discourse markers in the passage examined depends on its strategic position, as it is the *incipit* of both the meeting between Gorgias and Socrates and the Plato–Socrates' argumentation, thus playing a crucial role in the construction of both. This is particularly true in view of the fact that the passage includes the basic definition of rhetoric. Plato's basic line of argumentation in the dialogue is that both this definition and the discipline it tries to capture have to be rejected: according to Plato, the former is unsatisfactory and the latter is harmful.

The phrase *ὡς ἔπος εἰπεῖν* ("so to say") appears in 450b when Gorgias explains to Socrates why one should not call all arts having to do with discourse "rhetorics." The phrase is a parenthetical final clause introduced by the subordinating polyvalent conjunction *ὡς*. It is an etymological figure resulting from the alliterative adjacency of the accusative, the internal direct object *ἔπος* ("word," "discourse"), and the infinitive with the same root *εἰπεῖν* ("to say," "to talk"). Liddell, Scott, and Jones (1968: 676) give the following phraseological uses for the entry *ἔπος*:

> *ὡς ἔπος εἰπεῖν almost, practically,* qualifying a too absolute expression, esp. with *πᾶς* and *οὐδείς* (not with metaphors). Pl. *Ap.* 17a, *Phd.,* 78e, *Grg.* 456a, al., Arist. *Metaph.* $1009^b$ 16, *Pol.* $1252^b$ 29, D. 9-47, etc.; opp. *ὄντως* or *ἀκριβεῖ λόγῳ*.

The phrase *ὡς ἔπος εἰπεῖν* is used by Socrates to echo Gorgias in 450d and also appears in a number of other passages in the dialogue: in 456a (Gorgias), 466e (Socrates), 501a (Socrates), 505a (Socrates), 517b (Socrates). The first occurrence of the phrase (in 450b), however, is the only one Dodds specifically deals with, in a note in his authorized edition of *Gorgias* (Dodds, 1985: 196) that I discuss in the next section.

## 5. Contextualization of the Passage (*Grg. 450b*)

Gorgias, the brilliant rhetorician from Leontini at the top of his triumphal career, has just held a successful speech in front of a large audience that is now gradually scattering.[3] Callicles, who is part of this audience, expresses regret that Socrates and Chaerephon have not listened to Gorgias' performance (447a). However, he reassures them, they will have a chance to talk to Gorgias, as he is staying at his place. Suddenly Gorgias comes up and Socrates says he would like to ask a few questions about the true nature of his art, that is, its *quidditas* (rather than its quality): what rhetoric is about and how Gorgias defines himself (448e). Socrates' questions become more and more pressing.

The following is the co-textual environment of the passage under scrutiny; the latter is presented in both the English version and the original.[4]

| | |
|---|---|
| SOC. | Come now, answer me in the same way about rhetoric: with what particular thing is its skill concerned? |
| GORG. | With speech. |
| SOC. | What kind of speech, Gorgias? Do you mean that which shows by what regimen sick people could get well? |
| GORG. | No. |
| SOC. | The rhetoric is not concerned with all kinds of speech. |
| GORG. | No, I say. |
| SOC. | Yet it does make men able to speak. |
| GORG. | Yes. |
| SOC. | And to understand also the things about which they speak. |
| GORG. | Of course. |
| SOC. | Now, does the medical art, which we mentioned just now, make men able to understand and speak about the sick? |
| GORG. | It must. |
| SOC. | Hence the medical art also, it seems, is concerned with speech. |
| GORG. | Yes. |

[3] As a historical figure, Gorgias from Leontini (Siracuse, Sicily, 480 B.C. ca. to 380 B.C. ca.), a sophist (but see Dodds, 1985 [1959]), was the leading practitioner and teacher of rhetoric. He had among his masters Empedocles, Corax, and Tisias. The only certain date in his biography is 427 B.C., incidentally the same year Plato was born, when he headed an embassy in Athens where he gave lectures on rhetoric. His prose, very mannered and refined, is exercised at its best in the *Encomium of Helen*, and in the *Palamedes*. It may be worthwhile recalling here that the performances held by rhetoricians in ancient times should be imagined as a happening closer to a pop-concert than to a meeting of stiff, detached academics.

[4] The English translation employed here is by W. R. M. Lamb (Plato, 1961: 269–271). Plato (1985 [1959]) has also been considered. I have also made reference to two lexicons: Ast, 1956 (Lipsiae, 1835), Vol. I: 2; Liddell, Scott, and Jones, 1968.

SOC. That is, speech about diseases?

GORG. Certainly.

SOC. Now, is gymnastic also concerned with speech about the good and bad condition of our bodies?

GORG. Quite so.

SOC. And moreover it is the same, Gorgias, with all the other arts; each of them is concerned with that kind of speech which deals with the subject matter of that particular art.

GORG. Apparently.

SOC. Then why, pray, do you not give the name "rhetorical" to those other arts, when they are concerned with speech, if you call that "rhetoric" which has to do with speech?

GORG. Because, Socrates, the skill in those other arts is almost wholly concerned with manual work and similar activities, whereas in rhetoric there is no such manual working, but its whole activity and efficacy is by means of speech. For this reason I claim for the rhetorical art that it is concerned with speech, and it is a correct description, I maintain.

ΓΟΡ. Ὅτι, ὦ Σώκρατες, τῶν μέν ἄλλων τεχνῶν περὶ χειρουργίας τε καὶ τοιαύτας πράξεις ὡς ἔμος εἰπεῖν πᾶσά ἐστιν ἡ ἐπιστήμη, τῆς δέ ῥητορικῆς οὐδέν ἐστιν τοιοῦτον χειρούργημα, ἀλλὰ πᾶσα ἡ πρᾶξις καὶ ἡ κύρωσις διὰ λόγων ἐστίν. διὰ ταῦτ᾽ ἐγὼ τὴν ῥητορικὴν τέχνην ἀξιῶ εἶναι περὶ λόγους, ὀρθῶς λέγων, ὡς ἐγώ φημι.

Gorgias is tired after his speech and has probably already realized that he cannot expect anything good from Socrates. However, he patiently defends himself and his art. From a structural point of view, his answer to Socrates' question is made up of two parts. The first part is the explanation of why he does not define other arts as rhetoric. This section develops around the main contrast between these arts and rhetoric itself. The second part includes a definition of what rhetoric is, as opposed to the preceding explanation of what it is not. Finally, the closing of this second part is a self-evaluation of the correctness of what he has just said. Gorgias carefully weighs his words (at least if we adopt the mitigating interpretation of the phrase I am going to examine), while at the same time sounding fully aware and proud of his role. On the one hand, in the first part of his reply, he identifies the main difference between rhetoric and other arts, mitigating his statement by acknowledging its partial inadequacy. On the other hand, in the second part of his turn, in a crescendo of self-awareness and assertiveness, he boosts his utterance by fully committing himself to it ("*ἐγὼ τὴν ῥητορικὴν τέχνην ἀξιῶ εἶναι περὶ λόγους*", "for this reason I claim for the rhetorical art that it is concerned with speech") and proclaiming its correctness ("*ὀρθῶς λέγων, ὡς ἐγώ φημι*", "and it is a correct description, I maintain").

Nevertheless, Gorgias' definition of rhetoric is strongly ambivalent. Formal elements in the first part of the turn signal attenuation, whereas formal elements in the second part signal reinforcement. As a result, the stylistic contour of the passage is characterized by a fluctuating movement in two opposite modulation directions, that is, attenuation and reinforcement. This is the most common interpretation given to the two series of phrases occurring in Gorgias' turn.

As it is easy to gather, Gorgias' turn is of paramount importance for both the Sicilian rhetorician himself and rhetoric in general. The first phrase *ὡς ἔπος εἰπεῖν* seems to attenuate a statement that is too strong. This interpretation is also given in the authorized edition of *Gorgias* by Dodds (1985: 196), who, in full agreement with the translation suggested by Liddell, Scott, and Jones (1968), writes:

> *ὡς ἔπος εἰπεῖν*, *not* "so to speak", as if apologizing for a metaphor, but "practically", "one might almost say", qualifying a too sweeping statement (Lat. *paene dixerim*). (original emphasis)

But which statement is "too sweeping"? It is the one where Gorgias says that in other arts, *πᾶσά* [...] *ἡ ἐπιστήμη*, that is, *all* knowledge is non-verbal. According to Ast (1956 [1853]) and Liddell, Scott and Jones (1968), *εἶπον* usually collocates with the universal quantifier *πᾶς*, as exemplified in this passage. Indeed, what Gorgias says is that the knowledge characterizing other arts is *almost wholly* non-verbal; other arts are concerned *practically entirely* with non-verbal manual instruments and techniques. In this way Gorgias makes sure he is safe from the refutation already present, *in nuce*, in Socrates' question. Stating that other arts are *almost* only effective at a non-verbal level implies acknowledging Socrates' claim that they do employ discourse to some extent. Gorgias grants the truth of this point, while contrastively emphasizing rhetoric's distinctive feature: namely, the exclusive role that only it ascribes to discourse. In so doing, he introduces a factor of graduality into the contrast between rhetoric and other disciplines. This weakens the opposition between them as the contrast ceases to be dichotomous.

## 6. The Weakening Interpretation: The Marker as an Approximator

I believe the finest definition of markers like "almost," that is, the English translation of *ὡς ἔπος εἰπεῖν* suggested by Dodds, is the one given by the seventeenth-century rhetorician Matteo Peregrini (1639). In his treatise *Delle acutezze*, Peregrini employs the label "tempering particles" to refer to all the markers a speaker may use to acknowledge her/his inaccuracy. The following is Peregrini's (1960 [1639]: 60) list: *quasi* (almost, practically), *come* (as if), *forse* (maybe), *diresti* (you would say), *siami lecito* (let me say), *pare* (it seems), *per così dire* (so to say). Here, suffice it to say that tempering particles can be defined as markers expressing meta-pragmatic awareness (cf. Caffi, 1994) and operating as approximating devices. Three hundred and thirty-three years later, George Lakoff (1973 [1972]: 196) put both "practically" and "so to say" in the list of tempering particles he calls "hedges."[5]

Now, Peregrini's, Lakoff's, and Dodds' lists of tempering phrases contain items that actually center on different abstract scopes. On the one hand, Peregrini's "*quasi*" (almost), Lakoff's "practically," and Dodds' "almost" (like "*forse*," "*pare*") all signal an approximation of the propositional content. On the other hand, phrases like "so to say" or "one might almost say" (like "*siami lecito*") indicate a meta-linguistic self-evaluation focusing on the whole utterance act rather than on the proposition: the inaccuracy that the speaker acknowledges by them refers not merely to the proposition but to the act itself of saying. A first distinction can be drawn between these cases: while the modal devices "practically" or "*quasi*" belong to epistemic modality and hence typically occur in assertive speech acts, phrases like "so to say" or "one might almost say," which focus on an utterance's appropriateness in a given co-text and context rather than on its claim to truth, can also be employed in non-assertive illocutionary acts.

A further point can be made drawing on Authier-Revuz's (1995) substantial work on the "*non-coïncidences du dire*." The author analyzes the various uses of the French equivalent of "so to say," namely "*pour ainsi dire*." In particular, she observes:

> The use of *pour ainsi dire* covers the whole field of '*pas vraiment*' ('not really'), of an utterance to which the speaker does not '*pleinement*' ('fully') subscribe, since the word does not '*strictement*' ('strictly') correspond to the thing (Authier-Revuz, 1995: 652, my translation, C.C.).[6]

Here, the author distinguishes between two kinds of naming that are not fully adequate, that is:[7]

a. metaphorical naming;
b. approximating naming, where the shift with respect to the full correspondence between word and thing is due to a "*pas tout à fait*" ("not completely") (Authier-Revuz, 1995: 653). This case is opposed to the case of "contradiction" that takes place in a metaphor.

To go back to the analysis of the passage from *Gorgias*, we may well agree with Dodds that the marker used in Plato's dialogue has two possible English equivalents, namely it can be translated

---

[5] For general discussions of "hedges" see, among others, Kolde (1989), Markkanen and Schröder (1997) and Diewald (2006).

[6] Here the passage in the French original: "l'emploi du *pour ainsi dire* recouvre tout le champ du 'pas vraiment', d'un dire, auquel l'énonciateur n'adhère 'pas pleinement', le mot ne coïncidant 'pas strictement' à la chose."

[7] What strikes attention in the elegant and minute work by Authier-Revuz is a kind of terminological reductionism by which the instances considered here are viewed as 'naming', or as failures to "fit words to things." In fact, "naming," "words," and "things" are misleading hyperonyms used to refer to a wide variety of speaker's acts (acts of reference, acts of predication, illocutionary acts, etc.) and to linguistic phenomena like discourse markers, which cannot be described in extensional terms or even lack reference altogether.

with "practically" with the attenuating meaning of "almost," or it can be translated with "one might almost say." Having accepted that these are the two possible English translations of *ὡς ἔπος εἰπεῖν*, if we consider the scopes of these two markers, we can claim that they are heterogeneous: the former (i.e., "practically") focuses on the proposition, whereas the latter (i.e., "one might almost say") focuses on the utterance act. Clearly, it is not easy to identify the exact scopes of discourse markers as they are, by definition, not integrated into the syntactic structure of the utterance. In fact, as Authier-Revuz (1995: 653–654, my translation, C.C.) points out, their scopes are often vague and difficult to pin down, being often shifts that are vague, difficult to locate, producing a non-correspondence to the utterance of X, something like a halo of uncertainty, a diffuse feeling of unattained correspondence.[8] Despite this, my point is that the contributions of discourse markers to meaning construction and to the monitoring of communicative distances often change precisely because of differences between their scopes. At this juncture, let me briefly recall the empirically grounded typology of mitigating devices I have introduced elsewhere (cf. Caffi, 1999, 2001, 2007), which is based on the identification of three different scopes of mitigation: the *proposition* (and within it reference and predication), the *illocution* in its various dimensions, and the *deictic origin* of the utterance (Bühler, 1934; Benveniste, 1970). Three corresponding classes of mitigating devices can be clustered around these scopes: "bushes" (propositional), "hedges" (illocutionary), and "shields" (deictic). In Hare's (1970) terminology, bushes correspond to a de-intensification of the phrastic, whereas hedges signal a de-intensification of the neustic. In other words, bushes lessen the commitment to an utterance's propositional content, whereas hedges reduce the commitment to its illocutionary force (cf. Hübler, 1983). In contrast to these two first classes of mitigators, shields result in an overall dislocation of responsibility, for instance by introducing a new speaker or by deleting the "I-here-now" of the utterance. A concept that perfectly fits this definition of shields is Goffman's (1979) idea of different kinds of footing, typically realized by impersonalization strategies.

What is relevant for my present purposes is that there is a *continuum* between quotational shields, meta-linguistic cautionary markers ("so to say"), and approximating bushes ("practically") (cf. Caffi, 2007). In quotational shields, the speaker introduces a meta-level by means of expressions like "as X says" that explicitly signal that the words being used are someone else's in order to avoid committing her/himself to the utterance.[9] In other words, the

[8] The original passage sounds as follows: "écarts vagues non 'localisables', affectant le dire de X d'une non-coïncidence floue comme d'un halo d'incertitude ou d'un sentiment diffus de coïncidence non atteinte." Bolinger (1972: 227) speaks of the "halo effect" in dealing with "quite" vs. "entirely" and the different restrictions on their use as intensifiers.

[9] For systematic treatments of various forms of reported speech see, among others, Mortara Garavelli (1985); Mey (1999); Calaresu (2004). For a comprehensive account of French meta-linguistic expressions see Authier-Revuz (1995).

signaled suspension of literal meaning implies that the speaker's subscription – both cognitive and emotive – to her/his utterance, or part of it, is suspended too. The use of markers like "so to say" produces similar effects. However, in this latter case, to use Goffman's distinction between participation roles, in addition to being the "animator" of the message, the speaker is also its "author" (cf. Goffman, 1979, 1981). There is a sort of *continuum* along a scale of decreasing transparency (cf. Hölker, 1988), from

(1) quotational shields (e.g., "as X says," "in quotes"); through
(2) meta-linguistic cautionary markers (e.g., "so to say"); to
(3) approximating bushes (e.g., "practically").

To clarify the differences between these types, it may be useful to begin with the observation that, on the one hand, markers introducing actual quotations are linked to literality, namely a general dichotomous feature of communication. On the other hand, cautionary markers indicate at the meta-linguistic level the incomplete fulfillment of Austin's (1962) first B condition: the procedure must be correct. Finally, the approximating bushes, signal, without introducing a meta-level, what can be considered a lack of fulfillment of Austin's (1962) second B condition, namely the condition concerning the complete execution of the procedure. The resulting effect is vagueness (cf., among others, Channell, 1994; Jucker et al., 2003). Bazzanella *et al.* (1991) have labeled this scalar dimension "precision of propositional content." The focus of "so to say," that is, the meaning to be assigned to the indexical particle *par excellence* "so" (which is absent from the Greek expression), and the interpretation of "say" (cf. Grice, 1989) are all determined by the context.

Returning to the passage from *Gorgias*, we may claim that, according to Dodds (1985), the use of *ὡς ἔπος εἰπεῖν* corresponds to Authier-Revuz's (1995: 653) second interpretation of "*pour ainsi dire*" as an approximating device, or bush, to use the terminology adopted here. As we have seen (cf. Section 5), the possibility that the expression is used to introduce a metaphor – the first interpretation identified by Authier-Revuz, that is, the metaphorical naming – is completely excluded by Dodds.

Now, was this exclusion of the metaphorical use necessary? Even if we took the word "metaphorical" in Dodds' note to mean "non literal," is there really anything in the text that would bring us to assume that *ὡς ἔπος εἰπεῖν* is introducing a metaphor? Or rather, does this "unnecessary" note by Dodds implicitly confirm that the passage is hyper-rhetorical and overburdened with sense? Apparently, Dodds feels the need, if not to clarify the ultimate sense of the phrase, at least to exclude some other possible meanings.

## 7. The Adjacent Co-Text

Moving to the second modulation at the end of Gorgias' turn, we cannot but be amazed by the number of strengthening devices used. Two adjacent meta-linguistic formulae, that is, *ὀρθῶς λέγων* ("it is a correct description," literally, "speaking correctly") and *ὥς ἐγώ φημι* ("I maintain") evaluate the correctness of the definition just given while at the same time foregrounding the speaker by means of the first person singular. The latter has already been assertively pointed out by the first person singular, present tense *ἀξιῶ* ("I claim") (an explicit illocutionary device) introducing the utterance. This corresponds – almost performatively – to a declaration of propositional attitude (a *Bezeugung einer propositionalen Einstellung*[10]) confirming the speaker's responsibility for an opinion (a *δόξα*), as paradigmatically opposed to knowledge (*ἐπιστήμη*).

There is no room for reticence or a possible retreat here (Socrates will immediately reply with his counter-argument); there is neither caution nor *deminutio*. On the contrary, there is a full, proud, even pretentious commitment to the utterance, which may well be said to flout Leech's (1983) modesty maxim and even Grice's maxim of manner, more specifically the sub-maxim "be brief" (cf. Grice, 1989: 27). This is all the more striking since Gorgias has just boasted of being a master of conciseness (449c). The contrast with the uncertainty of the previous attenuating modulation and the clumsiness of the resulting definition are transparent.

Socrates' general criticism of inconsistency is harsh. What he says later on in the text, addressing Callicles, sounds decidedly unflattering: "[y]ou are spoiling your first statements, Callicles, and you can no longer be a fit partner with me in probing the truth, if you are going to speak against your own convictions" (495a). Now, is Gorgias' modulatory oscillation responsible for some kind of inconsistency that undermines his credibility? Regardless of possible conjectures, it is a matter of fact that the discourse identities projected by the two series of modulations within this single turn are incongruous. The former is cautious, whereas the latter is aggressive: Gorgias is prudent one moment, pretentious the next.

Within his overall argumentative strategy, Plato exploits these modulations and their connotations to construct the antagonist Gorgias. The anti-rhetorician Plato-Socrates seems to convey meta-communicatively to the implied reader, "look at this man, the founding master of the 'art of saying'; look at the way he talks. He is pretentious even when he does not know exactly what he is talking about." Plato does not say this overtly; rather, subtly, and much more convincingly, he points out that Gorgias claims he can teach people how to speak effectively without even knowing the subject of his own discourse. Is there any better strategy than this personification of inconsistency to demonstrate the basic assumption of the dialogue that rhetoric is an art or empirical knack (*ἐμπειρία*) rather than science (*τέχνη*), a messy collection of merely extrinsic devices which neither presuppose nor produce knowledge? Following Plato, rhetorical persuasion is irrational (*πειθῴ*). Based on psychagogy, the magical power of flattering, and

---

[10] The *Bezeugung einer propositionalen Einstellung* is a category that, according to Lang and Steinitz (1978), is paradigmatically opposite to the *Beschreibung einer propositionalen Einstellung*.

seducing words (*κολαλεία*), it disregards the truth and can therefore be condemned. Gorgias is precisely the symbol of rhetoric. Although acclaimed by a large audience, he is condemned by his own style of speaking even before having to surrender to Socrates' straightforward arguments. In contrast to Socrates' "irony on the upbeat" (Jankélévitch, 1964; my translation, C.C.), his style is confused and emphatic, and he is much more interested in personal success than in the search for truth. He therefore becomes entangled in a contradictory form of face-work that continually shifts between caution and self-assertiveness, and in doing so betrays his weakness. Instead of giving unambiguous definitions, he only *claims* to give them, not just antiphrastically, but following a kind of implicit inverse scale: the less clear his definitions are, the clearer Gorgias needs to claim they are.

Despite his self-proclaimed conciseness, Gorgias is inconsistent, maybe tired, or unable because of professional bias to give up pleonastic formulae, circumlocutions, and tortuous reasoning. Is this a way of taking time and weighing words before the *ad personam* attack that he rightly foresees? Is it *ὡς ἔπος εἰπεῖν* a sophist's habit, the surface trace of a compromise between the elegance of a clear definition and the need not to trigger a possible objection by Socrates which is already in the air? Or is it possible, after all, to interpret this marker, or "autonymic connotation," to use Authier-Revuz' (1995: 30ff.) term, in a totally different way?

## 8. The Strengthening Interpretation: The Marker as an Underscorer

It is certainly not common to be able to historically reconstruct the steps through which a given expression becomes grammaticalized as a stereotyped, desemantized locution. And it may be even more rare that we are able to date the first specific use of a given marker. According to Reinberg (1981), however, it is reasonable to conjecture that the marker *ὡς ἔπος εἰπεῖν* is found for the first time in *The Persians* by Aeschylus. Reinberg examines the passage where queen Atossa answers the question asked by the ghost of Darius, who urges her to be concise about the destiny of the Persian power. Here, in the lines 713–714 of Aeschylus' tragedy is Atossa's answer:

*πάντα γάρ, Δαρεῖ, ἀκούσῃ μῦθον ἐν βραχεῖ λόγῳ*
*διαπεπόρθηται τὰ Περσῶν πράγμαθ', ὡς εἰπεῖν ἔπος*[11]

Reinberg is above all interested in pointing out that Aeschylus' audience was able to trace the origin of *διαπορθέω* (be destroyed) to the root *πέρθω*, thus interpreting the word *Πέρσαι* from an

[11] The English translation by Herbert Weir Smyth (Aeschylus, 1956: 166, ll. 713–714) confirms the reinforcing interpretation of the marker in that particular context. This is the following: "O Darius, thou shalt hear in brief space of time. The power of Persia is ruined well-nigh utterly".

etymological standpoint. She finds an argument for her etymological thesis also in the occurrence of the locution *ὡς ἔπος εἰπεῖν* in the lines quoted above. Although, Reinberg notes, after Aeschylus, the locution has a predominantly attenuating function, in these lines of *The Persians*:

> it would be meaningless to use expressions like 'so to say' or 'generally' after the revelation of the Persian defeat, the more so since Darius has invited Atossa to be brief and avoid long-winded discourse (cf. *σαφές*, l.705). The phrase has not yet become a stereotype and is used here metalinguistically (and perhaps for the first time) to mean 'to say the right word', i.e. the word that suits the situation and can best summarize the destiny of the Persians, since it is the etymon itself of the Persians name. (Reinberg, 1981: 44; my translation, C.C.)

As to the subsequent use of the expression, Reinberg points out that in Euripides, as well as in the political prose of the fifth and fourth centuries B.C., the phrase is employed as both a stereotyped weakening device and a strengthening device, the latter highlighting a word that is particularly 'strong' but also indispensable to textual expressiveness (*ibid.*: 45). Hence, the original use of the phrase, which is metalinguistic and reinforcing, can be found in Aeschylus (Salvaneschi, 1978). According to this hypothesis, here, *ἔπος* is not yet watered down to an indexical pro-form. Rather, it actually highlights the meaningfulness of the utterance and could even be interpreted as an antonomastic synecdoche, which is translatable roughly as "to call things by their names," "to tell the right word." The said word becomes "the" word by antonomasia. The marker becomes an underscorer in the sense of the term advanced by Edmondson and House (1981: 76–77).

To sum up, although the reflexivity of the marker is assumed to be centered on contextual appropriateness in the weakening interpretation, it is assumed to be centered on the code – and hence assumed to be metalinguistic – in the strengthening interpretation.

The next point of my argumentation is that, as a matter of fact, this locution in its full meaning and in its strengthening function can be found in Plato's dialogues. This is supported by the fact that Ast (1956 [1853]: 632) records both mitigating and reinforcing uses of the expression in his *Lexicon Vocum Platonicarum*. In particular, Ast writes: "hac modesta loquutione [sic] Attici utuntur etiam in affirmatione vel asseveratione" ("Attics use this modest locution in statements as well as in emphatic declarations", *ibid.*; my translation, C.C.). Ast considers the marker in its emphatic use similar to German expressions like "*kann man sagen, kann man mit Recht sagen, in der Tat sagen, in Wahrheit, wirklich*" (*ibid.*). In this interpretation, the marker is used to underline the legitimacy and ground of what is said. In this reinforcing interpretation, the locution signals that, precisely because what is being said depicts the truth, not only can it not be expressed by means of an approximation, but that it *must* be said using exactly that word, ultimately, that the word introduced by the locution is the *right* word.

## 9. A Case of "Enantiopraxy"?

Considering (inter-textually) the reinforcing uses of *ὡς ἔπος εἰπεῖν* in Plato's dialogues and (co-textually) other reinforcing expressions in Gorgias' turn, we may well say that the marker in this passage is ambivalent. In other words, we may envisage the coexistence of two opposite functions of the marker: approximating and weakening on the one hand, and strengthening and underscoring proper word use on the other.

In Gricean terms, both interpretations, despite being apparently mutually exclusive, are crucially related to the maxim of Quantity: "make your contribution as informative as required" (Grice, 1989: 26). The weakening interpretation ("so to say," "practically") signals a partial fulfillment of the maxim of Quantity. The strengthening interpretation ("to say it in one word"), is in full compliance with the maxim of Quantity and thereby also in compliance with the maxim of Manner: "be perspicuous" (in particular with the sub-maxim "be brief") (Grice, 1989: 27). These two interpretations affect the construction of the character and the general textual and argumentative strategy used to attack Gorgias in different, although not incompatible, ways.

In conclusion, one of the means used perfidiously by Plato to destroy the credibility of his interlocutor is to "stuff" the last part of Gorgias' turn with expressions highlighting Gorgias' complacency about his knowledge. To this strategy we could ascribe Plato's subtle use of an expression, *ὡς ἔπος εἰπεῖν*, that works like a parody at the crucial juncture when the master of rhetoric is defining the essence of his art. It can be argued that in this passage Plato disqualifies Gorgias by making his message equivocal. The technique highlights Plato's main thesis that Gorgias' displayed knowledge is only a bluff and opens the way for subsequent criticisms that the over-emphatic Sicilian rhetorician lacks modesty.

Future in-depth studies of *Gorgias* and of Plato's work in general could test the following hypothesis: the two meanings and functions attributed to the marker discussed here – the weakening interpretation and the strengthening interpretation – coexist "*en filigrane*" in the passage analyzed; and both can be activated, although with different argumentative isotopies and different results, in the construction of Gorgias' character.

It is well-known that polysemy and multifunctionality are two defining features of discourse markers. In the passage of *Gorgias* I have dealt with here, it is reasonable to hypothesize that the ambivalence of *ὡς ἔπος εἰπεῖν* is exploited in the service of a complex, polyphonic, multi-layered, argumentative game. A single marker can have opposite meanings and functions not only from both diachronic and synchronic points of view, not only within the work of the same author[12] but also within a single occurrence in the same text. Owing to this semantic and

[12] As noted earlier, the reinforcing use of the locution *ὡς ἔπος εἰπεῖν* in Plato's works is registered by Ast (1956 [1853]).

functional ambivalence, such a marker can be interpreted as either an attenuating modulation or a strengthening modulation. By analogy with what Lepschy (1981: 153–166, 1982: 349–378; cf. also Ogden, 1967 [1932]) labels "enantiosemy," that is, a word having two opposite meanings, this can be called a case of "pragmatic enantiosemy" or "enantiopraxy," that is a marker having two opposite functions.

## 10. Conclusions

In Plato's unflattering, mischievous, hyper-rhetorical attack on rhetoric, we sense a deliberately biased interpretation of rhetoric as a mere set of tools for attaining lowly practical personal goals like wealth and power. The suggestion is that such goals are inferior to the noble, higher objectives of the speculative disciplines. The first Platonic objection to rhetoric is hence that it enables virtually anyone – not only philosophers – to reach goals by manipulating others' perceptions of events, and such ethical indifference goes hand in hand with a degradation of values (Dodds, 1985: 10). This motivates the second Platonic objection, which is that rhetoric, in contrast to dialectics, shifts the focus from what is true to what only *seems* to be true, from what is necessary to what is only *possible*, and from what is certain to what is only *probable*. This second objection could be raised against today's pragmatics as well, as pragmatics operates largely on the basis of abduction and probabilistic inferences. But the first objection certainly does not apply, as ethical concern is inherent in pragmatics, not only historically (for example, in the connections at the very beginning of the Oxford school between analytical philosophy and philosophy of law) but also by virtue of theoretical contiguity between notions of "act," "sincerity," "commitment," and so on that are central to both pragmatics and ethics. A whole branch of modern pragmatics is linked to the guiding concept of responsibility. As I have more than once suggested (Caffi, 1990, 2001, 2006, 2007), mitigation – be it deontic or epistemic, be it motivated by politeness or caution – relies on (different types of) weakening of responsibility. It is compatible with the key pragmatic concept of language as action and indirectly confirms this very concept. Precisely because language *is* action, speakers must be cautious and weigh their words, constantly adjusting these to changing aims and contexts, and monitoring their appropriateness to the *καιρός* of a given exchange. Pragmatics lends itself easily to functioning critically and analytically as a sort of ecology of communication in symbiosis with civil life, exactly as rhetoric originally did. Moreover, the fact that it provides a relatively "weak" theory of different types of discourses (rather than a theory of one specialized type of discourse) is precisely why it is potentially adequate as a broad form of integrated knowledge that rejects simplistic, sterile, technical definitions of its subject matter.

I admit to siding somewhat with Gorgias, for whom I feel a sort of peer sympathy. Like Gorgias' rhetoric, pragmatics has been defined as a "wastebasket," a loose domain, a messy mixture of heterogeneous studies yielding only partial descriptions of data or untestable hypotheses lacking "strong," stable, rational evaluative criteria.

In this chapter, I have assumed that there is a continuity between ancient rhetoric and pragmatics. With respect to their object of study, rhetoric and pragmatics both focus on language in movement, language set in motion by a *voluntas*, that is, a communicative intention and aim by someone directed to someone else. Regardless of whether this communicative intention is thought of mainly as emotional, manipulative, or logical, both disciplines investigate a polytropic message that is continuously being modulated and adjusted to the addressee and the situation (cf. Rostagni, 1955; Mortara Garavelli, 1997 [1988]; Venier, 2008). As to the speaking subject, that is, the model-speaker, this is in both cases an intermittent speaking subject that is not compact and transparent and most of the time does not fully identify with the utterance, nor can be exhausted by it. This is a subject that says and steps back, does and undoes, is involved with the utterance while at the same time keeping her/his distance from it. The micro-analysis of the passage from Plato's *Gorgias* has shown precisely some forms of this ambiguity that can be traced even in the use of a single marker. Pragmatic tools allow us to analyze the ways this antiphrastic, paradoxical tension between two opposite functions of the same expression work.

## Acknowledgments

I thank Enrica Salvaneschi (Genova) and Giulio Lepschy (London) for their insightful comments on earlier drafts.

## References

Aeschylus (1956). *Persians*. Translated by H. W. Smyth. London/Cambridge, MA: William Heinemann/ Harvard University Press.

Aristotle (1975). *The art of rhetoric*. Translated by J. H. Freese. London/Cambridge, MA: Heinemann/Harvard University Press.

Austin, J. L. (1962). *How to do things with words*. London: Oxford University Press.

Authier-Revuz, J. (1995). *Ces mots qui ne vont pas de soi. Boucles réflexives et non-coïncidences du dire. 2 Vols.* Paris: Larousse.

Bally, C. (1970 [1909]). *Traité de stylistique française. 2 Vols.* Genève: Librairie de l'Université Georg & Cie S.A.

Bazzanella, C., C. Caffi and M. Sbisà (1991). "Scalar dimensions of illocutionary force", in I. Žagar (ed.), *Speech acts: Fiction or reality?* Ljubjana: IprA, 63–76.

Benveniste, E. (1970). "L'appareil formel de l'énonciation". *Langages* **17**. Reprinted in Id., *Problèmes de linguistique générale*, II. Paris: Gallimard (1974), 79–88.

Bolinger, D. (1972). *Degree words*. The Hague, Paris: Mouton de Gruyter.

Brown, P. and S. Levinson (1978). "Universals in language usage: Politeness phenomena", in E. Goody (ed.), *Questions and politeness: Strategies in social interaction*. Cambridge: Cambridge University Press, 56–311. Reprinted in: *Politeness. Some universals in language usage*. Cambridge: Cambridge University Press (1987).

Bühler, K. (1934). *Sprachtheorie*. Jena: Fisher.

Caffi, C. (1990). "Modulazione, mitigazione, litote", in M.-E. Conte, A. Giacalone Ramat and P. Ramat (eds.), *Dimensioni della linguistica*. Milano: Angeli, 169–199.

Caffi, C (1994). "Metapragmatics", in R. Asher and J. Simpson (eds.), *The encyclopedia of language and linguistics*, Oxford: Pergamon. Reprinted in Brown, K. (ed.) (2006). *The encyclopedia of language and linguistics*, 2nd Edition, Oxford: Elsevier, pp. 82–88.

Caffi, C. (1999). "On mitigation". *Journal of Pragmatics* **31** (**2**): 881–909.

Caffi, C. (2001). *La mitigazione. Un approccio pragmatico alla comunicazione nei contesti terapeutici*. Münster: LIT Verlag.

Caffi, C. (2006). "Mitigation", in K. Brown (ed.), *The encyclopedia of language and linguistics. 2nd Edition*. Oxford: Elsevier, 171–175.

Caffi, C. (2007). *Mitigation*. Amsterdam/Tokyo: Elsevier.

Calaresu, E. (2004). *Testuali parole. La dimensione pragmatica e testuale del discorso riportato*. Milano: Angeli.

Castiglione, B. (2002 [1528]). in D. Javitsch (ed.), *The book of the courtier*. New York: Norton.

Channell, J. (1994). *Vague language*. Oxford: Oxford University Press.

Diewald, G. (2006). "Hecken und Heckenausdrücke. Versuch einer Neudefinition", in E. Calaresu, C. Guardiano and K. Hölker (eds.), *Italienisch und Deutsch als Wissenschaftssprachen. Bestandsaufnahmen, Analysen, Perspektiven. Italiano e tedesco come lingue della comunicazione scientifica. Ricognizioni, analisi e prospettive*. Münster: LIT Verlag, 295–315.

Dodds, E. R. (1985 [1959]). *Introduction, in Plato, Gorgias*. Oxford: Clarendon.

Edmondson, W. and J. House (1981). *Let's talk and talk about it. A pedagogical interactional grammar of English*. München, Wien, Baltimore: Urban & Schwarzenberg.

Giles, H., K. R. Scherer and D. M. Taylor (1979). "Speech markers in social interaction", in K. Scherer and H. Giles (eds.), *Social markers in speech*. Cambridge: Cambridge University Press, 343–381.

Goffman, E. (1979). "Footing". *Semiotica* **25**: 1–19. Reprinted in Id., *Forms of talk*. Oxford: Basil Blackwell (1981), 124–157.

Grice, P. H. (1975). "Logic and conversation", in P. Cole and J. L. Morgan (eds.), *Syntax and semantics. Speech acts*. New York & London: Academic Press, 41–58. Reprinted in Id., 1989, 22–40.

Grice, P. H. (1989). *Studies in the way of words*. Cambridge, MA: Harvard University Press.

Habermas, J. (1987 [1981]). *The theory of communicative action*. Vol. 2. Life world and system: A critique of functionalist reason. Translated by Thomas McCarthy. Cambridge: Polity Press.

Hare, R. M. (1970). "Meaning and speech acts". *Philosophical Review* **79**. Reprinted in Id., *Practical inferences*. London: MacMillan (1971), 74–93.

Hill, J. and J. T. Irvine (eds.) (1993). *Responsibility and evidence in oral discourse*. Cambridge: Cambridge University Press.

Hölker, K. (1988). *Zur Analyse von Markern*. Stuttgart: Franz Steiner Verlag.

Hübler, A. (1983). *Understatements and hedges in English*. Amsterdam/Philadelphia: Benjamins.

Jankélévitch, V. (1964). *L'ironie*. Paris: Flammarion.

Joly, H. (1990). "Sur la tête de Gorgias. Le 'parler beau' et le 'dire vrai' dans *Le Banquet* de Platon", in S. Borutti (ed.), *Rhetoric in the history of philosophy, Argumentation*, **4** (**1**): 5–33.

Jucker, A. H., S. W. Smith and T. Lüdge (2003). "Interactive aspects of vagueness in conversation". *Journal of Pragmatics* **35** (**12**): 1737–1769.

Kolde, G. (1989). "Probleme der Beschreibung von sogenannten. Heckenausdrücken im allgemeinen einsprachigen Wörterbuch", in H. Steger and H. E. Wiegand (eds.), *Handbücher zur Sprach - und Kommunikationswissenschaft*. Berlin, New York: Mouton de Gruyter.

Lakoff, G. (1973 [1972]). "Hedges: A study in meaning criteria and the logic of fuzzy concepts". *Journal of Philosophical Logic* **2**: 458–508.

Lang, E. and R. Steinitz (1978). "Können Satzadverbiale performativ gebraucht werden?" in W. Motsch (ed.), *Kontexte der Grammatiktheorie. Studia Grammatica XVII*. Berlin: Akademie-Verlag, 51–80.

Leech, G. (1981). "Pragmatics and conversational rhetoric", in H. Parret, M. Sbisà and J. Verschueren (eds.), *Possibilities and limitations of pragmatics*. Amsterdam: Benjamins, 413–441.

Leech, G. (1983). *Principles of pragmatics*. London, New York: Longman.

Lepschy, G. (1981). "Enantiosemy and irony in Italian lexis". *The Italianist* **1**: 82–88.

Lepschy, G. (1982). "Freud, Abel e gli opposti", in F. Fornari (ed.), *La comunicazione spiritosa. Il motto di spirito da Freud ad oggi*. Firenze: Sansoni, 39–68. Reprinted in Id., *Sulla linguistica moderna*, Il Bologna: Mulino (1989), 349–378

Markkanen, R. and H. Schröder (1997). "Hedging: A challenge for pragmatics and discourse analysis", in R. Markkanen and H. Schröder (eds.), *Hedging and discourse. Approaches to the analysis of a pragmatic phenomenon in academic texts*. Berlin, New York: Mouton de Gruyter, 3–18.

Mey, J. L. (1999). *When voices clash. A study in literary pragmatics*. Berlin, New York: de Gruyter.

Mortara Garavelli, B. (1985). *La parola d'altri*. Palermo: Sellerio.

Mortara Garavelli, B. (1997 [1988]). *Manuale di retorica*. Milano: Bompiani.

Ogden, C. K. (1967 [1932]). *Opposition. A linguistic and psychological analysis*. Bloomington: Indiana University Press.

Ossola, C. (1987). *Dal "cortegiano" all' "uomo di mondo"*. Torino: Einaudi.

Peregrini, M. (1960 [1639]). "Delle acutezze che altrimenti spiriti, vivezze e concetti volgarmente si appellano", in E. Raimondi (ed.), *Trattatisti e narratori del Seicento*. Milano-Napoli: Ricciardi, 113–168.

Perelman, C. (1955). "La méthode dialectique et le rôle de l'interlocuteur dans le dialogue". *Revue de Métaphysique et de Morale* **I**: 26–31. Reprinted in Id., *Rhétoriques*, Éditions de l'Université de Bruxelles: Bruxelles (1989), 53–60.

Plato (1961). *Gorgias, in Plato with an English translation*. Translated by W. R. M. Lamb. London/ Cambridge, MA: Heinemann/Harvard University Press.

Plato (1985 [1959]). *Gorgias*, in E. R. Dodds (ed.), *A revised text with introduction and commentary*. Oxford: Clarendon.

Plett, H. F. (1985). "Rhetoric", in T. van Dijk (ed.), *Discourse and literature*. Amsterdam: Benjamins, 59–84.

Reinberg, C. (1981). "Etimologia in Eschilo: modalità e significato della riflessione linguistica in un testo poetico". *Sandalion* **4**: 31–57.

Rostagni, A. (1955). "Un nuovo capitolo nella storia della retorica e della sofistica", in Id., *Scritti minori. Aesthetica*, Bottega d'Erasmo: Torino, 1–59.

Salvaneschi, E. (1978). "Sincretismo semantico in un passo di Eschilo", *Philologus. Zeitschrift für klassische Philologie*, Band 122, Heft 2, 320–327.

Schneider, S. (2007). *Reduced parenthetical clauses as mitigators. A corpus study of spoken French, Italian and Spanish*. Amsterdam/Philadelphia: Benjamins.

Segre, C. (1985). "L'analisi del testo letterario", in Id., *Avviamento all'analisi del testo letterario*, Einaudi: Torino, 5–159.

Urmson, J. O. (1952). "Parenthetical verbs". *Mind* **61**: 480–496.

Venier, F. (1991). *La modalizzazione assertiva*. Milano: Angeli.

Venier, F. (2008). *Il potere del discorso. Retorica e pragmatica linguistica*. Roma: Carocci.

## Lexicons

Ast, F. (1956 [Lipsiae 1835]), *Lexicon Platonicum sive Vocum Platonicarum Index*. Vol. I. Bonn: Rudolf Habelt Verlag.

Liddell Henry, G., R. Scott and H. S. Jones (1968). *A Greek-English Lexicon*. revised by Sir Henry Stuart Jones, with a supplement. *9th Edition*. Oxford: Clarendon Press.

New Approaches to Hedging
Edited by Gunther Kaltenböck, Wiltrud Mihatsch and Stefan Schneider


# 9

# Position and Scope of Epistemic Phrases in Planned and Unplanned American English

*Elise Kärkkäinen*

## Abstract

High-frequency epistemic phrases like *I think, I don't know, I guess, I thought,* and *I remember* have received considerable attention in linguistic research on different varieties of English. This chapter offers a quantitative survey of their occurrence in American English conversation, in a large database of almost 23 hours, with special reference to the semantic-pragmatic scope of these items. The chapter explores whether their scope extends over something yet to be verbalized in the turn-in-progress (forward scope), as opposed to having something in their scope that was just verbalized in the immediately preceding turn-so-far (backward scope). These issues will be examined primarily in two varieties of spoken American English, unplanned everyday speech and planned institutional speech, with a third variety, task-related talk, as a reference point in between. It is established that in all three data sets, there is a clear prevalence of clausal over phrasal scope and a prevalence of a forward-looking scope over scope pointing back in the immediately preceding discourse. The chapter further argues that the differences in scope observed between British English and American English are not really due to different types of data (i.e. that planned and/or monologic speech types in general manifest a different pattern from everyday dialogic speech), but more likely reflect a deeper grammaticization difference between the two varieties of English.

## 1. Introduction

This chapter examines the scope of high-frequency epistemic phrases like *I think, I don't know, I guess, I thought,* and *I remember* in spoken American English. More specifically, the chapter explores whether their scope extends over something yet to be verbalized in the turn-in-progress (forward scope), as opposed to having something in their scope that was just verbalized in the immediately preceding turn-so-far (backward scope). A further focus of attention will be to what extent these phrases can have phrasal as opposed to clausal scope in American English. These issues will be examined primarily in two varieties of spoken American English, unplanned everyday speech and planned institutional speech, with a third variety, task-related talk, as a reference point in between.

The determination of the scope of an epistemic phrase deserves some attention here. It is important to point out that I do not refer to a strictly syntactic scope, as in most cases the utterances in question do not contain any elements of syntactic subordination or superordination (such as the subordinator/complementizer *that*). By scope, then, I primarily understand semantic-pragmatic scope (see Kaltenböck, 2007 for a similar view), or "the stretch of language affected by the meaning of a particular form, even if it does not coincide with the scope of that form as just defined" (Crystal, 2003: 407). In most cases epistemic phrases can be seen to be doing very local work in conversational interaction and commonly have only one clause or phrase in their scope, and their pragmatic scope is then also in most cases quite local. In the case of some epistemic phrases, however, the pragmatic scope has been shown to extend beyond the associated clause; for example in multi-clause turns *I think* may project forward beyond the clause or utterance that it occurs in and thereby have more global pragmatic scope (Kärkkäinen, 2003), whereas *I don't know* may mark topic closing when it appears at the end of an extended turn or of a sub-sequence in the turn (Scheibman, 2000). But such functions can only be determined through a careful functional analysis of the sequential context in which an item occurs, and in this chapter, we confine ourselves to clausal and phrasal scope only. Very often turns also consist of only one clause, in which case even the pragmatic scope can really extend only over the associated clause.

However, the scope of epistemic phrases is shaped not only by their position in clause, sentence, conversational turn, or sequence of turns but also by the prosodic realization of the phrase and of the associated utterance as a whole. Kaltenböck (2007, 2008) establishes four types of prosodic binding between comment clauses (cf. epistemic phrases) and their host constructions in British English: in descending order of frequency these are left-binding, prosodically independent, left-right binding, and right-binding comment clauses. In contrast to this, Kärkkäinen (2003) found that the right-binding prosody was by far the most frequent in everyday unplanned speech, that is the epistemic phrase was prosodically integrated into the pitch contour of the following intonation unit (IU), most commonly a clausal one, whereas prosodically independent phrases were the next most frequent category, and the two others hardly occurred at all. An attempt is made here to find further evidence for these observed tendencies in an essentially larger database of everyday speech and to further examine whether they also hold for more planned and task-oriented varieties of spoken American English. The database for the present study consists of parts 1–4 of the Santa Barbara Corpus of Spoken American English (SBCSAE) (Du Bois *et al.*, 2000, 2003; Du Bois and Englebretson, 2004, 2005). As will be seen, there is ample evidence that the same trends hold for a larger sample of everyday speech, but there is also clear indication that those trends are prevalent in the other two varieties, even though the observed frequencies are much lower. This chapter therefore argues that the differences in scope observed between British English and American English are not really due to different types of data (i.e. that planned and/or monologic speech types in general manifest a different pattern from everyday dialogic speech), but more likely reflect a deeper grammaticization difference between the two varieties of English.

The database in Kärkkäinen (2003) consisted of five conversational excerpts of everyday conversation from part 1 of the SBCSAE data (amounting to about 1 hour 43 min).[1] The present database is substantially larger, amounting in all to 22 h 52 min, and consisting of *unplanned everyday talk* (13 h 34 min), *planned institutional talk* (5 h 36 min) and, as a genre that can be considered to lie somewhere between the two, *task-related talk* (3 h 42 min). A list of all 60 conversations can be found in Appendix 1.

## 2. Epistemic Phrases Included and Their Overall Frequency in the Three Speech Varieties

One of the observed tendencies in Kärkkäinen (2003), where initially all types of epistemic stance markers were included, was that *explicitly personalized epistemic phrases* that make reference to the speaker with the first person pronoun *I* were the most frequent type in everyday American English (see also Biber *et al.*, 1999: 667–669; Scheibman, 2001, 2002; Thompson, 2002 for similar observations). Focus will be placed on those in the present study. Such linguistic items have elsewhere been treated under the term "parenthetical clause" or "comment clause" (Urmson, 1963; Markkanen, 1985; Quirk *et al.*, 1985; Thompson and Mulac, 1991a, 1991b; Givón, 1993; Biber *et al.*, 1999; Wichmann, 2001; Kaltenböck, 2007, 2008). However, I prefer to use the term "epistemic phrase" (Thompson and Mulac, 1991a, 1991b) or even "epistemic fragment" (Thompson, 2002). As has been argued by Thompson (2002), the most frequent of these phrases, notably the ones with first-person subjects, have become relatively fixed epistemic formulas in American English (e.g. *I think/I don't think/I thought/I didn't think*), used by speakers to provide a certain type of perspective or stance toward the action that is performed in the associated utterance.

[1] The analysis of *I think* in Kärkkäinen (2003) additionally made use of another eight conversations.

Thompson (2002: 141) indeed proposes a view of grammar overall as consisting of *reusable fragments*, to be used as turns or parts of turns, i.e. as practices of turn construction.

I thus steer away from a strictly syntactic orientation and lean toward a more interactionally based analysis and interpretation (see also a discussion of this in Kärkkäinen, 2003: 39–42). Such an approach is also represented by studies that have used designations like "pragmatic markers" (van Bogaert, 2006) or "modal particles" (Aijmer, 1997) for the items in question. For one, these items are not really parenthetical in nature in the sense that they would occur equally at the beginnings, middles, or ends of clauses, but show a distinct preference for initial placement (see Sections 4.1 and 4.2). Moreover, it is often problematic to distinguish in real discourse data between a definitive/compositional meaning and a hedging/tentative meaning of a given verb (*I believe that there is a God.* = "I assert the belief that there is a God." vs. *There is a God, I believe.* = "There may be a God;" Quirk *et al.*, 1985: 1113; see also example (56) later in text) and consequently between a matrix clause and a comment clause use of the epistemic expression in question.[2] Even the presence of the complementizer *that* cannot be relied upon as an aid: in the present database *that* was almost consistently absent and occurred only 34 times out of the total number of occurrences, 1.496, of the phrases examined (or 2.3%, which is close to the 3.8% observed by van Bogaert, 2006, for *I guess* in the ICE-GB data).

Not only were explicitly personalized epistemic phrases the most common in the smaller data set in Kärkkäinen (2003), but it was also established that *epistemic stance-marking is highly routinized*, as only a small set of high-frequency items tended to be used by speakers (this finding has later found support in the studies of Precht, 2003, and Kaltenböck, 2007, 2008). Such markers included *I think, I don't know, I thought, I guess, I'm thinking*, and *I remember*. An attempt was therefore made to establish which phrases are the most common in the present database. It turned out that the aforementioned list needs only very small modification, notably the inclusion also of *I know* in the list of high-frequency phrases, whereas *I remember* turned out to be slightly less common than expected.[3]

---

[2] Kärkkäinen (2003, p. 41) presents an example where the cognitive verb *know* clearly has semantic substance beyond a mere hedge, yet there is no complementizer in the utterance: *Yeah but I do know, it it's an awfully, it's it's an awfully presumptuous thing, to sit down and write a book about death, when you haven't died* (SBCSAE tape 5).

[3] I have excluded the hearsay evidential *I said* or *s/he said* from the present study. These were in fact found to be quite frequent in Kärkkäinen (2003), especially the third person phrase *s/he said*, but as many studies do not consider them on a par with constructions involving a cognitive verb, I decided to leave them out. This of course does not make my results directly comparable with some other syntactically oriented studies such as Kaltenböck (2007, 2008), which include reporting clauses like *I was told*, *it appears*, and *I/you said* that do not contain a specific source of information. Somewhat in contradiction, I have included a frequent epistemic phrase *I'm sure* and its negative *I'm not sure*, even though it does not contain a cognitive verb but an adjective denoting epistemic certainty (as is also the case with *I know*).

**Table 9.1.** Frequency of epistemic phrases in unplanned everyday speech, task-related speech and planned speech (number of occurrences per minutes of data in each variety)

| Epistemic phrase | Unplanned everyday speech (814 min) | Task-related speech (222 min) | Planned speech (336 min) |
|---|---|---|---|
| I think | 2.8 | 2.2 | 6.6 |
| I don't know | 3.2 | 4.0 | 15.3 |
| I know | 4.7 | 9.3 | 19.8 |
| I thought | 5.6 | *17.1* | *56.0* |
| I guess | 9.7 | *8.2* | *48.0* |
| I don't think | 15.1 | 27.8 | 30.5 |
| I remember | 23.3 | 111.0 | 37.3 |
| I'm sure | 54.3 | 111.0 | 56.0 |
| I hope | 54.3 | 111.0 | 48.0 |

If we now turn to look at the present database, Table 9.1 presents the frequencies of the most common epistemic phrases in each variety of speech.

As we can see, the frequency of these phrases is by far the highest in everyday speech, with for example *I think* occurring about once every 3 minutes of speech and *I don't know, I know* and *I thought* only slightly less often. On the contrary, there is a clear drop after the five most common phrases, and *I'm sure* and *I hope* no longer occur more than about once in (a little less than) an hour. In the case of task-related speech, the figures for the top three phrases are not unlike those for everyday speech. If anything *I think* is even more frequent in conversations revolving around some practical task like game playing, cooking, or workplace chores. The order of *I guess* and *I thought* are reversed: as can be seen, the italicized figures deviate from the general ascending pattern and *I thought* in particular is not very common in this variety. For more planned institutional speech, finally, the frequencies are much lower overall. The only exception is made up of the phrases *I'm sure* and *I hope*, which are equally frequent as in everyday speech. However, *I hope* and also *I remember* occur in the sermon (tape 21 *Fear*) of particularly one speaker, and the figures are thus perhaps not so representative.

In all, the result that everyday speech shows a much higher density of epistemic stance marking is in line with the observation made by Kaltenböck (2007: 7) on the ICE-GB data, where there is also a clear preference for dialogic text types, both private and public (as opposed to unscripted and scripted monologues). This he takes to be an indication of the strong interactive character of comment clauses, which the present study also clearly corroborates. The order of the most frequent epistemic verbs is roughly the same in my data as in the British data in Kaltenböck (2008), with three notable exceptions. *Suppose* is much more frequent in British English (ICE-GB data) and *guess* in American English. Although *I guess* is among the high-frequency items in the present corpus and has indeed been found to be more prevalent in American than in British English (Kärkkäinen, 2007), *I suppose* occurred only in all 5 times and is by far more typical of British English (informal) speech (van Bogaert, 2006: 143). Finally, *I believe* is even less frequent in the present data and is much more common in British English (but in formal rather than informal contexts; van Bogaert, 2006: 143).

## 3. Role of Prosody: Intonation Units as Units of Transcription

The Santa Barbara corpus applies a transcription system somewhat different from most existing methodologies (see Appendix 2 for the transcription conventions). The transcription methodology used draws primarily from two sources, from the techniques commonly used in conversation analysis (e.g. in Sacks *et al.*, 1978) and from the work of Chafe (1979, 1987, 1988, 1994), which acknowledges the importance of the *Intonation Unit* (IU), variously referred to as tone group, tone unit, or intonational phrase in earlier prosodic research, as the fundamental unit of discourse production. Thus, the data are transcribed into IUs, or stretches of speech uttered under a single intonation contour, such that each line represents one IU. Du Bois *et al.* (1991: 100) also define four other criteria for identifying and classifying these units (these criteria owe to the work of Cruttenden, 1986). They include a resetting of the baseline pitch level at the beginning of the unit, a pause at the beginning of the unit, a sequence of accelerated syllables at the beginning of the unit, and a prosodic lengthening of syllable(s) at the end of the unit. They also observe that the presence of these cues is neither a necessary nor a sufficient criterion of IU status. There can further be more than one primary accent in an IU, but it is also possible for none to be present (Du Bois *et al.*, 1993: 57). The transcription process of the SBCSAE corpus involved a team of transcribers, whose training involved several rounds of transcription and checking, with repeated reconciliation sessions to arrive at an accepted version of some problematic point. In general, the interrater reliability accomplished in the perceptual identification of IUs was very high (cf. however Stelma and Cameron, 2007, on lower levels of interrater agreement in their data in less fluent stretches of talk, see Section 4.3).

The IU is thus the most important type of prosodic feature transcribed in the data. In addition, *transitional continuity* of intonation is marked consistently at the end of each IU. Of special relevance for this chapter is the distinction between continuing and final intonation at the ends of IUs. Thus, a unit may end in a way that implies that the present speaker intends to continue talking, most typically in a low rising intonation marked by a comma, or in a way that implies that a speaker change is possible, as when the unit ends in a distinctly falling intonation marked by a full stop, or in a high rising intonation marked by a question mark. In all, the transcription and also the present analysis are based on auditory, or perceptual, rather than instrumental analysis. Even though instrumental analysis could clearly confirm many of the analyses made, including the prosodic cues used in the perceptual identification of IUs, it is extremely time-consuming and is simply not feasible on a large number of data such as the present (see also Wichmann, 2001).

## 4. Position and Scope of Epistemic Phrases in Everyday Unplanned Speech

As will become obvious, no great differences in scope were observable in the three varieties of speech examined, everyday, task-related, and planned. In all three data sets, there is a clear prevalence of clausal over phrasal scope and a prevalence of a forward-looking scope over scope pointing back in the immediately preceding discourse. I will exemplify this by first taking a careful look at everyday unplanned speech, because it is the variety that shows by far the highest density of epistemic phrases. Following this, planned speech and task-related speech will be discussed primarily with a view to observed differences compare to everyday speech. Table 9.2 lays out the position of epistemic markers in view of IUs in the data and also presents a crude specification of their scope.

### 4.1. Clausal forward scope: IU-initial/clause-initial

We can see from Table 9.2 that about one-half (51.8% or 571 items) of the occurrences of epistemic phrases occur clause-initially and simultaneously IU-initially. What lies within their scope is then easy to determine: they have the upcoming proposition, that is a full clause, in their scope. This also means that their scope reaches forward rather than backward in discourse. This interpretation is supported above all by the prosodic encoding of the utterance, that is the epistemic phrase falls under the same coherent intonation contour with the upcoming clause. The IUs/clauses show a distinct tendency to end in a final intonation contour, which indicates that such clausal units are complete and that a legitimate speaker change may occur at this point. Such clauses are also often preceded by a pause (indicated by two or three periods), lending further support for a forward scope. It is also worth noting that very often the IU in question is preceded by an inbreath (H), which usually indicates a new beginning of some sort in talk. The following are examples of this very pervasive pattern in the data (the numbers in angle brackets refer to the tape number followed by the relevant line number in the transcript).[4]

[4] The line number is the first number taken from the longer code number appearing in front of each line in the transcripts. Several subsequent lines may on occasion have the same initial number because the transcript is time stamped with respect to the audio recording, but the lines are nevertheless easily recoverable. I have occasionally deleted overlap brackets from the examples where the overlap is with talk not shown in the example.

**Table 9.2.** Position and scope of epistemic phrases in unplanned everyday speech

| Epistemic phrase | IU-initial | | | | Separate IU | | | | | | Medial position in IU | | | | | | Final position in IU | | TOTAL | |
|---|---|---|---|---|---|---|---|---|---|---|---|---|---|---|---|---|---|---|---|---|
| | Clause-initial | % | Phrase-initial | % | Scope forward | % | Scope back | % | Indeterminate scope | % | Scope forward | % | Scope back | % | Indeterminate scope | % | | % | *n* | % |
| I think | **214** | 72.8 | 29 | 9.9 | 15 | 5.1 | 6 | 2.0 | 1 | 0.3 | 8 | 2.7 | 5 | 1.7 | | 0.0 | 16 | 5.4 | 294 | 100.0 |
| I dont know | **97** | 38.6 | 19 | 7.6 | **52** | 20.7 | **72** | 28.7 | | 0.0 | | 0.0 | 3 | 1.2 | | 0.0 | 8 | 3.2 | 251 | 100.0 |
| I know | **39** | 22.7 | 20 | 11.6 | **40** | 23.3 | **71** | 41.3 | | 0.0 | | 0.0 | 2 | 1.2 | | 0.0 | | 0.0 | 172 | 100.0 |
| I thought | **84** | 57.5 | 13 | 8.9 | **35** | 24 | 1 | 0.7 | | 0.0 | 6 | 4.1 | 2 | 1.4 | 1 | 0.7 | 4 | 2.7 | 146 | 100.0 |
| I guess | **44** | 52.4 | 10 | 11.9 | 8 | 9.5 | 10 | 11.9 | 1 | 1.2 | 3 | 3.6 | 1 | 1.2 | 1 | 1.2 | 6 | 7.1 | 84 | 100.0 |
| I dont think | **48** | 88.9 | 2 | 3.7 | | 0.0 | 1 | 1.9 | | 0.0 | 2 | 3.7 | | 0.0 | | 0.0 | 1 | 1.9 | 54 | 100.0 |
| I remember | 12 | 34.3 | 15 | 42.9 | 5 | 14.3 | | 0.0 | 1 | 2.9 | 2 | 5.7 | | 0.0 | | 0.0 | | 0.0 | 35 | 100.0 |
| Im sure | 9 | 60.0 | | 0.0 | | 0.0 | 2 | 13.3 | | 0.0 | 1 | 6.7 | | 0.0 | | 0.0 | 3 | 20.0 | 15 | 100.0 |
| I hope | 12 | 80.0 | 2 | 13.3 | 1 | 6.7 | | 0.0 | | 0.0 | | 0.0 | | 0.0 | | 0.0 | | 0.0 | 15 | 100.0 |
| Im thinking | 1 | 7.1 | 2 | 14.3 | 11 | 78.6 | | 0.0 | | 0.0 | | 0.0 | | 0.0 | | 0.0 | | 0.0 | 14 | 100.0 |
| Im not sure | 1 | 14.3 | 1 | 14.3 | | 0.0 | 5 | 71.4 | | 0.0 | | 0.0 | | 0.0 | | 0.0 | | 0.0 | 7 | 100.0 |
| I suppose | 3 | 75.0 | 1 | 25.0 | | 0.0 | | 0.0 | | 0.0 | | 0.0 | | 0.0 | | 0.0 | | 0.0 | 4 | 100.0 |

| | | | | | | | | | | | | | | | | | | | | |
|---|---|---|---|---|---|---|---|---|---|---|---|---|---|---|---|---|---|---|---|---|
| I cant imagine | 2 | 66.7 | 1 | 33.3 | | 0.0 | | 0.0 | | 0.0 | | 0.0 | | 0.0 | | 0.0 | | 0.0 | 3 | 100.0 |
| I would imagine | 2 | 66.7 | 1 | 33.3 | | 0.0 | | 0.0 | | 0.0 | | 0.0 | | 0.0 | | 0.0 | | 0.0 | 3 | 100.0 |
| I cant believe | | 0.0 | 2 | 100.0 | | 0.0 | | 0.0 | | 0.0 | | 0.0 | | 0.0 | | 0.0 | | 0.0 | 2 | 100.0 |
| I imagine | 1 | 50.0 | | 0.0 | 1 | 50.0 | | 0.0 | | 0.0 | | 0.0 | | 0.0 | | 0.0 | | 0.0 | 2 | 100.0 |
| I believe | 2 | 100.0 | | 0.0 | | 0.0 | | 0.0 | | 0.0 | | 0.0 | | 0.0 | | 0.0 | | 0.0 | 2 | 100.0 |
| **TOTAL** | **571** | **51.8** | **118** | **10.7** | **168** | **15.2** | **168** | **15.2** | 3 | 0.3 | 22 | 2.0 | 13 | 1.2 | 2 | 0.2 | 38 | 3.4 | **1103** | 100.0 |

(1) ... (H) **I think** that's cold. (SBCSAE 1/1020)
(2) Oh **I think** they're good like that. (SBCSAE 3/813)
(3) **I think** thei=r motives must .. be pretty solid, (SBCSAE 13/1549)
(4) (H) ... **I think** .. m=aybe .. Forster wanted him to be that way, (SBCSAE 23/213)
(5) .. (H) (TSK) Yeah **I think** he was trying to get a girl to go with him but, (SBCSAE 28/664)
(6) but **I think** they're gonna let it s=it another day, (SBCSAE 31/468)
(7) ... Well **I think** what ~Jennifer said .. is correct. (SBCSAE 33/205)
(8) ... **I don't know** what to do with this. (SBCSAE 42/801)
(9) ... **I don't know** if it's .. just the way people are in general now. (SBCSAE 36/741)
(10) **I know** ~Tommy's having the red wine. (SBCSAE 32/2)
(11) (H) <F But **I thought** it was very pragmatic of her to ask about that in June F>. (SBCSAE 5/804)
(12) ... **I thought** you already brought the cake in. (SBCSAE 13/609)
(13) .. **I guess** we ought to put those in the oven, (SBCSAE 3/1464)
(14) ... but **I guess** you still have to go out and do some banking now and then. (SBCSAE 43/454)
(15) **I don't think** it's sterling silver, (SBCSAE 52/472)
(16) **I don't think** ~Kathy ever buys him socks. (SBCSAE 59/187)
(17) ... (H) **I remember** I was pregnant with !Nicky. (SBCSAE 7/1187)
(18) **I hope** it's not too big? (SBCSAE 48/76)
(19) **I'm sure** he practices to=ns every day. (SBCSAE 19/429)
(20) ... **I believe** it was the paper this morning. (SBCSAE 60/1192)

As can be seen from examples (2), (5), (6), (7), (11), and (14), I have included under IU-/clause-initial cases where the epistemic phrase is preceded by a connective (*but*, *well*, *and*, *or*, *so*, *cause*; Chafe, 1988) or a short marker like *oh* or *yeah*, as these may mark the position of the current utterance within the longer sequence or the speaker's (epistemic) reception of the preceding turn (Heritage, 1984).

Of all epistemic phrases in the database, *I think* is by far the most common and has been shown to have a range of interactional functions when it occurs initially and with a forward scope. Kärkkäinen (2003) lists the following: bringing in a personalized speaker perspective to mark boundaries in discourse or to mark that the upcoming turn will bring in a new or different perspective compared to the prior turn, and (with a more full semantic content) maintaining face in interaction. Similarly, *I guess* has been shown to act as an intersubjective stance frame that projects a certain type of stance, based on inference, to be expressed in the utterance to follow (Kärkkäinen, 2007). Initial *I don't know* can still take a *wh*-complement, of which a *what*-complement and a conditional *if*-complement are by far the most common, as in examples (8) and (9), respectively. In the case of *I know*, however, no complementizer usually appears, as in example (10). These epistemic phrases then also act as epistemic fragments and stance frames for the upcoming utterance (see also Beach and Metzger,

1997; Scheibman, 2000). With both *I don't know* and *I know*, however, their encoding as separate IU, and thereby as a reactive token, is by far more common (Sections 4.3 and 4.4).

A new finding concerning the frequency and interactional functions of *I thought* emerged from the data. Even though its exact meaning and degree of semantic weakening cannot be judged without a close contextual analysis (Jucker *et al.*, 2003), even a cursory look at the data provided strong evidence that *I thought* is part of a social action format or a recurrent linguistic routine or conversational pattern used by speakers for taking a stance: in 68 cases out of a total of 146 in everyday speech, it is followed by an explicitly stanced phrase or clause such as *it was funny*, *it was pretty neat*, or *it was beautiful*, or by direct reported speech or thought embodying a clear speaker stance. The subject of the phrase has been claimed to be weak or general in reference, and also its past time reference loses importance at the expense of the significance of the action for the present interaction (Scheibman, 2001: 71); in example (12) ... *I thought you already brought the cake in.* (said about a birthday cake at a party), the speaker is not conveying something that she thought in the past so much as simply framing the current situation.[5]

*I don't think* is also one of the most frequent epistemic phrases (occurring about once every 15 minutes in everyday interaction) and occurs only clause-initially and without a complementizer in the database, as in examples (15) and (16). Finally, a few examples are given of the less frequent epistemic phrases *I remember*, *I hope*, *I'm sure* and *I believe* in examples (17)–(20).

I have made no distinction above between cases where the epistemic phrase is followed by a complementizer (of which there are very few, with the exception of *I don't know*) and have also included all initial occurrences even if they are not separated from what follows by a pause or hesitation sounds or fillers (cf. Kaltenböck, 2007: 6, for arguments for excluding these from his analysis and thus adopting a more cautious approach). I would like to claim, however, that there is already a great deal of evidence in the literature that the initial phrases discussed above have indeed become relatively fixed epistemic formulas and are used simply to provide a stance frame on what follows and thus perform a function not unlike comment clauses in discourse (Thompson and Mulac, 1991a, 1991b; Scheibman, 2000, 2001, 2002; Thompson, 2002; Kärkkäinen, 2003, 2008).

### 4.2. Phrasal forward scope: IU-initial/phrase-initial

Kärkkäinen (2003), using part 1 of SBCSAE as data, found that for everyday conversation the phrasal scope is not very frequent. When epistemic phrases do have phrasal scope, this is most commonly an *upcoming* (rather than preceding) NP, PP, or a clause fragment that is produced

[5] I thank an anonymous referee for pointing out that much depends on the prosodic realization of the utterance. Had the speaker put maximal prominence on *thought*, the meaning of the utterance would have implied a prior thinking process that now proves correct ("I knew it and you did"). Here, however, maximal prominence falls on *brought*.

within the same coherent intonation contour as the phrase. This is a much less frequent pattern in the data than clausal scope, however, with only 10.7% or 118 instances out of the total number (1,103). By comparison, Kaltenböck (2007, 2008) found for the ICE-GB database that their overall frequency can be as high as 23% (vs. 77% for clausal scope). Yet, in the present database no accurate overall figures can be given except for the IU-initial cases, because in the other three categories (separate IU, medial position in IU, and final position in IU), no attempt was made to actually count the exact occurrences of clausal vs. phrasal cases; that would have been extremely time-consuming and would have required contextual analysis of hundreds of cases.

The data show that speakers very often display problems in the production and formulation of an issue at these points, or cases of self-repair and online planning, as well as qualifying commitment on the fly, that is when they are already well into the utterance. Kaltenböck (2007: 19) also observes that the function of comment clauses may then have shifted from epistemic shields, marking speaker commitment, to acting as approximators, or making some aspect of the utterance less precise. This is the case in examples (21), (22), and (23). On occasion this may result in a redirection (or even abandonment) of the turn-in-progress, as in example (24).

(21) KEN: it was illegal,
.. you know,
from like the .. time of Cath- –
.. the Castro revolution,
up until,
**I think** the early seventies, (SBCSAE 3/82)

(22) LISA: there was two days in a row though,
cause there was one in Louisiana,
**I think** yesterday,
and one the day before that in Kansas. (SBCSAE 36/755)

(23) H)= We .. we we stayed in a f=irst rate,
.. **I guess** what you call today a four star hotel but, (SBCSAE 60/779)

(24) PATTY: ... [(TSK)(H)] **I think** Margaret though,
LINDA: [Mhm].
PATTY: I- % –
... I don't think we can underestimate her (Hx). (SBCSAE 23/21)

Sometimes the phrasal scope is more of an "accidental" pattern, where the issue being formulated could equally well have been produced as a single clausal IU.

(25) MATT: **I can't imagine** that dog,
GARY: @@@[@]
MATT: [weighing] seventy-two pounds. (SBCSAE 56/816)

Some further examples of scope over an NP are the following.[6]

(26) **I don't know** the .. the details. (SBCSAE 28/1072)
(27) ... **I know** that feeling. (SBCSAE 49/71)
(28) **I know** a bunch of em. (SBCSAE 32/818)

It is further of interest that some phrases, notably *I remember* and *I thought*, can be followed by a phrase and appear then to be rhetoric alternatives to clause-initial encoding, possibly to display that the upcoming telling or stance is going to be longer than just one clause long. *I thought* may be followed by phrases like *oh my lord*, *good heavens, gosh, oh my gosh,* or *fine*, that is a stanced item that strongly projects more to come in the way of stance-taking.

(29) **I remember** this story, (SBCSAE 45/779)
(30) ... (H) So **I thought** .. God. (SBCSAE 5/852)

### 4.3. Phrasal or clausal forward scope: separate intonation units

As regards all pre-positioned epistemic phrases, there are cases in the data where they do not come under the same intonation contour but as a separate IU before a clause or a phrase (168 items or 15.2%). In the case of most epistemic phrases, such usage is restricted to rather special interactional environments, namely instances of online planning, hesitant speech, word searches, and repair (see also Wichmann, 2001: 186, 189, 190 and Kaltenböck, 2007: 32–33 for similar observations). The determination of their scope in such cases depends on the design of the unfolding conversational turn in which the item occurs: sometimes these phrases quite clearly extend over a single phrase only, whereas at other times it is not quite clear whether they target a phrase within the clause or the whole clause (which may be realized over several IUs).

(31) Clausal scope
CAROLYN: [(H) They're just giving –
**I think**,
it sounds,
like,
to me,
they're giving you a lot of sh=it for no @reason. (SBCSAE 4/486)

[6] I thank an anonymous referee for the observation that in examples (26)–(29), and later with examples (54) and (55) on *remember*, the cognitive verbs in question appear to have full lexical meaning and their status as (parenthetical) epistemic fragments is not clear. However, as I have not carried out close contextual analysis of the data, I have included these cases for completeness.

(32) Phrasal scope
JILL: It was really quick YWN>.
**I think,**
um,
.. like mid-August. (SBCSAE 28/725)

(33) Unclear scope
HAROLD: So=,
**I guess,**
... I mean thi- this- thi- this just happened?
Or, (SBCSAE 2/388)

The fact that such usage is rare and restricted to rather special interactional environments in the data serves as indirect evidence for the prevalence of IU-initial encoding: that epistemic phrases occur as a separate IU in such instances can be seen as an exception to the general tendency to package a clause/proposition (and less commonly an NP or a PP or other phrase) in the same IU with the epistemic phrase.

While encoding *I thought* as a separate IU can be seen as yet another rhetoric alternative to the more usual clause-initial encoding (35 vs. 84 occurrences), the reverse is true of *I'm thinking*, which tends to occur on its own in the data (11 vs. 1 occurrences).

(34) ANGELA: .. (H) And **I thought**,
oh my lord, <SBCSAE 11/473>

(35) PATRICK: ... s=o=,
... **I'm thinking**,
okay just for a joke,
we should pull over or say something. <SBCSAE 45/389>

In the case of two high-frequency phrases encoded as separate IUs, *I don't know* and *I know*, the decision was made that they were assigned (a) forward scope when they end in non-final intonation, in which case the present speaker will continue talking, and (b) backward scope when they end in final intonation, in which case there is at least a temporary termination point enabling speaker change in the discourse at that point (see Section 4.4. for the cases in (b)). It is worth noting that simultaneously with the non-final intonation contour the phrase *I don't know* was also preceded by a pause (in 27/52 cases), and so was *I know* (in 14/40 cases), thus further strengthening the interpretation that the unit/phrase is clearly not integrated into the preceding talk. A pause also often preceded phrases ending in a final intonation contour: *I don't know* (44/72), *I know* (26/71). This can be taken as further indication of the grammaticization of these two phrases into the function of an independent reactive token in discourse (Section 4.4); in the cases below they point forward in the sense that the speaker first expresses alignment and affiliation with the prior speaker but continues to elaborate his or her like-mindedness immediately thereafter [examples (36)–(38)]. Example (39) is a rare instance of a separate IU actually constituting clause-initial occurrence; *I don't know* goes with the upcoming element in the turn and could have been produced as one IU with it, but was not.

(36) GARY: ... (TSK) (H) What happened to ~Matt.
JULIE: ... % **I don't know,**
I think he wandered off. (SBCSAE 56/279)

(37) KENDRA: ... **I know=,**
I've been sleeping about ten hou=rs,
every nigh=t. (SBCSAE 13/185)

(38) ALICE: **I know,**
that really sucks. (SBCSAE 7/1065)

(39) WESS: But he must've pushed it up there or something,
**I don't know,**
how he got it up there.[7] (SBCSAE 59/48)

**4.4. Phrasal or clausal backward scope: separate intonation units**

In the examples found of post-positioned epistemic phrases encoded as separate IUs (168 cases or 15.2 %), they are added after the speaker has already verbalized a clause (a proposition) or a phrase and may then come after a syntactic, pragmatic, and intonational completion point. Below *I think* and *I guess* are used to retrospectively qualify the speaker's commitment to the preceding phrase (40) or clause (41).

(40) DIANE: y- yeah,
in % .. Out of Africa,
**I think,**
is about this same time period. (SBCSAE 23/486)

(41) DARRYL: ... That's because I have my own ideas about it,
**I guess.**
That I'm .. pretty comfortable with. (SBCSAE 5/146)

Occasionally in the data we get examples like the following, where the phrase comes at (what is intended to be a) turn-final position, in which case it then pursues a recipient uptake.

(42) DORIS: (H) and 'they go there to ^walk.
ANGELA: (H)[=]
DORIS: [**I ^think**]. (SBCSAE 11/765)

[7] The speaker produces the clause in a rhythmically distinct manner: *I don't know* is said with a strong primary stress and a lengthened vowel sound on *^kno=w*, thus perhaps emphasizing its lexical meaning, while the rest is in faster speech, <A *how he got it up there* A>.

A pause also often precedes phrases ending in a final intonation contour, especially with *I don't know* (44/72 cases) and *I know* (26/71 cases). This can be taken as further indication of the grammaticization of these two phrases into the function of independent reactive tokens in discourse, which can also be seen from the relatively high number of separate-IU encodings of the two phrases in Table 9.2 (figures in bold) – this trend is even slightly higher in the case of *I know* than of *I don't know.*

(43) JULIE: [(H) he] is a cutie.
I mean he .. he's –
He models for Shepler's magazine.
... Really nice looking young fellow.
... **I don't know.** (SBCSAE 56/538)

(44) PATTY: It doesn't measure your creativity,
[it doesn't <X measure you know so X>] –
STEPHANIE: [Mom,
**I know.** (SBCSAE 35/58)

**4.5. Forward and backward scope: medial position in an intonation unit**

A frequent environment for epistemic phrases to occur medially in an IU is in connection with self- and other-repair, which may result in the fronting of the repairing element, as in the following example, in which the epistemic phrasee has phrasal backward scope.

(45) STEPHANIE: it's t=en o'clock,
... or no.
It was –
PATTY: ... Nine thirty **I thought** you said. (SBCSAE 35/842)

Unless the speaker leaves the repairing element last in the utterance and produces a more unmarked alternative, *I thought you said nine thirty*, the epistemic phrase unavoidably ends up in the middle of the sentence. Nevertheless, this is a much less common pattern and only occurs with any frequency in cases of repair or when some kind of hedging or modifying element appears first in the clause (as in *for some reason I think he likes students*). The following is a rare exception to this, where the epistemic phrase has forward clausal scope.

(46) JULIE: [(H) Like with uh ~Peggy's horse,
I looked at twenty-eight horses in ten [days.
GARY: [(WHISTLE)].
JULIE: be]fore I found the one that **I thought** would suit her. (SBCSAE 56/589)

In sum, then, the data provide evidence for the observation made by Wichmann (2001: 185) that medial comment clauses like *I think* and *I suppose* tend to be prosodically integrated.

### 4.6. Clausal and phrasal backward scope: final position in the intonation unit

Finally, there are some instances in the data where the epistemic phrase appears last in the IU, which may consist of a clause or a phrase. Again the interactional environments are somewhat special. In example (47) the speaker expresses a degree of disagreement with the previous speaker and maintains that the referent *she* does not in fact enjoy her present living conditions in her new school, even though she does enjoy the actual school itself. The phrase *I think* is tagged on after the disagreeing turn and softens the force of the disagreement.

(47) TOM_2: .. She told me that she was enjoying it.
TOM_1: .. (H) [Well],
TOM_2: [But] she was,
TOM_1: (H) [2she is enjoying the school **I think**2]. (SBCSAE 32/1071)

A little later in the discourse in example (48), still on the same topic, the same speaker produces the IU- and phrase-final *I think*, which on a closer inspection turns out to be (in a sense) clause-final. Yet the phrase *very well I think* is an increment, which speakers produce in talk for a variety of interactional reasons, such as problems with recipiency (Ford *et al.*, 2002). Even if it continues the syntactic structure of the initial clause, its incremental production points to the fact that it was not actually planned for by the speaker at the outset.

(48) TOM_1: [(TSK) (H) Yeah she] likes [2all that2],
TOM_2: [2uh2],
TOM_1: [3very well **I think**3]. (SBCSAE 32/1151)

In example (49), the speaker redirects her turn after *Because* and produces a stanced digression on the fly, which perhaps accounts for the clause-final position of the actual stance frame.

(49) SHERI: Cause I wanna put these uh,
.. geraniums,
... in a pot.
Because,
... why they aren't dead **I don't know**,
because all I do is take them to the brink of death
all the time and, (SBCSAE 58/452)

In the last example, the speaker is bad-mouthing the referent *he* and again inserts a quick positive assessment of the restaurant before getting to the less favorable features of this referent.

(50) ALINA: [He's a waiter].
.. He's a waiter at Rosa's.
out there [in Ontario].

LENORE: [(Hx)]
ALINA: which is a very nice restaurant **I'm sure**,
but,
.. he wants to open his own restaurant someday,
and he thinks,
.. we're gonna finance it. (SBCSAE 6/505)

By way of conclusion, we can say that in unplanned everyday speech, the scope of epistemic phrases extends forward in discourse in the great majority of cases (79.7% if we add up all occurrences in the relevant categories in Table 9.2),[8] whereas in about a fifth of the cases (19.9%) the scope extends back in discourse. Clausal scope is by far more common than phrasal scope: this is clear from the high number of occurrences in one category alone, that is IU-initial/Clause-initial position, in Table 9.2 (571 of the total of 1,103). In the case of separate IUs or IU-medial position, we do not always know whether the scope is clausal or phrasal without doing contextual analysis. Yet the fact that two items, *I know* and *I don't know*, are responsible for the majority of separate IU occurrences and have largely grammaticized into independent reactive tokens makes it rather irrelevant to talk about clausal or phrasal scope in these cases. As for final position in an IU, clausal scope is generally more common here as well, even though no figures are actually presented in Table 9.2. All in all we can safely conclude, then, that clausal scope is prevalent for epistemic phrases in everyday interaction.

## 5. Position and Scope of Epistemic Phrases in Planned Speech

The 14 recordings representing planned speech in the SBCSAE comprise teaching discussions, organized discussions, sermons, lectures, a demo presentation, a storytelling performance, an interview, a small claims court, and even a judo class. Some of these are clearly monologic, but very often they also contain dialogic elements and some degree of engagement with an audience. Overall we can say that the tendencies observed for everyday speech hold fairly consistently for planned speech as well, even if the general frequencies are lower (even in proportion to the total duration of speech in each variety, see Table 9.1).

The order of the most frequent epistemic phrases is almost the same, but *I thought* and *I guess* are clearly less frequent than in everyday speech. We can also observe from Table 9.3 that *I know* and *I don't know* do not show similar clusterings in the two separate-IU columns as they did for everyday speech but tend to appear either clause- or phrase-initially, that is reactive tokens are not used with similar frequency in planned speech, very likely because of the predominance of

---

[8] We leave the few cases in the data where the scope is indeterminate out of the calculations.

**Table 9.3.** Position and scope of epistemic phrases in planned speech

| Epistemic phrase | IU-initial | | | | Separate IU | | | | | | Medial position in IU | | | | | | Final position in IU | | TOTAL | |
|---|---|---|---|---|---|---|---|---|---|---|---|---|---|---|---|---|---|---|---|---|
| | Clause-initial | % | Phrase-initial | % | Scope forward | % | Scope back | % | Indeterminate scope | % | Scope forward | % | Scope back | % | Indeterminate scope | % | | % | *n* | % |
| I think | **25** | 49.0 | **12** | 23.5 | 6 | 11.8 | | 0.0 | 2 | 3.9 | 1 | 2.0 | 1 | 2.0 | 2 | 3.9 | 2 | 3.9 | 51 | 100.0 |
| I dont know | **11** | 50.0 | 2 | 9.1 | 4 | 18.2 | 5 | 22.7 | | 0.0 | | 0.0 | | 0.0 | | 0.0 | | 0.0 | 22 | 100.0 |
| I know | **8** | 47.1 | 3 | 17.6 | 3 | 17.6 | 1 | 5.9 | | 0.0 | 1 | 5.9 | | 0.0 | | 0.0 | 1 | 5.9 | 17 | 100.0 |
| I thought | 5 | 83.3 | 1 | 16.7 | | 0.0 | | 0.0 | | 0.0 | | 0.0 | | 0.0 | | 0.0 | | 0.0 | 6 | 100.0 |
| I guess | 2 | 28.6 | 1 | 14.3 | 1 | 14.3 | 1 | 14.3 | | 0.0 | | 0.0 | | 0.0 | | 0.0 | 2 | 28.6 | 7 | 100.0 |
| I dont think | **11** | 100.0 | | 0.0 | | 0.0 | | 0.0 | | 0.0 | | 0.0 | | 0.0 | | 0.0 | | 0.0 | 11 | 100.0 |
| I remember | 2 | 22.2 | 6 | 66.7 | | 0.0 | 1 | 11.1 | | 0.0 | | 0.0 | | 0.0 | | 0.0 | | 0.0 | 9 | 100.0 |
| Im sure | 3 | 50.0 | | 0.0 | 1 | 16.7 | 1 | 16.7 | | 0.0 | | 0.0 | | 0.0 | | 0.0 | 1 | 16.7 | 6 | 100.0 |
| I hope | 7 | 100.0 | | 0.0 | | 0.0 | | 0.0 | | 0.0 | | 0.0 | | 0.0 | | 0.0 | | 0.0 | 7 | 100.0 |
| Im thinking | | 0.0 | | 0.0 | 1 | 100.0 | | 0.0 | | 0.0 | | 0.0 | | 0.0 | | 0.0 | | 0.0 | 1 | 100.0 |
| Im not sure | 1 | 50.0 | 1 | 50.0 | | 0.0 | | 0.0 | | 0.0 | | 0.0 | | 0.0 | | 0.0 | | 0.0 | 2 | 100.0 |
| I suppose | 1 | 100.0 | | 0.0 | | 0.0 | | 0.0 | | 0.0 | | 0.0 | | 0.0 | | 0.0 | | 0.0 | 1 | 100.0 |

**Table 9.3.** (*Continued*)

| Epistemic phrase | IU-initial | | | | Separate IU | | | | | | Medial position in IU | | | | | | Final position in IU | | TOTAL | |
|---|---|---|---|---|---|---|---|---|---|---|---|---|---|---|---|---|---|---|---|---|
| | Clause-initial | % | Phrase-initial | % | Scope forward | % | Scope back | % | Indeterminate scope | % | Scope forward | % | Scope back | % | Indeterminate scope | % | | % | *n* | % |
| I cant believe | 2 | 100.0 | | 0.0 | | 0.0 | | 0.0 | | 0.0 | | 0.0 | | 0.0 | | 0.0 | | 0.0 | 2 | 100.0 |
| I cant imagine | | | | | | | | | | | | | | | | | | | 0 | 0.0 |
| I would imagine | | 0.0 | | 0.0 | | 0.0 | | 0.0 | | 0.0 | | 0.0 | | 0.0 | | 0.0 | 1 | 100.0 | 1 | 100.0 |
| I imagine | | | | | | | | | | | | | | | | | | | 0 | 0.0 |
| I believe | 2 | 50.0 | 2 | 50.0 | | 0.0 | | 0.0 | | 0.0 | | 0.0 | | 0.0 | | 0.0 | | 0.0 | 4 | 100.0 |
| **TOTAL** | **80** | **54.4** | **28** | **19.0** | **16** | **10.9** | 9 | 6.1 | 2 | 1.4 | 2 | 1.4 | 1 | 0.7 | 2 | 1.4 | 7 | 4.8 | **147** | 100.0 |

monologic speech. As far as the relative frequencies of the different positions and scope types are concerned, we can see that in planned speech the scope of epistemic phrases shows an even higher tendency to extend forward in discourse: 85.7% as opposed to 79.7% for everyday speech. Consequently, backward scope obtains a lower percentage here: 11.6% as opposed to 19.9% for everyday speech. Clausal scope is again more prevalent than phrasal scope: 80 of 147 occurrences are definitely clausal, whereas on the basis of an impressionistic analysis clausal scope is more prevalent in IU-final cases as well.

We confine ourselves here to look at some examples from planned speech, especially where they deviate from everyday usage.

In IU-initial and simultaneously clause-initial position, the phrases may be followed by the complementizer *that* rather more often than in everyday speech (but the frequencies are small), as in:

(51) RUBEN: ... **I think that** it's more ... eye-opening,
.. to see,
.. that,
.. this doesn't exist,
... more than it does. (SBCSAE 12/1311)

(52) FOSTER: (H) **I don't think that** he would (Hx) .. acknowledge original sin. (SBCSAE 25/143)

(53) CYNTHIA: .. A=nd **I hope that** some of you would be able to come. (SBCSAE 54/54)

Some items have phrasal scope relatively more often in planned than in everyday speech, notably *I remember*:

(54) WALT: ... (H) And **I remember** all of the fears that were in m=y life. (SBCSAE 21/1308)

(55) WOOD: ... **I remember** Toshiko= (H) Takaezu, (SBCSAE 55/610)

Finally, one item, *I believe*, is slightly more common in formal planned speech (four instances) than informal speech (see van Bogaert, 2006: 143 for a similar finding concerning British English). In example (56) it modifies a prepositional phrase, whereas in example (57) it is clause-initial, even though the clause is produced haltingly over several IUs (the second occurrence in example (57) would be classified as phrase-initial in the present system, however, because the IU contains no verb).

(56) MATTHEW: .. After the agreement was entered into,
... he had been on the job for about a week or so,
... and,
it was time,
... **I believe** for the-,
... first or second pay ... period for his men, (SBCSAE 53/836)

| (57) | WALT: | ... (H) You know I wanna talk a little bit about f=ear today, |
|---|---|---|
| | AUD: | ... X |
| | WALT: | (TSK) Uh, |
| | | (H) cause **I believe** it's something that keeps us, |
| | | ... % .. from doing everything we can do, |
| | | as .. human beings, |
| | | ... the potential that God has given us, |
| | | ... and **I believe** it also, |
| | | ... really keeps us [from=], |
| | AUD: | [(SNEEZE)] |
| | WALT: | ... a=, |
| | | ... s=trong s=piritual .. walk with God. (SBCSAE 21/511) |

## 6. Position and scope of epistemic phrases in task-related speech

The 11 recordings representing task-related talk in the SBCSAE consist of different types of workplace talk, talk at home while cooking, two service encounters, a witness preparation, game playing situation, appointments with a doctor and a dietician, and a trainee feedback session. These were separated from planned speech on the one hand and everyday speech on the other, because they tend to be more dialogic in type than the more highly institutional planned speech in Section 5, but because they also do not represent mundane unplanned everyday interaction of the kind discussed in Section 4. Even though the above is by no means a hard and fast distinction that can be maintained consistently and be argued to hold throughout a given recording, for example, it was decided upon to get a clearer distinction between unplanned vs. planned speech (and because it was not clear which variety the task-related recordings should have been subsumed into).[9] As it turned out, task-related speech (Table 9.4) is somewhere between the two ends of the continuum from unplanned to planned, yet perhaps approaching the planned variety.

We can again see the same overall pattern of the most frequent epistemic phrases (see also Table 9.1), with slight modifications. Although *I think* is even slightly more common than in everyday speech, *I thought* is clearly less common, *I guess* about the same, and the rest of the high-frequency items of everyday speech are not really high-frequency here (see the few and small numbers below the double line). From the summary below (Table 9.5) we can see that the tendency for forward scope in task-related speech is between that of the other two varieties, but

[9] For example, it can be argued that tapes 9 *Zero Equals Zero* (math tutoring), 23 *Howard's End* (book club discussion), and 3 *Conceptual Pesticides* (involving some cooking) of unplanned everyday data could equally well have been included under the task-related variety.

**Table 9.4.** Position and scope of epistemic phrases in task-related speech

| Epistemic phrase | IU-initial | | | | Separate IU | | | | | | Medial position in IU | | | | | | Final position in IU | | TOTAL | |
|---|---|---|---|---|---|---|---|---|---|---|---|---|---|---|---|---|---|---|---|---|
| | Clause-initial | % | Phrase-initial | % | Scope forward | % | Scope back | % | Indeterminate scope | % | Scope forward | % | Scope back | % | Indeterminate scope | % | | % | *n* | % |
| I think | **58** | 56.9 | 8 | 7.8 | 19 | 18.6 | 6 | 5.9 | 4 | 3.9 | 3 | 2.9 | | 0.0 | 1 | 1.0 | 3 | 2.9 | 102 | 100.0 |
| I dont know | **29** | 52.7 | 3 | 5.5 | 7 | 12.7 | 16 | 29.1 | | 0.0 | | 0.0 | | 0.0 | | 0.0 | | 0.0 | 55 | 100.0 |
| I know | **10** | 41.7 | 3 | 12.5 | 5 | 20.8 | 5 | 20.8 | | 0.0 | 1 | 4.2 | | 0.0 | | 0.0 | | 0.0 | 24 | 100.0 |
| I thought | **13** | 100.0 | | 0.0 | | 0.0 | | 0.0 | | 0.0 | | 0.0 | | 0.0 | | 0.0 | | 0.0 | 13 | 100.0 |
| I guess | **17** | 63.0 | 6 | 22.2 | 1 | 3.7 | 1 | 3.7 | | 0.0 | | 0.0 | | 0.0 | | 0.0 | 2 | 7.4 | 27 | 100.0 |
| I dont think | 7 | 87.5 | | 0.0 | | 0.0 | 1 | 12.5 | | 0.0 | | 0.0 | | 0.0 | | 0.0 | | 0.0 | 8 | 100.0 |
| I remember | | 0.0 | 1 | 50.0 | | 0.0 | 1 | 50.0 | | 0.0 | | 0.0 | | 0.0 | | 0.0 | | 0.0 | 2 | 100.0 |
| Im sure | 2 | 100.0 | | 0.0 | | 0.0 | | 0.0 | | 0.0 | | 0.0 | | 0.0 | | 0.0 | | 0.0 | 2 | 100.0 |
| I hope | 2 | 100.0 | | 0.0 | | 0.0 | | 0.0 | | 0.0 | | 0.0 | | 0.0 | | 0.0 | | 0.0 | 2 | 100.0 |
| Im thinking | | 0.0 | | 0.0 | | 0.0 | | 0.0 | | 0.0 | 1 | 100.0 | | 0.0 | | 0.0 | | 0.0 | 1 | 100.0 |
| Im not sure | 3 | 60.0 | 1 | 20.0 | 1 | 20.0 | | 0.0 | | 0.0 | | 0.0 | | 0.0 | | 0.0 | | 0.0 | 5 | 100.0 |
| I suppose | | | | | | | | | | | | | | | | | | | 0 | 0.0 |

**Table 9.4.** (*Continued*)

| Epistemic phrase | IU-initial | | | | Separate IU | | | | | | Medial position in IU | | | | | | Final position in IU | | TOTAL | |
|---|---|---|---|---|---|---|---|---|---|---|---|---|---|---|---|---|---|---|---|---|
| | Clause-initial | % | Phrase-initial | % | Scope forward | % | Scope back | % | Indeterminate scope | % | Scope forward | % | Scope back | % | Indeterminate scope | % | | % | *n* | % |
| I cant believe | 1 | 100.0 | | 0.0 | | 0.0 | | 0.0 | | 0.0 | | 0.0 | | 0.0 | | 0.0 | | 0.0 | 1 | 100.0 |
| I cant imagine | | | | | | | | | | | | | | | | | | | 0 | 0.0 |
| I would imagine | | | | | | | | | | | | | | | | | | | 0 | 0.0 |
| I imagine | 2 | 100.0 | | 0.0 | | 0.0 | | 0.0 | | 0.0 | | 0.0 | | 0.0 | | 0.0 | | 0.0 | 2 | 100.0 |
| I believe | 1 | 50.0 | | 0.0 | | 0.0 | | 0.0 | | 0.0 | | 0.0 | 1 | 50.0 | | 0.0 | | 0.0 | 2 | 100.0 |
| **TOTAL** | **145** | **58.9** | **22** | **8.9** | **33** | **13.4** | **30** | **12.2** | 4 | 1.6 | 5 | 2.0 | 1 | 0.4 | 1 | 0.4 | 5 | 2.0 | **246** | 100.0 |

closer to planned than everyday speech. The same is true of backward scope: it is between the two varieties but closer to the low figure of planned speech.

**Table 9.5.** Forward and backward scope according to speech type

| | **Forward scope (%)** | **Backward scope (%)** |
|---|---|---|
| Everyday speech | 79.9 | 19.9 |
| Task-related speech | 83.3 | 14.6 |
| Planned speech | 85.7 | 11.6 |

As for clausal vs. phrasal scope in IU-initial cases, task-related speech does not really fit into the above pattern but stands out in showing by far the highest clausal scope percentage and consequently a lower phrasal scope percentage (Table 9.6). It is difficult to postulate reasons for

**Table 9.6.** Clausal and phrasal scope in IU-initial cases according to speech type

| | **Clausal scope (%)** | **Phrasal scope (%)** |
|---|---|---|
| Everyday speech | 51.8 | 10.7 |
| Task-related speech | 58.9 | 8.9 |
| Planned speech | 54.4 | 19.0 |

this, but a wild guess could be that when speakers are dealing with a (possibly urgent) task at hand, they are more likely to talk in a brisk and to-the-point manner, that is in full and brief clauses.

I conclude by presenting some examples from task-related conversations of patterns that have not been exemplified before.

Line 1 in example (58) shows a very rare occurrence of IU-medial *I know. I think* on line 5 shows an instance that is not frequent in the whole database (6 in everyday speech, 6 here), that is a separate IU with a scope backward in discourse. It seems to be responsive to Randy's less than enthusiastic reception of Lance's turn on line 1: by toning down his earlier claim (also on line 3 with *it seems*), Lance seems to be pursuing a stronger display of affiliation or acceptance from Randy, the experienced air traffic controller, while Lance is still training to be one. It is worth noting that a little later (line 12) Lance reverts back to the unmarked IU- and clause-initial pattern, which Randy also adopts (line 16).

(58) 01 LANCE: ..(H) Jet Speed [is th- **I know** fast on the] pr-departure,
02 RANDY: [AM-Flight].
03 LANCE: it seems.
04 RANDY: .. Yeah.
05 LANCE: ... % **I think**.
06 ..It .. seems like that was the one,
07 but,
08 yeah AM-Flight,
09 when they fly the later jet.
10 (H) Um,
11 yeah.
12 And **I think** I might have said for delta niners or to,
13 no delay,
14 or some[thing like that and],
15 RANDY: [Yeah.
16 **I think** you did]. (SBCSAE 22/684)

Finally, an example of a similarly infrequent pattern in the data is *I don't think* encoded as a separate IU and looking backward in discourse (two instances). Note that even if it has the preceding clause in its scope, it seems to show a degree of independency and mobility (like *I don't know*) as it comes after a short pause and is clearly an IU of its own. Example (60) is an extraordinarily cautious formulation of the subject matter, which the patient may have suffered from posterior cruciate before.

(59) JENNIFER: ... I'm not gonna be able to wipe this striped guy out yet.
... **I don't think**. (SBCSAE 24/591)

(60) REED: or posterior cruciate we call it.
DARREN: ... (SNIFF)
REED: ... (TSK) Uh,
... seems to be the problem,
.. (H) but it's not uh,
... **I'm not sure** you didn't have a little bit of that problem before. (SBCSAE 46/416)

## 7. Conclusion

This chapter has found clear support for the tendencies observed in Kärkkäinen (2003) that epistemic phrases are most commonly prosodically integrated into the pitch contour of the IU in progress, most commonly a clausal one, and appear initially in these units. Prosodically independent phrases are the next most frequent category, whereas medial and final encoding within an IU hardly occur at all. We thus observed a clear prevalence in American English speech of the right-binding prosody of epistemic phrases and a scope that extends forward rather than backward in discourse. It is also safe to say that the high-frequency (and also less high-frequency) items most commonly have clausal rather than phrasal scope. These patterns were seen to be equally predominant in everyday, planned, and task-related varieties of American English. This is in rather stark contrast with the results of Kaltenböck (2007, 2008) for British English, where a left-binding prosody was the most common and a right-binding prosody was the least frequent. Even though the much higher proportion of right-binding prosody in the present study is probably an artifact of the inclusion of a larger number of initially occurring epistemic phrases (because a less cautious approach and more "liberal" criteria were adopted), it still appears that British English is more versatile in the way epistemic phrases pattern, especially in how they may frequently point backward in discourse. It seems likely that American English shows a different and perhaps a more conservative grammaticization pattern of epistemic phrases: they are not as mobile as they are in British English, but have largely preserved the erstwhile main clause + complement clause syntactic pattern.

Traugott (1995: 38–39) sheds some light on why this appears to be the case. She argues for the most frequent phrase *I think* that this verbal construction is undergoing a change, first from main clause status to a parenthetical construction (with greater freedom of position), and gradually to a fixed phrase indicating speaker's epistemic attitude. The subjectification of its meaning also involves the choice of mostly first-person subjects, and the tendency for the subject to gradually lose referential properties and become a mere *starting-point of a perspective* (see also Scheibman, 2001 and 2002 for support for this claim). Traugott's claim seems to lend strong support to Thompson's (2002) later claim about the most frequent epistemic (and evidential and evaluative) fragments with first-person subjects having become fixed formulas in American English and being used by speakers to provide a certain type of perspective or stance toward the action that is performed in the associated (mostly upcoming) utterance.

Relatedly, Bybee (2004) stresses the importance of *frequency* and *repetition* in grammaticization. She views grammaticization as a process "by which a frequently used sequence of words or morphemes becomes automated as a single processing unit" (2004: 603). This process involves the following five changes, most of which have a bearing on the high-frequency epistemic phrases discussed earlier.

First, high type and token frequency of an item or a grammaticizing construction is seen to lead to the weakening of semantic force. Kärkkäinen (2003) observed the weak or general referentiality of the subject pronoun in *I think*, to the point that it is sometimes omitted completely (as is also noted by Traugott, 1995: 38). In the present database, also *I guess*, *I thought*, and *I don't know* are found on occasion to occur without the subject pronoun.

(61) ... Guess I'll put it o=n, (SBCSAE 1/765)
... Thought I was gonna get you. (SBCSAE 3/1254).
... Don't know. (SBCSAE 50/647)

Evidence has also been presented in the literature that the actual cognitive verbs involved "are not being used to inform participants of the speaker's cognitive activities," but for a subjective pragmatic function (Scheibman, 2001: 71; see also Thompson, 2002).

Second, grammaticization brings with it a reduction of phonological form, which is again said to be conditioned by the high frequency of the given item or construction. Bybee (2004: 617) gives as an example the phonological fusion of *don't*: out of many more possible combinations of *don't* + verb, the reduction of *don't* is most extreme in phrases in which it most commonly occurs, these being *I don't know* and *I don't think*. According to Bybee, these two phrases have come to be stored and processed in one chunk. Kärkkäinen (2003) also found that in some of its uses *I think* has become phonologically reduced, either on the pronoun or the verb, and the construction is clearly produced as one chunk. What has happened with other high-frequency epistemic phrases awaits further study.

Third, increased frequency conditions a greater autonomy from other instances of the same morphemes, that is they grow increasingly independent of their composite morphemes (*go*, *ing*, and *to* in *be going to*) but also other instances of the same construction. Although this has also to be proven by further study, there is evidence that at least the pragmatic functions of *I think* vs. *I'm thinking* or *I thought* (or *I don't think* for that matter) have diverged and are specific to each construction.

Fourth, the autonomy of grammaticizing phrases makes it possible that they acquire new pragmatic functions. Bybee (2004: 618) again illustrates this with *I don't know* in colloquial American English, where it can be used with its literal meaning (as an answer to a question) but also increasingly to mitigate an assertion and to politely disagree or refuse something being offered (see also other functions proposed for this phrase by Beach and Metzger, 1997). In the latter functions, it has lost its association with the individual words from which it derives (Bybee, 2004: 618). In addition to the pragmatic functions identified for *I think* (Kärkkäinen, 2003) and *I guess* (Kärkkäinen, 2007), we have seen some evidence here for the pragmatic function of *I thought* as a stance frame, that is a new pragmatic function.

The fifth change involved in grammaticization and semantic change concerns autonomy of a frequent phrase, which makes it more entrenched in the language and may help preserve a more conservative structure (e.g. the syntactic properties associated with the English modal auxiliaries were once properties of all verbs but have become conventionalized in these high-frequency verbs, whereas all others have changed with the changing syntax of the language). This is a change that does not at first blush appear to relate to epistemic markers. However, by a more conservative structure, we may understand their persistent utterance- or clause-initial position, that is that they have in a sense preserved the erstwhile main clause + complement clause syntactic pattern.

In all, there is ample evidence that the high-frequency items in the present study (and perhaps also the less high-frequency ones) are processed as single processing units, which with surprising regularity tend to occur initially in clauses and, less frequently, in phrases. Why do they then not display a greater variety of positions and greater mobility possible for a parenthetical construction? The explanation must be looked for in the interaction between speakers and recipients. Traugott and Dasher (2002) also argue that meanings in grammaticization and in semantic change in general tend to become not only subjective (Traugott, 1995) but *intersubjective*, or grounded in the speaker–hearer relationship. Thus, despite the first person pronoun in *I think* or *I guess*, they may acknowledge various "image-saving" needs of addressees (or readers), that is be used as expressions of politeness, hedges, and other mitigators (Traugott and Dasher, 2002: 91). Maybe one indication of this is that of the very-high-frequency items in the data, *I think* is followed by the first-person pronoun only in 29 cases (out of 294, or 9.9 %) in everyday speech (as in *I think I'd hate to be in business right now.* <11/345>), *I know* in 4 cases (2.3%), *I thought* in 2 cases (1.4%), *I guess* in 3 cases (3.6%), and *I don't think* in 5 cases (9.3%). And even these utterances can on occasion be interpreted as more hearer- than speaker-oriented (as in ... *Well I think I told you this.* <11/1210>). Thus, we may conclude that the interactional work that they are doing is best done in initial position rather than later in the utterance or turn.

## References

Aijmer, K. (1997). "*I think* – an English modal particle", in T. Swan and O. Jansen Westvik (eds.), *Modality in Germanic languages – Historical and comparative perspectives*. Berlin: Mouton de Gruyter, 1–47.

Beach, W. A. and T. R. Metzger (1997). "Claiming insufficient knowledge". *Human Communication Research* **23**: 560–585.

Biber, D., S. Johansson, G. Leech, E. Finegan and S. Conrad (1999). *The Longman grammar of spoken and written English*. London: Longman.

Bybee, J. (2004). "Mechanisms of change in grammaticization: The role of frequency", in B. D. Joseph and R. D. Janda (eds.), *The handbook of historical linguistics*. Malden, MA: Blackwell Publishing, 602–623.

Chafe, W. (1979). "The flow of thought and the flow of language", in T. Givón (ed.), *Discourse and syntax*. New York: Academic Press, 159–181.

Chafe, W. (1987). "Cognitive constraints on information flow", in R. S. Tomlin (ed.), *Coherence and grounding in discourse*. Amsterdam: Benjamins, 21–51.

Chafe, W. (1988). "Linking intonation units in spoken English", in J. Haiman and S. A. Thompson (eds.), *Clause combining in grammar and discourse*. Amsterdam: Benjamins, 1–27.

Chafe, W. (1994). *Discourse, consciousness, and time: The flow and displacement of conscious experience in speaking and writing*. Chicago: University of Chicago Press.

Cruttenden, A. (1986). *Intonation*. Cambridge: Cambridge University Press.

Crystal, D. (2003). *A dictionary of linguistics & phonetics*. Oxford, UK: Blackwell Publishing.

Du Bois, J. W., Schuetze-Coburn, S., Paolino, D., and Cumming, S. (1991). "Discourse transcription". Manuscript, University of California, Santa Barbara.

Du Bois, J. W., S. Schuetze-Coburn, S. Cumming and D. Paolino (1993). "An outline of discourse transcription", in J. Edwards and M. Lampert (eds.), *Talking data: Transcription and coding in discourse research*. Hillsdale, NJ: Lawrence Erlbaum, 45–87.

Du Bois, J. W., W. L. Chafe, C. Meyer and S. A. Thompson (2000). *Santa Barbara corpus of spoken American English, Part 1*. Philadelphia: Linguistic Data Consortium.

Du Bois, J. W., W. L. Chafe, C. Meyer, S. A. Thompson and M. Nii (2003). *Santa Barbara corpus of spoken American English, Part 2*. Philadelphia: Linguistic Data Consortium.

Du Bois, J. W. and R. Englebretson (2004). *Santa Barbara corpus of spoken American English, Part 3*. Philadelphia: Linguistic Data Consortium.

Du Bois, J. W. and R. Englebretson (2005). *Santa Barbara corpus of spoken American English, Part 4*. Philadelphia: Linguistic Data Consortium.

Ford, C., B. Fox and S. A. Thompson (2002). "Constituency and the grammar of turn increments", in C. Ford, B. Fox and S. A. Thompson (eds.), *The language of turn and sequence*. Oxford: Oxford University Press, 14–38.

Givón, T. (1993). *English grammar. A function-based introduction. Vols. I and II*. Amsterdam: Benjamins.

Heritage, J. (1984). "A change-of-state token and aspects of its sequential placement", in J. M. Atkinson and J. Heritage (eds.), *Structures of social action: Studies in conversation analysis*. Cambridge: Cambridge University Press, 299–345.

Jucker, A. H., S. W. Smith and T. Lüdge (2003). "Interactive aspects of vagueness in conversation". *Journal of Pragmatics* **35**: 1737–1769.

Kaltenböck, G. (2007). "Position, prosody, and scope: The case of English comment clauses". *Vienna English Working Papers (VIEWS)* **16 (1)**: 3–38.

Kaltenböck, G. (2008). "Prosody and function of English comment clauses". *Folia Linguistica* **42 (1–2)**: 83–134.

Kärkkäinen, E. (2003). *Epistemic stance in English conversation. A description of its interactional functions, with a focus on I think*. Amsterdam: John Benjamins.

Kärkkäinen, E. (2007). "The role of *I guess* in conversational stancetaking", in R. Englebretson (ed.), *Stancetaking in discourse: Subjectivity, evaluation, interaction*. Amsterdam: Benjamins, 183–219.

Markkanen, R. (1985). "English parenthetical clauses of the type 'I believe/ you know' and their Finnish equivalents", in R. Markkanen (ed.), *Cross-language studies in pragmatics*. Department of English, University of Jyväskylä, 41–63.

Precht, K. (2003). "Stance moods in spoken English: Evidentiality and affect in British and American conversation". *Text. Special issue: Negotiating Heteroglossia: Social perspectives on evaluation* **23 (2)**: 239–257.

Quirk, R., S. Greenbaum, G. Leech and J. Svartvik (1985). *A comprehensive grammar of the English language*. London: Longman.

Sacks, H., E. Schegloff and G. Jefferson (1978). "A simplest systematics for the organization of turn-taking for conversation", in J. Schenkein (ed.), *Studies in the organization of conversational interaction*. New York: Academic Press, 7–55.

Scheibman, J. (2000). "I *dunno* ... A usage-based account of the phonological reduction of *don't* in American English conversation". *Journal of Pragmatics* **32**: 105–124.

Scheibman, J. (2001). "Local patterns of subjectivity in person and verb type in American English conversation", in J. Bybee and P. Hopper (eds.), *Frequency and the emergence of linguistic structure*. Amsterdam: Benjamins, 61–89.

Scheibman, J. (2002). *Point of view and grammar: Structural patterns of subjectivity in American English conversation*. Amsterdam: Benjamins.

Stelma, J. H. and L. J. Cameron (2007). "Intonation units in spoken interaction: Developing transcription skills". *Text & Talk* **27** (**3**): 361–393.

Thompson, S. A. (2002). "'Object complements' and conversation: Towards a realistic account". *Studies in Language* **26** (**1**): 125–163.

Thompson, S. A. and A. Mulac (1991a). "A quantitative perspective on the grammaticization of epistemic parentheticals in English", in E. C. Traugott and B. Heine (eds.), *Approaches to grammaticalization Vol. 1–2*. Amsterdam: John Benjamins, 313–329.

Thompson, S. A. and A. Mulac (1991b). "The discourse conditions for the use of the complementizer *that* in conversational English". *Journal of Pragmatics* **15**: 237–251.

Traugott, E. C. (1995). "Subjectification in grammaticalisation", in D. Stein and S. Wright (eds.), *Subjectivity and subjectivisation: Linguistic perspectives*. Cambridge: Cambridge University Press, 31–54.

Traugott, E. C. and R. B. Dasher (2002). *Regularity in semantic change*. Cambridge: Cambridge University Press.

Urmson, J. O. (1963). "Parenthetical verbs", in C. E. Caton (ed.), *Philosophy and ordinary language*. Urbana: University of Illinois Press, 220–240.

van Bogaert, J. (2006). "*I guess, I suppose* and *I believe* as pragmatic markers: Grammaticalization and functions". *BELL (Belgian Journal of English Language and Literatures) New Series* **4**: 129–149.

Wichmann, A. (2001). "Spoken parentheticals", in K. Aijmer (ed.), *A wealth of English. Studies in honour of Göran Kjellmer*. Gothenburg: Acta Universitatis Gothoburgiensis, 177–193.

## Appendix 1

| No. | Name of tape | Type | Length |
|---|---|---|---|
| UNPLANNED EVERYDAY: | | | |
| 1 | *Actual Blacksmithing* | Face-to face | 25 min 16 s |
| 2 | *Lambada* | Face-to face | 23 min 58 s |
| 3 | *Conceptual Pesticides* | Face-to face | 26 min 7 s |
| 4 | *Raging Bureaucracy* | Face-to face | 19 min 22 s |
| 5 | *A Book about Death* | Face-to face | 20 min 28 s |
| 6 | *Cuz* | Face-to face | 27 min 16 s |
| 7 | *A Tree's Life* | Face-to face | 23 min 6 s |
| 9 | *Zero Equals Zero* | Face-to-face (math tutoring) | 25 min |
| 11 | *This Retirement Bit* | Face-to face | 20 min 31 s |
| 13 | *Appease the Monster* | Face-to face | 27 min 25 s |
| 15 | *Deadly Diseases* | Face-to face | 25 min 19 s |
| 17 | *Wonderful Abstract Notions* | Face-to face | 10 min 21 s |

## Appendix 1 *(Continued)*

| No. | Name of tape | Type | Length |
|---|---|---|---|
| 19 | *Doesn't Work in This Household* | Face-to face | 21 min 46 s |
| 23 | *Howard's End* | Face-to-face (book club discussion) | 24 min 25 s |
| 28 | *Hey Cutie Pie* | Telephone conversation | 25 min 6 s |
| 31 | *Tastes Very Special* | Face-to-face | 24 min 38 s |
| 32 | *Handshakes All Around* | Face-to-face | 24 min 47 s |
| 33 | *Guilt* | Face-to-face | 10 min 47 s |
| 34 | *What Time Is It Now?* | Face-to-face | 24 min 40 s |
| 35 | *Hold My Breath* | Face-to-face | 19 min 30 s |
| 36 | *Judgmental on People* | Face-to-face | 26 min 51 s |
| 42 | *Stay out of It* | Face-to-face | 19 min 17 s |
| 43 | *Try a Couple Spoonfuls* | Face-to-face | 25 min 1 s |
| 44 | *He Knows* | Face-to-face | 29 min 7 s |
| 45 | *The Classic Hooker* | Face-to-face | 30 min 15 s |
| 47 | *On the Lot* | Face-to-face | 20 min 12 s |
| 48 | *Mickey Mouse Watch* | Face-to-face | 18 min 5 s |
| 49 | *Noise Pollution* | Face-to-face | 18 min 58 s |
| 50 | *Just Wanna Hang* | Face-to-face | 16 min 32 s |
| 51 | *New Yorkers Anonymous* | Face-to-face | 25 min 48 s |
| 52 | *Oh You Need a Breadbox* | Telephone conversation | 25 min 53 s |
| 56 | *What Is a Brand Inspection* | Face-to-face | 30 min 30 s |
| 58 | *Swingin' Kid* | Face-to-face | 25 min 47 s |
| 59 | *You Baked* | Face-to-face | 27 min 54 s |
| 60 | *Shaggy Dog Story* | Face-to-face | 24 min 49 s |
| | | | Total **13 h 34 min 47 s** |
| TASK-RELATED SPEECH: | | | |
| 8 | *Tell the Jury That* | Witness preparation | 25 min 25 s |
| 10 | *Letter of Concerns* | Workplace talk | 15 min 41 s |

**Appendix 1** (*Continued*)

| No. | Name of tape | Type | Length |
|---|---|---|---|
| 14 | *Bank Products* | Workplace talk | 28 min 17 s |
| 16 | *Tape Deck* | Service encounter | 12 min 9 s |
| 18 | *Vet Morning* | Workplace talk | 11 min 59 s |
| 22 | *Runway Heading* | Trainee feedback session | 13 min 53 s |
| 24 | *Risk* | Game playing | 26 min 20 s |
| 29 | *Ancient Furnace* | Service encounter | 26 min 56 s |
| 37 | *Very Good Tamales* | Cooking | 26 min 30 s |
| 41 | *X Units of Insulin* | Dietician's appointment | 20 min 33 s |
| 46 | *Flumpity-Bump Down the Hill* | Orthopedist's appointment | 15 min 6 s |
| | | | Total **3 h 42 min 49 s** |
| PLANNED SPEECH: | | | |
| 12 | *American Democracy is Dying* | Teaching/discussion | 25 min 41 s |
| 20 | *God's Love* | Sermon | 25 min 7 s |
| 21 | *Fear* | Sermon | 27 min 51 s |
| 25 | *The Egg Which Luther Hatched* | Lecture | 22 min 8 s |
| 26 | *A Hundred Million Dollars* | Organized discussion (city meeting) | 26 min 33 s |
| 27 | *Atoms Hanging Out* | Teaching/discussion (science lecture) | 16 min 30 s |
| 30 | *Vision* | Sermon | 25 min 56 s |
| 38 | *Good Strong Dam* | Lecture | 24 min 15 s |
| 39 | *Pretty Busy Bird* | Teaching/discussion | 25 min 32 s |
| 40 | *Beaten on a Regular Basis* | Presentation/demo | 22 min 33 s |
| 53 | *I will appeal* | Small claims court | 21 min |
| 54 | *That's Good Said the Tiger* | Arranged storytelling performance | 19 min 22 s |
| 55 | *The Mama of Dada* | Interview/oral history | 27 min 22 s |
| 57 | *Throw Me* | Judo workout/class | 26 min 12 s |
| | | | Total **5 h 36 min 2 s** |
| | | | **TOTAL CORPUS 22 h 52 min 38 s** |

## Appendix 2. Symbols used in transcription (from Du Bois *et al.*, 1993)

| UNITS | | |
|---|---|---|
| Intonation unit | {carriage return} | |
| Truncated intonation unit | – | |
| Truncated word | - | |
| TRANSITIONAL CONTINUITY | | |
| Final | . | |
| Continuing | , | |
| Appeal (seeking a validating response from listener) | ? | |
| SPEAKERS | | |
| Speech overlap | [ ] | |
| (numbers inside brackets index overlaps) | | |
| LENGTHENING | | |
| Lengthening | = | |
| PAUSE | | |
| Long and medium | ... | |
| Short (brief break in speech rhythm) | .. | |
| Latching | (0) | |
| VOCAL NOISES | | |
| e.g. (TSK), (SNIFF), (YAWN), (DRINK) | | |
| Glottal stop | % | |
| Exhalation | (Hx) | |
| Inhalation | (H) | |
| Laughter (one pulse) | @ | |
| QUALITY | | |
| Loudness | | |
| Forte: loud | <F | F> |
| Piano: soft | <P | P> |
| Pitch | | |
| Higher pitch level | <HI | HI> |
| Lowered pitch level | <LO | LO> |
| Parenthetical prosody | <PAR | PAR> |
| Tempo and rhythm | | |
| Allegro: rapid speech | <A | A> |
| Lento: slow speech | <L | L> |
| Marcato: each word distinct and emphasized | <MRC | MRC> |
| Arrhythmic: halting speech | <ARH | ARH> |
| Voice quality | | |
| Whispered | <WH | WH> |
| Breathy | <BR | BR> |
| Creaky | <% | %> |
| Crying | <CRY | CRY> |
| Yawning | <YWN | YWN> |
| TRANSCRIBER'S PERSPECTIVE | | |
| Uncertain hearing | <X | X> |

New Approaches to Hedging
Edited by Gunther Kaltenböck, Wiltrud Mihatsch and Stefan Schneider


# 10

# Pragmatic Functions of Parenthetical *I Think*

*Gunther Kaltenböck*

## Abstract

This chapter explores the pragmatic functions of parenthetical *I think* based on 379 spoken occurrences in the British component of the *International Corpus of English*. Taking into account the parameters of position, prosody, scope and co-occurrence facts, it identifies four core functions: shield function, approximator function, structural function and booster function. These are related to an underlying abstract core meaning, which is activated in different ways depending on the concrete co-textual realisation of *I think*.

## 1. Introduction

This chapter investigates the pragmatic functions of parenthetical *I think* in spoken language, based on an analysis of 379 occurrences in a corpus of modern British English, viz. ICE-GB, the British component of the *International Corpus of English* (cf. Nelson *et al*., 2002). Parenthetical *I think* (e.g. Urmson, 1952; Huddleston and Pullum, 2002: 895) is also commonly referred to as a comment clause (e.g. Quirk *et al*., 1985: 1112; Stenström, 1995; Biber *et al*., 1999: 197) or reduced parenthetical clause (e.g. Kaltenböck, 2005, 2007a; Schneider, 2007). Owing to its formulaic nature and high degree of grammaticalisation (cf. Thompson and Mulac, 1991; Traugott, 1995: 38–39; Palander-Collin, 1999) or pragmaticalisation (cf. Aijmer, 1997), *I think* shows a strong affinity to discourse markers and is sometimes also subsumed under that term (e.g. Mindt, 2003). As a parenthetical element *I think* is only semantically-pragmatically but not syntactically linked to some host construction (cf. Burton-Roberts, 1999: 40; Peterson, 1999: 237) and therefore highly flexible in its position, as illustrated by the examples in (1).[1]

(1a) **I think** <,> I'd like to answer that in a slightly different way (s1a-001-117)
(1b) We're going to have a very small set **I think** at Brave for Edward (s1b-045-110)
(1c) Uhm it's quite fast **I think** (s1a-029-69)

The aim of the chapter is twofold. First of all, it provides a detailed description of the different uses of *I think*, based on large numbers of authentic examples. In this it differs from previous accounts (cf. Section 2 for an overview) by including a systematic analysis of the prosodic realisation and syntactic position of *I think* and linking them to the question of scope. More precisely, it shows that the scope of *I think* is not always clausal, as generally assumed, i.e. covering the entire host clause, but may also be phrasal, e.g. singling out parts of the host construction.[2] By taking into account the parameters of scope, prosody, position and co-occurrence features, four basic communicative functions of *I think* are identified: shield function, approximator function, structural function and booster function. These are basic in the sense that they allow the derivation of further, more specific uses.

The second aim of the chapter is to show that the functional flexibility of *I think* is not random but can be accounted for in terms of the interaction of *I think* with its co-text, which in turn gives rise to different pragmatic interpretations depending on the larger situational context. Section 5 therefore proposes a model for the multifunctionality of parenthetical *I think* which derives the four communicative functions identified earlier from an underlying abstract core meaning. The different functions are activated by the different ways in which *I think* interacts with formal co-textual features. Such an essentially monosemous account has the advantage of systematising the co-textual functions of *I think* while leaving sufficient room for more specific contextual uses. It is also compatible with a diachronic perspective which suggests a process of semantic bleaching for *I think*.

After an overview of previous studies of *I think* in Section 2 and a brief discussion of corpus retrieval and frequencies in Section 3, Section 4 offers a detailed investigation of core communicative functions, viz. shield function (Section 4.1), approximator function (Section 4.2), structural function (Section 4.3) and booster function (Section 4.4). Section 5, finally, provides a unified explanation for the different uses based on a monosemous account of parenthetical *I think*.

---

[1] The notation <,> indicates a short pause, <,,> indicates a long pause.

[2] Cf. also Kärkkäinen (this volume), for an analysis of the scope of epistemic phrases in American English.

## 2. Previous Accounts

There are only few studies that focus explicitly on the use of *I think*, most of which are from the recent past. The first discussions of *I think* are limited to its semantics. Arndt (1987: 27), for instance, distinguishes the following two meanings of *I think*: 'expression of personal attitude' (as in *I think he's a fool*) and 'insufficient evidence' (as in *I think he's a carpenter*). Persson (1993), though not exclusively focussing on *I think*, identifies four different meanings of *think* in general: cogitation, probability, pure opinion and subjective evaluation.

A pragmatic account of *I think* is provided for the first time by Holmes (1984: 359, 1990: 187), who observes that *I think* may have not only tentative function but also deliberative function, conveying certainty and reassurance. What matters for the distinction between these two uses is its prosody and syntactic position, and also contextual factors such as the relationship between the participants, the topic, and the formality of the interaction (Holmes, 1990: 200).

The first large-scale corpus analysis of *I think* was carried out by Stenström (1995) as part of a broader investigation of comment clauses. Although its main concern is not a functional one, this study provides interesting data on frequency and prosodic patterns of *I think*.

The first in-depth corpus treatment of *I think* is Aijmer (1997), who investigates 1,757 instances of *I think* in the *London-Lund Corpus*, including both matrix clauses and parenthetical uses. Aijmer (1997: 21–23) takes up Holmes' (1990) distinction of tentative and deliberative functions, which she aligns with rather fixed prosodic and positional patterns. Thus, *I think* is classified as deliberative only in initial position if it has a nuclear tone or prosodic booster or if it is followed by a *that*-complementiser. This definition yields a total of 15 per cent of deliberative uses in the corpus. Although the study can be criticised for being too mechanistic in assigning the different functions (cf. Kärkkäinen, 2003: 113), it represents the first attempt at applying functional sub-classifications to a large set of data. Aijmer's work is also notable for its proposal of a polysemic model of the semantics of *think*, which takes 'cogitation' as a semantic prototype from which the other meanings, 'belief', 'opinion' and 'intention', are derived by inferencing (Aijmer, 1997: 11–13).

In a study of *I think* in political discourse Simon-Vandenbergen (2000) highlights the importance of text type and wider context for the functional interpretation of *I think*. Comparing the use of *I think* in political interviews and casual conversation (on the basis of samples of 100 instances from each), she finds that political discourse typically makes use of deliberative *I think*, whereas tentative *I think* is rare. From this she concludes that in political interviews speakers do not primarily use *I think* to express uncertainty but to signal authority ('this is my opinion'; Simon-Vandenbergen, 2000: 60).

In a recent corpus study, Mindt (2003) tries to answer the question whether *I think* is a discourse marker. Using the British component of the *International Corpus of English* as her database, she finds a total of 1,724 occurrences of *I think* (96 per cent of which are spoken), which include both syntactically detached (i.e. parenthetical) uses and those involving various forms of complementation (e.g. governing a direct object). She identifies four semantic meanings for *I think*, 'have an opinion/a belief', bleached meaning, 'remember/imagine', 'use one's mind', which are mapped onto two pragmatic functions, viz. textual and interpersonal function. Analysing the correlations of the semantic, pragmatic and the syntactic levels, she concludes that *I think* can be classified as discourse marker if it is semantically bleached, syntactically detached and conveys textual function. This is the case in 23.6 per cent of all instances.

The most comprehensive study of the functions of *I think* to date is Kärkkäinen (2003: 105–182, 2006: 706–711). Based on an analysis of data from the *Santa Barbara Corpus of Spoken American English*, she investigates the function of 41 occurrences of *I think* from a predominantly interactional perspective. *I think* is viewed as a stance taking device with stance being seen as a dynamic and interactional activity of the conversational co-participants, "rather than a way of framing an isolated 'thought' or position of an individual speaker" (Kärkkäinen, 2006: 711). Taking into account position, prosodic aspects and the co(n)textual situation, Kärkkäinen (2003) identifies the following functions of *I think*, all of which are interactionally contingent: starting point function (for marking boundaries or routinely bringing in speaker perspective), recipient-oriented design of utterances, online planning, signalling and pursuing a response. Unlike previous studies, which have limited the interactional function of *I think* to questions of politeness (e.g. for facework), Kärkkäinen for the first time highlights the interactional motivation for the expression of stance.

As far as the identification of pragmatic functions of *I think* is concerned, the above-mentioned studies differ considerably in methodology. Thus, Aijmer (1997), for instance, adopts a fairly mechanistic approach by equating all instances of nuclear tone or prosodic booster on initial *I think* with deliberative function, and all others with tentative function. This has the advantage of being applicable to a large set of corpus data but bears the risk of overgeneralisation. Kärkkäinen (2003), on the other hand, takes into account the specific contextual situation of each occurrence and is therefore able to identify very specific pragmatic functions of *I think*. The present study, by comparison, steers a middle course. While providing a detailed account of co-textual features, especially prosody, based on a large set of corpus data, it proposes categories general enough to allow for a high degree of systematicity and flexible enough to accommodate more fine-grained functional analyses.

## 3. Corpus Frequencies

Previous studies (as discussed in Section 2) have typically included all occurrences of *I think*, i.e. irrespective of whether it is a parenthetical or a matrix clause. While this approach has the advantage of facilitating corpus retrieval, it conflates two linguistic categories that might also be functionally different. The present study therefore restricts the investigation to clear cases of parenthetical *I think*, in an attempt to increase the functional homogeneity of the class.

Delimiting parenthetical *I think* from matrix clauses is, however, not an easy task. Unlike final and medial *I think*, which are always parenthetical, clause-initial *I think* is difficult to distinguish from a matrix clause (which is equivalent to syntactic dependence of the following clause), especially if the *that*-complementiser has been omitted. Compare, for instance, example (2).

(2) **I think** (that) John is in London

Various views have been expressed on the status of such initial clauses with and without *that* complementiser. They are either taken to be parenthetical (e.g. Kruisinga, 1932: 486; Ross, 1973; Thompson and Mulac, 1991; Thompson, 2002; Kärkkäinen, 2003), matrix clauses (e.g. Svensson, 1976: 375; Stenström, 1995: 293, 296; Peterson, 1999: 236) or ambiguous, i.e. allowing interpretation as both matrix clause and parenthetical clause depending on context and type of 'matrix' predicate (e.g. Urmson, 1952: 481; Aijmer, 1972: 46; Quirk *et al.*, 1985: 1113; Biber *et al.*, 1999: 197; Huddleston and Pullum, 2002: 896).[3]

In the absence of hard and fast evidence for any of the different positions, the present study takes a cautious approach which tries to filter out all potentially ambiguous cases. It therefore excludes all instances of initial *I think* with a *that*-complementiser and only takes into account cases of zero *that*-clauses if they are separated from initial *I think* by means of a pause or some intervening material such as hesitation sounds (*uh, uhm*) or other fillers (*you know, I mean*).[4]

Corpus retrieval of parenthetical *I think* is greatly facilitated by the syntactic annotation of ICE-GB, more precisely the category 'detached function'. However, many cases of *I think* in the corpus turned out to be somewhat inconsistently labelled as independent main clauses, which made is necessary to double-check all tokens of *I think* manually. Overall, the spoken section of ICE-GB, which comprises a total of 600,000 words, yielded 379 instances of parenthetical *I think*. As illustrated in Table 10.1, parenthetical *I think* prefers the dialogic text types, which can be taken as an indication of a strong interactive character.

## 4. Core Communicative Functions

This section gives an overview of the main functions of parenthetical *I think* based on an analysis of its co-textual realisation, i.e. prosody, position and co-occurrence facts. The corpus data show that in order to capture the communicative use of parenthetical *I think* it is also

---

[3] For a discussion of the function of *that*-omission in a specific type of matrix clause cf. Kaltenböck (2006a).

[4] Most studies agree that a pause separating the two clauses signals parenthetical use of the first. Cf. also Kaltenböck (2009), which shows that there is little difference in the prosodic realisation of initial *I think* followed by a *that*-complementiser and initial *I think* followed by zero.

**Table 10.1.** Distribution of parenthetical *I think* in the ICE-GB text categories (normalised per 10,000 words)

| | *n* | **10,000 words** |
|---|---|---|
| Private dialogue (s1a) | 158 | 7.9 |
| Public dialogue (s1b) | 134 | 8.4 |
| Unscripted monologue (s2a) | 70 | 5.0 |
| Scripted monologue (s2b) | 17 | 1.7 |
| TOTAL | 379 | 6.3 |

necessary to take into account the type of material *I think* is associated with or has scope over. This scope is of course not to be understood as syntactic scope (in terms of c-command; cf. e.g. Haegeman, 1991; Peterson, 1999) but in semantic-pragmatic terms, i.e. the 'topic' to which the 'comment' of *I think* applies. Establishing the scope of *I think* may also be crucial for identifying its position in relation to the host construction. Take for instance example (3).

(3) Nine is report too **I think** an interesting document which uhm Professor Greenbaum initiated and which I hope everybody uh will have had a chance to digest (s1b-075-128)

In its written form the attachment of *I think* and hence its position is unclear: it may either be initial with scope over *an interesting document which ...* or final with scope over *Nine is report too*. What clarifies the situation is the prosodic realisation of *I think*, which clearly signals attachment to the right and therefore marks the parenthetical as initial. Example (3) also illustrates another important point. It shows that, contrary to the commonly held assumption in the literature, *I think* may not only have scope over clausal host constructions but also over phrasal ones (see Section 4.2 for details).

Based on the co-textual realisation of parenthetical *I think* it is possible to identify four core communicative functions, viz. shield function, approximation function, structural function and booster function, which will be discussed in turn below.

### 4.1. Shield function

The function typically attributed to parenthetical *I think* in the literature is that of an epistemic marker expressing the speaker's tentativeness, lack of certainty or commitment with regard to the truth value of its host (e.g. Hübler, 1983: 114; Quirk *et al.*, 1985: 1114; Thompson and Mulac, 1991: 313; Stenström, 1995: 295; Aijmer, 1997: 21; Wierzbicka, 2006:208). In the terminology of Prince *et al.* (1982: 89), *I think* is a 'shield', which signals that the speaker "is not fully committed in the usual or 'unmarked' way to the belief that the relevant state of affairs actually obtains". As such, *I think* mitigates the 'neustic' (Hare, 1970; cf. also Schneider, 2007: 127–139).

This shield function of *I think* is closely linked with clausal scope, i.e. scope over a clausal host construction which expresses a full proposition. More precisely, *I think* introduces, in Prince *et al.*'s (1982: 85) terms, a "fuzziness in the relationship between the propositional content and the speaker, that is in the speaker's commitment to the truth of the proposition conveyed". Typical examples of such clausal scope uses with shield function are given in (4).

(4a) **I think** <,> I'd like to answer that in a slightly different way (s1a-001-117)
(4b) Uhm it's quite fast **I think** (s1a-029-69)
(4c) And she uhm <,> uh was quite high up **I think** cos she had a degree (s1a-019-248)

Clausal scope *I think* of the type illustrated in (4) is by far the most frequent use in the corpus. With 309 instances (of a total of 379), clausal scope *I think* accounts for a clear majority of 81.5 per cent. As such, clausal scope *I think* with its concomitant shield function represents the default or unmarked use of parenthetical *I think* in the corpus (cf. Givón, 1995 on frequency distribution as a criterion for markedness).

Figure 10.1 provides a schematic (and simplified) overview of the positional distribution of 246 clausal *I think* in the host construction (not included are 53 instances in subordinate clauses, 3 in coordination, 4 in other positions and 3 in NPs; for detailed figures cf. Tables 10.A.1 and 10.A.2 in the Appendix). A typical example of each of the six main insertion points (labelled a – f) is given in (5).

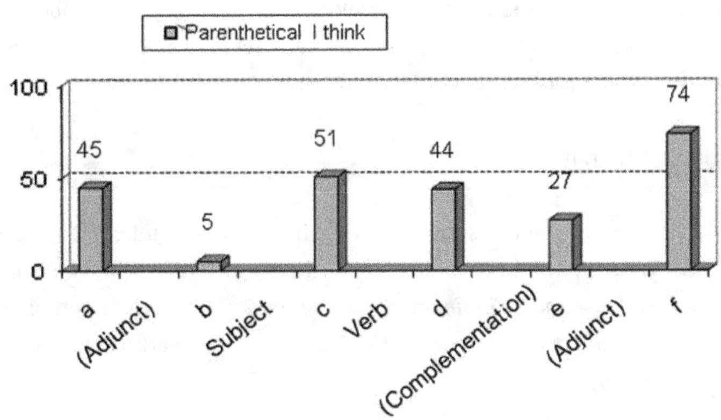


**Figure 10.1.** Schematic and simplified representation of the syntactic positions of 246 clausal *I think* (a–f = points of insertion).

(5a) **I think** <,> I'd like to answer that in a slightly different way (s1a-001-117)
(5b) First of all **I think** <,> relying on lecture notes alone is not enough for for any work you're going to hand in (s1b-007-1)

(5c) The voters **I think** just have an opportunity to stick two fingers up to whoever seems to be on top at the moment (s1b-029-92)

(5d) Uh i it's not uh **I think** legitimate to go out to kill him uhm (s1b-027-49)

(5e) There is no hiding place **I think** anywhere around the world now for Saddam Hussein (s1b-036-59)

(5f) I mean I'm too lazy really for that **I think** (s1a-002-12)

We can see that clausal *I think* occurs at all major constituent boundaries, but is most frequent in final position. It is also substantially represented in initial position, between Subject and VP as well as between main verb and some form of complementation (e.g. object, subject complement). The figures for initial *I think* are considerably lower than those given by other studies, which typically include all forms of *I think* in initial position, i.e. also those followed by a *that*-complementiser. As pointed out in Section 3, the present study has adopted a restrictive definition of initial position, which, for methodological reasons, excludes cases of potential syntactic ambiguity between matrix and parenthetical use. The ratios of mid-position (127 instances) and final position (74 instances), however, are comparable to the findings of other studies. Simon-Vandenbergen (2000: 48), for instance, reports a total of 167 initial, 26 medial and 7 final occurrences in casual conversation and political interviews and Mindt (2003: 478) 1,256 occurrences in front position, 374 in mid-position, and 94 in end-position in the entire ICE-GB, i.e. including written texts.[5]

The functional label of 'shield', of course, has to be seen as referring to a very general concept which is based on the interaction of *I think* with its immediate co-text, i.e. the host construction or rather its proposition. As such, the notion of shield can be expanded and elaborated, for instance in terms of politeness and mitigation (e.g. Holmes, 1990; Schneider, 2007), by taking into account the larger situational context (cf. Section 5).

### 4.2. Approximator function

Contrary to the commonly held assumption in the literature, parenthetical *I think* does not only have a clausal host construction in its scope (cf. Kaltenböck, 2007b, 2008). As noted above, the corpus data show that the scope of *I think* may also be phrasal, i.e. over a non-clausal constituent. Although this use is, with only 18.5 per cent (70 instances), a marked option, it is nonetheless clearly attested in the corpus.

[5] Kärkkäinen (2003: 109) found 32 instances of *I think* in intonation-initial position, and 3 in intonation-unit medial position (6 had a separate intonation unit). Aijmer's (1997: 23) results are noticeably different: in the *London-Lund Corpus* she found 1,377 instances in front-position, 159 in mid-position and 221 in end-position in the "utterance", without however defining the term in any way.

This raises the question how we can identify phrasal scope, or, put differently, how the speaker signals divergence from unmarked clausal scope. To narrow down the scope of *I think* the speaker can make use of essentially two formal signals: position and/or prosodic realisation of *I think*.

Let us first look at the position of *I think* in the host construction as a possibility of restricting the scope and singling out, as it were, a phrasal constituent. A useful tool for establishing the exact scope of *I think* in this connection is the movement test. This involves moving *I think* to a different position in the host construction and checking whether its scope changes (cf. Schneider, 2007: 195). The corpus data show that there are certain positions that are exclusively linked to phrasal scope. These are the positions between a preposition and its NP complement, as in example (6a), and between an NP head and its pre-head dependent (determiner or adjective), as in example (6b) (square brackets indicate scope; for an overview of attested positions with phrasal scope cf. Tables 10.A.1 and 10.A.2 in the Appendix)

(6a) Father McDade d'you remember in **I think** [lecture three] uh Rabbi Sacks said at one point faith is not measured by acts of worship alone (s1b-028-88)

(6b) Uh in the uhm <,> **I think** [October issue] of Computational uh Linguistics there's an attempt to do something of this type (s1a-024-105)

In addition to cases such as these, where *I think* is inserted within a NP or PP, phrasal scope is also the only possibility with non-clausal host constructions, i.e. elliptical or incomplete hosts, as in (7) (scope indicated by square brackets).

(7a) I mean most pagan marriages like **I think** [ninety per cent] that's what happens (s1a-071-234)

(7b) A: When when exactly is it on
B: It's the twenty-seventh **I think** [two o'clock in the afternoon] (s1a-005-113)

Apart from clear positional cues, phrasal scope can also be signalled by prosodic means, more precisely by prosodic binding of *I think* to the left or right. This concerns positions where there is a phrasal constituent in the immediate vicinity of *I think*, i.e. a possible candidate for phrasal scope, such as between main verb and non-clausal complementation, between a VP and non-clausal adjunct, and in clause-final position (cf. Biii, Ci, Ciii, respectively in Table 10.A.1). In these positions, prosodic integration of *I think* with the material on its right or, less frequently, on its left can signal association with a phrasal constituent while other prosodic patterns, i.e. complete prosodic integration (left–right binding) or a separate tone unit for *I think* (prosodic independence), generally lack the ability to single out phrasal constituents.[6]

---

[6] For a detailed discussion of the prosodic patterns of comment clauses in English cf. Kaltenböck (2008).

Prosodic binding to the right is illustrated by the example in (8), where *I think* is prosodically integrated into the pitch contour of the following tone unit but immediately preceded by a tone unit boundary.[7] Figure 10.2 gives the corresponding intonation contour as analysed by PRAAT 4.4.33 (Boersma and Weenink, 2008) (brackets indicate binding to the right or left).

(8) Now one of the things that begins to happen **I think** in the seventeen seventies <,> in particular is the uh is the caricaturist that picks on particular individuals and presents a kind of unrelenting uh sort of repetition of a particular way of looking at them uhm a particular image of them if you like (s2a-057-72)

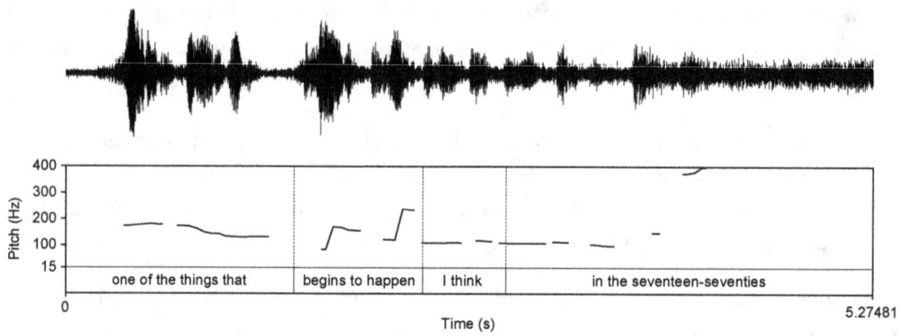


**Figure 10. 2.** One of the things that begins to happen (*I think* in the seventeen-seventies).

Prosodic binding to the left is exemplified in (9) and the corresponding pitch contour in Figure 10.3. Here, *I think* is integrated as tail into the pitch contour (a fall-rise) initiated on *Monday.* This tone unit (*Monday I think*), in turn, is separated from the preceding tone unit by pitch change (a step up by about 100 Hz) and a pause.

(9) The House knows that this matter may be debated on the Queens's speech specifically tomorrow and again on uh Monday **I think** (s1b-052-3)

[7] What exactly constitutes a tone unit boundary is, of course, not always easy to determine (cf. e.g. Cruttenden, 1997: 29–37). Phonetic cues such as pauses, anacrusis, final syllable lengthening or change of pitch level/direction of unaccented syllables may provide some 'external' indication for a prosodic boundary but they are by no means conclusive. They may just as well be simply markers of hesitation. As noted by Cruttenden (1997: 32), for instance, "pauses do not always mark intonation boundaries, nor are intonation boundaries always marked by pauses" (cf. also Fagyal, 2002: 94). These 'external' phonetic criteria therefore have to be complemented by 'internal' ones, i.e. whether the suspected tone unit in fact has the internal structure of one. By definition a tone unit must contain a pitch accent or nucleus (tonic).

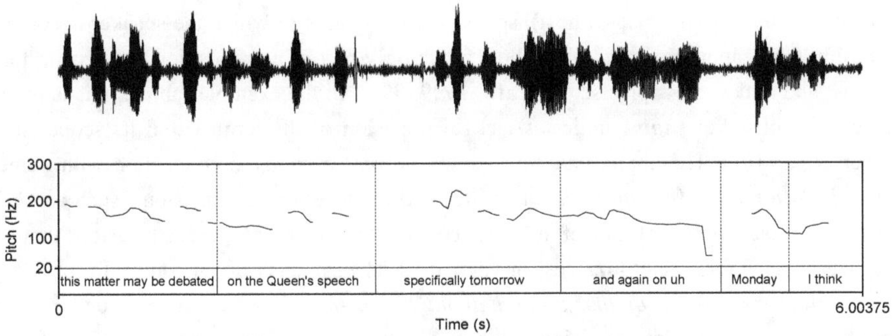


**Figure 10.3.** This matter may be decided on the Queen's speech specifically tomorrow and again on uh Monday *I think.*

The corpus data thus show that, although the default option for *I think* is to have scope over a clausal host, occasionally the speaker may choose to narrow down the scope of *I think* by means of its position or prosody to single out a phrasal constituent. This marked use may be indicative of a special communicative function, as the following examples suggest (some repeated from above).

(10a) Uh in the uhm <,> **I think** [October issue] of Computation al uh Linguistics there's an attempt to do something of this type (s1a-024-105)

(10b) Father McDade d'you remember in **I think** [lecture three] uh Rabbi Sacks said at one point faith is not measured by acts of worship alone (s1b-028-88)

(10c) A plea uh uh a uh a an amended defence containing a plea of justification <,,> uh is in lieu of the <,> uh previous plea of fair comment <,,> uh was uh <,> uh completed <,> uh in **I think** [September] of uh nineteen eighty-nine (s2a-063-58)

(10d) And it sloped down <,> uh for <,> uhm a distance of uhm uh <,,> **I think** [four three or four] <,> uhm feet or possibly more <,> than the length of the slope (s2a-067-3)

(10e) She is wearing <,> a lime green suit carrying <,> a dark blue (**I think** [handbag] <,> white gloves <,> and a pale hat <,> with a <,> rather pretty lime green bobble in it Not a good word but bobble (s2a-019-63/64)

(10f) We're going to have a very small set (**I think** [at Brave] for Edward <,> (s1b-045-110)

These examples differ from the shield uses discussed in the previous section in that they do not so much operate on the relationship between propositional content and speaker but introduce a fuzziness "within the propositional content proper" (Prince *et al.*, 1982: 85). As such, they operate proposition-internally and mitigate the 'phrastic' (Hare, 1970; cf. also Schneider, 2007) and therefore qualify for classification as approximators, in Prince *et al.*'s (1982) terms, or what Caffi (1999) calls 'bushes'. Unlike shields (or in Caffi's terminology 'hedges'), which affect an entire proposition (i.e. the clausal host), specifying the degree to which the speaker is committed to its truth value, approximators (or bushes) affect only part of a proposition, a referring term or predicate, and make it less precise (cf. Caffi, 1999: 890). In the examples above, this is precisely what we can observe: *I think* indicates lack of precision of the term within its scope, such as *October issue* (10a). The approximating function is most obvious in connection with numerals, such as *lecture three* (10b), *three or four* (10d) and other terms of 'precision', such as *October issue* (10a), *September* (10c). In fact, it is the semantic 'precision' of these expressions that seems to trigger the need for greater fuzziness or vagueness. The same is true, of course, for prototypical approximators, such as *sort of, like, around, about, approximately*, which can be found in a similar linguistic environment. Not surprisingly, these prototypical approximators can replace *I think* in the examples above, e.g. *in the (something) like October issue, in about/like/sort of lecture three.* The approximative function of *I think* can, however, also be found with other lexical items which lack the precision of numerals and proper nouns. This is illustrated by example (10e), a radio commentator's description of the Queen's attire, where *I think* is used as an approximator for the semantic category handbag. This use can be explained by the fact that handbags also come in non-prototypical shapes, e.g. shoulder bags or clutch purses (note also the commentator's apparent insecurity in naming fashion items in his use of *bobble* in the immediately following text).

Approximative uses of *I think*, however, differ somewhat from prototypical approximators (e.g. *sort of*) since examples such as (10a), *in the I think October issue* and example (10b) *in I think lecture three* cannot be judged semantically false in a context where the factual truth lies clearly outside a plausible categorial range, say *February issue, lecture 51.*[8] However, in such contexts examples (10a) and (10b) would be regarded as infelicitous or at least uncooperative. This is because the approximative function is derived via conversational implicature in accordance with the conversational maxims. As such, approximative *I think* still reduces speaker commitment but more indirectly than shields. In other words, the speaker will be held less responsible for a statement like *She is carrying a blue I think handbag* (10e) than for *She is carrying a blue sort of handbag*. However, interpretation of the former in terms of categorial fuzziness (i.e. *type of handbag, handbag-like*) will be pragmatically more plausible.

Approximative function of *I think* thus does not exclude reduced speaker commitment. It is simply that in most cases such distancing of the speaker from a term or predicate by *I think* will be interpreted pragmatically by the listener as approximative of the actual truth in accordance with the cooperative principle. This mechanism could be paraphrased as follows: if the speaker signals uncertainty about the truth value of a certain term/predicate, the listener assumes the speaker will try to approximate the truth as much as possible (despite limitations of memory or knowledge) by

[8] Cf. Sadock (1977), who argues that even ordinary approximations have to be treated as almost unfalisfiable.

choosing a term/predicate close to the actually intended, in accordance with the maxim of quality. For such an approximative interpretation much depends on the actual co(n)text, more precisely whether it permits scalar approximation. This is why numerals, days of the week/month, etc. lend themselves particularly well to approximation.[9]

On a more general level, there is also a close link between approximation and precision of categorial delimitation in the sense that approximative use presupposes clear category boundaries. This is why referring terms and predicates are the natural environment for approximators or bushes. Entire propositions or 'states of affairs' (cf. Prince *et al.*, 1982: 89), on the other hand, are by their very nature less clearly delimited. Speaker distance in these cases will therefore be interpreted as lack of commitment rather than approximation. A similar cotext-sensitive interpretation applies, for instance, to *like* (although with reverse diachronic development): if used with phrasal scope (e.g. *He's like 35 years old*) it has approximative function. If used with clausal scope (e.g. *He's like John's a liar*), however, it has quotative function and as such is used as Attribution shield (Prince *et al.*, 1982), which reduces speaker commitment in the sense that the speaker indicates that s/he is simply reporting and therefore not necessarily committed to the truth of the proposition (cf. Andersen 2001 for the pragmatic function of *like*).

Approximative uses of *I think* thus remind us that the distinction between categories such as approximator and shield, which is essentially one between semantics and pragmatics, is far from clear-cut and that we have to allow for intersective gradience (Aarts, 2004).[10] Although a semantic concept which operates proposition-internally and affects the truth condition of that proposition, an approximator is also sensitive to contextual factors (as argued already by Wachtel, 1980). More precisely, what affects the interpretation of *I think* as approximator is the type of host it has scope over and to what extent it lends itself to scalar implicature (as noted above). For a better understanding of the communicative function of *I think* it is therefore necessary to take into account its immediate co-text. In Section 5 I will show how this co-textual information can be incorporated into a model of the pragmatic functions of *I think*.

---

[9] Other terms are less prone to an approximative interpretation. Compare, for instance, *He went to I think Rome*. Here the geographical location *Rome* lends itself less to an approximative interpretation. However, even here an approximative reading is possible either along the lines of "... or some other Italian city", "... or some other European capital", depending on context.

[10] Aarts (2004: 1) defines intersective gradience as "an inter-categorial phenomenon which is characterised by two form classes 'converging' on each other". I am using the term in a wider sense here to include also functional categories. On the link between approximation and shields cf. also Mihatsch (this volume).

### 4.3. Structural function

With a total of 379 occurrences (6.3 per 10,000 words), parenthetical *I think* is a highly frequent linguistic category. It is also by far the most frequent lexical type of all comment clauses (cf. Kaltenböck, 2006b, 2008). As a high-frequency lexical item *I think* has been subject to considerable semantic bleaching (e.g. Bybee and Thompson, 1997: 378). A well-known concomitant effect of such semantic erosion is that of phonetic reduction, which can also be observed with *I think*. Apart from phonetic reduction of the pronoun *I*, to the extent of total omission (e.g. *∅ Think I have a slide feed problem* – s2a-029-97), a substantial number of parenthetical *I think* are also prosodically fully integrated into the host clause. This is illustrated, for instance, in example (11) and its corresponding pitch contour in Figure 10.4.

(11) blinkered **I think** is a nice word if you're describing someone that you don't like (s1a-037-217)

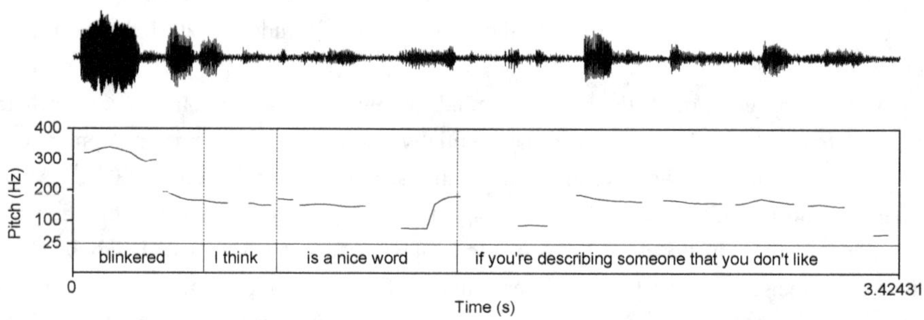


**Figure 10.4.** Blinkered *I think* is a nice word if you're describing someone that you don't like.

In contrast to the prosodic patterns of left-binding and right-binding (discussed in Section 4.2), this is a case of left-right binding, where *I think* is integrated in the middle of a larger pitch contour and does not contain an accented syllable. This prosodic pattern, in fact, is with 117 instances the most frequent one for parenthetical *I think* in the corpus, followed by left-binding (105), right-binding (83) and an independent tone unit (72) (two had no sound file).

With such prosodically integrated, semantically weakened instances of *I think* the scope is often not so clear. Although all non-phrasal cases of *I think* have been classified by default as clausal (cf. Tables 10.A.1 and 10.A.2 in the Appendix), there are many cases, especially if prosodically fully integrated, where the notion of scope does not really apply. This can be explained by the lack of semantic substance, which often makes it difficult to interpret *I think* as 'comment' on some sort of 'commentatum' (Posner, 1973). Take, for instance, example (12a), where the main function of *I think* is not so much that of an epistemic marker (shield) but that of a filler, like the items surrounding it (*I mean, really, uhm*). Similarly, in example (12b), where an epistemic reading of *I think* would be in conflict with the certainty expressed by the subsequent adverbial (*certainly*).

(12a) I mean **I think** really uhm <,,> it's very difficult to to to produce any form of art unless you are driven <,> (s1a-015-145)
(12b) Uh that **I think** is uh uh certainly a new factor (s2b-013-45)

The reduction of semantic substance of *I think*, especially of prosodically integrated cases, can be seen as the result of a general grammaticalisation (pragmaticalisation) process of comment clauses, as outlined for instance by Thompson and Mulac (1991). This grammaticalisation process has been described as a change from main clause status to epistemic parenthetical.[11] In view of corpus data such as in (12), however, it seems reasonable to assume that the grammaticalisation process does not stop there but may involve even further bleaching, changing epistemic *I think* (with shield function) into a pleonastic structuring device (cf. Mindt, 2003 for a similar observation). As such, *I think* is no longer used predominantly as epistemic comment but functions as a textual device for linking purposes and the structuring of information flow (cf. Taglicht, 1984: 22–28; Ziv, 2002). From a diachronic point of view it can be assumed that the narrowing of scope from clausal to phrasal noted for approximative uses (cf. Section 4.2) represents an intermediary step in this development away from an epistemic comment with shield function (cf. Section 4.1) to a pleonastic structuring device.[12] Whereas shield function has preserved the original clausal scope of *I think*, semantic erosion leads to diffusion of scope. The effect is that *I think* may operate also over non-clausal elements (phrasal scope) or, in the extreme case of pleonastic use, scope is no longer clearly identifiable at all. In what follows, I will provide some further illustration of the semantic erosion of *I think.*

Evidence for a structural or filler function of *I think* comes, for instance, from co-occurrence patterns. The corpus data show that *I think* has a strong tendency to occur together with disfluency features such as fillers (e.g. *you know, I mean*), hesitation sounds (*uhm, uh*), word repetitions, pauses (<,> short, <,,> long) and backtracking/restarts. Compare, for instance, example (13).

[11] In this view, comment clauses have developed out of matrix clauses which were re-analysed as epistemic parentheticals (e.g. Thompson and Mulac, 1991; Traugott, 1995: 38–39). Alternative views have been proposed by Brinton (1996: 239–254), who argues that comment clauses have developed out of adverbial/relative structures such as *as I think*, and Fischer (2007a: 304–305, 2007b: 106), who agrees with Brinton in principle but classifies the anaphoric connective element as adverbial derived from a demonstrative pronoun.

[12] Although it is difficult to find conclusive evidence for a grammaticalisation development as outlined above, because of the unavailability of comparable spoken data from previous periods, an analysis of *I think* in the *Oxford English Dictionary* quotation database shows that phrasal uses are only attested from 1621 (*They hurt and crucify themselves, sometimes in lax clothes, an hundred yards I think in a gown, a sleeve* Burton *Anat. Mel.* III, ii. III. iii. 474). Clausal use, by contrast, is attested from around 1300.

(13) Took them uh **I think** some some something like ten to fifteen years to complete it (s1a-009-87)

Disfluency features as these, immediately preceding or following *I think*, occur in 38 per cent of all cases (i.e. 144 out of 379). Of these, 60.4 per cent (87 instances) have one disfluency feature, 27.1 per cent (39 instances) have two disfluency features, 11.1 per cent (16) three and 1.4 per cent (2) four disfluency features. Table 10.2 gives a more detailed overview.

**Table 10.2.** Disfluency features immediately preceding or following *I think*

| | **Preceding *I think*** | **Following *I think*** |
|---|---|---|
| Filler (*you know, I mean, oh*) | 28 | 25 |
| Hesitation sound, repetition | 32 | 46 |
| Pause | 28 | 50 |
| Backtracking/restarts | – | 12 |

Further evidence for the semantic erosion of parenthetical *I think* comes from the observation that it frequently co-occurs with epistemic markers of certainty without obvious semantic clash. This is illustrated in examples (14a) and (14b) (cf. also 12b above).

(14a) Uh and it it's **certainly** uh **I think** a fair assumption that uh when talking about innovation most people assume that innovation is something that's carried out within the industrial context (s2a-037-3)

(14b) B: **I'm sure** Richard Burton stars in this **I think** C: Does he (s1a-049-182/183)

This evidence, of course, is far from conclusive as we have to allow for the possibility of a speaker adapting to newly assessed discourse requirements in the communicative process and re-shaping his/her utterance accordingly (cf. Goodwin, 1979). Moreover, it is unclear whether adverbs such as *certainly* really enhance the truth value or force of a sentence. Although this has been claimed by Quirk *et al.* (1985: 485) and Palmer (1986: 28f), Lyons (1977: 809) disagrees. These open questions notwithstanding, it is interesting that even in close proximity *I think* shows no apparent semantic incompatibility with markers of certainty, which can be explained if we interpret these uses of *I think* not so much as epistemic markers (shields) but as semantically weak structural devices.

Depending on their actual use in context, bleached uses of *I think* may adopt a range of different pragmatic functions. In interactive text types clause-final *I think* frequently marks the end of a speaker contribution, which in turn is interpreted by the interlocutor as an invitation to respond, as in example (14b) above. Such a response eliciting function, where *I think* marks the end of a speaker turn, can be found in 36.1 per cent of all clause-final occurrences of *I think* in Private or Public dialogue (s1a, s1b).

In initial position, structural *I think* often has important stalling function, which allows the speaker to buy time to prepare his/her upcoming utterance. This is especially important if the speaker takes the turn, which is the case in 26.8 per cent of all initial occurrences of *I think* in Private or Public dialogue (s1a, s1b). In this position, structural *I think* also frequently has its own tone unit (for a detailed prosodic analysis of intial *I think* cf. Kaltenböck, 2009).

In medial position, structural *I think* has a similar gap-filling function, and it also functions as an important text structuring device. Medial *I think* shows a certain preference for insertion at key structural points in the host construction, notably between subject and predicate, and between main verb (predicator) and complementation, and after relative elements (cf. Table 10.A.1), where it ensures smooth online production (especially with syntactically complex constituents) or structures the message to highlight certain parts or enhance a thematic link with the preceding discourse. Let me illustrate this with the following examples.

(15a) The the next <,,> next what occurs **I think** is that if we look at the diary entry <,> uh at page seventy-two <,,> there is the <,> reference in your diary at that point on the ninth of September nineteen eighty-two nineteen eighty-six <,> uh to a telephone conversation with Ferndale Business Services (s1b-064-94)

(15b) And and also apt to take you know very completely irrational hates against people for what **I think** were probably several reasons (s1a-031-101)

(15c) B that much of the fault for this lies with teachers and their various uh hangers-on the su so-called experts who **I think** uh <,> Prince Charles called educationalists the other day <,> in the educational establishment (s2a-021-21)

In example (15a) *I think* occurs between subject and predicate and as such has important structural function separating the topic (or theme) from the comment (or rheme). In Taglicht's (1984: 22) terminology *I think* represents a "partition", which turns the preceding constituent (i.e. the subject) into a "marked theme". Such a marked theme, according to Ziv (2002: 3), functions as a link between the utterance in which it occurs and the preceding discourse. This linking function seems to be largely independent of the semantics of the parenthetical but derives exclusively from "its linear position and the intonational and segmentational properties that are associated with it" (*ibid.*). This is illustrated by example (15a), where *I think* functions as a structuring device separating a clausal topic from a syntactically (and informationally) complex comment. The topic, moreover, is low in informational value and merely links the new information of the comment to the preceding discourse. Similar structural explanations can be given for examples (15b) and (15c). In both cases *I think* separates a subject from its predicate in complex constructions involving a subordinate clause. It not only highlights the thematic structure of the subordinate clause, with concomitant linking function of the marked theme, but also provides a convenient 'breathing space' for the production of a syntactically complex construction (note the disfluency manifested in the pause and hesitation sound in 15c).

A special structural use of *I think* is that of marking off the beginning or end of a communicative chunk, or what Schiffrin (1987: 31) calls "bracket[ing] units of talk". This is illustrated in example (16), where *I think* signals the end of the main message, before the addition of an afterthought introduced by the discourse marker *you know*. Often this can involve a double use, as in (17), where *I think* is used twice to 'frame' some part of the message, not unlike inverted commas, as if to set it off from the rest of the utterance.

(16) Probably worthwhile doing that **I think** you know just to say <,> how do you think I rate <,> (s1a-035-88)

(17a) I mean I do know that it does take up time and I do feel that I have to be there for every activity that I set up and **I think** that's probably right **I think** <,> (s1b-078-214)

(17b) And the work that I've done with him <,> in the early stages has uhm <,> **I think** helped <,> a lot <,> **I think** (s1a-003-90)

This function closely resembles the boundary marking function noted by Kärkkäinen (2003: 128), who points out that *I think* can be used as "a bracket at a boundary in discourse, at a point in transition, or a shift to meta-discourse or subsidiary information, or a shift back to an earlier or to a completely new point".

To conclude, structural *I think*, which is the result of a high degree of semantic bleaching, may have a range of more specific pragmatic functions, depending on contextual requirements. Thus, it may be used to segment text, structure information flow, signal and alleviate disfluencies, or for the sequential organisation of talk. The process of semantic bleaching is, however, not one that is completed. Instead, various degrees of semantic reduction exist side by side and, depending on the specific use of *I think*, its epistemic meaning may still be activated to varying degrees. In the following section I will look at such a case of activation.

### 4.4. Booster function

As discussed in Section 4.1, *I think* with clausal scope has shield function and expresses an epistemic qualification of the host proposition, which reduces the speaker's commitment to that proposition, i.e. makes it more tentative. Depending on the prosodic realisation of *I think*, however, the opposite effect is also possible. If given sufficient prosodic prominence, *I think* may even have the pragmatic effect of strengthening the proposition rather than attenuating it. In this function, *I think* represents what Holmes (1984: 359) refers to as booster. Similarly, Kärkkäinen (2006: 710) notes the possibility of heightened speaker commitment and Aijmer (1997: 21) speaks of deliberative uses of *I think*. While Aijmer equates nuclear prominence on *I think* with deliberative use, my corpus results suggest that a nuclear tone alone (i.e. independent tone unit) may not be enough to turn *I think* into a booster. There are many cases of *I think* with an independent tone unit in the corpus (19 per cent in total), which consequently have their own nuclear tone, but these may just as well have shield function. While it is not always easy to determine exactly when the function of *I think* changes from lack of commitment (shield) to full commitment (booster) (as noted, for instance, by Simon-Vandenbergen, 2000: 52), what seems to matter is the amount of pitch movement on *I think*: a nuclear tone with a high starting point spanning a wide pitch range will normally have the effect of boosting the force of the host proposition. The tone itself may be a fall, which was noted by Simon-Vandenbergen (2000: 51) to frequently occur in the rather assertive text category 'political interview' (as opposed to casual conversation). This tone is illustrated in the pitch contour of example (18) (cf. Figure 10.5), which expresses the conviction of a theatre critic.

(18) **I think** uh Opera North is always inventive (s1b-044-42)

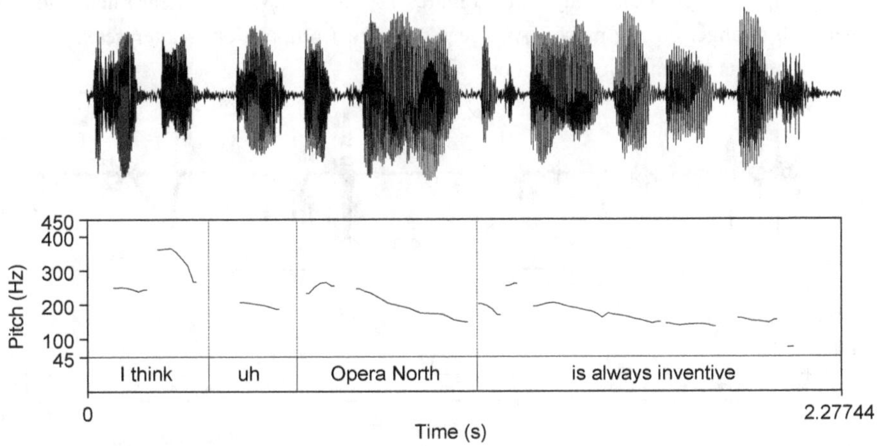


**Figure 10.5.** *I think* uh Opera North is always inventive.

However, the tone may also be a different one, such as the rise-fall in example (19), provided the relative pitch height makes *I think* stand out from its immediate co-text (Figure 10.6).

(19) The reason for it is **I think** that when they're walking round the school so are thousands of tourists (s1a-054-163)

Apart from pitch movement, the boosting function of *I think* can also be activated by tonicity, i.e. the location of the tonic (or nucleus) in the tone unit. These are cases where the nuclear tone is not on the predicate *think* but on the subject *I*, which gives rise to an implicit contrastive interpretation (*I* as opposed to someone else). Compare, for instance, examples (20) and (21),

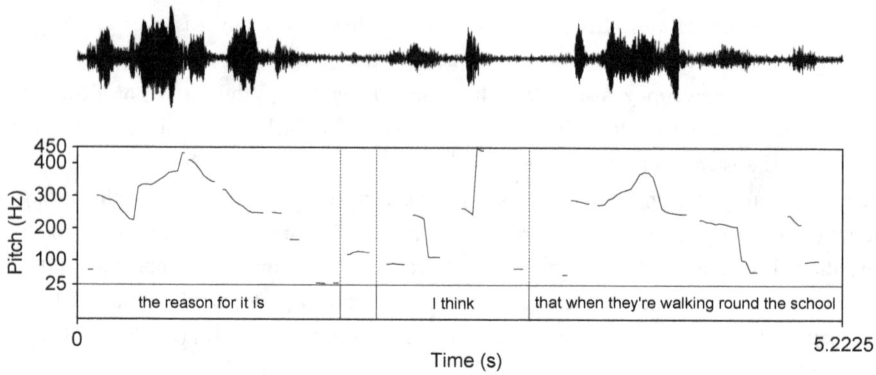


**Figure 10.6.** The reason for it is *I think* that when they're walking round the school.

where the respective prosodic analyses (in Figures 10.7 and 10.8) show clear pitch change on *I* together with stronger energy pulses. As a result, the host proposition is interpreted as a strong assertion rather than a tentative suggestion.

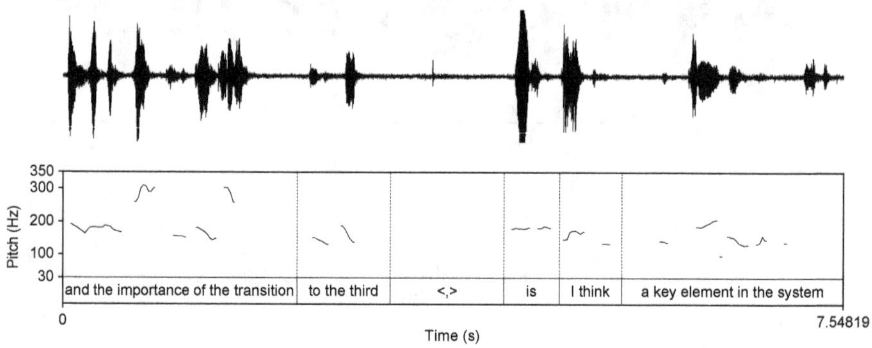


**Figure 10.7.** And the importance of the transition to the third <,> is I think a key element in the system.

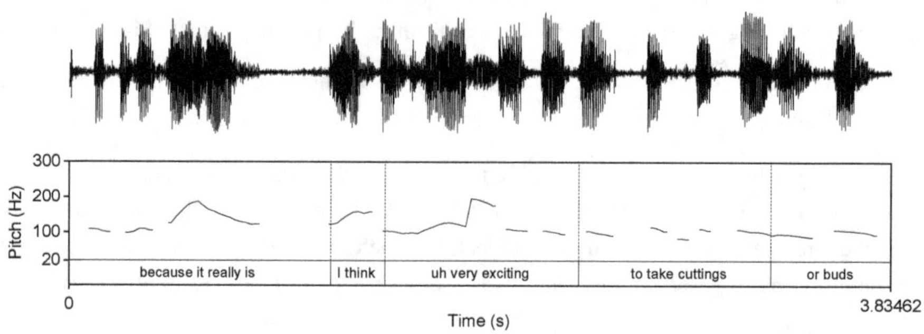


**Figure 10.8.** Because it really is *I think* uh very exciting to take cuttings or buds.

(20) But the reality of the second age for a woman <,> and the importance of the transition to the third <,> is **I think** a key element in the system (s2a-038-56)

(21) I'm glad you're doing this because it really is **I think** uh very exciting to take cuttings or buds (s1b-025-104)

## 5. A Unified Account

In the previous sections I have identified an inventory of basic communicative functions of parenthetical *I think*. These functions are basic in the sense that they take into account the interaction of *I think* with its immediate co-text and formal textual features such as prosody and position, but not the larger situational context. As such, they can be further refined and specified depending on exact contextual use, that is by relating *I think* to contextual features (e.g. roles and purpose of interlocutors, situation, socio-cultural knowledge). The preceding discussion has shown that already on a basic textual level it is possible to distinguish a number of highly diverse uses of *I think*. These range from the expression of lack of commitment (shield), approximative and structural uses, to the expression of speaker assertion (booster) and it may be asked how such disparate uses, which seem to it have little in common, can be meaningfully related to the same lexical expression. In the present section I will try to answer this question by providing a unified explanation based on a monosemous account of parenthetical *I think*.

The key argument for the proposal outlined here is the observation that the interpretation of parenthetical *I think* crucially depends on its interaction with the linguistic co-text. Thus, it was shown, for instance, that shield function is closely associated with clausal scope, whereas approximative uses presuppose phrasal scope, which, in turn, is signalled by the formal features prosody and/or position. Structural function, by contrast, lacks clearly identifiable scope altogether as a result of semantic bleaching. Booster function, by comparison, depends on a particular prosodic realisation.

Further evidence for the strong influence of the linguistic co-text of *I think* is easy to find. Various studies have highlighted the extreme semantic flexibility of *I think*. Aijmer (1997: 12), for instance, identifies 'belief' and 'opinion' as distinct meanings of *I think* (cf. also Arndt, 1987). An even more elaborate classification was proposed by Persson (1993), who distinguishes between 'probability', 'pure opinion' and 'subjective evaluation'. All these different meanings, which are here subsumed under shield,[13] can be shown to be co-text dependent. More specifically, the interpretation of *I think* depends on the type of proposition in its scope: if the proposition is

---

[13] Persson's notion of 'pure opinion' (e.g. *I think we should help him*) is of course close to the booster function. However, he does not refer to prosodic realisation, which is the defining criterion for the booster function. In its default prosodic realisation the above example would not take a nucleus on *I think*. Consequently, the pragmatic interpretation of the sentence is such that it contrasts with *I know/I'm sure we should help him* and therefore lacks full commitment of the speaker.

verifiable or falsifiable, as in *I think John is in London*, *I think* assumes the function of 'belief/ insufficient evidence/probability-based opinion'. Conversely, a proposition which is not objectively verifiable, such as *I think Mary is pretty*, will trigger a 'personal attitude/opinion/ subjective evaluation' meaning for *I think*. Of course, such a classification leaves considerable room for indeterminate cases, as propositions may only be partly verifiable. In such unclear cases, where the linguistic co-text provides only insufficient cues, the interpretation of *I think* will depend to a large extent on the situational context. The importance of context for the interpretation of *I think* has been noted by Kärkkäinen (2003: 111), who, quoting Chafe, points out that for *I think it's time to go* only the context determines whether the meaning of *I think* is that of opinion or insufficient evidence.

What these examples and the functions identified in Section 4 illustrate is thus, first of all, a high degree of functional flexibility of *I think*, as a result of the ongoing process of semantic bleaching, and, secondly, a close interaction of *I think* with contextual features, which shape its exact meaning. The notion of context, of course, has to be seen as including the linguistic co-text as well as the situational, social and socio-cultural context (cf. Fetzer, 2004). In an attempt to systematise the influence of context on the interpretation of *I think* I focus here on the verbal co-text, as it offers a limited number of interaction possibilities and can therefore be more easily accounted for than the more complex and essentially infinite constellations of the situational context. From an interpretative point of view, the verbal co-text may also be seen as more basic in the sense that it provides the basis for a more specific contextual interpretation. In this view, then, context interacts on different levels, i.e. on the level of verbal co-text and the level of situational and socio-cultural context, with some abstract underlying core meaning of *I think*, which gives rise to a number of more concrete instantiations of meaning. An obvious candidate for the underlying core meaning of *I think* is that of 'speaker cogitation' (cf. Aijmer, 1997: 12; also Schneider, 1988: 42ff; Persson, 1993: 4), which corresponds with the literal meaning of *think*, reflected most fully in the non-parenthetical uses (e.g. *I am thinking about what you said*).[14]

To capture the link between the underlying semantic meaning of *I think* and its various pragmatic meanings in actual use an essentially monosemous model seems to be most appropriate. I use the term monosemous here in a wide sense as denoting an approach that associates all uses of parenthetical *I think* with an underlying, abstract core meaning from which the different concrete interpretations arise via processes of interaction with the verbal co-text and the situational context.[15] Such a model is sketched out in Figure 10.9 and explained below.

[14] This is the meaning the *Oxford English Dictionary* refers to as significance I: "To conceive in the mind, exercise in the mind, etc.". It can be assumed that the literal meaning of cogitation also reflects the historic origin of *think* out of which the parenthetical uses (e.g. epistemic meaning) have developed by a process of grammaticalisation (cf. Thompson and Mulac, 1991).

[15] For a discussion of approaches to polifunctionality cf. e.g. Fischer (2006: 12ff).

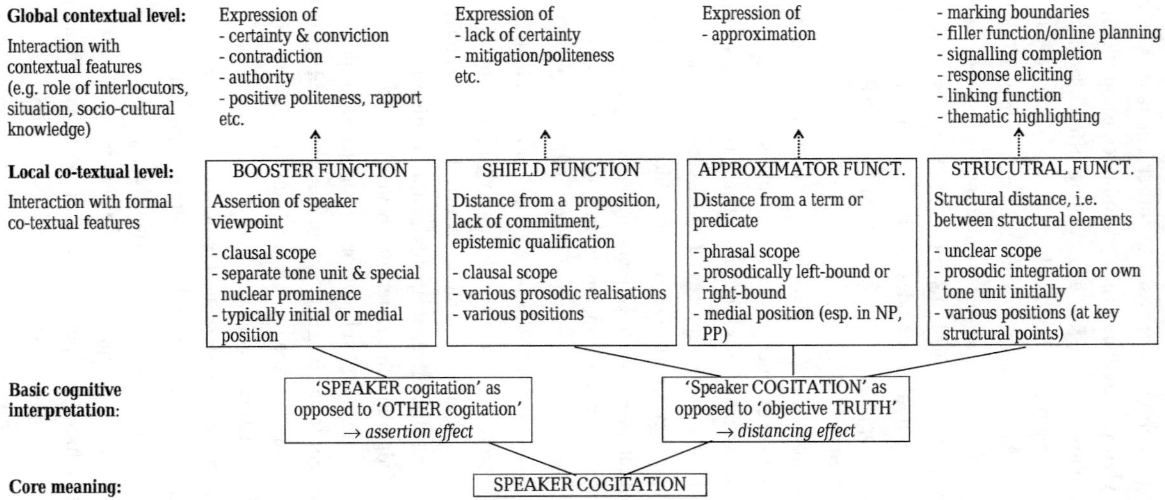


**Figure 10.9.** Monosemous account of the functions of parenthetical *I think*.

The underlying core meaning of parenthetical *I think* is an abstract notion of highest generality, identified here as 'speaker cogitation'. This abstract meaning can cognitively be construed in two ways: either as '**speaker** cogitation' as opposed to '**other** cogitation', which lends itself to an assertion of the speaker's view (given appropriate prosodic realisation) or as 'speaker **cogitation'** as opposed to 'objective **truth'**, which has a distancing effect, separating for instance some speaker proposition from objective truth. Which of the two interpretations will be activated depends on how the core meaning interacts with the local co-textual level, i.e. how *I think* is realised in terms of formal textual features such as position and prosody and consequently scope. Essentially, this level is what Mosegaard Hansen (2006: 29) refers to as "micro-level syntactic and prosodic information", and also includes local-level semantic information such as the proposition types of the host (opinion vs. verifiable fact) or to what extent a phrasal host allows for scalar interpretation (cf. Section 4.2).

More specifically, realisation of *I think* as a separate tone unit with extra pitch prominence (signalled by wide pitch range or nucleus on *I*) and clausal scope will activate the booster function. By contrast, lack of extra prosodic prominence but clear clausal scope signals the unmarked option of shield function. In this case *I think* creates a distance between the clausal proposition of the host and some objective reality, which is interpreted as lack of speaker commitment to the truth of the proposition. Depending on the type of proposition, this epistemic qualification will be interpreted as opinion, probability or subjective evaluation (cf. Persson's 1993 classification). If, however, the interaction of *I think* with co-textual features is such that it is associated with phrasal scope, as a result of its position and/or prosodic binding to the left or right, the effect is that of approximation. In this case, the underlying distancing effect is interpreted as holding between some term or predicate and factual reality. Provided the phrasal host is amenable to scalar interpretation, the result is that of approximation (This may also require some more global socio-cultural knowledge and therefore goes beyond the local co-textual level). Finally, *I think* may surface on the textual level without clear scope, especially in the form of a prosodically integrated element (or an independent tone unit in initial position). The effect is that of a pleonastic structural device. Here the underlying distancing effect is present only on a purely linear level, separating two structural elements.

The four categories have to be understood as a basic frame of reference which has to allow for a certain amount of overlap and fuzzy boundaries between the categories, thus representing a functional cline. As basic categories on the co-textual level, the four functions can be further refined and specified by taking into account the next level of interaction, which is that of the more global context. This level includes the specific details of the speech situation, such as the social relationship between the interlocutors, their discourse roles and communicative purpose as well as more general social-cultural information (cf. Fetzer, 2004). Only more detailed information about a specific speech situation will allow us to specify, for instance, whether a booster *I think* is used to express certainty, contradiction or "positive politeness and rapport" (Aijmer, 1997: 22), or whether a shield *I think* signals mere lack of certainty or is used for the purpose of mitigation, i.e. is more recipient-oriented. Similarly, only the larger context can help us decide on the exact *raison d'être* of structural *I think*: e.g. to elicit a response, act as a filler or reinforce the link with the preceding sentence (cf. Ziv, 2002), highlight the thematic structure of a sentence (cf. Taglicht, 1984) or mark boundaries (cf. Kärkkäinen, 2003).[16]

Apart from systematising the different uses of parenthetical *I think*, a monosemous model as the one sketched out above also has the advantage of being in line with the presumed diachronic development of *think* from the original expression of cogitation to epistemic markers (e.g. Thompson and Mulac, 1991) and increased bleaching and diffusion of scope. In the synchronic model in Figure 10.9, this diachronic dimension is represented by the horizontal axis from left to right. The semantic bleaching of *I think* may raise the question how such a process is compatible with the notion of an invariant core meaning in a monosemous model. This can be explained by the fact that the ongoing semantic change is not a qualitative but a quantitative one: any change in the underlying meaning would only involve a weakening of its force not a qualitative shift in meaning. Moreover, it can be argued that even extreme cases of bleaching, i.e. the structural uses of *I think*, are not semantically empty but have retained a trace of the underlying meaning of 'distance' in their function as structural markers which mark and simultaneously bridge the linear distance between constituents. All it takes to activate the core meaning more fully are slight changes in co-textual realisation.

## 6. Conclusion

The analysis of 379 occurrences of parenthetical *I think* in the spoken text categories of ICE-GB has shown that it exhibits great functional flexibility, with the pragmatic function of *I think* being shaped to a considerable extent by its formal co-textual realisation. One important parameter in this respect turned out to be the scope of *I think*, which, depending on prosodic realisation, position and degree of semantic bleaching, can range from covering entire clauses to singling out phrasal constituents and cases of unclear scope. By taking into account the different

[16] Although Kärkkäinen's (2003: 115–175, 2006: 706–711) approach is a different one, i.e. one which views stance as a dynamic interactional activity, the model outlined here may accommodate her functional distinctions too. For intonation unit initial *I think* Kärkkäinen notes a 'starting point function' for marking boundaries or routinely attending to interactional trouble. Both these functions can be seen as specific uses of structural *I think*, possibly with some overlap with the shield function. Her 'recipient-oriented design of utterance' may be associated with booster or shield function. For *I think* with separate intonation unit the function 'online planning' (in pre-position) and 'signalling completion and pursuing a response' (in post-position) are identified, both of which may qualify for inclusion as special uses of structural *I think*.

types of scope together with prosodic realisation and co-occurrence facts, four core communicative functions of *I think* have been identified: shield function (Section 4.1), approximator function (Section 4.2), structural function (Section 4.3) and booster function (Section 4.4). These functions are considered to be basic in the sense that they are co-textual only and may adopt more specific pragmatic functions depending on the specificities and requirements of the situational context.

The final section (Section 5) has attempted to provide a unified explanation for the different core functions, which at first sight seem to have little in common. It has been shown that the assumption of an underlying abstract core meaning of 'speaker cogitation' can provide a unifying semantic 'bracket' for all four communicative functions, with the different meanings deriving from the specific co-textual realisation of parenthetical *I think*, i.e. prosodic realisation, position and scope. Such an essentially monosemous view has the advantage of providing a framework for a systematic approach to seemingly disparate uses of *I think* and the basis for a more fine-grained classification of the functions of parenthetical *I think* depending on its contextual use.

## References

Aarts, B. (2004). "Modelling linguistic gradience". *Studies in Language* **28** (**1**): 1–49.

Aijmer, K. (1972). *Some aspects of psychological predicates in English*. Stockholm: Almqvist & Wiksell.

Aijmer, K. (1997). "*I think* – An English modal particle", in T. Swan and O. J. Westvik (eds.), *Modality in Germanic languages. Historical and comparative perspectives*. Berlin: Mouton de Gruyter, 1–47.

Andersen, G. (2001). *Pragmatic markers and sociolinguistic variation*. Amsterdam: Benjamins.

Arndt, H. (1987). "Cognitive verbs and the indication of utterance function", in J. Monaghan (ed.), *Grammar in the construction of texts*. London: Frances Pinter, 24–36.

Biber, D., S. Johansson, G. Leech, S. Conrad and E. Finegan (1999). *Longman grammar of spoken and written English*. Harlow: Longman.

Boersma, P. and Weenink, D. (2008). Praat: doing phonetics by computer (Version 4.4.33) [Computer programme] Retrieved December 2005, from http://www.praat.org

Brinton, L. J. (1996). *Pragmatic markers in English. Grammaticalization and discourse functions*. Berlin: Mouton de Gruyter.

Burton-Roberts, N. (1999). "Language, linear precedence and parentheticals", in P. Collins and D. Lee (eds.), *The clause in English*. Amsterdam: Benjamins, 33–52.

Bybee, J. and S. Thompson (1997). "Three frequency effects in syntax". *Proceedings of the 23 Annual Meeting of the Berkeley Linguistics Society*: 378–388.

Caffi, C. (1999). "On mitigation". *Journal of Pragmatics* **31**: 881–909.

Cruttenden, A. (1997). *Intonation. 2nd Edition*. Cambridge: Cambridge University Press.

Fagyal, Z. (2002). "Prosodic boundaries in the vicinity of utterance-medial parentheticals in French". *Probus* **14**: 93–111.

Fetzer, A. (2004). *Recontextualizing context*. Amsterdam, Philadelphia: John Benjamins.

Fischer, K. (2006). "Towards an understanding of the spectrum of approaches to discourse particles: introduction to the volume", in K. Fischer (ed.), *Approaches to discourse particles*. Amsterdam, New York: Elsevier, 1–20.

Fischer, O. (2007). *Morphosyntactic change. Functional and formal perspectives*. Oxford: Oxford University Press.

Fischer, O. (2007). "The development of English parentheticals: A case of grammaticalization? in U. Smit, et al. (eds.), *Tracing English through time*. Wien: Braumüller, 99–114.

Givón, T. (1995). *Functionalism and grammar*. Amsterdam: John Benjamins.

Goodwin, C. (1979). "The interactive construction of a sentence in natural conversation", in G. Psathas (ed.), *Everyday language studies in ethnomethodology*. New York: Irvington, 97–119.

Haegeman, L. (1991). "Parenthetical adverbials: The radical orphanage approach", in S. Chiba, et al. (eds.), *Aspects of modern English linguistics. Papers presented to Masamoto Ukaji on his 60th birthday*. Tokyo: Kaitakushi, 232–254.

Hare, R. M. (1970). "Meaning and speech acts". *Philosophical Review* **79**: 3–24.

Holmes, J. (1984). "Modifying illocutionary force". *Journal of Pragmatics* **8**: 345–365.

Holmes, J. (1990). "Hedges and boosters in women's and men's speech". *Language and Communication* **10** (**3**): 185–205.

Hübler, A. (1983). *Understatements and hedges in English*. Amsterdam: John Benjamins.

Huddleston, R. and G. K. Pullum (2002). *The Cambridge grammar of the English language*. Cambridge: Cambridge University Press.

Kaltenböck, G. (2005). "Charting the boundaries of syntax: A taxonomy of spoken parenthetical clauses". *Vienna English Working Papers (VIEWS)* **14** (**1**): 21–53.

Kaltenböck, G. (2006a). "'... That is the question': Complementizer omission in extraposed *that*-clauses". *English Language and Linguistics* **10** (**2**): 371–396.

Kaltenböck, G. (2006b). "Some comments on comment clauses: A semantic classification", in R. Povolná and O. Dontcheva-Navratilova (eds.), *Discourse and interaction 2*. Brno: Masarykova Univserszita, 71–87.

Kaltenböck, G. (2007a). "Spoken parenthetical clauses in English: A taxonomy", in N. Dehé and Y. Kavalova (eds.), *Parentheticals*. . Amsterdam: Benjamins.

Kaltenböck, G. (2007b). "Position, prosody, and scope: The case of English comment clauses". *Vienna English Working Papers (VIEWS)* **16** (**1**): 3–38.

Kaltenböck, G. (2008). "Prosody and function of English comment clauses". *Folia Linguistica* **42** (**1**): 83–134.

Kaltenböck, G. (2009). "Initial *I think*: main or comment clause?" *Discourse and Interaction* **2** (**1**): 49–70.

Kärkkäinen, E. (2003). *Epistemic stance in English conversation. A description of its interactional functions, with a focus on I think*. Amsterdam: John Benjamins.

Kärkkäinen, E. (2006). "Stance taking in conversation: From subjectivity to intersubjectivity". *Text and Talk* **26** (**6**): 699–731.

Kruisinga, E. (1932). *A handbook of present-day English. Part II*. Groningen: Noordhoff.

Lyons, J. (1977). *Semantics. Vol. 2*. Cambridge: Cambridge University Press.

Mindt, I. (2003). "Is *I think* a discourse marker?", in E. Mengel, et al. (eds.), *Proceedings Anglistentag 2002 Bayreuth*. Trier: WVT, 473–483.

Mosegaard Hansen, M.-B. (2006). "A dynamic polysemy approach to the lexical semantics of discourse markers (with an exemplary analysis of French toujours)", in K. Fischer (ed.), *Approaches to discourse particles*. Amsterdam, New York: Elsevier, 21–41.

Nelson, G., S. Wallis and B. Aarts (2002). *Exploring natural language. Working with the British Component of the International Corpus of English.* Amsterdam, Philadelphia: John Benjamins.

Palander-Collin, M. (1999). *Grammaticalization and social embedding. I think and methinks in Middle and Early Modern English.* Helsinki: Société Néophilologique.

Palmer, F. R. (1986). *Mood and modality.* Cambridge: Cambridge University Press.

Persson, G. (1993). "Think in a panchronic perspective". *Studia Neophilologica* **65**: 3–18.

Peterson, P. (1999). "On the boundaries of syntax: Non-syntagmatic relations", in P. Collins and D. Lee (eds.), *The clause in English.* Amsterdam, Philadelphia: Benjamins, 229–250.

Posner, R. (1973). "Redekommentierung. In *Funk-Kolleg Sprache Vol. 2.* Frankfurt: Fischer, 124–133.

Prince, E. F., J. Frader and C. Bosk (1982). "On hedging in physician-physician discourse", in R. J. Pietro (ed.), *Linguistics and the professions. Proceedings of the Second Annual Delaware Symposium on Language Studies.* Norwood (NJ): Ablex, 83–97.

Quirk, R., S. Greenbaum, G. Leech and J. Svartvik (1985). *A Comprehensive grammar of the English language.* Harlow: Longman.

Ross, J. R. (1973). "Slifting", in M. Gross, M. Halle and M.-P. Schützenberger (eds.), *The formal analysis of natural languages.* The Hague: Mouton, 133–169.

Sadock, J. M. (1977). "Truth and approximations". *Proceedings of the Third Annual Meeting of the Berkeley Linguistics Society*: 430–439.

Schiffrin, D. (1987). *Discourse markers.* Cambridge: Cambridge University Press.

Schneider, E. W. (1988). *Variabilität, Polysemie und Unschärfe der Wortbedeutung. Vol. 2.* Tübingen: Max Niemeyer.

Schneider, S. (2007). *Reduced parenthetical clauses as mitigators. A corpus study of spoken French, Italian and Spanish.* Amsterdam: Benjamins.

Simon-Vandenbergen, A.-M. (2000). "The functions of *I think* in political discourse". *International Journal of Applied Linguistics* **10 (1)**: 41–63.

Stenström, A.-B. (1995). "Some remarks on comment clauses", in B. Aarts and C. F. Meyer (eds.), *The verb in contemporary English.* Cambridge: Cambridge University Press, 290–299.

Svensson, J. (1976). "Reportindicators and other parentheticals", in F. Karlsson (ed.), *Papers from the Third Scandinavian Conference of Linguistics.* Turku: Textlinguistics Research Group, Academy of Finland, 369–380.

Taglicht, J. (1984). *Message and emphasis. On focus and scope in English.* London, New York: Longman.

Thompson, S. A. (2002). "'Object complements' and conversation. Towards a realistic account". *Studies in Language* **26 (1)**: 125–164.

Thompson, S. A. and A. Mulac (1991). "The discourse conditions for the use of the complementizer *that* in conversational English". *Journal of Pragmatics* **15**: 237–251.

Traugott, E. C. (1995). "Subjectification in grammaticalization", in D. Stein and S. Wright (eds.), *Subjectivity and subjectivisation.* Cambridge: Cambridge University Press, 31–54.

Urmson, J. O. (1952). "Parenthetical verbs". *Mind* **61**: 480–496.

Wachtel, T. (1980). "Pragmatic approximations". *Journal of Pragmatics* **4**: 201–211.

Wierzbicka, A. (2006). *English. Meaning and culture.* Oxford: Oxford University Press.

Ziv, Y. (2002). This, I believe, is a processing instruction: discourse linking via parentheticals. http://micro5.mscc.huji.ac.il/~english/IATL/18/Ziv.pdf (Dec. 2006)

## APPENDIX

**Table 10.A.1.** Syntactic position of parenthetical *I think* with predominantly clausal scope

| | | Clausal scope | Phrasal scope |
|---|---|---|---|
| A. | Prenuclear position | | |
| (i) | Initial | 45 | – |
| (ii) | Adjunct # Subject | 5 | 1 |
| B. | Middle Position | | |
| (i) | Subject # VP (MV, Copula, Aux+MV) | 44 | 1 |
| (ii) | Aux # MV | 7 | 1 |
| (iii) | MV # Non-clausal complementation (Od., SC, other) | 26 | 4 |
| (iv) | MV # Finite clausal complementation (Obj. cl., Subj. compl. cl., Compl. cl.) | 11 | – |
| (v) | MV # Non-finite clausal complementation | 7 | – |
| (vi) | Subordinate clauses: | | |
| | – Subordinator # Adverbial clause/Noun clause[a] | 6 | – |
| | – Relative element # Relative clause[b] | 42 | – |
| | – Noun # Relative element | 5 | – |
| (vii) | Coordination (various)[c] | 3 | 2 |
| (viii) | Other | 4 | – |
| C. | Postnuclear Position | | |
| (i) | VP # Adjunct (non-clausal) | 14 | 13 |
| (ii) | VP # Adjunct (clausal) | 12 | – |
| (iii) | Between adjuncts: A # A′ | 1 | – |
| (iv) | Final | 74 | 4 |
| | TOTAL | 306 | 26 |

*Notes*: # = point of insertion, MV = main verb.

[a]This category captures only CCs following the subordinator in adverbial clauses. Those preceding it are grouped under C(ii).

[b]Including 1 case of zero relative element.

[c]In all these cases of coordination the CC comes immediately after the coordinator. Cases of clausal coordination where the CC comes before the coordinator have been classified as final, i.e. C(iii).

**Table 10.A.2.** Syntactic position of parenthetical *I think* with predominantly phrasal scope

| | | **Clausal scope** | **Phrasal scope** |
|---|---|---|---|
| (a) | Initial (elliptical/non-clausal Host) | – | 9 |
| (b) | Within PP: P # NP | – | 4 |
| (c) | Within NP | | |
| | - Prehead position | – | 5 |
| | - Posthead position | 3 | 5 |
| (d) | Final (elliptical/non-clausal Host) | – | 19 |
| (e) | Other (elliptical Host, phrase internal) | – | 2 |
| | TOTAL | 3 | 44 |

*Note*: # = point of insertion.

New Approaches to Hedging
Edited by Gunther Kaltenböck, Wiltrud Mihatsch and Stefan Schneider


# 11

# PARENTHETICAL HEDGED PERFORMATIVES ☆

*Stefan Schneider*

## ABSTRACT

This contribution investigates the use of parenthetical hedged performatives in spoken English, French, Italian and Spanish. It reviews the different devices by which a performative may be hedged and the various forms actually occurring in corpora of spoken discourse. The performatives are mostly based on Engl. *say* and its equivalents in the other three languages. Formally, hedged performatives resemble descriptions of state of affairs rather than indications of illocutionary force and thus produce an overt discrepancy, as they pretend to describe a speech act which at the same time is being performed. The discrepancy causes the violation of a conversational maxim, which is resolved by a conversational implicature and reinterpreted as a mitigation of speaker commitment. The analysis of the illocutionary force indicating function of parenthetical hedged performatives evidences that in many cases they preserve little or nothing of their original function.

## 1. BACKGROUND

Although performative clauses are sometimes cited as the most obvious device for indicating the illocutionary force of an utterance (cf. Yule, 1996: 49), it has been recognized that in everyday speech utterances introduced by performative clauses are less common than expected. The

☆ Previous versions of this chapter were read at the *Grazer Linguistisches Kolloquium* of the University of Graz and at the *Linguistischer Arbeitskreis* of the University of Hannover.

illocutionary force is often clear from other linguistic cues (word order, intonation, particles, etc.) or from the context, and it is unnecessary to use a clause to indicate it. Liedtke (1997: 208f.; see also Bublitz, 2009: 148f.) points to the fact that the use of a performative clause depends on particular circumstances. I suggest that one of these circumstances may be the speaker's need to downgrade her[1] commitment, which is one of the fundamental reasons for using hedged performatives. Performatives thus reveal their utility insofar as they provide a place where to attach a mitigating device.

Lakoff (1972: 213), observing that hedges may act on performatives, introduces the concept of 'hedged performative'. But it was not until Fraser (1975) that the concept was fully developed. According to Fraser (1975: 187f.), a hedged performative contains a modal or a semi-modal. It counts as the performance of the illocutionary act denoted by the performative verb, although the meaning of, for example, Engl. *I must advise* is not identical to the meaning of Engl. *I advise*, since the first clause states that the speaker has the obligation to advise, whereas the second one states that the speaker is advising. Other hedged performatives may mean that the preconditions for carrying out the speech act are met or that the speaker intends to perform the act (cf. Brehmer, 2003: 40). Fraser (1975) distinguishes strong performatives such as Engl. *I must advise*, whose performative use can easily be understood, from weak performatives such as, for example, Engl. *I can claim*, *I might order* or *I could warn*, whose performative use is dubious. Fraser (1975: 188, 208f.) makes clear that the clauses in his examples do not exhaust the variety of expressions that can be used as hedged performatives. As possible expressions he mentions clauses such as Engl. *I am happy to inform you* or *I am sorry to have to fire you*, as well as sequences of modals and embedded hedged performatives.

Since Fraser (1975), very little research on hedged performatives has been done. Brown and Levinson (1978) dedicate some pages to "performative hedges", that is, to hedges on illocutionary force. Although they explicitly refer to Fraser (1975), in their examples these hedges (e.g., adverbs, particles, adverbial clauses) do not directly act on a performative clause because the latter has been deleted. Moreover, according to Brown and Levinson (1978: 152), the difference between hedges on performative force and hedges on propositional content is of little importance in assertions. So it seems that Brown and Levinson's (1978) performative hedges are mainly hedges directly expressing speaker commitment or affecting the propositional content, rather than modifying a performative verb. A few other studies, however, follow Fraser's suggestion and focus on infinitives of performative verbs governed by modals. Interestingly, most of these are dedicated to hedged performatives in German (see Brünner, 1981; Greifeld, 1981; Wunderlich, 1983; Werlen, 1984; Koch, 1986; Gloning, 1997). Brehmer (2003) analyzes them in Russian,

[1] In this chapter, I conventionally assume that the speaker is female and the interlocutor male.

Polish, and Czech directives and expressives. Miecznikowski (2009) studies Italian performatives hedged by the conditional form.

Unhedged and hedged performatives may appear as superordinate clauses, but they may also be parenthetical clauses. However, apart from Schneider (2007), parenthetical hedged performatives have not yet been taken into consideration. The present contribution analyzes the use of parenthetical hedged performatives in spoken English, French, Italian and Spanish. Its aims are (1) to examine the effects of non-parenthetical and parenthetical hedged performatives on the speech act, (2) to provide an overview of parenthetical hedged performatives actually occurring in corpora of spoken discourse and of the different devices by which performatives may be hedged, and (3) to speculate on the illocutionary force indicating function of parenthetical hedged performatives.

## 2. Performative Clauses and Performative Utterances

Sentences consist of propositions and a number of illocutionary force indicating devices. Performative clauses, that is, clauses containing performative verbs, represent one of many different ways to indicate the illocutionary force. From a grammatical point of view, they may be superordinate clauses, parenthetical clauses (in initial, medial, or final position) or even independent clauses. Notwithstanding their name, performative clauses do not by themselves constitute performances of acts; they are like labels, attached to sentences to make their intent clear (see Urmson, 1977: 263). Since their main function consists in the indication of the illocutionary force, they could also be called *illocutionary force indicating clauses*. They are not necessary ingredients of the speech act (cf. Garrido Medina, 1999: 3894). To take a famous example, the following sentences, under the appropriate circumstances and with the appropriate intonation, count as warnings with or without the initial or final Engl. *I warn you*:

(1a) **I warn you** that there is a bull in that field.
(1b) **I warn you**, there is a bull in that field.
(1c) There is a bull in that field, **I warn you**.
(1d) **I warn you**. There is a bull in that field.

In the examples above, the performative clauses are clearly recognizable and contain a performative verb in the first person singular of the non-progressive present indicative.

Certain conventional actions and rituals are carried out by reciting partially or completely fixed formulae. Such an action cannot be performed without the reciting of the formula, or in other words, the reciting of the formula is a constitutive feature of the action. The formula has the grammatical form of a simple clause. If it contains a performative verb, it does not merely act as a facultative illocutionary force indicating device, but as an obligatory constituent of the formula and the entire speech act.[2] Austin (1976 [1962]: 5) calls these formulae *performative utterances*. Typical examples of these utterances are:

(2) I name this ship the Queen Elizabeth.
(3a) I apologize to the lovely state of New Jersey.
(4) Rien ne va plus.
'No more bets'

As can be seen in example (4), a performative utterance does not necessarily have to contain a performative verb. The completeness of the formulaic wording is more important that the presence of a performative verb. Some formulae contain Engl. *hereby* (see Austin, 1976 [1962]: 57, 61, 75) or, rarely though, Fr. *avec cela* 'with that' or *par cela* 'by that', It. *con queste mie parole* 'with these my words' (see Fava, 1995: 26), and Sp. *con eso* 'with that'. To several other formulae, these words may be added to underline their performative character. Even if a performative utterance contains a performative verb, in most cases the grammatical structure of the performative utterance does not permit a clear-cut distinction between propositional content and performative clause (cf. Searle, 1976: 13).

Summing up, we can differentiate between three functions or uses of verbs of 'saying' that are relevant for the present discussion: the illocutionary force indicating function, the doing or performative function and, finally, the purely descriptive function. The last function can be seen in the following examples:

(1e) **He warns you** that there is a bull in that field.
(1f) **I warned you** that there is a bull in that field.

Note that an English clause such as, for example, *I warn you* + p ordinarily indicates an ongoing warning, but in some speech situations it could also describe the act of warning:

(1g) A: What do you do if you see a bull in that field?
B: **I warn you** that there is a bull in that field.

Fraser (1975) does not distinguish between the illocutionary force indicating character of performative clauses and the doing, executing or accomplishing character of performative utterances. In fact, the term *hedged performative* leaves open what exactly is hedged: a performative clause, a performative utterance or maybe only a performative verb? However, virtually all examples discussed by Fraser (1975) are performative clauses. Therefore, we should

[2] In Schneider (2007: 101) the verbs contained in performative clauses are called *saying-and-doing verbs*, those in performative utterances *saying-is-doing verbs*.

bear in mind that when Fraser (1975) analyzes the performativity of, for example, Engl. *I must advise*, he actually discusses its illocutionary force indicating function.

Fraser (1975) is concerned with modals and semi-modals applied to performative verbs within performative clauses, but there is no doubt that performative verbs of performative utterances may also be hedged. Jary (2007: 227ff.) reports attested performative utterances whose verbs are hedged by modals or semi-modals, for example:

(3b) I must hereby apologize to the lovely state of New Jersey.
(5) I want to hereby publicly thank PK for making this great tool freely available.

The presence of *hereby* shows that these utterances, albeit modified, retain their performing character.

## 3. The Performativity of Hedged Performatives

To explain how performative verbs modified by modals and semi-modals maintain their performative or, as we can say, their non-descriptive character, Fraser (1975: 194ff.) posits a number of conversational principles and inferences. One of these is the principle of efficiency, which is formulated as follows:

> Given nothing to suggest the contrary, whenever a further utterance would be redundant one can infer that the speaker need not make the utterance but that he will operate as if he had made it and will expect the hearer to operate similarly. (Fraser, 1975: 195)

It applies to several cases of hedged performatives. Here, as an example, I summarize Fraser's (1975: 200) line of reasoning regarding the 'can'-case, as far as relevant for the present discussion. The hearer's interpretation of, for example, Engl. *I can say* + p could comprise the following steps:

a. The speaker has indicated that she has the ability to perform the illocutionary act of saying.
b. The speaker would not have told me unless she intended to use this ability.
c. Thus, I can conclude that the speaker will perform the act in question.
d. As a consequence of the principle of efficiency formulated above, there is no need to actually utter the redundant sentence *I say* + p, and we both can act as if it had been uttered.

Owing to its centrality in the reasoning, step (b) should be reformulated and formalized into a principle of expressed ability:

> Given nothing to suggest the contrary, whenever someone indicates that he has a new ability to act one can infer that he intends to exercise this ability. (Fraser, 1975: 200)

Guided by these principles and reasonings, the hearer may interpret any sentence with the form *I can* + performative verb + p as having the force denoted by the performative verb, for example, *I can say* + p as having the same illocutionary force as *I say* + p.

Literally, with *I can say* + p, the speaker conveys the idea that she has the capability or is in the condition to perform the speech act indicated by the performative, but not that she is performing it. The fact that she is performing it is inferred by the hearer guided by the aforementioned principles. That is the reason why Engl. *can* may be accompanied by some adverbial such as *now*, *finally*, *at last*, and so on (cf. Fraser, 1975: 199), which underlines its performative nature. In fact, due to the frequent combination of Engl. *can* with time adverbials, Fraser (1975: 200) posits a principle of time-qualified ability, which, however, need not concern us here. In spoken language, we rarely find adverbials and other modifiers in parentheticals, as they tend to be as short and reduced as possible.

There are several diagnostic tests by which the illocutionary force indicating character of a performative clause and the doing or executing character of a performative utterance can be determined. These can also be applied to hedged performatives. The best-known test is the one with Engl. *hereby* suggested by Austin (1976 [1962]: 57, 61, 75). Stubbs (1996: 243) criticizes the test as not reliable. Owing to the extremely low frequency of the word *hereby* – it almost never occurs in spoken corpora and only sporadically in very large written corpora – the test is inappropriate for judgements based on intuition. However, as we have seen in the preceding section, Jary (2007: 227ff.) reports attested performative utterances hedged by modals or semi-modals containing *hereby*. It is almost impossible, though, to find performative clauses with *hereby*. Another difficulty is that the Romance equivalents for *hereby*, Fr. *avec cela* 'with that' or *par cela* 'by that', It. *con queste mie parole* 'with these my words' (see Fava, 1995: 26), and Sp. *con eso* 'with that', are even less common.

According to Stubbs (1996: 243), the only possibility to distinguish performatives from other verbs is the insertion of Engl. *you*:

(1a) I warn **you** that there is a bull in that field.
(6) *I deplore **you** what he's done.

The insertion of *you*, however, points to differences between classes of verbs, rather than to differences between uses of the same verb. The English performative *I warn* as well as the non-performative *he warned*, for instance, can take *you*.

Another possible test is the insertion of an optional modal sentence adverb such as, for example, Engl. *perhaps* or *maybe*. Such adverbs automatically cancel any performative function of an utterance, probably even making it grammatically unacceptable:

(3c) ?**Perhaps** I apologize to the lovely state of New Jersey.

If *I apologize* is interpreted as 'I will apologize', the sentence above might be marginally acceptable. Performative clauses with modal sentence adverbs lose their illocutionary force indicating function and assume a descriptive meaning:

(1h) **Perhaps** I warn you that there is a bull in that field.

Sentences with hedged performatives, as in the following French example, retain their grammatical acceptability with *peut-être* 'perhaps, maybe', but change their meaning. If the resulting sentence is inappropriate in a given speech context the superordinate clause is likely to be a hedged performative:

(7a) EMA: [...] **je dirais** que la partie est pratiquement gagnée [...] (COR-FR.FPUBDL03)[3]
I say-COND.1SG that the match is practically won
'I would say that the match is practically won'

(7b) **Peut-être je dirais** que la partie est pratiquement gagnée.
'Perhaps I would say that the match is practically won'

The sentence with Fr. *peut-être* is acceptable only if interpreted as a description of what the speaker would say if certain conditions are met and not as an indication of an ongoing speech act; an interpretation that is not appropriate within the context of (7a).

A descriptive, that is, non-performative sentence can be felicitously confirmed or denied by, for example, Engl. *Yes*, *No*, *That's true* whereas a performative utterance cannot (cf. Bublitz, 2009: 74f.):

(3d) A: I apologize to the lovely state of New Jersey.
B: *Yes / *No / *That's true.

The same can be said of a sentence with a performative clause:

(1i) A: I warn you that there is a bull in that field.
B: *Yes / *No / *That's true.

Sentences with hedged performatives, as in the following Italian example, can be confirmed or denied with *Sì* 'yes', *È vero* 'that's true', *No* 'no' or *Non è vero* 'That's not true', but the answers would be understood as confirmations or denials of the propositional content of the subordinate clause:

(8a) D: [...] **devo dire** che noi abbiamo già un accordo
Must-1SG say-INF that we have already an agreement
con l'UNICEF per l'inoltro dei fondi [...] (CLIP.MC9)
with the UNICEF for the delivery of.the funds
'I must say that we already have an agreement with UNICEF for the delivery of the funds'

[3] For bibliographical information regarding the cited corpora please refer to the list at the end of the contribution.

(8b) A: **Devo dire** che noi abbiamo già un accordo con l'UNICEF per l' inoltro dei fondi.
B: Sì / È vero / No / Non è vero.

Thus, in the example above, the interlocutor B confirms or denies that 'we already have an agreement with UNICEF for the delivery of the funds' and not that A must say something.

The test with interrogative tags such as, for example, Engl. *don't I*, yields similar results (cf. Bublitz, 2009: 74, for a similar test):

(3e) *I apologize to the lovely state of New Jersey, don't I?
(1j) *I warn you that there is a bull in that field, don't I?
(9a) [. . . ] I was quite startled **I must say** to find that this pedestal is still in situ [. . . ] (ICE-GB.S2A-026-074)
(9b) I must say that I was quite startled to find that this pedestal is still in situ, ?mustn't I / wasn't I?

In sentences with hedged performatives, as in example (9b), the interrogative tag may have the performative clause or the subordinate clause in its scope. This depends on its morphological form. The first possibility is only marginally acceptable (cf. Cattel, 1973: 620ff.), whereas the second one is unproblematic.

Summing up, the test with the insertion of a modal sentence adverb, the confirmation or denial test, and the interrogative tag test can be applied to performative utterances as well as to unhedged and hedged performative clauses. The tests unequivocally confirm the performative character or the illocutionary force indicating character of the expressions in question.

## 4. How do Hedged Performatives Hedge?

Hedged performatives have several communicative functions (cf. Gloning, 1997: 317–323; Miecznikowski, 2009), most prominently the expression of mitigated speaker commitment. Exactly how is *I say* + p mitigated by *can*? Fraser (1975: 202) does not insist on the issue; he only affirms that the use of Engl. *can* in the performative gives the interlocutor an option, as he can deny the implied force of an utterance:

(10) A: **I can now admit** that it was I who sent that telegram.
B: Oh, please don't do that. I don't want to talk about the matter any more.

If my interpretation is correct, Fraser (1975: 202) suggests that the hedging effect is achieved by conceding an option to the interlocutor. Although this seems a viable explanation, I would like to explore and propose another one, which relates hedged performatives to Grice's (1975, 1978) maxims.

As I said before, an English clause such as, for example, *I warn you* + p ordinarily indicates the performance of a warning, but in some speech situations it could also describe the act of warning. Performative clauses have the potential to function as descriptions, but their form (first person singular present indicative) is maximally congruent with the speech act indicating function, which therefore clearly prevails. The form of hedged performatives, on the contrary, is more congruent with descriptions and much less with the speech act indication. With the exception of those forms that shift the person deixis from the first person singular to the first person plural, hedged performatives are more like descriptions of state of affairs than indications of illocutionary force.

Hedged performatives constitute an overt discrepancy because they pretend to describe a speech act that at the same time is being performed (cf. Gloning 1997: 310f.). With principles such as those proposed by Fraser (1975), the discrepancy can be resolved by the interlocutor. Nevertheless, hedged performatives represent the violation of a conversational maxim, most probably either the maxim of quality or the maxim of manner. The speaker is not quietly violating the maxim nor opting out from the cooperation nor facing a clash with other maxims (cf. Grice, 1975: 49), but she overtly fails to respect the maxim. Provided that she observes the cooperative principle, such a situation gives rise to conversational implicatures. Its interpretation involves several steps that can be tentatively formalized along the following lines:

a. The speaker qualifies her own speech act as if it were not taking place at that moment while she is actually performing it at the same time.
b. The speaker uses the hedged performative as an illocutionary force indicating device, that is, as a performative clause (by virtue of the inferences illustrated in the preceding section).
c. The speaker flouts a maxim while apparently cooperating conversationally.
d. Implicature: The speech act could possibly not be performed.
e. Implicature: The speaker's commitment regarding her speech act is not complete.

As mentioned, the reasoning above should be valid for all hedged performative clauses with the exception of those forms shifting person deixis from the first person singular to the first person plural. It provides a common basis to which the specific meanings of a particular hedging device are added, for example, reference to ability in the 'can'-case, reference to obligation in the 'must'-case, and so forth.

## 5. Characterization of Reduced Parenthetical Clauses

Since the concept of 'parenthesis' can be understood in a number of ways (see Dehé and Kavalova, 2007; Schneider, 2007: 19–35) and its definition crucially depends on the adopted approach, it is necessary to make clear which expressions are analyzed in this chapter. When I use the term *parenthetical clause*, I actually refer to the *reduced parenthetical clause* (cf. Schneider,

2007). Except the distinction between *clause* and *verb*, the characterization of reduced parenthetical clauses I propose in this section is in line with the main points of Urmson's (1952) original definition of *parenthetical verbs*.

The English, French and Spanish utterances in examples (9a)–(12a) show typical examples of reduced parenthetical clauses with hedged performatives:

(9a) [...] I was quite startled **I must say** to find that this pedestal is still in situ [...] (ICE-GB.S2A-026-074)

(11a) L1 [...] - la plupart du temps ils n'arrivent pas à faire le lien
the most of the time they not arrive not to make-INF the connection
entre l'enseignement euh - **je dirais** théorique [...] (CRFP.LYO-PRO001)
between the teaching HESITATION I say-COND.1SG theoretical
'Most of the time, they can't make the connection between the, I would say, theoretical teaching'

(12a) Nie: [...] / no se pierde nada de espacio /
not REFL lose-3SG nothing of space
se pierde muy poco / **quiero decir** / (COR-ES.EFAMDL19)
REFL lose-3SG very little want-1SG say-INF
'One doesn't lose space, one doesn't lose much, I want to say'

The expressions in italics are neither main clauses nor subordinate clauses. They are inserted into or adjoined to the beginning or end of a host clause in a way similar to sentence adverbs (in other aspects, though, they behave differently from sentence adverbs). As all adjuncts, they are optional, that is, they can be added or dropped without affecting the grammatical acceptability of the host. For instance, example (11a) is perfectly acceptable without Fr. *je dirais* 'I would say':

(11b) La plupart du temps ils n'arrivent pas à faire le lien entre l'enseignement théorique...

Theoretically, the mobility of reduced parenthetical clauses within the host clause is almost unlimited. But if preservation of meaning is a criterion, their mobility depends on their scope (cf. Schneider, 2007: 184–190). For example, Engl. *I must say* in example (9a) and Sp. *quiero decir* 'I want to say' in example (12a) have entire clauses in their scope and could occur in several other positions within their respective hosts, without altering the meaning of the sentences:

(9c) I was **I must say** quite startled to find that this pedestal is still in situ.
(9d) **I must say** I was quite startled to find that this pedestal is still in situ.
(12b) No se pierde nada de espacio, **quiero decir** se pierde muy poco.
(12c) No se pierde nada de espacio, se pierde **quiero decir** muy poco.

The action of Fr. *je dirais* 'I would say' in example (11a), on the contrary, focuses on the adjective *théorique* 'theoretical', and its mobility is thus restricted to the immediate surroundings of the adjective phrase:

(11c) La plupart du temps ils n'arrivent pas à faire le lien entre l'enseignement théorique **je dirais** . . .

If placed further away from the immediate surroundings of the adjective phrase, the scope of *je dirais* changes:

(11d) La plupart du temps **je dirais** ils n'arrivent pas à faire le lien entre l'enseignement théorique . . .
(11e) **Je dirais** que la plupart du temps ils n'arrivent pas à faire le lien entre l'enseignement théorique . . .

In other words, in the case of example (11a), moving Fr. *je dirais* to a position distanced from its original scope will automatically result in changes of scope and meaning.

There is no overt syntactic link between the parenthetical and the host apart from adjacency. Nevertheless, the expressions in italics in examples (9a)–(12a) are pragmatically connected to their hosts, a conclusion shared by virtually all studies on parentheticals since Urmson (1952). I call them *reduced* because the verbs they contain lack one of the arguments required by their respective valencies. A restriction I want to introduce at this point is that the transformation of the host into a clause governed by the verb of the reduced parenthetical should always be possible, regardless of a possible change in scope:

(12d) No se pierde nada de espacio, se pierde muy poco **quiero decir**. → No se pierde nada de espacio, **quiero decir que** se pierde muy poco.

That means that the verb's missing argument should be represented semantically by the host itself and that the missing information can be recovered from the host.

## 6. Data

The examples cited in the present study have two main sources: the data on which the studies in Kaltenböck (2006, 2007, this volume) are based and those on which Schneider (2007) is based. Both derive from spoken language. Kaltenböck (2006, 2007, this volume) analyses the use and semantic properties of 830 tokens of parenthetical clauses in the spoken part of the British component of the *International Corpus of English* (ICE-GB). The texts in the ICE-GB date from 1990 to 1993 and contain a total of 600,000 words in different text types (private dialogue, public dialogue, unscripted monologue, scripted monologue). In Kaltenböck (2006), these 830 tokens are assigned to 89 types, 8 of which are hedged performatives. The data base for Schneider (2007) consists of 2,868 parentheticals extracted from a collection of 22 corpora of French, Italian and Spanish comprising a total amount of 3,975,500 words and documenting spoken language of the last 30 years. The collection comprises, for each language, at least two large reference corpora exhibiting appropriate variation in regional origin, social background, profession, sex, and the age of speakers and in speech situation, theme and register. The pragmatic functions of a selected subset of these parentheticals (1,939 instances) are then analyzed in detail.

## 7. Review of Hedging Devices and Forms

Hedges can have many different grammatical forms, but since Fraser (1975) there has been a tacit agreement that a hedged performative consists of a modal or semi-modal applied to a performative verb. I maintain the basic idea of this assumption, but extend its field of application. That is, besides modals and semi-modals, I take into consideration verbal suffixes, which play an important role in the Romance languages examined. To be sure, considering the variety of hedging devices, this is as arbitrary as Fraser's (1975) initial decision to consider only modals and semi-modals.

An analysis based on the meaning of the modifying expression (modal or semi-modal verb, conditional or temporal suffix) and on its morphosyntactic person–number agreement yields at least six types of devices hedging the parenthetical performative (cf. also Brehmer, 2003: 42ff.; Schneider, 2007: 109f.):

1. devices referring to capability
2. devices referring to obligation
3. devices expressing desire or intention
4. devices expressing conditionality
5. devices producing a shift in person deixis
6. devices producing a shift in temporal deixis

As we see in this section, two devices may also appear together and combine their effects on the performative.

The review in the following subsections will show that the forms are almost all based on the verb 'say', the only exception being Engl. *I've got to admit*, *I would suggest* and Fr. *j'ajouterais* 'I would add'. That is, in comparison with the diversity of performatives tested by Fraser (1975), for example, Engl. *advise*, *admit*, *claim*, *order*, *warn*, and several others, the performatives analyzed in this chapter do not display great variety. The reasons are simple: (1) Unlike Fraser (1975), the present list is based on real data or, more specifically, on corpora of spoken language. (2) The parenthetical position reduces the variety of possible forms (cf. Schneider, 2007: 78ff.).

In Schneider (2007: 109f.) I distinguish between three strategies by which the downgrading of speaker commitment can be brought about: by *alleviating* responsibility, by *removing* responsibility and by *sharing* responsibility. The first consists in directly reducing the burden of one's own communicative responsibility (e.g., with English parentheticals such as *I think* or *I believe*), without trying to move it away or to share it with somebody else. The second and third strategies are relevant in the case of parenthetical hedged performatives. The speaker moves the communicative responsibility away from herself, for example, by suggesting that she is not performing the speech act but that she is capable of doing so, that she intends to do so or that she would perform it under certain conditions. The speaker shares responsibility by allocating part of it to the other participants of the verbal interaction.

### 7.1. Capability

The Italian parenthetical *posso dire* 'I can say' is the only hedged performative occurring in the data cited earlier whose hedging device expresses capability exclusively:

(13) E: il modo di reagire delle persone
the manner of reacting of the persons
'people's ways of reacting'
A: i comportamenti e il modo di reagire delle persone
the behaviors and the manner of reacting of the persons
'people's behaviors and ways of reacting'
E: **posso dire** anche le emozioni_ i sentimenti emozioni [ . . . ] (CLIP.RC8)
can-1SG say-INF also the emotions the feelings emotions
'I can say, also the emotions, the feelings'

We have already discussed the 'can'-case in Sections 3 and 4. However, most of the times reference to capability does not appear in isolation but is combined with conditionality and/or a shift in person deixis.

### 7.2. Obligation

Hedges referring to obligation are found in parentheticals such as Engl. *I should say, I've got to admit, I have to say, I must say,* and It. *devo dire* 'I must say' and *devo dire sinceramente* 'I must say sincerely'. Example (9a) provides an English example; in example (8a) we see an Italian non-parenthetical hedged performative with 'must'. By using 'must', the speaker says that she is obliged to perform a particular speech act and, at the same time, she implies that she wants to be partly relieved of the burden of its consequences (Fraser, 1975: 196). In the case of a statement, this means that the speaker wants to reduce her claim to truth, in the case of a confession, that she wants to protect her self-image and her self-respect, that is, her positive face. I interpret 'I must say' as a particular case of responsibility removing. The speaker is actually performing the speech act, but by suggesting that she is obliged to do so the communicative responsibility is reallocated to the obligating entity (which, of course, remains unspecified). By using a hedged performative such as 'I must say', the speaker also sheds doubts on the speech act actually being performed and thus reduces her commitment. Fraser (1975: 196) suggests that 'must' implies a sense of helplessness with respect to what the speaker is obliged to do. Bach and Harnish (1979: 219) claim that performatives modified by 'must' indicate speech acts that the speaker is reluctant to perform (cf. also Gloning 1997: 348ff.). Jary (2007: 229), however, points out that the speaker could be very keen to perform the act as she is under an obligation to do so.

### 7.3. Desire or intention

Devices expressing desire yield parenthetical hedged performatives such as Fr. *je veux dire*, It. *voglio dire* and Sp. *quiero decir*, all meaning 'I want to say'. The Spanish example (12a) shows such a performative. Engl. *I am tempted to say* is special insofar as it refers to the speaker's desire indirectly by saying that she is only tempted to speak. A device expressing intention is contained in the Italian hedged performative *intendo dire* 'I intend to say'. The semantic difference between 'want' and 'intend' is slight but occasionally can be important: Wanting to do something does not necessarily mean intending to do it and vice versa. The inferences required from the hearer by 'want' and 'intend' partly differ. However, the effects of 'want' and 'intend' on the speech act are similar: In both cases the speaker conveys the idea that she is not actually performing the speech act indicated by the performative, but she only wants or intends to do so. Thus, the speaker cannot be held fully responsible for its consequences (cf. Bastian, 2002: 51). The hearer, on the contrary, as in the case of 'can' described earlier, might have the option of rejecting the performative force implied by the utterance (see Fraser, 1975: 204). Both types of hedged performatives are typical instances of responsibility removing.

### 7.4. Conditionality

Several performatives are hedged by conditionality (cf. Miecznikowski, 2009), as can be seen in the French example (11a). With Engl. *I would say*, the speaker literally declares that she performs the act of saying only if certain (generally unspecified) conditions are satisfied, that is, the performance of the speech act is made dependent on other circumstances. Therefore, I interpret conditionality hedges as examples of responsibility removing. As in the 'can'- and 'want'-cases, the speaker sheds doubt on her performing the act. The same is true of Engl. *I would suggest.*

In Fr. *je dirais*, It. *direi*, *io direi*, Sp. *diría*, *yo diría* and *diría yo*, all meaning 'I would say', and in Fr. *j'ajouterais* 'I would add', the same type of conditionality is expressed by a conditional suffix. Conditionality is frequently combined with capability, with desire or with a shift in person deixis. For example, by using It. *potrei dire* or Sp. *podría decir*, both meaning 'I could say', the speaker refers explicitly to the fact that her capability of performing the act depends on other circumstances. With It. *vorrei dire* 'I would like to say' the speaker refers to the fact that her desire to perform the act depends on other circumstances.

In Fraser's (1975: 207f.) view, performatives such as, for example, Engl. *I would claim* are sentences with an implicit conditional clause such as, for example, *if you were to ask my opinion* or *since you have asked my opinion*. These performatives are appropriate when the speaker feels that it would be reasonable to offer her opinion, whether being asked or not. In other words, the condition is irrelevant and Engl. *I would claim* is directly interpreted as *I claim*. The interpretation of these performatives does not require any conversational principle. Hence the 'would'-case seems to be different from the other cases so far illustrated.

If a conditional clause is hypothesized, be it implicit or not, I suggest that its relation to the ongoing speech act should somehow be accounted for. In my view, the speaker behaves as if any condition possibly contained in the elliptical clause is met. The following principle of satisfied condition could account for this behaviour:

> In absence of evidence to the contrary, whenever a speaker makes her speech act dependent on a condition that remains unexpressed and unspecified one can infer that she will perform the act as if the condition were satisfied.

This seems to be more plausible than claiming that what is implied in the implicit clause has no influence whatsoever on the speech act. Such a claim would contradict the very nature of a condition.

### 7.5. Shift in person deixis

Performatives are also hedged by a shift of person deixis, that is, the first person singular is shifted to the first person plural (cf. Austin, 1976 [1962]: 57) or to an impersonal form. This can be seen as a type of impersonalization strategy (cf. Brown and Levinson, 1978, 1987), deictic displacement (cf. Caffi, 1999, 2001, 2007) or responsibility sharing (cf. Schneider, 2007: 109f). The speaker allocates part of the communicative responsibility to the addressee and/or someone else (inclusive or exclusive 'we') or to anybody and thus shields herself from the possible risks of the verbal interaction. In the data analyzed here, a deictic person shift is usually associated with conditionality (with the exception of Fr. *on peut dire* and It. *si può dire*, both meaning 'one can say'). In Sp. *diríamos* 'we would say', for instance, the speaker indicates that she herself and other unspecified persons perform the act and links the performance to an unspecified condition:

(14) <H1> [...] no la lección ordinaria de cada día, sino,
not the lecture ordinary of every day but
**diríamos**, una conferencia de cierto relieve en la universidad [...] (COREC.BHUM029A)
say-COND.1PL a lecture of certain importance at the university
'not the ordinary everyday lecture but, we would say, a lecture of a certain importance at the university'

Engl. *we could say* and Sp. *podríamos decir* 'we could say' are comparable to 'we would say', the only difference being that the condition is linked to the capability of performing the act. With Fr. *on dirait* 'one would say' the speech act is literally marked as being performed by an unspecified person and linked to an unspecified condition.[4]

The shift of the person deixis from 'I' to inclusive or exclusive 'we' or to the impersonal form does not in itself endanger the performative character of a clause. However, the performative requires an additional interpretative effort by the addressee because he has to figure out who actually is the subject or author of the ongoing speech act. In the default case, the addressee comes to the conclusion that neither he himself nor anyone else is a likely author (or coauthor), and thus he will interpret the 'we' or 'one' as an 'I'.

### 7.6. Shift in temporal deixis

The French parenthetical performative *j'allais dire* 'I was going to say' (cf. also Bastian, 2002) is the only parenthetical hedged performative in our data that produces a shift in temporal deixis:

(15) L2 [...] pour soulager les collègues de façon à ce que
to relieve the colleagues in manner to this that
eux n'aient à gérer **j'allais dire** que les clients de petits débits [...] (CRFP.GRE-PRO001)
they not have-SUBJ.3PL to manage I went say-INF than the clients of small turnovers
'to relieve the colleagues so that they can manage, I was going to say, only the clients with small turnovers'

Since it combines the semi-modal *aller* 'go', which indicates near future, with a past tense (*imparfait*) suffix, the shift is twofold: future in the past. The speaker presents the passage in

[4] We should not forget, however, that in French *on* 'one' is often used instead of *nous* 'we'.

question as if she was going to or intended to perform it in the past. Although the passage is actually expressed, by this strategy she implies that it might not have been expressed and so succeeds in reducing her commitment.

## 8. Illocutionary Force Indication and Parenthesis

In Section 3, I explained how, according to Fraser (1975), performative verbs modified by modals and semi-modals maintain their performative function, and I tacitly assumed that this is also true if the performative verbs occur in parenthetical position. In fact it is an assumption shared by several linguists (e.g., Lyons 1977: 738; Holdcroft 1978: 64) that performatives in parenthetical position maintain their performative function or illocutionary force indicating function. In a footnote, Fraser (1975: 188) explicitly mentions the possibility that a performative occurs in parenthetical position, an idea that dates back to Urmson (1952):

(16) I will be there, **I promise you**.
(17) I was, **I admit**, a little late.

In a contribution on French parenthetical verbs, Récanati (1984: 347) discusses examples with performatives such as the following:

(18) Viens ici, **je te prie**.
come-IMP.2SG here I you beg
'come here, I beg you'

Later studies focus on the illocutionary force indicating function of utterance verbs, rather than on their performative function. Kerbrat-Orecchioni (2001: 37) includes postposed clauses like the one above in the class of French illocutionary force indicating devices. In Italian, according to Fava (1995: 45f.), four of Austin's five classes of speech acts may be indicated by final parentheticals (exercitives, commissives, behabitives and expositives; see Austin, 1976 [1962]: 148–164); see, for example, the following exercitive:

(19) Adesso dimmelo, **te lo ordino**.
now say-IMP.2SG.me.it you it order-1SG
'now tell me, I order you'

For Garrido Medina (1999: 3894f.) the postposed clauses in the following two Spanish examples are descriptive and interpretative rather than performative:

(20) Ven aquí, **te lo ruego**.
come-IMP.2SG here you it beg-1SG
'come here, I beg you'

(21) Juan está en casa **digo yo**.
Juan is in home say I
'Juan is at home, I say'

However, Garrido Medina's (1999) understanding of the descriptive and interpretative functions of verbs of 'saying' is virtually the same as the common one of the illocutionary force indicating function. In fact, since the deictic centre of the performative clause and the speech act are concomitant, all performative clauses, parenthetical and non-parenthetical, indicate the ongoing speech act by simply describing it.

The question whether expressions like those in the examples (16)–(21) are parentheticals or not is discussed in Schneider (2007: 104ff.) and, at this stage, does not require further comment. We should bear in mind that the examples (16)–(21) have all been construed by the respective authors. Our corpus-based analysis shows that with the exception of Sp. *digo yo* 'I say' the parentheticals in examples (16)–(21) are extremely rare or even non-existent. However, the corpus analysis also shows that hedged performatives habitually occur in parenthetical position. In that case, do they retain their illocutionary force indicating function? There are at least two facts that suggest a partly negative answer.

As I said before, the parentheticals detected in the corpora are almost all based on English and Romance forms of 'say', the few exceptions being Engl. *I've got to admit*, *I would suggest* and Fr. *j'ajouterais* 'I would add'. The English verb *say* and its Romance equivalents are unspecific performatives. Commonly they occur in statements but with a 'want'-hedge they may also be found in questions and directives, as in the following French and Italian examples:

(22) L1 [...] **je veux dire** est-ce que la Corse est française [...] (CRFP.COR-PUB001)
I want say is this that the Corsica is French
'I want to say, is Corsica French?'

(23) B: [...] # # cioè **voglio dire** dagli due colpi [...] (CLIP.MB64)
that is want-1SG say give-IMP.2SG.him two blows
'that is, I want to say, give him two blows'

In other words, 'say' by default indicates statements in a very general way, without specifying a particular subtype, and in some circumstances, it may even be used to indicate other speech acts.

Second, as we saw in Section 5, a parenthetical hedged performative may have only a part of an utterance in its scope. I repeat the French example:

(11a) L1 [...] - la plupart du temps ils n'arrivent pas à faire le lien
the most of the time they not arrive not to make-INF the connection
entre l'enseignement euh - **je dirais** théorique [...] (CRFP.LYO-PRO001)
between the teaching HESITATION I say-COND.1SG theoretical
'Most of the time, they can't make the connection between the, I would say, theoretical teaching'

Since the scope of Fr. *je dirais* 'I would say' is limited to the adjective *théorique* 'theoretical', the parenthetical, at least in the example above, cannot function as an illocutionary force indicating verb for the whole sentence. Arguably a parenthetical hedged performative can act as an illocutionary force indicator only if it has an entire sentence in its scope.

## 9. Conclusion

Regarding the three research aims formulated in the initial section, some conclusions can now be drawn. Owing to their form, hedged performatives resemble descriptions of state of affairs rather than indications of illocutionary force and thus produce an overt discrepancy, as they pretend to describe a speech act which at the same time is being performed. The discrepancy causes the violation of a conversational maxim (quality or manner), which is resolved by a conversational implicature and reinterpreted as a reduction of speaker commitment. Owing to their special status, parenthetical hedged performatives, even more than non-parenthetical ones, are interpreted as hedges and as metatextual comments rather than as descriptions of states of affairs. The overview of the parenthetical hedged performatives actually occurring in the corpora reveals six types of hedging devices (devices referring to capability, devices referring to obligation, devices expressing desire or intention, devices expressing conditionality, devices producing a shift in person deixis and devices producing a shift in temporal deixis) and shows that the forms are almost exclusively based on the performative 'say'. Two facts, namely that 'say' is an unspecific verb that can indicate several speech acts and that parenthetical hedged performatives often do not have an entire clause in their scope, suggest that in many cases these expressions do not retain more than a minimal aspect of their illocutionary force indicating function.

## Acknowledgments

I also want to express my gratitude to Karin Aijmer, Klaus Hölker and Johanna Miecznikowski for their critical comments and helpful suggestions, and I thank Georg Marko for his accurate stylistic corrections.

## Corpora

CLIP = Corpus del lessico di frequenza dell'italiano parlato (De Mauro, T., Mancini, F., Vedovelli, M. and Voghera, M. [1993], Lessico di frequenza dell'italiano parlato, Etas Libri, Milano, or <http://badip.uni-graz.at>).

COREC = Corpus oral de referencia del español contemporáneo (<http://www.lllf.uam.es/~fmarcos/informes/corpus/corpusix.html>).

COR-ES and COR-FR = Spanish and French components of the C-ORAL-ROM Corpus (Cresti, E. and Moneglia, M. [Eds.] [2005], C-ORAL-ROM. Integrated reference corpora for spoken Romance languages, Benjamins, Amsterdam/Philadelphia).

CRFP = Corpus de référence du français parlé (unpublished).

ICE-GB = British component of the International Corpus of English (Nelson, G., Wallis, S. and Aarts, B. [Eds.] [2006], The International Corpus of English. The British component, CD-ROM Release 2, Survey of English Usage, University College London, London).

## References

Austin, J. L. (1976 [1962]). *How to do things with words*. The William James Lectures delivered at Harvard University in 1955. Edited by J. O. Urmson and Marina Sbisà, 2nd Edition, Oxford University Press, London.

Bach, K. and R. M. Harnish (1979). *Linguistic communication and speech acts*. Cambridge, MA: MIT Press.

Bastian, S. (2002). "'J'allais dire ... - Ich sag' mal ...'. Formen und Funktionen metakommunikativer Kommentierungen in mündlicher Argumentation", in S. Bastian and F. Hammer (eds.), *'Aber wie sagt man doch so schön ...' Beiträge zu Metakommunikation und Reformulierung in argumentativen Texten*. Frankfurt am Main: Peter Lang, 49–61.

Brehmer, B. (2003)."Beobachtungen zum Gebrauch von 'hedged performatives' im Ost- und Westslavischen", in R. Blankenhorn, J. Blaszcak and R. Mazari (eds.), *Beiträge der Europäischen Slavistischen Linguistik* (POLYSLAV), Bd.6. München: Sager, 21–28.

Brown, P. and S. Levinson (1978). "Universals in language usage: Politeness phenomena", in E. N. Goody (ed.), *Questions and politeness. Strategies in social interaction*. Cambridge: Cambridge University Press, 56–311.

Brown, P. and S. Levinson (1987). *Politeness: Some universals in language usage*. Cambridge: Cambridge University Press.

Brünner, G. (1981). "Modalverben und die Realisierung von Sprechhandlungen", in I. Rosengren (ed.), *Sprache und Pragmatik*. Lunder Symposium 1980. Lund: Gleerup, 91–101.

Bublitz, W. (2009). *Englische Pragmatik. Eine Einführung. 2nd Edition*. Berlin: Erich Schmidt.

Caffi, C. (1999). "On mitigation". *Journal of Pragmatics* **31**: 881–909.

Caffi, C. (2001). *La mitigazione. Un approccio pragmatico alla comunicazione nei contesti terapeutici*. Münster: LIT.

Caffi, C. (2007). *Mitigation*. Amsterdam: Elsevier.

Cattel, R. (1973). "Negative transportation and tag questions". *Language* **49**: 612–639.

Dehé, N. and Y. Kavalova (eds.) (2007). *Parentheticals*. Amsterdam/Philadelphia: Benjamins.

Fava, E. (1995). "Tipi di atti e tipi di frasi", in L. Renzi, G. Salvi and A. Cardinaletti (eds.), *Grande grammatica italiana di consultazione. Vol. 3. Tipi di frasi, deissi, formazione delle parole*. Bologna: Il Mulino, 19–48.

Fraser, B. (1975). "Hedged performatives", in P. Cole and J. L. Morgan (eds.), *Syntax and semantics. Vol. 3. Speech acts*. New York: Academic Press, 187–210.

Garrido Medina, J. (1999). "Los actos de habla. Las oraciones imperativas", in I. Bosque and V. Demonte (eds.), *Gramática descriptiva de la lengua española*. Madrid: Espasa Calpe, 3879–3928.

Gloning, Th. (1997). "Modalisierte Sprechakte mit Modalverben. Semantische, pragmatische und sprachgeschichtliche Untersuchungen", in G. Fritz and Th. Gloning (eds.), *Untersuchungen zur semantischen Entwicklungsgeschichte der Modalverben im Deutschen*. Tübingen: Niemeyer, 307–437.

Greifeld, B. (1981). *Modalverben in Sprechakten*. Trier: LAUT.

Grice, H. P. (1975). "Logic and conversation", in P. Cole and J. L. Morgan (eds.), *Syntax and semantics. Vol. 3. Speech acts*. New York: Academic Press, 41–58.

Grice, H. P. (1978). "Further notes on logic and conversation", in P. Cole (ed.), *Syntax and semantics. Vol. 9. Pragmatics*. New York: Academic Press, 113–127.

Holdcroft, D. (1978). *Words and deeds*. Oxford: Oxford University Press.

Jary, M. (2007). "Are explicit performatives assertions? *Linguistics and Philosophy* **30**: 207–234.

Kaltenböck, G. (2006). "Some comments on comment clauses: A semantic classification", in R. Povolná and O. Dontcheva-Navratilova (eds.), *Discourse and interaction Vol. 2*. Brno: Masarykova Univerzita, 71–87.

Kaltenböck, G. (2007). "Spoken parenthetical clauses in English: a taxonomy", in N. Dehé and Y. Kavalova (eds.), *Parentheticals*. Amsterdam/Philadelphia: Benjamins, 25–52.

Kerbrat-Orecchioni, C. (2001). *Les actes de langage dans le discours. Théorie et fonctionnement*. Paris: Nathan.

Koch, W. (1986). "Das Modalverb als Handlungsevaluator", in W. E. Weiss, H. E. Wiegand and M. Reis (eds.), *Textlinguistik kontra Stilistik. Akten des VII. Kongresses der Internationalen Vereinigung für germanische Sprach- und Literaturwissenschaft Bd. 3*. Tübingen: Niemeyer, 381–392.

Lakoff, G. (1972). "Hedges: A study in meaning criteria and the logic of fuzzy concepts", in P. M. Peranteau, J. N. Levi and G. C. Phares (eds.), *Papers from the Eighth Regional Meeting of the Chicago Linguistic Society*, Chicago Linguistic Society, Chicago, 183–228.

Liedtke, F. (1997). "Gesagt - getan: über illokutionäre Indikatoren", in E. Rolf (ed.), *Pragmatik, Implikaturen und Sprechakte*. Opladen: Westdeutscher Verlag, 180–213.

Lyons, J. (1977). *Semantics*. Cambridge: Cambridge University Press.

Miecznikowski, J. (2009). "Tratti attenuativi e rafforzativi del condizionale italiano con i verbi performativi", in B. Gili Fivela and C. Bazzanella (eds.), *Fenomeni di intensità nell'italiano parlato*. Firenze: Franco Cesati, 115–126.

Récanati, F. (1984). "Remarques sur les verbes parenthétiques", in P. Attal and C. Muller (eds.), *De la syntaxe à la pragmatique. Actes du colloque de Rennes Vol. 8*. Amsterdam/Philadelphia: Benjamins, 319–352.

Schneider, S. (2007). *Reduced parenthetical clauses as mitigators. A corpus study of spoken French, Italian and Spanish*. Amsterdam/Philadelphia: Benjamins.

Searle, J. R. (1976). "A classification of illocutionary acts". *Language in Society* **5**: 1–23.

Stubbs, M. (1996). *Text and corpus analysis. Computer-assisted studies of language and culture*. Oxford: Blackwell.

Yule, G. (1996). *Pragmatics*. Oxford: Oxford University Press.

Urmson, J. O. (1952). "Parenthetical verbs". *Mind* **61**: 480–496.

Urmson, J. O. (1977). "Performative utterances", in P. A. French, Th. E. Uehling and H. K. Wettstein (eds.), *Contemporary perspectives in the philosophy of language*. Minneapolis: University of Minnesota Press, 260–267.

Werlen, I. (1984). *Ritual und Sprache. Zum Verhältnis von Sprechen und Handeln in Ritualen*. Tübingen: Narr.

Wunderlich, D. (1983). "Modalisierte Sprechakte", in G. Brünner and A. Redder (eds.), *Studien zur Verwendung von Modalverben*. Tübingen: Narr, 226–245.

New Approaches to Hedging
Edited by Gunther Kaltenböck, Wiltrud Mihatsch and Stefan Schneider


# 12

# On the Relationship between Attenuation, Discourse Particles and Position

*Antonio Briz and Maria Estellés*

## Abstract

This chapter aims to provide evidence for the direct interaction between the meaning of discourse particles and their situation with respect to discourse units. Changes in position bring corresponding changes in meaning and, more importantly for our purpose, they may trigger or inhibit attenuation. Examples taken from the *Diccionario de partículas discursivas del español* (DPDE, www.dpde.es) provide evidence for the existence of some discourse particles whose core meaning is mitigating, and some others where an attenuating meaning arises in particular contexts. The former particles are *prototypically* attenuating, but their position with respect to discourse is determinant for them to finally work as such; the latter, by contrast, may develop a contextual, *peripheral* attenuating meaning if their position in discourse is changed.

## 1. Introduction

The term *attenuation*[1] accounts for a particular argumentative strategy aiming to get other people's agreement or acceptance (including social acceptance). It consists in a downgrading of what is said and of the fact of saying it: of what is said, because utterances containing this strategy

---

[1] The terms *attenuation, mitigation* and *hedge* will all be considered synonyms.

become blurred or less explicit; of the fact of saying it, because attenuation allows speakers to soften the strength of their actions and intentions. Attenuating or mitigating devices are the verbal tactics used to reach the intended attenuation. (Fraser, 1980, 1999; Caffi, 1999, 2007; Briz, 2005; Briz and Montañez, 2008; for a particular study on *no sé*, see Schneider, 2007):

(1) P: Carlos no sé es un poco raro
'P: Carlos, I don't know, he's a little weird'

In (1), P's pretended ignorance, expressed by *no sé* 'I don't know', mitigates or diminishes the strength of both the act of stating and the statement, that is, the weirdness of Carlos (this last role can be played by the quantifier *poco* as well). Attenuation saves the face of the speaker, allowing him or her to avoid responsibility.

In (2), the use of *bueno,* insofar as it is a concessive prelude, downgrades the following opinion, which contrasts with the one stated by the interlocutor L and, hence, disagrees with her. The attenuation, thus, is also of a polite nature: it watches over the other's face:

(2) L: a mí me ha encantado la conferencia
S: bueno/ yo esperaba otra cosa
'L: I loved the lecture
S: well/ I was expecting something else'

Finally, in (3), by using *a lo mejor,* the speaker in E2 is trying to mitigate (again, in a polite way) the disagreement and the conflict provoked by E1's previous assertion. Thus, the speaker's face is preserved:

(3) E1: la culpa puede ser de los dos
C1: no me digas que soy yo culpable de nada
E2: quiero decir que a lo mejor tú tampoco estás actuando bien
'E1: both of you can be blamed for it
C1: Surely you are not telling me I'm guilty of anything
E2: I mean that perhaps you are not acting properly either'

Here, C1 interprets E1's utterance as face-threatening and, consequently, C1 reacts showing disagreement. In order to avoid tension, E1 must restore harmony by using a reformulation strategy, introducing the connective *quiero decir* 'I mean' first, and reinforcing it with the use of the hedge *a lo mejor* 'perhaps', thus attenuating the strength or harshness of the utterance.

Three facts can be noted in the light of the above-mentioned examples:

(i) The first fact has to do with the various ways of understanding attenuation (Puga Larraín, 1997; Bravo, 1999, 2001; Caffi, 1999; Hernández Flores, 2002; Albelda, 2004; Kerbrat-Orecchioni, 2004; Álvarez, 2005):

– as a mechanism for minimizing the speaker's actions (for instance, of 1P's opinion). Attenuation here acts as a sort of protecting shield.
– as a mechanism for minimizing a possible threat to the other's face or rights, that is, a mechanism for watching over one's face and rights as well as – especially – everybody else's (as in 2S). The hedge has then a preventive function.
– as a mechanism for repairing actions that have previously damaged the other's face or have invaded his space (as in 3E2.) The purpose of the hedge is then 'healing'.
In summary, the hedge has a part in both speaker's and speaker/hearer's activities; these activities affect both of them and, therefore, are often related to politeness.
(ii) The second remarkable fact is that these attenuating operations can be marked via discourse particles: in the examples above, *no sé*, *bueno* and *a lo mejor* are the mechanisms used for mitigation (Martín Zorraquino, 1992; Briz, 1994: 384, 2001, 2006; Ruiz Gurillo and Pons, 1995; Casado Velarde, 1998: 66; Martín Zorraquino and Portolés, 1999; Pons, 2000: 210; Montolío, 2003, 2006).
(iii) Finally, the third fact, not yet mentioned, is that markers seem to occupy different positions in relation to the chunk of discourse they affect: *no sé* in (1) and *a lo mejor* in (3) are in the medial position, whereas in (2) *bueno* appears in the initial position.

In summary, some discourse particles are hedging devices and they have either a self-protecting, preventive or a repairing function, and they can appear in different positions. However, a question arises when considering the third fact highlighted above: is the position of the attenuating particle arbitrary? Can particles take any place in discourse, as examples (1–3) seem to suggest? We think the answer is no.

In the next sections, some examples will be provided to show that there is a correspondence or relationship between attenuation and the position of the particle (Briz and Val.Es.Co., 2003; Cortés and Camacho 2005; Briz, 2006; Briz and Montañez, 2008; Briz and Pons, 2010). It is important to note, however, that position cannot be thought of in absolute terms; position is always a relative concept and, as far as discourse particles are concerned, the reference point is the discourse unit to which they relate. Therefore, Section 2 will briefly sketch some theoretical principles of Val.Es.Co.'s (*Valencia español coloquial*) theory of discourse units. This theoretical framework will support the particular examples studied in Section 3, taken from the *Diccionario de partículas discursivas del español* (DPDE).[2] These examples will attempt to show that attenuation results from an interaction between the meaning of the particle and the position it

[2] The DPDE is available at http://www.dpde.es. This online dictionary is edited by Antonio Briz and Salvador Pons (Universitat de València) and José Portolés (Universidad Autónoma de Madrid), and is coordinated in the University of Valencia. Currently, the DPDE consists of circa 65 discourse particles, although the number of entries is still growing; the dictionary provides a global definition of each particle, considering meaning and contextual use, as well as data about pronunciation, prosody, register, syntax, position, conversational formulae in which they appear, and all the formal variants.

occupies with respect to the discourse unit. Finally, Section 4 will summarize the main conclusions.

## 2. Towards a System of Discourse Units: Val.Es.Co.'s Theory

Organizing discourse into pragmatic units has been the goal of many scholars (Roulet *et al.*, 1985; Roulet, 1991; Roulet *et al.*, 2001; Cortés and Camacho, 2005). The Val.Es.Co. model also aims to reach a clear-cut systematization of discourse units (Briz and Val.Es.Co., 2003; Briz and Pons, 2010), but this model adds a different nuance: units are delimited according to semantic, pragmatic and prosodic aspects. These are the best explanatory criteria in oral discourse and, besides, they account for those phenomena not yet fully explained by sentence grammar and semantics (such as indexicals, implicit meanings, emphasis, vocal focalizations, alterations in word order, etc.).

According to Val.Es.Co. (Hidalgo and Padilla, 2006: 3), the system of discourse units is distributed as shown in Table 12.1.

**Table 12.1.** Discourse units

| Levels | Dimensions | | |
|---|---|---|---|
| | **Structural** | **Social** | **Informative** |
| Dialogic | Dialogue Exchange | Turn-taking | |
| Monologic | Intervention Act | Turn | Subact |

We will not be using all of these terms in this chapter. Therefore, we will merely give an outline for the terms *intervention* and *act* (the complete model can be found in, among others, Briz and Val.Es.Co. (2003) and Briz and Pons (2010); for a brief introduction in English see Pons and Estellés (2009)).

In Pons and Estellés' (2009) words, interventions:

> are somehow "natural" units and can be automatically recognized by the change of speaker; they belong to the *structural* dimension of talk. Turns, instead, are defined by the *acceptance* of the co-interlocutor. Their recognition deals with the presence in the other's interventions of traces of the previous turn (an answer to a question, anaphoric indexes, lexical chains, and so on). Turns are not produced automatically, but are conceded by co-interlocutors; they belong to the *social* dimension of talk. Interventions and turns are the maximal monological units in the structural, as well as in the social dimensions of talk.

| Intervention | Maximal unit uttered by a single speaker. It belongs to the structural dimension. It triggers or is triggered by a linguistic reaction. According to these possibilities, two kinds of intervention are delimited: |
|---|---|
| | ***Initiative*** It triggers a hearer's further contribution |
| | ***Reactive*** It is triggered by an initiative intervention |
| | ***Reactive-initiative*** They are triggered by a previous intervention and eventually trigger a further reaction. |

**Figure 12.1.** Interventions and subtypes (Cabedo Nebot, 2009)

Interventions are defined and sub-categorized as shown in Figure 12.1.

Acts, in turn, are smaller units than the intervention. They can be recognized according to two criteria: isolability and identifiability.

> Interventions have immediate constituents, called acts (following Roulet *et al.*, 1985). An act is characterized by two features: it is an identifiable and an isolable unit. According to the first feature, every act can be the only constituent of an intervention (this means that it is the bearer of its illocutive force). The second feature imposes a formal, recognizable limit to this kind of constituent (Pons and Estellés, 2009).

These defining features are best explained with an example, provided by Briz and Pons (2010):

(4) P1: #a ese paso no adelgazarás ¿eeh?#
#síi↑# # he perdido un poquito↑#

'P1: #you won't lose weight at this rate#
#Yees# #I lost a little#'

[ ... ] Isolability is proved because an act can become an intervention, that is, it may be initiative or reactive. For instance, C1 contains two acts, given that each one, taken in isolation, may be the reaction to P1[3]:

(4b) P1: A este paso no adelgazarás, ¿eh?
a. C1: #síii↑#
b. C1:#he perdido un poquito↑#

These two notions provide sufficient theoretical basis to continue with the analysis. In Section 3, some Spanish discourse particles will be analysed. The data will show that the position of the particle with respect to the discourse unit produces an attenuation meaning of the particle.

## 3. A Case Study: Spanish Discourse Particles Of Attenuation

### 3.1. Attenuation in discourse particles. Core hedging value vs. subsidiary hedging value

Discourse particles are linguistic ways to control discourse, as well as guides to interpret it. Connection, modality and phatic control are the three functions performed by discourse particles in Spanish, be it in a main, subsidiary or exclusive way. In other words, these forms, also known as discourse markers (DMs), pragmatic connectives, etc., develop predominantly or prototypically one of these three functions.[4]

For instance, particles such as *además* 'besides' or *por un lado ... por otro lado* 'on the one hand ... on the other hand' are instances of connection, either argumentative (*además* adds a new argument and connects it to one previously introduced, both of them being co-oriented towards the same conclusion) or structural (*por un lado ... por otro lado* puts the discourse in order). The phatic control is present in forms such as *¿eh?, ¿sabes?* 'you know?', *mira* 'look', *oye* 'listen'. And modalization, which means either an intensification or an attenuation of utterances and stances, can be represented with forms such as *¡;ojo!* 'watch out!', *por supuesto* 'of course', *hombre / mujer*, 'man', *tío-a* 'dude', *en principio* 'in principle', *a lo mejor* 'perhaps', *no sé* 'I do not know' and so forth.

---

[3] "Dicha aislabilidad se corrobora cuando cada uno de esos segmentos puede constituirse en intervención, esto es, puede ser inicio o reacción. Por ejemplo, C1 está formada por dos actos, ya que cualquiera de ellos, de forma aislada, puede constituir la reacción a P1" (Briz and Pons, forthcoming).

[4] It is beyond the purpose of this article to discuss whether or not focalization is a fourth function.

A brief look into the DPDE corroborates the above mentioned (what the DPDE calls the particle's base or core meanings[5]). The lexicographic entry in the DPDE shows that particles such as *al parecer* 'apparently', *por así decir* 'so to speak', *por lo visto* 'seemingly', *digamos* 'let's say', etc., essentially play an attenuating role, whereas other particles such as *a decir verdad* 'to tell the truth', *es un decir* 'it's (just) a manner of speaking', *mejor dicho* 'or rather', *más bien* 'more like', *o sea* 'that is' or 'I mean', *igual* 'maybe', etc., develop this value only in certain contexts (in DPDE, 'contextual uses',[6] that is, particular contextual situations under which this value, which is different from their core meaning, comes to light).

This contrast can be better illustrated with an example: let us compare two discourse particles in Spanish: *al parecer*, on the one hand, and *a decir verdad*, on the other hand.

In the DPDE's definition of *al parecer*, Albelda (DPDE, www.dpde.es, entry *al parecer*) highlights its attenuating nature, particularly hedging the truthfulness of the statement it affects:

> Using *al parecer* the speaker/writer expresses that the information s/he is presenting is not first-hand but rather, s/he has obtained it from other external sources. When using this particle, the speaker/writer indicates that this information is objective and, at the same time, that s/he is not responsible for the truth of it:[7]
>
> Me dicen por el aparato que solemos tener para escuchar la comunicación con los realizadores que nos vamos primero al Palacio de Exposiciones y Congresos, donde *al parecer* hay ¡;últimos datos! Allí se encuentra nuestra compañera, Beatriz Ariño. Beatriz Ariño, buenas noches. Hola, buenas noches. ¿Hay alguna comunicación oficial, tenéis datos? (Oral, España, CREA, 1991)
>
> 'Through this thing we use for communicating with the producer, I'm being informed that we are first connecting with the Conference and Exhibition Hall, where *apparently* they have latest news! Our reporter, Beatriz Ariño, is there. Beatriz Ariño, good evening. Hello, good evening. Is there any official press release, do you have any information?'

By contrast, Fernández (DPDE, www.dpde.es, entry *a decir verdad*), when describing the contextual uses of *a decir verdad,* notes that, "if it [*a decir verdad*] accompanies a member of the

[5] 'Significados de base o fundamentales de las partículas'.

[6] 'Usos contextuales'.

[7] Indica que el hablante no es testigo directo de la información transmitida y que la ha adquirido por fuentes externas a él mismo. Manifiesta, por tanto, que es una información objetiva y, a su vez, que no es responsable de su verdad.

discourse which is likely to damage the speaker's or the other's face, *a decir verdad* acts as a hedge".[8] She points out that this particle can soften the severity of an assertion:

– ¿Cómo contempla en estos momentos el legado del Instituto Warburg [ ... ]?
– A decir verdad con cierto escepticismo. Compruebo que muchos de mis colegas más jóvenes son cada vez menos warburgianos.
  (Juan Manuel Bonet, in ABC Cultural, 7/02/1992, 38)
  '- ¿How do you regard the legacy of the Wartburg Institute at the moment? [ ... ]?
– To tell the truth, with a certain skepticism. I see that many of my youngest colleagues are less and less Wartburgians.'

or of a reply which shows disagreement with the previously uttered discourse:

– ¿Y qué dudas te asaltan, qué negros presentimientos te asedian, amigo?
– A decir verdad no se trata de presentimientos, sino de reflexiones.
  (Cerezales, Escaleras en el limbo, España, CREA, 1991)
  '–¿What doubts do you have, what black premonitions besiege you?
  To tell you the truth, it is not about premonitions, but about reflections'

Consequently,

(a) attenuation is one of the modalizing functions of DMs. It has to do with argumentative weakening (Montolío, 2006) or minimization of illocutive force;
(b) dialogically, it is related to a way of softening disagreement, preventing and avoiding conflict, easing tension in discourse or, simply, preventing it.
(c) Attenuation can be either the core meaning of particles or a contextually acquired sense.

### 3.2. Attenuation and position in discourse. Some case studies

Some particles, as mentioned above, have several functions. However, that diversity in operation is tightly related to two parameters: the position of the particle and the discourse unit in which the particle appears (see Section 2). In this section, a group of particles taken from the DPDE will be analysed. When comparing the different meanings these particles may show, it is noticeable that position plays a major role in eventually triggering or inhibiting attenuation. To better illustrate this fact, four particles will be considered.

---

[8] Si acompaña a un miembro del discurso que pueda dañar la imagen del hablante o la de otro, a *decir verdad* actúa como un atenuador.

*3.2.1. Bueno.* As an example, let us take the Spanish discourse particle *bueno* 'well', which develops three different functions depending on its position in the discourse units:

(a) In initial position, the particle *bueno* is always attenuating (see also example (2)). In example (5B) below, according to Val.Es.Co.'s theory of discourse units, *bueno* is heading a discourse unit, specifically a reactive intervention, that is, a speaker's utterance reacting to another interlocutor's:

(5) A: ¿qué te ha parecido la conferencia de nuestro antiguo profesor?
B: *bueno*/ no ha estado mal
'A: how did you like our old professor's lecture?
B: *well*/ not bad'

(b) By contrast, *bueno* works as a reformulative connective when located *inside an intervention*, between acts (for instance, in (6) between a fragment such as *hablas poco* 'you don't speak much' and its reformulation, *parece que no tienes muchas ganas de charlar* 'it seems you don't feel like chatting'. Here, only occasionally is the reformulation linked to an attenuating function, as in (6L):

(6) L: hablas poco *bueno* parece que no tienes muchas ganas de charlar
'L: you don't speak much, *well*, it seems you don't feel like chatting'

(c) When *heading an initiative intervention* (an intervention which triggers further utterances but not a response to previous interventions), the particle signals the beginning of a new dialogical as well as thematic sequence; in fact, *bueno* can act as digression marker or topic shifter (see Pons and Estellés, 2009):[9]

(7) *bueno* hablemos ahora del gobierno /que es algo que me pone.
'*now then*, let's talk about the government/ something that really turns me on'

Examples (5), (6) and (7) suggest that the abstract function as well as the concrete meaning of these forms are tightly interrelated to both the positional trait and the discourse unit hosting the particle: the modal, attenuating predominance of *bueno* is linked to the *initial* position; the connection (reformulative) appears when *bueno* is located between acts, *inside* an intervention (together with a contextual value of mitigation); finally, if *bueno* heads an intervention which is additionally the starting point of a dialogical sequence – as in (6) – the particle is meant to be a topic shifter.

---

[9] This does not mean that a topic shift excludes a strategic preventive mechanism, or a way of repairing a virtual disagreement.

*3.2.2. O sea.* According to Briz (DPDE, www.dpde.es, entry *o sea 2*), *o sea* in its second meaning "specifies or rectifies the previous discourse [. . . ]. This rectification often adds a tinge of attenuation in problematic situations when the speaker/hearer's face is at stake".[10] This nuance, however, again depends on a positional criterion:

(a) When the connective functions as an explicative reformulative, it can act at the same time as a repairing attenuation of the damaged or threatened face (Briz, 2001, 2002). In other words, in (8) and (9) connection and, in particular, explanatory reformulation, is the core value of *o sea 2,* although this reformulative operation safeguards both S and C's face.

As it might be seen in (8) and (9), *o sea* is located inside the intervention, between the reformulated segment and the reformulation. Here medial position confers the particle a connective function to which a related attenuating role is added. The speaker has uttered a potentially threatening sentence: *lo primero va a ser blanquearme los dientes* 'the first thing to do is to whiten my teeth', which may lead the hearer to think the speaker's teeth are stained or unclean. To avoid this possible interpretation, S adds mitigation headed by *o sea*, to clarify that the speaker's teeth are white, and the whitening must be considered, not as a need for the speaker, but as an incentive for the speaker to quitting smoking:

(8) (S quit smoking, but still feels the need)
S: sí// peroo muchísimas/ yy según me han dicho cada vez voy a tener más[11] // entonces↓// lo primero↑/ va a ser blanquearme los dientes// que eso ya me dará un punto↑/ paraaa/ intentar no fumar/ *o sea* los tengo blancos que me- aunque no los tengoo/ yo los tengo bien↓ (l)os dientes ¿no?/ pero tengo que buscarme motivos// paraa olvidarme de- de fumar↓ porque/ últimamente tengo de verdad/ muchas tentaciones ¿no? [AP.80.A.1.: 562–567]
'S: yes, I really need it. And I've heard that it will become worse and; then, the first thing to do is to whiten my teeth, because that will be an incentive to try giving up smoking. *I mean,* my teeth are white, although they are not . . . they are OK, my teeth, aren't they? but I must find some reason to forget about smoking, because I have really been tempted quite often, lately, haven't I?'

(9) C: La verdad es que no me gusta tu madre *o sea* es un poco agobiante
'The truth is, I don't like your mother, *I mean*, she's a bit of a pest'

---

[10] [. . . ] matiza o rectifica lo anterior [. . . ]. Con frecuencia, la rectificación añade un matiz de atenuación, especialmente en situaciones problemáticas en las que, por ejemplo, la imagen propia o ajena puede quedar afectada.

[11] Laughing.

(b) By contrast, in final position (in the intervention and the act), connection gives way to attenuative modalization, as in (10):

(10) Yo no sé, la mayoría de tus preguntas, para mí, no son lógicas, *o sea*...
'I don't know, most of your questions, for me, they are not logical, *I mean* ... ]'

In this place, the particle is but a mark of attenuation: it mitigates what has just been stated, clearly attempting to avoid responsibility. Therefore, the subsidiary, modalizing attenuative function becomes salient and exclusive of this particle in this particular position, at the end of an intervention. It is important to highlight, however, the general tendency towards the abuse of *o sea* in this position, which leads the particle to become a mere tag.

*3.2.3. No.* Briz (2006) points out the mitigating, polite function of the DM *no* (11):

(11) B: Es que mi vida ya no parece mía/ a mis amigos ya no los veo
A: no↓ yo SÉ que debería darte más tiempo↓ del que te doy
'B: The thing is, my life doesn't seem to belong to me anymore. I don't even see my friends
A: no, I know I should give you more time than I actually do ... '

Here the discourse particle *no* is part of a *reactive intervention*: an interlocutor reacts to or answers another interlocutor's previous intervention(s), and must mitigate negativity, objections or reproaches, accepting the latter's utterance(s). The particle *no* gets around these obstacles and shows agreement.

In example (12), A2 accepts S and J's recrimination using *no*, but, at the same time, he corrects their statements, explaining and clarifying his relapse with *pero* 'but'. The threatened face requires the attenuative use of *no*, used as a sort of shield, before starting the repairing movement:

(12) S1: ¿y por qué has fumao?
A1: y hoy– hoy he cogío y hoy me he fumao hoy cinco y este seis
S2: pues yaa/// (2") ¡;chee![12]
J1: aguanta
S3: dos meses ¿después de dos meses?
((,,,))
A2: *no*/ pero yo mee
[AP.80.A.1: pág, 149, lines 250–258]
'S1: and why have you smoked (again)?
A1: and today– today I go and smoke five! Six, with this one!

---

[12] Valencian interjection with a meaning of surprise.

S2: oooh/// (2") man!
J1: hold on!
S3: two months, after two months?
((,,,))
A2: *no*/ but I . . . '

Again, the modal function, the beginning of the reactive intervention and the absolute initial position are interrelated. Thus, when accounting for the functions of DMs and, specifically, the attenuating values of DMs, it seems necessary to take this positional criterion into consideration.

*3.2.4. Other functions: Phatic markers and fillers.* One interesting remark: if a marker with a modalizing function in an initial position, like *bueno* and *no*, shifts to a medial position, *inside an act,* it will frequently become a mere element of formulative support: Thus, in (13), *no* collaborates in restarting, and in (14), *bueno* seems to be a verbalized pause which gives the speaker time to think of the continuation of his/her speaking:[13]

(13) L: ¿pero tú no lo haces↓?
E: ¡;pero yo no lo hago/ o s(e)a↑/ yo estoy pensando quién está delante↓ porque para mí hay cosas más importantes que pasar una noche guay// y enrollarme con un tipo/// o sea↑/ yoo- yo/ *no*↓ verás- yo es que tengo muy claro con quién me voy a enrollar/ para mí eso es muy- muy importante
[L.15.A.2, p. 93, lines 472–477]
'L: But you don't do it?
E: ¡;But I don't do it/ I mean, I'm considering who's standing in front of me, because for me there are more important things than having a super night, and hooking up with someone . . . I mean, I . . . I . . . *no*, you see, I always know for sure who I'm hooking up with, that is really important for me'

(14) G: hombre↓yo al llegar aquí y noo/// bueno↓ no encontrar a nadie/ o s(e)a/// tía↓he llegao y he llamao all- ahí al- al veinticinco no- no abría nadie *¿no?* al veinticinco
[L.15.A.2, p. 83, lines 40–42]
'G: well, I . . . when I arrived here and I . . . you see, I didn't find anyone . . . I mean, woman, I arrived and I knocked there- on- number twenty-five *no*- nobody opened you know? On number twenty-five'

But as stated in Briz and Montañez (2008) and in the first acceptation of *¿eh?* in the DPDE, the particle *¿eh?,* whose core meaning is a search for agreement, sometimes acquires a sense of mitigating or attenuating politeness in the final position, especially when it follows a request,

[13] This formulative meaning is often adopted by some connective markers, sometimes as a mere tag, when they are placed inside acts, as in (9), (12) and (13).

question, advice, rejection or any kind of utterance which is face-threatening to some extent. The position is decisive: only at the end of the discourse unit can *¿eh?* be attenuating; however, the kind of speech act to which *¿eh?* is associated is the key. Compare (15), where *¿eh?* does not attenuate but controls communication, with (16), where G2 asks E1 not to pour too much whiskey, his request being downgraded by *¿eh?*

(15) C: sí sí sí↓ pero eso no se te ocurra vendérselo a ese tío por doscientas mil *¿eh?*
D: eso vale medio kilo
'C: OK, but don't even think about selling it to that guy for less than two-hundred thousand, *right*?
D: It is worth half a million'

(16) E1: te pongo un Jotabé↓ peroo/ hielo no hay↓ con agua/ si quieres
G1: no↓ solo solo
E2: ¿solo? ¡;ah! pues mejor/ te lo pongo porque como no hay hielo↑§
G2: § pero no pongas mucho *¿eh?*[14]
E3: no↓ no↓ yoo te saco la botella↑ y tú te pones el que quieras
(Briz and Val.Es.Co., 2002, 108, l. 1094–1099)
'E1: I'll serve you some JB, but ... I've run out of ice ... with water, if you prefer.
G1: no, straight
E2: straight? ah! better then/ I'll serve you some because there isn't any ice
G2: but not too much, *huh?*
E3: no, no, I give you the bottle and you pour yourself as much as you like.'

To summarize, in particles (such as *bueno* or *no*), which are basically hedging devices, the rise of attenuation as an exclusive feature mainly relates to the initial position of a reactive intervention. By contrast, when particles are located inside the unit, à connective function is added, and attenuation is no longer the only feature in the particle's meaning (as it is the case in *bueno*, *no sé*, *a lo mejor*). In some cases, the attenuating sense even disappears. Such is the case of *bueno* heading an *initiative intervention:* attenuation basically fades away and *bueno* becomes a topic introducer or shifter. Finally, it must be noted that in some cases, especially when the particle is used excessively, attenuation gives way to a mere formulation.

When attenuation is only a complement of the basic value, it prototypically arises together with some other functions, such as connection. This is the case, for instance, of the particle *o sea*: prototypically reformulative, its natural place of occurrence is to be found between acts. There, attenuation is but a complement of the main, connective value. Nevertheless, when *o sea*, moves to the less frequent initial or final positions of a discourse unit, it becomes a hedging modal. This

[14] It has been argued that *¿eh?* in this context could also be interpreted as a reinforcing device. However, the original sound recording shows no emphasis or ascending intonation, which, according to us, discards the reinforcing interpretation.

is also the case with phatic control markers such as *¿eh?* or *¿no?*: they *may* add attenuation to their own appellative or filling functions when they are located in the final position of an *initiative* (or *reactive-initiative*) *intervention*.

## 4. Conclusions

Discourse particles and attenuation are interconnected: some particles are essentially hedging devices and some others only function as such contextually or in a subsidiary way. However, having attenuation as the core, basic value does not mean that attenuation is always present: the mitigating value of essentially attenuating discourse particles depends on the place they take with respect to the discourse units, and the same happens with particles which are of a non-attenuating nature.

In general terms, in particles whose meaning is prototypically attenuating (*bueno*, *no*), attenuation seems to be linked to the initial position. If the particle is placed elsewhere (for instance, between acts), new meanings arise, different from attenuation; and, if a constant abuse of this particle in medial positions takes place (as is the case of *bueno*), the attenuating meaning may even completely disappear, giving place to a formulative or filling value as the only feature of the particle.

In particles whose core meaning is *not* attenuation, the mitigating meaning is usually associated with final position instead. Particles such as *o sea* are prototypically connectives. Thus, their natural position is between units (generally, *acts*). In that position, attenuation may exist, but just as a subsidiary meaning that arises contextually next to the main, reformulative one. However, when it is placed in less natural or frequent positions (such as initial and final position), it may become only attenuating. This is also the case with some phatic particles, such as *¿eh?*.

## Acknowledgment

This work has been funded by the Spanish Ministry of Education and Science, as well as by FEDER funds (Research project *Diccionario de partículas discursivas del español* [DPDE] in 2000 [BFF2000/1438] and 2004 [HUM2004-01453]).

## References

Albelda, M. (2004). “Cortesía en diferentes situaciones comunicativas, la conversación coloquial y la entrevista sociológica semiformal”, in D. Bravo and A. Briz (eds.), *Pragmática sociocultural, análisis del discurso de cortesía en español*. Barcelona: Ariel, 109–134.

Álvarez, A. (2005). *Cortesía y descortesía*. Mérida: Universidad de los Andes.

Bravo, D. (1999). "¿Imagen positiva vs. imagen negativa? Pragmática social y componentes del *face*". *Oralia* **2**: 155–184.

Bravo, D. (2001). "Sobre la cortesía lingüística, estratégica y conversacional en español". *Oralia* **4**: 299–314.

Briz, A. (1994). "Hacia un análisis argumentativo de un texto coloquial. La incidencia de los conectores pragmáticos". *Verba* **21**: 369–395.

Briz, A. (2001). "El uso de *o sea* en la conversación", in J. De Kock (ed.), *Gramática española. Enseñanza e investigación. Lingüística con corpus. Catorce aplicaciones sobre el español.* Salamanca: Ediciones Universidad, 287–318.

Briz, A. (2002). "Otra vez sobre *o sea*", in C. Saralegui and M. Casado, M (eds.), *Pulchre, bene, recte.* Estudios en Homenaje al Prof. Fernando González Ollé, Navarra, EUNSA, Universidad de Navarra, 169–190.

Briz, A. (2005). "Eficacia, imagen social e imagen de cortesía. Naturaleza de la estrategia atenuadora en la conversación coloquial española", in D. Bravo (ed.), *Estudios de la (des)cortesía en español. Categorías conceptuales y aplicaciones a corpus orales y escritos.* Stockholm, Buenos Aires: Dunken, 53–92.

Briz, A. (2006). "Unidades del discurso, partículas discursivas y atenuantes. El caso de *no/ tienes razón*", in J. Falk, J. Gille and F. Wachtmeister (eds.), *Discurso, interacción e identidad.* Homenaje al Profesor Lars Fant. Stockholm: Stockholms Universitet, 13–36.

Briz, A. and M. P. Montañez (2008). "La forma *¿eh?* en el *Diccionario de partículas discursivas del español* (DPDE)", in A. Álvarez Tejedor (ed.), *Lengua viva: estudios ofrecidos a César Hernández Alonso*, Valladolid: Universidad de Valladolid, 625–642.

Briz, A. and S. Pons (2010). "Unidades, marcadores discursivos y posición", in O. Loureda (ed.), *Los estudios sobre marcadores del discurso en espanol, hoy.* Madrid: Arco Libros, 327–358.

Briz, A. and Val.Es.Co (eds.) (2002), *Corpus de conversaciones coloquiales*, Madrid: Arco Libros.

Briz, A. and Val.Es.Co (2003). "Un sistema de unidades para el estudio del lenguaje coloquial". *Oralia* **6**: 7–61.

Cabedo Nebot, A. (2009). "Segmentacion prosodica en la conversación coloquial: sobre el grupo entonativo como mecanismo demarcativo de unidades minimas". Unpublished doctoral thesis, Universitat de Valencia, Valencia.

Caffi, C. (1999). "On mitigation". *Journal of Pragmatics* **31**: 881–909.

Caffi, C. (2007). *Mitigation.* Amsterdam: Elsevier.

Casado Velarde, M. (1998). "Lingüística del texto y marcadores del discurso", in M. A. Martín Zorraquino and E. Montolío (eds.), *Los marcadores del discurso.* Madrid: Arco/Libros, 55–70.

Cortés, L. and M. M. Camacho (2005). *Unidades de segmentación y marcadores del discurso.* Madrid: Arco/ Libros.

Fraser, B. (1980). "Conversational mitigation". *Journal of Pragmatics* **4**: 341–350.

Fraser, B. (1999). "What are discourse markers". *Journal of Pragmatics* **31**: 931–952.

Hernández Flores, N. (2002). *La cortesía en la conversación española de familiares y amigos; la búsqueda del equilibrio entre la imagen del hablante y la imagen del destinatario.* Aalborg: Institut for Sprog og Internationales Kulturstudier, Aalborg Universitet.

Hidalgo, A. and X. Padilla (2006). "Bases para el análisis de las unidades menores del discurso oral: los subactos". *Oralia* **9**: 109–143.

Kerbrat-Orecchioni, C. (2004). "¿Es universal la cortesía? in D. Bravo and A. Briz (eds.), *Pragmática sociocultural, análisis del discurso de cortesía en español.* Barcelona: Ariel, 39–53.

Martín Zorraquino, M. A. (1992). "Partículas y modalidad", in G. Holtus, et al. (eds.), *Lexikon der Romanistischen Linguistik Vol. VI, 1.* Tübingen: Niemeyer, 110–124.

Martín Zorraquino, M. A. and J. Portolés (1999). "Los marcadores del discurso", in I. Bosque and V. Demonte (eds.), *Gramática descriptiva de la lengua española*. Madrid: Espasa Calpe, 4051–4213.

Montolío, E. (2003). "Es una buen periodista, en principio. Sobre el operador discursivo en principio y su función modalizadora en el discurso periodístico". *Español actual* **79**: 45–58.

Montolío, E. (2006). "*Por ahora/de momento/por el momento es un tipo encantador.* Operadores de debilitamiento argumentativo de origen temporal", in J. Falk, J. Gille and F. Wachtmeister (eds.), *Discurso, interacción e identidad.* Homenaje al Profesor Lars Fant. Stockholm: Stockholms Universitet, 81–107.

Pons, S. (2000). "Los conectores", in Briz and grupo Val.Es.Co. (eds.), *¿Cómo se comenta un texto coloquial?* Barcelona: Ariel Practicum, 193–220.

Pons, S. and M. Estellés (2009). "Expressing digression linguistically: Do digressive markers exist? *Journal of Pragmatics* **41**: 921–936.

Puga Larraín, J. (1997). *La atenuación en el castellano de Chile, un estudio pragmalingüístico*. Valencia: Universitat de València.

Roulet, E. (1991). "Le modèle genevois d'analyse du discours: évolution et perspectives". *Pragmatics* **1**: 243–248.

Roulet, E., et al. (1985). *L'articulation du discours en français contemporain*. Bern: Peter Lang.

Roulet, E., et al. (2001). *Un modèle et un instrument d'analyse de l'organisation du discours*. Bern: Peter Lang.

Ruiz Gurillo, L. and S. Pons (1995). "Escalas morfológicas o escalas argumentativas". *Español actual* **64**: 53–74.

Schneider, S. (2007). *Reduced parenthetical clauses as mitigators. A corpus study of spoken French, Italian, and Spanish*. Amsterdam, Philadelphia: Benjamins.

# Subject Index

www.ingramcontent.com/pod-product-compliance
Lightning Source LLC
LaVergne TN
LVHW010625300926
849162LV00001B/60